METAPHYSICS

Problems, Paradoxes and Puzzles,

SOLVED?

Bob Doyle
The Information Philosopher
"beyond logic and language"

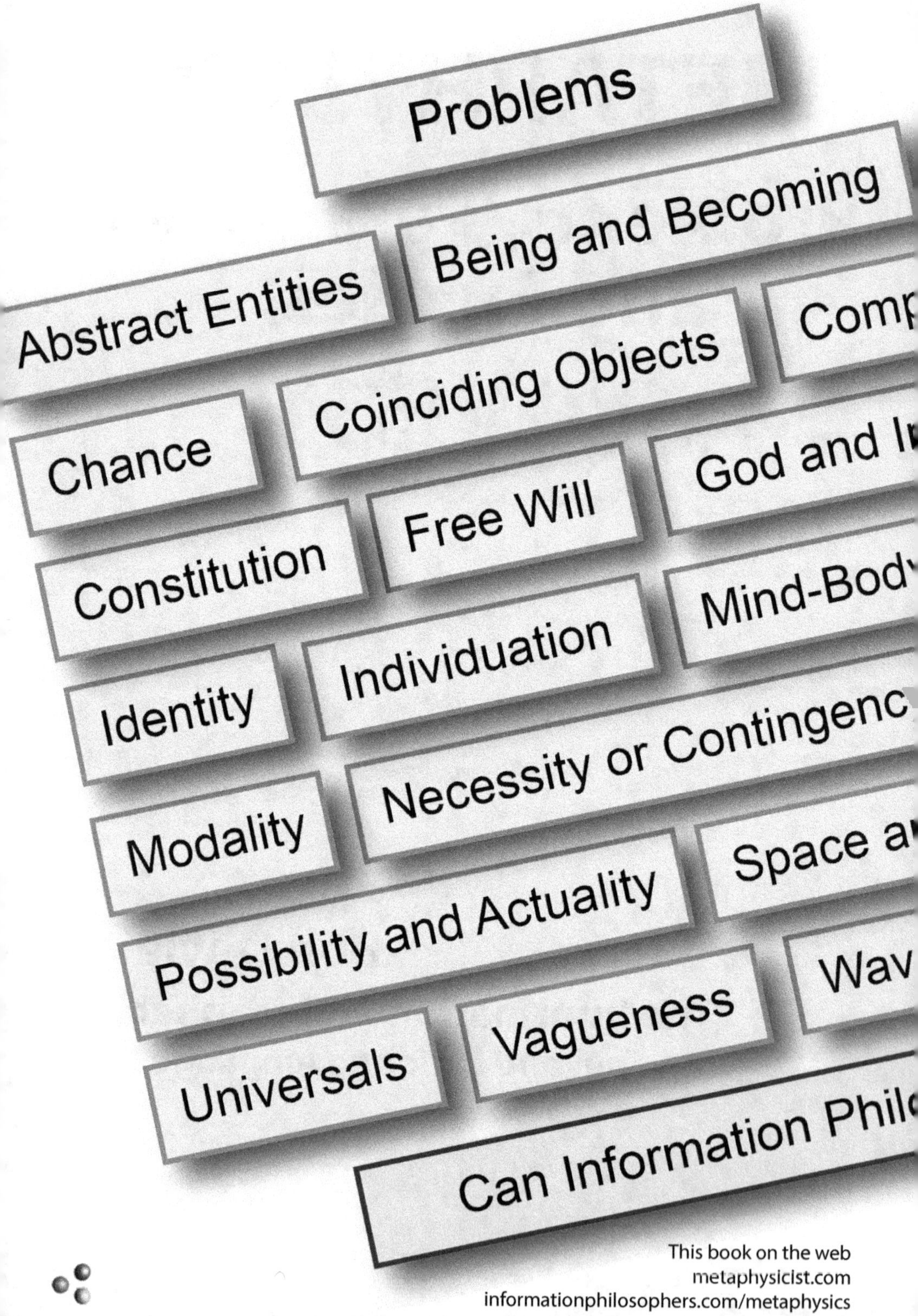

Problems

- Abstract Entities
- Being and Becoming
- Com[position]
- Chance
- Coinciding Objects
- God and I[mmortality]
- Constitution
- Free Will
- Mind-Body
- Identity
- Individuation
- Modality
- Necessity or Contingenc[y]
- Possibility and Actuality
- Space a[nd Time]
- Vagueness
- Wav[e-Particle Duality]
- Universals
- Can Information Phil[osophy...]

This book on the web
metaphysicist.com
informationphilosophers.com/metaphysics

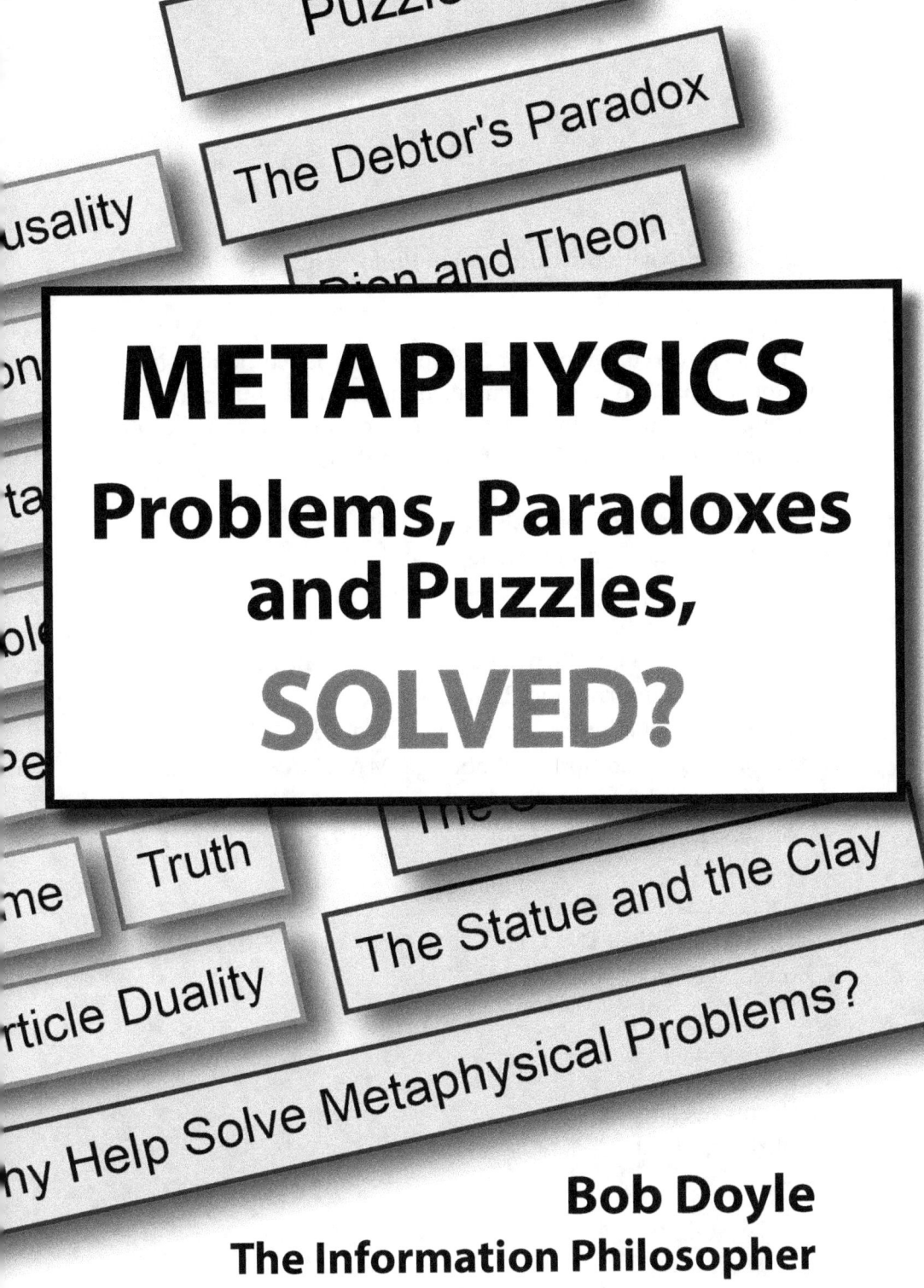

First edition, 2016
© 2016, Bob Doyle, The Information Philosopher

All rights reserved. No part of this book may be reproduced in any form by electronic or mechanical means (including photocopying, recording, or information storage and retrieval) without the prior permission of The Information Philosopher.

Publisher's Cataloging-In-Publication Data
(Prepared by The Donohue Group, Inc.)

Names: Doyle, Bob, 1936-
Title: Metaphysics : problems, paradoxes, and puzzles, solved? / Bob Doyle, the Information Philosopher.
Other Titles: Metaphysics : problems, paradoxes, puzzles
Description: First edition. | Cambridge, MA, USA : I-Phi Press, 2016. | Includes bibliographical references and index.
Identifiers: ISBN 978-0-9835802-6-3 | ISBN 978-0-9835802-2-5 (ebook)
Subjects: LCSH: Metaphysics.
Classification: LCC BD111 .D69 2016 (print) | LCC BD111 (ebook) | DDC 110--dc23

I-Phi Press
77 Huron Avenue
Cambridge, MA, USA

Dedication

To all the metaphysicians on the METAPHYSICIST.COM website.

Special thanks to many who have sent suggestions and corrections to ensure that their work is presented as accurately as possible for the students and young professionals who use the METAPHYSICIST and INFORMATION PHILOSOPHER websites as an entry point into some great intellectual problems that they may help to clarify and teach to others in the coming decades.

Information is like love. Giving it to others does not reduce it. It is not a scarce economic good. Sharing it increases the total information in human minds.

Information wants to be free.

Bob Doyle
Cambridge, MA
December, 2016

Contents

Preface — xi
How To Use This Book With The Metaphysicist Website — 1

1. **Introduction** — 3
   How We Proceed — 11
2. **Abstract Entities** — 13
   Information as a Physical Cause — 16; The Idea of Abstraction — 17; Colors as Abstract Entities — 18
3. **Being and Becoming** — 21
   Being and Becoming in Modern Physics — 22
4. **Causality** — 25
   What Counts as a Cause? — 26; The Problem of Induction — 30; Induction and the Scientific Method — 31
5. **Chance** — 35
   The Discovery of Ontological Chance — 43
6. **Change** — 47
   Cosmic Change as the Growth of Information Structures — 50
7. **Coinciding Objects** — 55
   An Information Analysis of "Coinciding Objects" — 59
8. **Composition** — 63
   Temporal Parts — 66; Mereology — 67; Mereological Essentialism — 69; Biomereological Essentialism — 72; Composition as Holism and Emergence — 73
9. **Constitution** — 75
   Is Constitution Identity? — 75
10. **Essentialism** — 79
    Intrinsic Information as Essence — 79; Natural Kinds and Mereological Essentialism — 80
11. **Free Will** — 83
    The Two-Stage Model of Free Will — 85; Does Ontological Chance Threaten Free Will? — 92
12. **God and Immortality** — 95
    No Creator, But There Was/Is A Creation — 96; The Ergod — 97; The Problem of Immortality — 98
13. **Identity** — 101
    Information Identity — 101; A Criterion for Identity — 101; A Criterion for Essence — 103; Background of the Problem — 104; Leibniz — 107; Leibniz's Laws — 108; Frege — 109; Peirce — 111; Principia Mathematica — 112; Wittgenstein — 113; Frank Ramsey on Identity — 114; Willard Van Orman Quine on Identity — 115; Ruth Barcan Marcus — 120; David Wiggins — 121; Saul Kripke on Identity — 122; Peter Geach on Relative Identity — 125;

David Lewis   126; Relative Identity   126; A = A   129; Identity through Time   130; Changes in Time   131; Personal Identity   132; Identity and Biology   132; Vague Identity   133

14. Individuation — 135
The History of Individuation   135; The Biology of Individuation   139; Individuation and Quantum Mechanics   140

15. Mind-Body Problem — 143
The Problem of Mental Causation   144; Mind as an Experience Recorder and Reproducer   146; Consciousness a Property of Mind   149

16. Modality — 151
Actual Possibles and Possible Possibles   155; The Many Possible Worlds in Our Actual World   156; Necessity of Identity and the Limits of Necessitism   157; Modal Realism and Possible Worlds   159

17. Necessity (or Contingency) — 161
The Logical Necessity of the Analytic and the *A Priori*   161; The Logical Necessity of Necessity   162; The Necessity of Identity   165; Separating Necessity from Analyticity and A Prioricity   167; Necessity and Free Will   170; No Logical Necessity in the Material World   172; Necessitism   173

18. Persistence — 175
Perdurance   177; Endurance   179; Temporal Parts?   179

19. Possibility — 181
Actual Possibles   183; Actualism   184; Possibilities in Quantum Mechanics   185; Shannon and Quantum Indeterminism   186; An Information Interpretation of Quantum Mechanics   189; Possible Worlds   190; Other Possible Worlds   193

20. Space and Time — 195
Space and Time in Quantum Physics   196; Nonlocality and Entanglement   200; Visualizing Entanglement   201; Can Metaphysics Solve the EPR Paradox?   203

21. Universals — 207
The One and the Many   211

22. Vagueness — 213
Vagueness and the Two-Slit Experiment   215

23. Wave-Particle Duality — 217
The Heart of the Puzzle   218; The History of Waves and Particles   221; Dueling Wave and Particle Theories   222; Dirac on Wave-Particle Duality   225

24. The Debtor's Paradox — 227
Information Philosophy Resolves the Debtor's Paradox   229

Contents

25. Dion and Theon — 233
What Chrysippus May Have Been Doing 234;
An Information Philosophy Analysis 237

26. Frege's Puzzle — 241
Names and Reference 243; Quine's Paradoxes 244;
The New Theory of Reference 246

27. The Growing Argument — 249

28. The Infinite Regress — 253

29. Porphyry's Fateful Question — 257

30. The Problem of the Many — 259
Peter Unger 261; Peter Geach 262

31. The Ship of Theseus — 265
How Information Philosophy Resolves the Paradox 265;
How to Make Two Ships Out of One. 266

32. Sorites Puzzle — 269
Liar Paradox 271

33. The Statue and the Clay — 273
How to Make Two Out of One 275

34. Tibbles, the Cat — 279

35. Metaphysicians — 285
David M. Armstrong 285; Michael Burke 287; Rudolf Carnap 292; David Chalmers 293; Roderick Chisholm 296; René Descartes 298; Peter Geach 300; David Hume 302; Immanuel Kant 304; Saul Kripke 305; David Lewis 315; E. Jonathan Lowe 316; Ruth Barcan Marcus 318; Trenton Merricks 319; Huw Price 323; Willard Van Orman Quine 325; Michael Rea 330; Alan Sidelle 332; Ted Sider 335; Peter Unger 339; Peter van Inwagen 340; Timothy Williamson 349

36. A History of Metaphysics — 353
The Presocratics 353; Socrates and Plato 354; Aristotle 354; The Stoics 356; Academic Skeptics 360; The Scholastics 360; Descartes 361; Leibniz 361; The Empiricists 364; Kant 365; Positivisms 366; Linguistic Analysis 369; Modal Logic 370; The Necessity of Identity 374; David Wiggins on Identity 375; Saul Kripke on Identity 377; David Lewis on Identity 378; Modal Logic and Possible Worlds 379; Why Modal Logic Is Not Metaphysics 381; The Return of Metaphysics and Its Paradoxes 384

Great Problems Solved? — 387

Bibliography — 397

Index — 404

Preface

Metaphysics has been rejuvenated in the past few decades, after nearly a century of attacks from logical positivists, logical empiricists, behaviorists, and eliminative materialists, with their loud cries that metaphysics is "meaningless" or "non-sense."

Traditional metaphysicians asked questions about the fundamental nature of physical reality. Modern metaphysicians claim to be looking into the *foundations* of metaphysics, sometimes called meta-metaphysics. Similarly, they are looking for a new basis for ontology, a meta-ontology.

They are also engaged in a critical review of why attacks on metaphysics were so successful in the past century. Some see many years of what can be looked at today as just verbal quibbling, what Kant once called "word-juggling " (*Wortklauberei*). Can the analysis of language, of concepts and their precise definitions, yield truths about the world? Many famous debates now appear to have been metaphysicians talking past each other, captivated by their elaborate conceptual schemes and dense jargon. Others think metaphysics might have had a more scientific approach.

Although few moderns draw much of metaphysical importance from today's sciences of physics, chemistry, biology, or psychology, for example, some do like a methodology of hypothetical axiomatic systems that may even offer the kind of experimental testing that is the watchword of modern science.

Some view the "naturalization" of epistemology by WILLARD VAN ORMAN QUINE as a step toward a more scientific metaphysics, but others criticize the limited "extensional" approach of Quine and RUDOLF CARNAP, in which meaning and truth of our words are to be found in the members of sets of objects.

Other "intensionalists" find meaning located in human intentions, either in initial speech acts or final interpretations of meanings in relevant contexts, but both of these are vulnerable to charges of relativism from modern skeptics. Proponents look to philosophers of science who are impressed by interpretations of

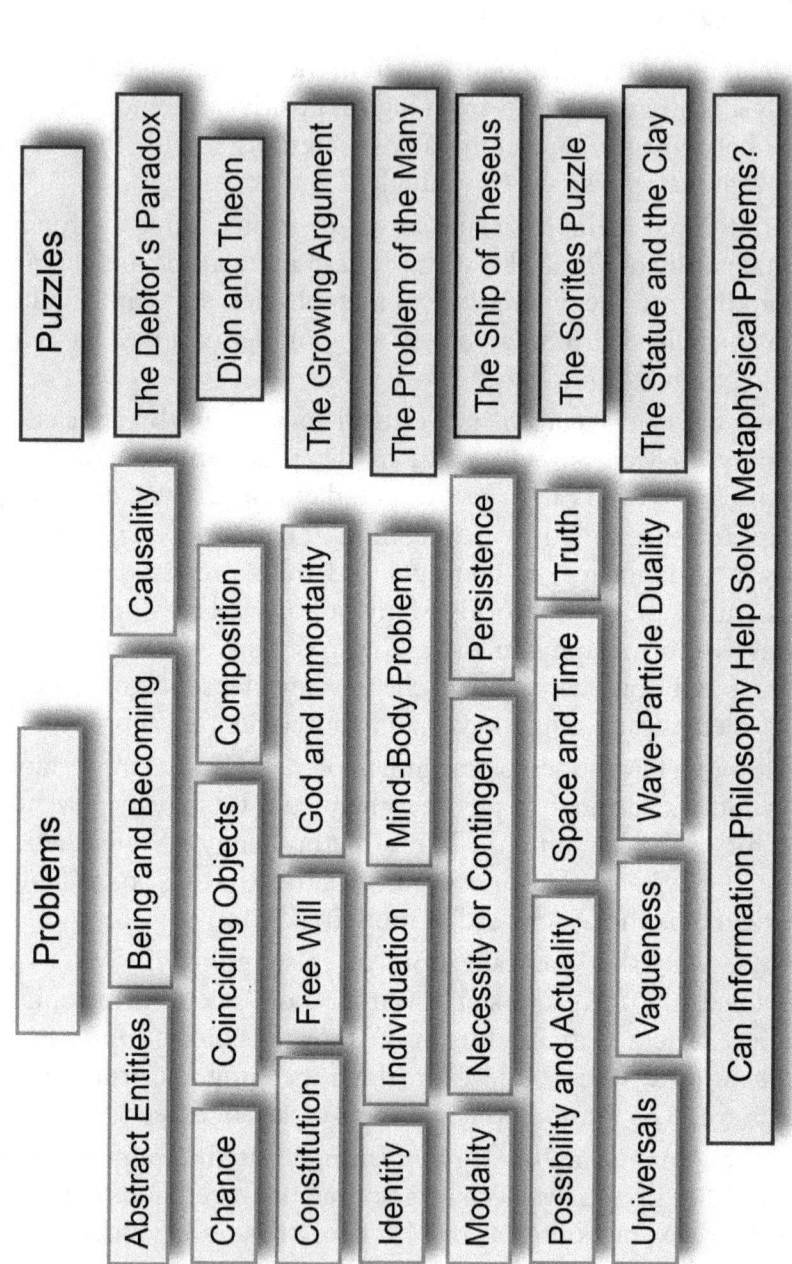

Figure iv-1. A taxonomy of metaphysical problems, puzzles, and paradoxes.

quantum physics that may indicate that reality is not an external, observer-independent entity.

Perhaps the most significant development in the rebirth of metaphysics has been the reintroduction of *modal* thinking that had been a vital part since Aristotle, but was more or less forgotten since the late-nineteenth century creation of second-order propositional logic by GOTTLOB FREGE.

Quine opposed the reintroduction of modality, but parallel to the existential and universal quantifiers he thought sufficed, modal logicians have added operators for possibility and necessity. Next to ∃, "there exists" or "for some," and ∀, "for all," modal logicians have added operators for ◊ "possibly" and □ "necessarily."

Necessity is defined as propositions true in all possible worlds. Possibility is defined as propositions true in some possible worlds.

But there is no room in the new modal logic and its many possible worlds for *contingent* statements, about the future for example, propositions that are not yet either true or false.

The possible worlds of DAVID LEWIS are in fact as eliminatively materialist and completely deterministic as the most classical physics. *There are no possibilities in Lewis's possible worlds.*

Leading metaphysicians who see the new modal logic *as metaphysics* have an opportunity to make a significant breakthrough in visualizing the fundamental nature of physical reality, if they can get beyond claims they have found an absolute *metaphysical necessity* - the necessity of identity, for example.

We will examine their arguments for the necessity of identity and offer a *criterion for identity,* one that establishes the existence of *relative identity*, as well as finding an *absolute identity,* which we find must be limited to cases of *self-identity.*

And we will make the case for the existence of *metaphysical possibilities*, which may allow metaphysics to become the ground for the so-called "quantum reality" of modern physics.

Without metaphysical possibility there can be no foundation for the possibility of metaphysics.

In part 1, chapters 1 to 23, we examine some classic problems in metaphysics, attempting to resolve them by analyzing their information content, not their logic or language.

Chapters 24 to 34, in part 2, look at some of the most ancient puzzles and paradoxes of metaphysics, still unsolved but now rejuvenated. We also look at a few modern puzzles.

These chapters are arranged alphabetically. They can be assigned for independent reading. As a result, there is considerable redundancy on some basic concepts.

Since this work is intended as a critical resource for students, we provide extensive quotations from original thinkers to avoid clumsy paraphrases in our words of their unique ideas.

In part 3 (chapter 35) we describe the works of some leading metaphysicians.

In part 4 (chapter 36) we briefly review the history of metaphysics.

In an appendix, we summarize a number of other problems in philosophy, physics, cosmology, psychology, and biology for which an information philosophy approach suggests plausible solutions.

Most of our chapters are supplemented by additional material on the web pages at **www.metaphysicist.com**.

Bob Doyle
bobdoyle@informationphilosopher.com
rodoyle@fas.harvard.edu
Astronomy Department
Harvard University
Cambridge, MA
December, 2016

How To Use This Book With The Metaphysicist Website

The content of this book comes from our new **metaphysicist.com** website and the **informationphilosopher.com** website. You will find multiple entry points into the websites from this book, with URLs for the chapters and in many of the footnotes. I hope that you agree that the combination of a printed book and an online knowledge-base website is a powerful way to do philosophy in the twenty-first century.

The Metaphysicist site has four drop-down menus - Problems, Puzzles, History, and Metaphysicians. Above these are the eight drop-down menus of the parent Information Philosopher website.

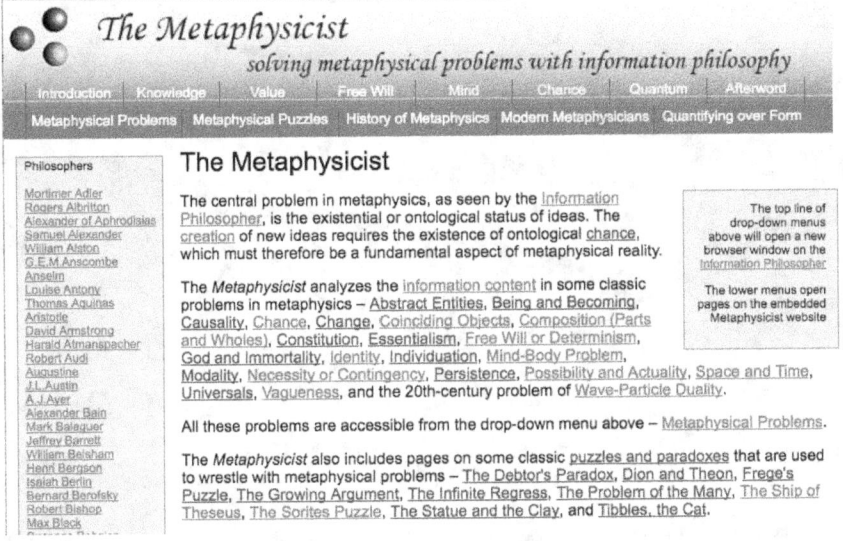

Figures in the text often are full-color *animated* images on the I-Phi website. All our images come from open-source websites.

Names in SMALL CAPS in the book are the hundreds of philosophers and scientists with their own web pages on the I-Phi website. Active links on the Metaphysicist site will jump to those thinkers on I-Phi.

Chapter 1

Introduction

Problems

Introduction

We apply methods of information philosophy to metaphysics and find solutions to several classic problems, puzzles and paradoxes. You can find them all on our website **metaphysicist.com**, the most important of which are the problem of absolute and relative identity, the problem of composition (parts/wholes) and of coinciding objects, Aristotelian essentialism, the need for a metaphysical possibility, and the semantics and modal logic of "possible worlds."

Many ancient puzzles are variations on the problem of coinciding objects, including Dion and Theon, the Growing Argument, and the Statue and the Clay. We solve these puzzles.

A central problem in information philosophy is the existential or ontological status of ideas. We show that while ideas exist in the physical world, they are not made of the matter and energy normally associated with "physical" objects. This in no way makes them supernatural or other-worldly. But ideas have a kind of physicality that deserves the name of metaphysical.

We solve the problem since at least RENÉ DESCARTES of how *immaterial* ideas in the mind have causal power over material objects like the body. The solution involves no intermediate material entity, such as his pineal gland.

We find that the *creation* of new ideas requires the existence of ontological chance. Metaphysical possibility must therefore be a fundamental aspect of metaphysical reality. Sadly, most modern metaphysicians embrace the notion of metaphysical necessity.

Information provides a unique explanation of self-identity and the *relative* identity of numerically distinct objects. It also explains the existential status of abstract entities and non-existent objects.

Metaphysics is an abstract human invention about the nature of concrete reality – *immaterial* thoughts about material things. Information philosophy explains the metaphysics of chance and possibilities, which always underlie the creation of new information structures. Without metaphysical possibilities, there can be no human creativity and no new knowledge.

Metaphysics

A materialist metaphysics asks questions about the underlying substrate presumed to *constitute* all the objects in the universe. Unfortunately, most modern philosophers are eliminative materialists and determinists who think there is "nothing but" the substrate of matter. As JAEGWON KIM puts it,

> "bits of matter and their aggregates in space-time exhaust the contents of the world. This means that one would be embracing an ontology that posits entities other than material substances — that is, immaterial minds, or souls, outside physical space, with immaterial, nonphysical properties." [1]

A formalist or idealist metaphysics asks about the *arrangement* and *organization* of matter that shapes material objects, what brings their forms into existence, and what causes their changes in space and time. Information philosophy defends a Platonic realm of *immaterial* ideas in a dualism with the realm of matter and energy. The information realm is physical and natural. It is not supernatural and "outside space and time." Ideas are embodied in matter and use energy for their communication. But they are neither matter nor energy. They are forms that inform.

The total amount of matter (and energy) in the universe is a conserved quantity. Because of the universe expansion, there is ever more room in space for each material particle, ever more ways to arrange the material, ever more possibilities. The total information in the universe is constantly increasing. This is the first contribution of information philosophy to metaphysics.

The second contribution is to restore a *dualist* idealism, based on the essential importance of information communication in all living things. Since the earliest forms of proto-life, information stored in each organism has been used to create the following generations, including the random variations that have evolved to become thinking human beings who invented the world of ideas that contains metaphysics. Abstract information is an essential, if *immaterial*, part of reality. Plato was right that his "ideas" (ἰδέας) are real.

Plato's forms inform.

---

[1] Kim (2007). Physicalism, or something near enough. *p.71*

A third contribution from information philosophy adds biology to the analysis of metaphysical problems which began in puzzles over change and growth. The parts of living things – we call them biomers – are communicating with one another, which integrates them into their "wholes" in a way impossible for mere material parts – a *biomereological essentialism.*

The arrangement of individual material particles and their interaction is abstract immaterial information. The metaphysics of information can also explain the cosmic creation process underlying the origin of all information structures in the universe and the communication of information between all living things, which we will show use a meaningful biological language, consisting of arbitrary symbols, that has evolved to become human language.

Ontology asks the question "what is there?"

Eliminative materialism claims that nothing exists but material particles, which makes many problems in ancient and modern metaphysics difficult if not insoluble. To be sure, we are made of the same material as the ancient metaphysicians. With every breath we take, we inspire 10 or 20 of the fixed number of molecules of air that sustained Aristotle. We can calculate this because the material in the universe is a constant.

But information is not a fixed quantity. The stuff of thought and creativity, information has been increasing since the beginning of the universe. There is ever more knowledge (but relatively little increase in wisdom?) With hundreds if not thousands of times as many philosophers as ancient Greece, should we still be debating the same ancient puzzles and paradoxes?

Information philosophy restores so-called "non-existent objects" to our ontology. Abstract entities consist of the same kind of information that provides the structure and process information of a concrete object. What we call a "concept" about an object is some subset of the immaterial information in the object, accurate to the extent that the concept is isomorphic to that subset.

Epistemology asks, "how do we know what there is?"

Immaterial information provides a new ground for epistemology, the theory of knowledge. We know something about the "things themselves" when we discover an isomorphism between our abstract ideas and the concrete objects in the material world. But words and names are not enough. Information philosophy goes beyond the logical puzzles and language games of analytic philosophy. It identifies knowledge as information in human minds and in the external artifacts of human culture.

Abstract information is the foundation – the metaphysical ground – of both logic and language as means of communication. It is a dual parallel to the material substrate that the Greeks called ὑποκείμενον - the "underlying." It gives matter its form and shape. Form informs.

Much of formal metaphysics is about necessary relationships between universal ideas, certain knowledge that we can believe independent of any experience, knowledge that is "*a priori*" and "analytic" (true by logic and reason alone, or by definition). These ideas appear to be unchanging, eternal truths in any possible world.

Information philosophy now shows that there is no necessity in the material world. Apodeictic certainty is just an idea. There is no *a priori* knowledge that was not first discovered empirically (*a posteriori*). Only after a fact is discovered do we see how to demonstrate it logically as *a priori*. And everything analytic is part of a humanly constructed language, and thus synthetic. All such "truths" are philosophical inventions, mere concepts, albeit some of the most powerful ideas ever to enter the universe.

Most important, a formal and idealistic metaphysics is about abstract entities, in logic and mathematics, some of which seem to be true independent of time and space. Aristotle, the first metaphysician, called them "first principles" (*archai, axioma*). GOTTFRIED LEIBNIZ said they are true in all possible worlds, which is to say their truth is independent of the actual world.

But if these abstract metaphysical truths are not material, where are these ideas in our world? Before their discovery, they *subsisted* as unknown properties. Once invented and discovered to be empirical facts, they are embedded in material objects, artifacts, and minds – the software in our hardware. Those ideas that are invented but not found empirically "real" (imagined fictions, flawed hypotheses, round squares) are also added to the sum of human knowledge, even if never exemplified or embodied.

Many unchanging abstract entities share a property that the early philosophers Parmenides, Plato, and Aristotle called "Being," to distinguish its nature from "Becoming," the property of all material objects that change with time. Certain truths cannot possibly change. They are eternal, seemingly "outside space and time."

It is unfortunate that information philosophy undermines the logical concepts of metaphysical necessity, certainty, the *a priori* and analytic, even truth itself, by limiting their analyticity to the unchanging abstract entities in the realm of Being. But, on the positive side, information philosophy now establishes the metaphysical possibility of ontological possibilities.

Possibilities depend on the existence of irreducible ontological chance and contingency, the antithesis of *necessity*. Without metaphysical possibilities, no new information can be created.

Information philosophy and metaphysics restore an *immaterial* mind to the impoverished and deflated metaphysics that we have had since empiricism and naturalism rejected the dualism of RENÉ DESCARTES and its troublesome mind-body problem.

Naturalism is a materialism. Just as existentialism is a humanism. Even stronger, naturalism is an eliminative materialism. It denies the immaterial and particularly the mental.

While information philosophy is a form of the great dualism of idealism versus materialism, it is not a substance dualism. Information is a physical, though immaterial, property of matter. Information philosophy is a property dualism.

Abstract information is neither matter nor energy, although it needs matter for its embodiment and energy for its communication.

Information is *immaterial*. It is the modern spirit, the ghost in the machine. It is the mind in the body. It is the soul. And when we die, our personal information and its communication perish. The matter remains.

Information is the underlying currency of all communication and language. Passive material objects in the universe contain information, which metaphysicians and scientists analyze to understand everything material. They are *information structures*. But passive material objects do not create, actively communicate, and process information, as do all living things.

Realism is the ontological commitment to the existence of *material* things. Information realism is equally committed to the existence or subsistence of *immaterial*, but physical, ideas.

Human language is the most highly evolved form of information communication in biology. But even the simplest organisms signal their condition and their needs, both internally among their smallest parts and externally as they compete with other living things in their environment.

Biosemioticians convincingly argue that all the messages in biology, from the intracellular genetic codes sent to the ribosomes to produce more of a specific protein, to the words in sentences like this one, are a meaningful part of one continuously evolving semantic system. All messaging is as purposeful as a human request for food, so biology is called *teleonomic*, though not teleological. This "telos" or purpose in life did not pre-exist life.

Like human language, the signs used in biological messages can be symbolic and arbitrary, having no iconic or indexical or any other intrinsic relation between a signifier and the signified concept or object.[2] Like human signs, the meaning of a biological sign is highly dependent on the context. Only four neurotransmitters act as primary messengers sent to a cell, inside of which one of dozens of secondary messengers may be activated to determine the use inside the particular cell - the ultimate Wittgensteinian "meaning as use" in the message.

---

2   Doyle (2016) *Great Problems in Philosophy and Physics*, Appendix G

Modern Anglo-American metaphysicians think problems in metaphysics can be treated as problems in language, potentially solved by conceptual analysis. They are analytical language philosophers. But language is too flexible, too ambiguous and full of metaphor, to be a diagnostic tool for metaphysics. We must go beyond language games and logical puzzles to the underlying information contained in a concept or object.

Information philosophy restores the metaphysical existence of a realm that is "beyond the natural" in the sense since at least DAVID HUME and IMMANUEL KANT that the "laws of nature" completely determine everything that exists, everything that happens, in the phenomenal and material world.

The immaterial realm of information is not "supernatural" in any way, but the creation of information throws considerable light on why so many humans, though few scientists, believe – correctly as it turns out – that there is a *providential* force in the universe.[3]

MARTIN HEIDEGGER, the philosopher of "Being," called FRIEDRICH NIETZSCHE the "last metaphysician." Nietzsche thought that everything in his *"lebensphilosophie"* was the creation of human beings. Indeed, when we are creative, what we create is new information, pure abstract ideas or material information structures.

Did we humans "discover" the abstract ideas, or did we "invent" them and then find them to be true of the world, including those true in any possible world? ALBERT EINSTEIN called them "free inventions of the human mind which admit of no *a priori* justification either through the nature of the human mind or in any other way at all."[4]

As opposed to an analytic language metaphysician, a metaphysicist searches for answers in the analysis of *immaterial* (but physical) information that can be *seen* when it is embodied in external material information structures. Otherwise it can only be *known* – in our minds.

Metaphysical truths are pure abstract information, subsisting in the realm of ideas.

---

3   See chapter 7 below.
4   Einstein. (1933) 'On the Methods of Theoretical Physics,' p.165

Metaphysical facts about the world are discovered when there are isomorphisms between abstract ideas and the concrete structures in the external world that embody those ideas.

Information philosophy bridges the ideal and material worlds of Plato and Aristotle and the noumenal and phenomenal worlds of Kant. It demonstrates how *immaterial* minds are a *causal* force in the material world, connecting the psychological and phenomenological with the "things themselves," which are perceptible *because* they are embodiments of our concepts, our ideas.

The causal force of ideas, combined with the existence of alternative possibilities, is the information philosophy basis for free will.

What are we to say about a field of human inquiry whose major problems have hardly changed over two millennia? Information philosophy looks at a wide range of problems in metaphysics, situating each problem in its historical framework and providing accounts of the best work by today's metaphysicians.

Metaphysicians today are analytic language philosophers, some of whom work on a very small number of metaphysical problems that began as puzzles and paradoxes two thousand years ago.

The *metaphysicist* adds biological knowledge and quantum physics to help investigate the fundamental nature of reality. DAVID WIGGINS called for the former and E. JONATHAN LOWE called for the latter. DAVID CHALMERS thinks information may help explain the "hard problem" of consciousness.

An information-based metaphysics provides a single explanation for the origin and evolution of the universe as well as life on Earth. Since the beginning of time, it is the creation of material information structures that underlies all possibilities.

From the appearance of the first living thing, biological communication of information has played a causal role in evolution.

Metaphysics must include both the study of matter and its *immaterial* form. A quantum particle is pure matter or energy. The quantum wave function is pure abstract information about possibilities.

The metaphysics of possibility grounds the very possibility of metaphysics.

How We Proceed

In part 1, we analyze the information content in twenty-two classic problems in metaphysics – Abstract Entities, Being and Becoming, Causality, Chance, Change, Coinciding Objects, Composition (Parts and Wholes), Constitution, Essentialism, Free Will or Determinism, God and Immortality, Identity, Individuation, Mind-Body Problem, Modality, Necessity or Contingency, Persistence, Possibility and Actuality, Space and Time, Universals, Vagueness, and the 20th-century quantum problem of Wave-Particle Duality.

In part 2, we apply the lessons learned from part 1 to some classic puzzles and paradoxes that are frequently used to wrestle with metaphysical problems – The Debtor's Paradox, Dion and Theon, Frege's Puzzle, The Growing Argument, The Infinite Regress, The Problem of the Many, The Ship of Theseus, The Sorites Puzzle, The Statue and the Clay, and Tibbles, the Cat.

In part 3, we take a closer look at the work of twenty-three metaphysicians who have made major contributions to the problems and puzzles above, including David Armstrong, Michael Burke, Rudolf Carnap, David Chalmers, Rod Chisholm, René Descartes, Peter Geach, David Hume, Immanuel Kant, David Lewis, E. Jonathan Lowe, Ruth Barcan Marcus, Trenton Merricks, Huw Price, Willard van Orman Quine, Michael Rea, Alan Sidelle, Ted Sider, Richard Taylor, Peter Unger, Peter van Inwagen, David Wiggins, and Timothy Williamson.

Part 4 is a brief history of metaphysics, touching on the introduction and development of our problems, puzzles, and paradoxes.

An appendix lists some of the great problems in philosophy, physics, cosmology, psychology, and biology that may soon be solved using the methods of information philosophy.

We hope readers will look at web pages on metaphysicist.com that correspond to each of the chapters of the book for further information, for corrections, and for your suggestions, which we will incorporate in future editions of *Metaphysics*.

Chapter 2

Problems

Abstract Entities

Abstract Entities

Rather than simply ask "Do abstract entities like numbers and properties exist," a metaphysicist prefers to ask in what way they might exist that is different from the way in which "concrete" objects exist.

Concrete objects can be seen and touched by our senses. They are material, with causal relations that obey the physical laws of nature.

Abstract entities are *immaterial*, but some of them can still play a causal role, for example when agents use them to decide on their actions, or when chance events (particularly at the quantum level) go this way instead of that.

Just as the mind is like software in the brain hardware, the abstract information in a material object is the same kind of immaterial stuff as the information in an abstract entity, a concept or a "non-existent object." Some philosophers say that such immaterial things "subsist," rather than exist.

Broadly speaking, the distinction between concrete and abstract objects corresponds to the distinction between the material and the ideal. Ideas in minds are *immaterial*. They need the matter of the brain to be embodied and some kind of energy to be communicated to other minds. But they are not themselves matter or energy. "Eliminativists," who believe the natural world contains only material things, deny the existence of ideas, of immaterial information, and of the mind itself.

Some ideas may be wholly fictitious and nonsensical, whether mere possibles or even impossibles, but most ideas correspond to actual objects or processes going on in the world. In either case, we can usually specify the information content of the idea.

Metaphysicists identify abstract entities with the information contained in them. They may be concepts that did not exist in the world until they were *invented*. Or the information may have pre-existed in material structures and so we say they were *discovered*. For example, the idea of the moon includes the concepts of a distinct shape, color, and even the appearance of a face.

This chapter on the web - metaphysicist.com/problems/abstract_entities

Many such ideas are mind-independent. Consider properties of the moon. Most observers agree the shape is round and the color is white. (Actually, the moon is blacker than most any terrestrial black object. It only appears white compared to the blackness of space.) Some metaphysicians deny the existence of a universal property such as roundness or whiteness. But metaphysicists see the information needed to specify circularity and the wavelengths of radiation that correspond to whiteness. And that information is embodied in the moon, just as a software program is embodied in computer hardware, and a mental idea is embodied in a brain.

Many ideas or concepts are created by human minds by "picking out" some of the information in physical objects. Whether such concepts "carve nature at the joints"[1] depends on their usefulness in understanding the world.

Plato's Theory of the Forms held that Ideas like the circle pre-exist material beings, whereas Aristotle argued that the Ideas are abstractions from the general properties in all the actual circles.

Information philosophy restores so-called "non-existent objects" to our ontology. They consist of the same kind of information that provides the structure and process information of a concrete object. What we call a "concept" about an object is some subset of the information in the object, accurate to the extent that the concept is *isomorphic* to that subset. By "picking out" different subsets, we can sort objects, classifying and categorizing them.

Information philosophy can then defend the claim that all this abstract information that represents our knowledge about both material and immaterial objects is itself a collection of abstract entities, mere concepts about objects and other concepts.

The abstract vs. concrete dichotomy maps well onto the ancient dichotomy between idealism and materialism. But in modern times, many philosophers distinguish a third realm beyond the ancient dualism of idealism and materialism. The apparently mind-independent ideas are described as "objective" or "intersubjective" by contrast with the purely "subjective."

---

1   Plato, *Phaedrus*, 265e

Consider the "triads" of GOTTLOB FREGE, KARL POPPER, CHARLES SANDERS PEIRCE.

Gottlob Frege's Three Realms
  An External Realm of Public Physical Things and Events
  An Internal Subjective Realm of Private Thoughts
  An "Objective" Platonic Realm of Ideal "Senses" (to which sentences refer, providing their meaning)

Karl Popper's Three Worlds (clearly influenced by Frege)
  World I - "the realm of physical things and processes"
  World II - "the realm of subjective human experience"
  World III - "the realm of culture and objective knowledge" - of human artifacts (our *Sum*)

C. S. Peirce's triad of Objects, Percepts, and Concepts is in the same order as Frege and Popper.

In information philosophy, we also divide the world into three fundamental parts, the material, the ideal (ideas are the same kind of abstraction as pure information), and the biological/human, a middle world that combines ideality and materiality, essentially mind and body, where we find the realm of subjective thoughts and actions - human experience.

We could also widen the definition of the middle human realm to include the biological realm. It would include the genetic content of all living things, the product of four billon years of evolution. The genetic information is not the nucleotides of DNA that embody it. Both kinds of knowledge, human and biological, are abstract entities.

Human knowledge (information) and biological knowledge are created, stored, and communicated by similar means. The creation of new information requires chance events. Its storage requires the embodiment of abstract symbols or patterns in material information structures.

Communication of those symbols requires transmission through a medium, via sound and sight at a distance, or touch, smell, and taste by contact. These all are evolutionary refinements of the chemical interactions inside living things. Assembled from arbitrary symbols, the syntax and semantics of messages from a cell nucleus to the ribosomes, or messages between cells, even signaling from the amygdala to the prefrontal cortex, are the progenitors of human prose and poetry.

Many centuries ago, the neoplatonist philosopher Porphyry asked what some called his "fateful question, "what is the existential status of the Platonic ideas?" Metaphysicists see our ideas as the information they contain. They have no existence as material, although they might be embodied in material. Our knowledge can be communicated in the form of energy or matter to other beings and to material things. But it is neither matter nor energy.

Information as a Physical Cause

Abstract entities are generally thought to be causally inert. Information philosophy demonstrates that abstract information (ideas) can initiate new causal chains starting in the minds of agents. Although the ideas are embodied in the material brains of the agents, their content is not material. New immaterial information generates new possibilities that are "free creations of the human mind," as Albert Einstein described them.

Many philosophers of mind are "physicalists" or "eliminative materialists." The mind and mental events are described as redundant causes that can be excluded, since they think that the material brain already provides physical events as the cause.

Since abstract entities lack any spatial or temporal positions, they are believed to be causally inert by eliminative materialists.

By contrast, some philosophers of mind hold "Platonist" views, for example that ideas such as sets and numbers have a place in our physical universe, if only a metaphysical place.

One approach that attempts to give causal power to knowledge is the so-called "causal theory of knowledge" associated with FRANK RAMSEY, ALVIN GOLDMAN, DAVID ARMSTRONG, HILARY KORNBLITH, and others. Their goal is to avoid the infinite regress of justifications that are implicit in the original Platonic idea that knowledge is "justified true belief." They argue that a causal connection explains why we have "reliable" knowledge, that is to say knowledge that can inform and affect our actions in a pragmatic sense.

This so-called causality can become trapped in an epistemological circle. Information philosophy hopes to breakout of that circle by showing how mere ideas, especially newly created ideas, have causal power over future events.

Pragmatic philosophers since C. S. Peirce have had a similar view, that knowledge is "true" when applying it to the world is efficacious. True knowledge has "cash value" as WILLIAM JAMES put it.

This is the ordinary common sense view, that ideas have changed material things, facts and events, in the physical world, not just ideas themselves or our knowledge of the world.

The Idea of Abstraction

An abstraction is literally something that can be drawn out of something else as its *essence*. Despite the fundamental abstract/concrete dichotomy of philosophical discourse, an abstract can be material that stimulates a particular sensation, like a smell that is the essence of a perfume or a "color" that is the essential "quale" of redness. The first is a molecule that elicits an olfactory response, the second photons of light of a particular wavelength.

Of course the essence of an abstract entity has no material content. It is just more pure information.

Metaphysicians think that words can list the "properties" of an entity, but these are poor and often vague and ambiguous approximations to the total information in an entity.

A metaphysicist says that the essence, the essential and metaphysical nature of all ideas is the information that they contain.

Of course, any concrete object that is discriminable from a background *contains* information. That information is the arrangement of the matter that embodies the information, the ship not its planks, the statue not the clay. And an arrangement of matter is pure form, pure abstract information.

Colors as Abstract Entities

Colors are thought to present some philosophical puzzles as well as raise deep metaphysical issues about both a mind-independent physical reality and about the philosophy of mind. Information philosophy can clarify these issues.

The puzzles include questions about the ontological property of color. Are the colors properties of physical objects or only visual perceptions? Are colors "real" or merely phenomenal illusions? Is the "quale" that we call "red" in the world or only in the mind.

Eliminativists and materialists who deny the "mind" may accept colors as "primary qualities" that are "really" possessed by physical objects. On the other hand, if colors are dependent on the perceiver, merely projected onto experience, they would be subjective. Puzzles then concern whether two persons might be having different internal experiences when looking at the same color.

Today we know that the eyes may perceive or interpret some light from an object as red when it actually contains no red photons, but only that the photons from the object are relatively longer wavelength than other objects in the scene. So there is definitely what some might regard as a subjective element. But this is mistaken.

In Edwin Land's demonstrations of his famous two-color theory of vision, he showed pictures of apples that were perceived as red when only green and yellow light was used.

The mind's *experience recorder and reproducer* is replaying information about past experiences of apples in varying light conditions to aid in this interpretation. But it is not just "subjective," because all observers experience the same non-intuitive phenomenon. It is "intersubjective" when there is agreement between observers.

Photons coming from a Macintosh apple, a cherry tomato, and a strawberry in ordinary daylight all have the standard wavelengths of red light. But the mind/brain can make up for drastically changed lighting conditions in which the photons landing on our retinas do not have the wavelength property of normal "red" light.

Philosophical theories of colors provide powerful examples of the confusions that arise when we assign words as names of abstract entities. Conceptual analyses of ordinary language and "folk-concepts" of color are mostly a lot of verbal quibbling.

The spectrum of colors sensible to human eyes is in fact a continuum of changing wavelengths (or frequencies) of light that is a tiny part of the spectrum of electromagnetic radiation. Animal eyes have evolved sensitivity to these wavelengths because they are the part of solar radiation that penetrates the earth's atmosphere.

Boundaries of the division into three primary and three secondary colors are as arbitrary and vague as many word or name definitions. There are no precise "color truths" to be found by a critical analysis of "color concepts."

Color science brings precision to a theory of colors by assigning quantitative meaning to "hue" (the wavelength of the predominant color), "saturation" (the amount of the dominant wavelength compared to all other wavelengths), and "intensity" (the total number of all photons). The very real perception of "whiteness" is in fact a combination of all visible colors in amounts that approximate their relative amounts in everyday sunlight. "Blackness" is the absence of any light.

When a metaphysicist examines a color as an abstract entity, the information content of the color provides a quantitative starting point for what is happening in the physical world.

But an objective or intersubjective description of what is being experienced by a specific observer is much more complex, dependent on all the past experiences of the individual and any physiological differences, such as color vision deficiencies in the photo-pigments of the three types of cones that respond to red, green, and blue light.

The author, for example, is red-green color blind, the most common deficiency and has never seen the color green.

Chapter 3

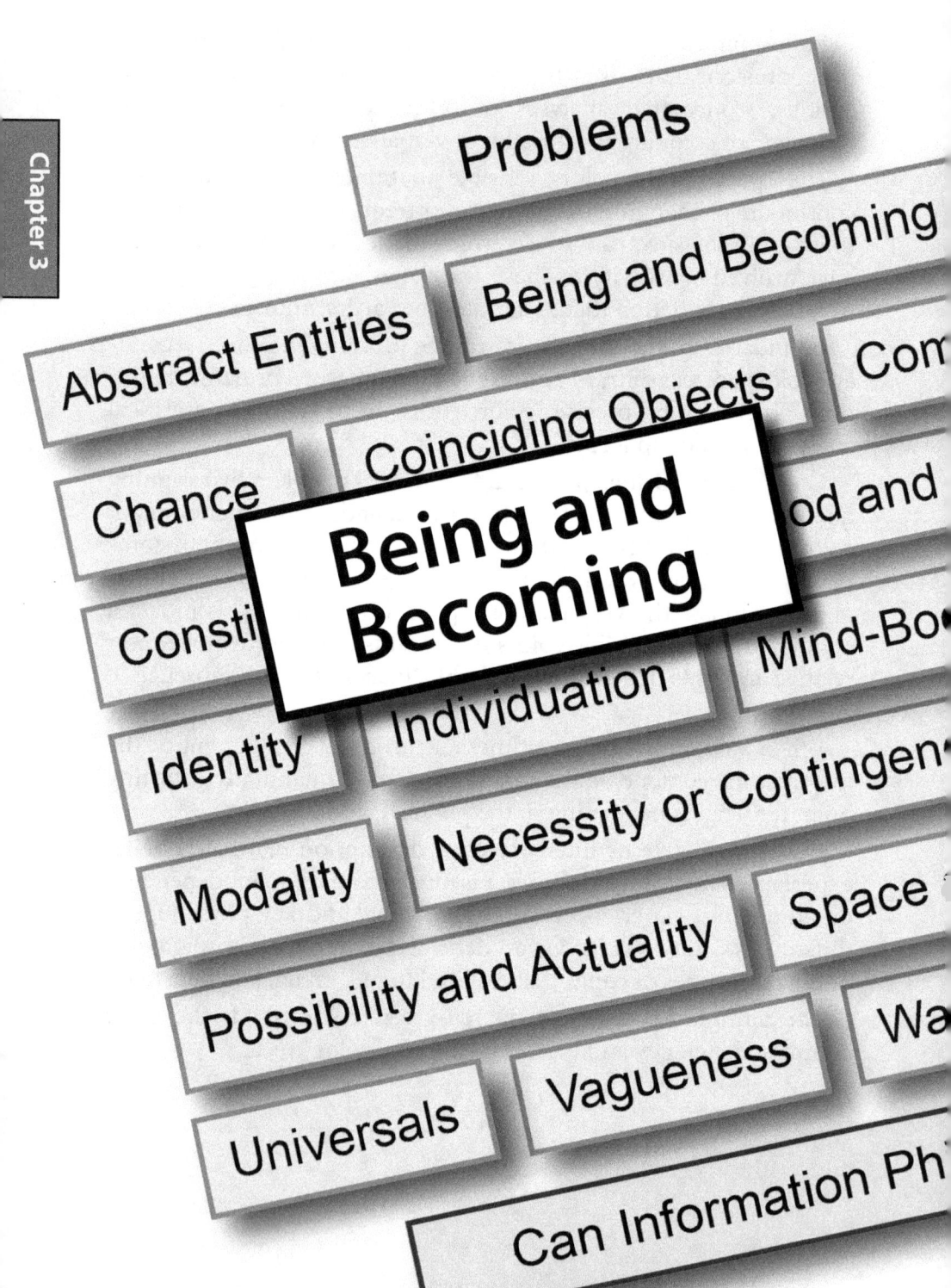

Being and Becoming

Information philosophy greatly simplifies the classic dichotomy between Being and Becoming that has bothered metaphysicians from Heraclitus and Parmenides, Plato and Aristotle down to Martin Heidegger.

Heraclitus argued that the only constants are change and the laws (logos) governing change. Plato said of his ideas:

> "Heraclitus, I believe, says that all things pass and nothing stays, and comparing existing things to the flow of a river, he says you could not step twice into the same river." [1]

By contrast, Parmenides argued that reality is a unity and that any change is merely an illusion.

Being is part of the essential nature of some abstract entities. They are ideas that exist in the immaterial realm of pure information and do not change.

Becoming is the essential nature of concrete material objects, which are always changing, at a minimum changing their positions relative to other objects.

Change in space and time is a characteristic of all concrete material objects.

Some abstract immaterial entities also change, like the time of day. Only those abstract entities that do not change in time are those with metaphysical "Being."

Information philosophy establishes that there is new information being created in the universe at all times, even as the second law of thermodynamics is destroying some information, sadly much more than is being created.

We can therefore limit the realm of "Being" to ideas and other abstract entities. Even the most elementary material particles are not resistant to a change in their "identity" when interacting with other particles. An isolated proton is thought to have an infinite lifetime in principle, but isolation is not possible in practice.

---

1   Plato, *Cratylus* 402a

Now metaphysicians, from Aristotle's original definitions to Heidegger's claim that we have forgotten the original pre-Socratic sense of "being," have talked about "being *qua* being." Even medieval scholars like THOMAS AQUINAS took "being" to be the fundamental ground of metaphysics.

Today's metaphysicians tend to describe fundamental questions about being as ontological and "being *qua* being" as a kind of "meta-ontology" or even "metametaphysics." Are these just verbal quibbles? Typical is the quibble between DAVID LEWIS and PETER VAN INWAGEN when counting existents in a room with two simples. Van Inwagen says that only the two things exist. Lewis sees three things, the simples and their composite.

Consider the statue made from that lump of clay in the metaphysical problem of colocation. It certainly looks to be unchanging as it sits on its pedestal. But with the earth's rapid rotation, its revolutionary travel around the sun, and our Milky Way flying around the Andromeda galaxy, the statue is dramatically moving in space and time, apart from the barely observable deterioration of its surface and the microscopic motions of its atomic constituents.

One could argue that if the statue could be positioned in the inertial frame of the cosmos, that average position of all the galaxies, surely it would sit still in space, but according to special relativity this too is wrong. In the infinitely many inertial frames in relative motion, the statue's space coordinates are changing, and its time coordinate changes inexorably in all frames.

Being and Becoming in Modern Physics

The special theory of relativity has encouraged many physicists and philosophers to think that time does not flow (there is no becoming), that the time dimension from past to future is "already there" in some sense. The physicist Hermann Minkowski described this as a "block universe." The philosopher John McTaggart and other idealists such as J.J.C. SMART described this as an atemporal "B" theory of time. All these theories are like Parmenides' denying the obvious evidence of change.

There is a strong correlation between "Being" and determinism, which is the idea that all the information in the future is already here at the present time, that information is a conserved quantity like matter and energy.

If everything that happens was certain to happen, as determinist philosophers claim, no new information would ever enter the universe. Information would be a universal constant. There would be "nothing new under the sun." Every past and future event could in principle be known by a god-like super-intelligence with access to the fixed totality of information (Laplace's Demon).

The strongest evidence that new information is entering the universe and that change ("Becoming") is real comes from the cosmological evidence that the universe itself came into existence 13.74 billion years ago in a state of maximal chaos and minimal information. There were not yet any "information structures," no atoms for nearly 400 thousand years and no galaxies, star, and planets for over 400 million years.

Now that we have planets, the history of biological evolution on our planet is local evidence for "Becoming," from the first appearance of life over four billion years ago to the creation "from so simple a beginning endless forms most beautiful and most wonderful ..."[2]

---

[2] last sentence of Darwin, *On the Origin of Species*.

Chapter 4

Problems

Abstract Entities
Being and Becoming
Coinciding Objects
Chance
Constitu...
Causality
Individuation
Mind-Bo...
Identity
Necessity or Contingen...
Modality
Space
Possibility and Actuality
Universals
Vagueness
Can Information Ph...

Causality

Belief in causality is deeply held by many philosophers and scientists. Many say it is the basis for all thought and knowledge of the external world.

The core idea of causality is closely related to the idea of determinism. But we can have a "soft" causality without strict determinism. and an adequate or statistical determinism that accommodates *indeterminism*.

And we will see that the departure from strict causality needed to negate determinism is very slight compared to the miraculous ideas associated with the *"causa sui"* (self-caused cause) of the ancients, which most modern thinkers find unintelligible (with the exception of aome theists who accept the idea of miracles).

Despite DAVID HUME's critical attack on the logical necessity of causes, which should have made us all skeptics about the logical necessity for causality, many philosophers embrace strict causal determinism strongly. Some even identify causality with the very possibility of logic and reason.

Few commentators note Hume's view that we all have an unshakable natural belief in causality, despite the impossibility of a logical proof of causality or successful attack on his skepticism.

BERTRAND RUSSELL thought a logical proof excessive,
"The law of causation, according to which later events can theoretically be predicted by means of earlier events, has often been held to be *a priori*, a necessity of thought, a category without which science would not be possible. These claims seem to me excessive." [1]

Now the assumption of deterministic causation underlies most successful scientific theories, with the critical exception of quantum mechanics. Some major objections to the causal determinism implied by Newtonian laws of motion are

---

1 Russell. (1914) *Our Knowledge of the External World*, p.232

- The complete predictability of future events is possible in principle (Laplace's Demon).
- There is only one possible future, even if unpredictable.
- The laws of motion are time reversible.
- Given enough time, all positions and motions will recur.

Information philosophy shows that all these objections can be removed by admitting a modest form of indeterminism into the world, at the microscopic level of quantum mechanics.[2]

The core idea of indeterminism is an event without a cause. Quantum mechanics does not go so far as to say that events have absolutely no causal connection with the events (the distribution of matter and motions) of the immediate past. What it does do is introduce events with a statistical cause. And quantum mechanics makes extremely accurate predictions of the probabilities for the different random outcomes.

So we can have an adequate or statistical causality without strict determinism, which otherwise implies complete predictability of events and only one possible future.

What Counts as a Cause?

For the ancients, a cause was an explanation (*aition*) or a story (*logos*) about how an event came about. For every event there is a cause, they argued. Aristotle famously argued in his *Metaphysics* that there are generally causal chains which he classified as material and formal, efficient and final.

ARISTOTLE's material cause is simply the matter in an object. The formal cause is the *arrangement* of the matter, its "form" or shape. That these are distinct became the basis for metaphysical controversies between the Stoics and the Skeptics. For example, in the puzzle of the Statue and the Clay, the clay is Aristotle's material cause, the shape is Aristotle's formal cause.

Aristotle's efficient cause was the agent who initiates the change, for example, the sculptor of the statue. His final cause was the goal or purpose, the telos or end, in this example, the desire to have a statue.

---

2   Doyle (2016) *Great Problems*, ch.25, Microscopic Irreversibility

In his *Physics* and *Metaphysics,* Aristotle also said there were "accidents" caused by "chance (τυχή)." In his *Physics,* he clearly reckoned chance among the causes. Aristotle considered adding chance as a fifth cause - an uncaused or self-caused cause - that happens when two causal chains come together by accident (συμβεβεκός). He noted that the early physicists found no place for chance among the causes.

In his *Metaphysics,* Aristotle makes the case for chance and uncaused causes (*causa sui*) and in the Nicomachean Ethics he shows our actions can be voluntary and "up to us" so that we can be morally responsible.

> "Nor is there any definite cause for an accident, but only chance (τυχόν), namely an indefinite (ἀόριστον) cause." [3]

Without such indefinite (uncaused) causes, everything would happen by necessity.

> "It is obvious that there are principles and causes which are generable and destructible apart from the actual processes of generation and destruction; for if this is not true, everything will be of necessity: that is, if there must necessarily be some cause, other than accidental, of that which is generated and destroyed. Will this be, or not? Yes, if this happens; otherwise not." [4]

Some determinist philosophers have claimed that Aristotle's "accident" as the convergence of two causal chains is quite compatible with determinism, but Aristotle himself is unequivocal in opposing strict necessity. Accidents are a consequence of chance.

Aristotle rejected the necessity of determinism in his statement on chance. Unfortunately, his description of chance as "obscure" (ἄδηλος) to human reason led centuries of philosophers to deny the existence of chance:

> "Causes from which chance results might happen are indeterminate; hence chance is obscure to human calculation and is a cause by accident."[5]

---

[3] Aristotle, *Metaphysics*, Book V, 1025a25
[4] *Ibid.*, Book VI, 1027a29
[5] *Ibid.*, Book XI, 1065a33

While it was Aristotle who first discussed the metaphysics of causality, it was IMMANUEL KANT in his "Copernican revolution" who called causality the "*crux metaphysicorum*."[6] David Hume had famously attacked metaphysics...

> "If we take in our hand any volume; of divinity or school metaphysics, for instance; let us ask, Does it contain any abstract reasoning concerning quantity or number? No. Does it contain any experimental reasoning concerning matter of fact and existence? No. Commit it then to the flames: for it can contain nothing but sophistry and illusion." [7]

Here Hume is distinguishing logical and mathematical reasoning, relations between ideas, in which the results can be known *a priori*, from experimental evidence concerning matters of fact, which can only be known *a posteriori*, after the fact itself. In modern discussions, this is called "Hume's fork," the distinction between *analytic* and *synthetic* knowledge, between logical truths and empirical facts, between the necessary and the contingent.

Information philosophy has established that nothing in the material world is necessary, no cause is logically pre-determined, because the *creation* of new information always involves indeterminism, the source of new possibilities in the universe. Necessity and apodeictic truth are concepts applicable only in math and logic.

An example of an event that is not strictly caused is one that depends on chance, like the flip of a coin. If the outcome is only probable, not certain, then the event can be said to have been caused by the coin flip, but the head or tails result itself was not pre-determined. Some events are at least partially caused by prior (uncaused) events, so they are not completely determined by prior events in a causal chain back to a primal first cause. The Aristotelian chain (ἄλυσις) has been broken by the uncaused cause. Uncaused events start new causal chains. Aristotle himself called these events "fresh starts," "new beginnings," or archai (ἀρχαί).

We can describe most events as "adequately determined" because the contributions of chance tend to cancel out when they

---

6   Kant (1783) *Prolegomena to Any Future Metaphysics*, §29
7   Hume (1748) *Enquiry Concerning Human Understanding* (last paragraph)

are averaged over large numbers of individual contributing causes. Thus microscopic randomness at the quantum level is normally averaged over, unless specific amplification mechanisms bring quantum indeterminism to the macroscopic level. Even in a world that contains quantum uncertainty, the behavior of most objects is determined to an extraordinary degree. Newton's laws of motion are deterministic to the limits of observational error for large objects.

The presence of quantum uncertainty leads philosophers to call the world "indeterministic." But indeterminism is seriously misleading when most events are overwhelmingly "adequately determined." No events are pre-determined in the Laplacian or theological senses.

It was Hume's approach defining causality that famously awakened Immanuel Kant from his "dogmatic slumbers." Kant said

"My object is to persuade all those who think Metaphysics worth studying, that it is absolutely necessary to pause a moment, and, neglecting all that has been done, to propose first the preliminary question, 'Whether such a thing as metaphysics be at all possible?'...

"Since the Essays of Locke and Leibniz, or rather since the origin of metaphysics so far as we know its history, nothing has ever happened which was more decisive to its fate than the attack made upon it by David Hume... Hume started from a single but important concept in Metaphysics, viz., that of Cause and Effect. He challenges reason, which pretends to have given birth to this idea from herself, to answer him by what right she thinks anything to be so constituted, that if that thing be posited, something else also must necessarily be posited; for this is the meaning of the concept of cause. He demonstrated irrefutably that it was perfectly impossible for reason to think a priori and by means of concepts a combination involving necessity." [8]

Kant's "synthetic a priori" project hoped to show that necessity, which is "analytic" (true by logic and reason alone), is a "concept of the understanding" that can apply to experience - the realm of empirical evidence and synthetic knowledge. Kant's stumbling block was his failure in the *Critiques of Reason* to distinguish deductive reasoning from inductive reasoning.

---

8   Kant, *Prolegomena*, (Introduction)

The Problem of Induction

Hume had described causality as merely the constant conjunction of cause and effect. But no number of such conjunctions establishes with certainty that the next appearance of the cause will necessarily produce the same effect. Even the sun may not rise tomorrow.

This is the problem of induction. Whereas deduction can establish the truth of a logical conclusion given the premises, induction at best is an accumulation of evidence in favor of a causal relation.

Francis Bacon described "genuine Induction" as the new method of science. Opposing his new idea to what he thought Aristotle's approach had been in his *Organon* (as misinterpreted by the medieval Scholastics), Bacon proposed that science builds up knowledge by the accumulation of data (information), which is of course correct.

This is simply the empirical method of collecting piece by piece the (statistical) evidence to support a theory. The "problem of induction" arises when we ask whether this form of reasoning can lead to apodeictic or "metaphysical" certainty about knowledge, as the Scholastics thought. Thomas Aquinas especially thought that certain knowledge can be built upon first principles, axioms, and deductive or logical reasoning. This certain knowledge does indeed exist, within a system of thought such as logic or mathematics. But it can prove nothing about the natural material world.

Bacon understood logical deduction, but like some protoempiricists among the Scholastics (notably JOHN DUNS SCOTUS and WILLIAM OF OCCAM), Bacon argued in his *Novum Organum* that knowledge of nature comes from studying nature, not from logical *a priori* reasoning in the ivory tower.

Bacon likely did not believe certainty can result from inductive reasoning, but his great contribution was to see that (empirical) knowledge gives us power over nature, by discovering what he called the form of nature, the real causes underlying events.

It was of course David Hume who pointed out the lack of certainty or logical necessity in the method of inferring causality from observations of the regular succession of "causes and effects." His great paradigm of scientific thinking, Isaac Newton, had championed induction as the source of his ideas. This is as if Newton's laws of motion were simply there in the data from Tycho Brahe's extensive observations and Johannes Kepler's elliptical orbits. "*Hypotheses non fingo,*" Newton famously said, denying the laws were his own ideas. Although since Newton it is a commonplace that the gravitational influence ("action at a distance") of the Sun causes the Earth and other planets to move around their orbits, Hume's skepticism led him to question whether we could really know, with certainty, anything about causality, when all we ever see in our inductive evidence is the regular succession of events.

Thus it was Hume who gave us the "problem of induction" that has bothered philosophers for centuries, spilling a great deal of philosophical ink. Hume's skepticism told him induction could never yield a logical proof. But Hume's mitigated skepticism saw a great deal of practical value gained by inferring a general rule from multiple occurrences, on the basis of what he saw as the uniformity of nature. It is reasonable to assume that what we have seen repeatedly in the past is likely to continue in the future.

So how is it that philosophers and scientists should establish causal relations between events? It turns out that it is neither logical deduction nor empirical induction alone, but rather by what CHARLES SANDERS PEIRCE called "abduction," to complete his triad.

Induction and the Scientific Method

Abduction is the creative formation of new hypotheses, one step in what some philosophers of science in the twentieth describe as the scientific method - the hypothetico-deductive-observational method. It can be described more simply as the combination of theories and experiments. Observations are very often the spur to theory formation, as the old inductive method emphasized. A scientist forms a hypothesis about possible causes for what is observed. Although the hypothesis is an immaterial idea, pure information, the abduction of a hypothesis creates new information in the universe, albeit in the minds of the scientists. By contrast, an experiment is a material and energetic interaction with the world that produces new information structures to be compared with theoretical predictions.

Experiments are Baconian accumulations of data that can never logically "prove" a theory (or hypothesis). But confirmation of any theory consists entirely of finding that the statistical outcomes of experiments match the theory's predictions, within reasonable experimental "error bars." The best confirmation of any scientific theory is when it predicts a phenomenon never before seen, such that when an experiment probes nature, that phenomenon is found to exist. These "surprising" results of great theories shows the extent to which science is not a mere "economic summary of the facts," as claimed by ERNST MACH, who was a primary exponent of logical positivism in science.

In his early years, ALBERT EINSTEIN thought himself a positivist disciple of Mach. He limited his theories to observable facts. Special relativity grew from the fact that absolute motions are not observable. But later when he realized the source of his greatest works were his own mental inventions, he changed his views. Although a great believer in determinism, Einstein argued for "free creations of the human mind." [9] Here is Einstein in 1936,

> "We now realize, with special clarity, how much in error are those theorists who believe that theory comes inductively from experience. Even the great Newton could not free himself from this error ("Hypotheses non fingo")...
>
> "There is no inductive method which could lead to the fundamental concepts of physics. Failure to understand this fact constituted the basic philosophical error of so many investigators of the nineteenth century. It was probably the reason why the molecular theory and Maxwell's theory were able to establish themselves only at a relatively late date. Logical thinking is necessarily deductive; it is based upon hypothetical concepts and axioms. How can we expect to choose the latter so that we might hope for a confirmation of the consequences derived from them?
>
> "The most satisfactory situation is evidently to be found in cases where the new fundamental hypotheses are suggested by the world of experience itself. The hypothesis of the non-existence of perpetual motion as a basis for thermodynamics affords such an example of a fundamental hypothesis suggested by experience; the same holds for Galileo's principle of inertia. In the same

---

9   Einstein. (1936), 'Physics and Reality,' p.291

category, moreover, we find the fundamental hypotheses of the theory of relativity, which theory has led to an unexpected expansion and broadening of the field theory, and to the superseding of the foundations of classical mechanics." [10]

And here, Einstein wrote in his 1949 autobiography about what may be the greatest of all the causal laws of nature...

"I have learned something else from the theory of gravitation: No ever so inclusive collection of empirical facts can ever lead to the setting up of such complicated equations. A theory can be tested by experience, but there is no way from experience to the setting up of a theory. Equations of such complexity as are the equations of the gravitational field can be found only through the discovery of a logically simple mathematical condition which determines the equations completely or [at least] almost completely." [11]

We can conclude that causality is not something that can be understood deductively as Kant's synthetic *a priori*, nor is explained as Hume's inductive constant conjunction of cause and effect.

Induction corresponds to the gathering of large numbers of observations or experiments, which today are seen as the statistical basis for accepting a scientific theory.

Deduction is an *a priori* tool that allows predictions to be derived logically and mathematically from the theory.

Deduction and induction are supplemented today with abduction, which is the free invention of theories or hypotheses to be tested against the results of experiments. Freely created theories, new information in the universe, are then seen to generate predictions about alternative possibilities and probabilities.

Experimental tests provide the statistical evidence that either confirms or denies those predictions.

Theories are probabilities. Experiments are statistics.

Causality and various causal laws are simply theories, as is determinism.

---

10 Einstein. (1936), 'Physics and Reality,' pp. 301, 307
11 Einstein (1949), 'Autobiographical Notes,' p.89

Chapter 5

Chance

Chance

The Stoic CHRYSIPPUS (200 B.C.E.) said that a single uncaused cause could destroy the universe (cosmos), a concern shared by some modern philosophers, for whom reason itself would fail.

> "Everything that happens is followed by something else which depends on it by causal necessity. Likewise, everything that happens is preceded by something with which it is causally connected. For nothing exists or has come into being in the cosmos without a cause. The universe will be disrupted and disintegrate into pieces and cease to be a unity functioning as a single system, if any uncaused movement is introduced into it."

The core idea of chance and indeterminism is closely related to the idea of causality. Indeterminism for some is simply an event without a cause, an uncaused cause or *causa sui* that starts a new causal chain. If we admit a limited number of uncaused causes, we can still have an "adequate" causality without the physical necessity of strict determinism, without complete predictability of events and only one possible future.

An example of an event that is not strictly caused is one that depends on chance, like the flip of a coin. If the outcome is only probable, not certain, then the event can be said to have been caused by the coin flip, but the head or tails result itself was not predictable. This "adequate" causality, which recognizes prior uncaused events as causal factors, admits new possibilities, although not the result of chance alone.

Even mathematical theorists of games of chance found ways to argue that the chance they described was somehow necessary and chance outcomes were actually determined. The greatest of these, PIERRE-SIMON LAPLACE, preferred to call his theory the "calculus of probabilities." With its connotation of approbation, probability was a more respectable term than chance, with its associations of gambling and lawlessness. For Laplace, the random outcomes are unpredictable only because we lack the detailed information to predict. As did the ancient Stoics, Laplace explained the appearance of chance as the result of human ignorance.

He said,

> "The word 'chance,' then expresses only our ignorance of the causes of the phenomena that we observe to occur and to succeed one another in no apparent order."

Decades before Laplace, ABRAHAM DE MOIVRE had discovered the normal distribution (the bell curve) of outcomes for ideal random processes, like the throw of dice. Perfectly random processes produce a regular distribution pattern for many independent trials (the law of large numbers). Inexplicably, the discovery of these regularities in various social phenomena led Laplace and others to conclude that the phenomena were determined, not

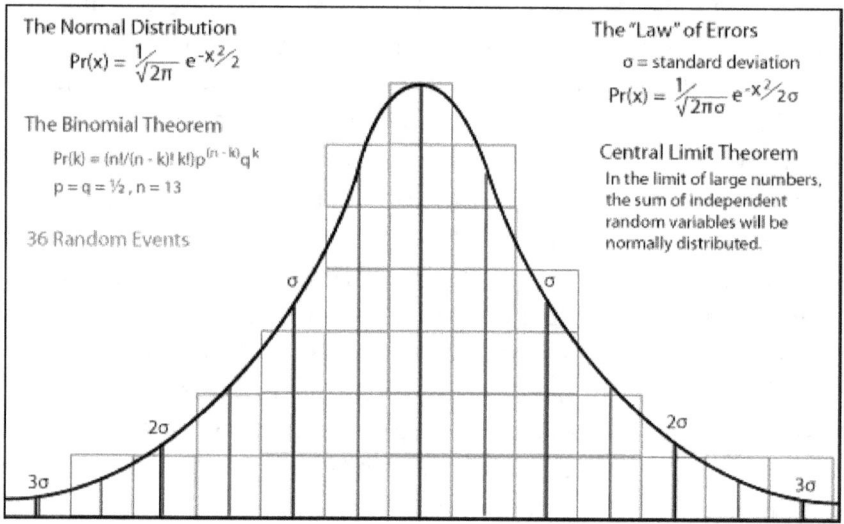

random. They simply denied chance in the world.

Chance is closely related to the ideas of uncertainty and indeterminacy. Uncertainty today is best known from WERNER HEISENBERG's principle in quantum mechanics. It states that the exact position and momentum of an atomic particle can only be known within certain (sic) limits. The product of the position uncertainty and the momentum uncertainty is equal to a multiple of MAX PLANCK's constant of action h. Ten years earlier, irreducible chance in physical processes had been discovered by ALBERT EINSTEIN in 1916, but he saw it as a "weakness in the theory."

The idea of real chance and uncertainty had already entered physics fifty years earlier than Heisenberg or Einstein, when Ludwig Boltzmann showed in 1877 that randomizing collisions between atomic particles in a gas could explain the increase in entropy that is the Second Law of Thermodynamics.

In 1866, when Boltzmann first derived Maxwell's velocity distribution of gas particles, he did it assuming that the physical motion of each particle (or atom) was determined exactly by Newton's laws. In 1872, when he showed how his kinetic theory of gases could explain the increase in entropy, he again used strictly deterministic physics. But Boltzmann's former teacher Josef Loschmidt objected to Boltzmann's derivation of the second law. Loschmidt said that if time was reversed, the deterministic laws of classical mechanics require that the entropy would go down, not up.

So in 1877 Boltzmann reformulated his derivation, assuming that each collision of gas particles was not determined, but random. He assumed that the directions and velocities of particles after a collision depended on chance, as long as energy and momentum were conserved. He could then argue that the particles would be located randomly in "phase space," based on the statistical assumption that individual cells of phase space were equally probable. Boltzmann's H-Theorem produced a quantity which would go only up, independent of the time direction. Laws of nature became statistical.

In particular, the macroscopic and phenomenological laws of thermodynamics were now based on a microscopic randomness that Boltzmann later called "molecular disorder." Classical mechanics became "statistical mechanics." Chance appeared to play a role in physics, but it would be forty years before Einstein clearly saw the existence of ontological chance, and it greatly bothered him because he thought physics must be deterministic.

Boltzmann's student Franz S. Exner defended the idea of absolute chance and indeterminism as a hypothesis that could never be ruled out on the basis of observational evidence, just as determinism can never be *proved* by any number of experiments.

Exner did this in his 1908 inaugural lecture at Vienna University as rector (two years after Boltzmann's death), and ten years later in his textbook written during World War I. But Exner's view was far from the standard view. Ever since Laplace's development of the calculus of probabilities, scientists and philosophers assumed that probabilities and statistical phenomena, including social statistics, were completely determined by some as yet to be discovered underlying laws. They thought that our inability to predict individual events was due simply to our ignorance of the details.

In his 1922 inaugural address at the University of Zurich, What Is a Law of Nature?, ERWIN SCHRÖDINGER said about his teacher,

> "It was the experimental physicist, Franz Exner, who for the first time, in 1919, launched a very acute philosophical criticism against the taken-for-granted manner in which the absolute determinism of molecular processes was accepted by everybody. He came to the conclusion that the assertion of determinism was certainly possible, yet by no means necessary, and when more closely examined not at all very probable.
>
> "Exner's assertion amounts to this: It is quite possible that Nature's laws are of thoroughly statistical character. The demand for an absolute law in the background of the statistical law — a demand which at the present day almost everybody considers imperative — *goes beyond the reach of experience.*" [1]

Ironically, just four years later, after developing his continuous and deterministic wave theory of quantum mechanics, Schrödinger would himself "go beyond the reach of experience" searching for deterministic laws underlying the discontinuous, discrete, statistical and probabilistic indeterminism of the Bohr-Heisenberg-Born school, to avoid the implications of absolute chance in quantum mechanics. Planck and Einstein too were repulsed by randomness and chance. "God does not play dice," was Einstein's famous remark.

A major achievement of the Ages of Reason and Enlightenment was to banish absolute chance as unintelligible and atheistic. Newton's Laws provided a powerful example of deterministic laws governing the motions of everything. Surely LEUCIPPUS' and DEMOCRITUS' original insights had been confirmed.

---

[1] Schrödinger (1922) 'What Is a Law of Nature?' pp.142,147.

In the early eighteenth cntury, De Moivre wrote a book called *The Doctrine of Chances*. It was very popular among gamblers. In the second edition (1738), he derived the mathematical form of the normal distribution of probabilities, but he vigorously denied the reality of chance. Because it implied events that God could not know, he labeled it atheistic.

> "Chance, in atheistical writings or discourse, is a sound utterly insignificant: It imports no determination to any mode of existence; nor indeed to existence itself, more than to non existence; it can neither be defined nor understood." [2]

As early as 1784, IMMANUEL KANT had argued that the observed regularities in social events from year to year showed that they must be determined by general laws of nature.

> "No matter what conception may form of the freedom of the will in metaphysics, the phenomenal appearances of the will, i.e., human actions, are determined by general laws of nature like any other event of nature...Thus marriages, the consequent births and the deaths, since the free will seems to have such a great influence on them, do not seem to be subject to any law according to which one could calculate their number beforehand. Yet the annual (statistical) tables about them in the major countries show that they occur according to stable natural laws." [3]

In the 1820's, JOSEPH FOURIER saw that statistics on the number of births, deaths, marriages, suicides, and various crimes in the city of Paris had remarkably stable averages from year to year. The mean values in a "normal distribution" (that follows the bell curve or "law of errors") of statistics took on the prestige of a social law.

The Belgian astronomer ADOLPHE QUÉTELET did more than anyone to claim these statistical regularities were evidence of determinism in human affairs. In 1835, Quételet published his book *Sur l'homme et le développement de ses facultés, ou Essai de physique sociale*. Quételet argued that these regularities in what he called "social physics" prove that individual apparently free choices like marriage and suicide must be determined by natural law.

---

2   De Moivre (1718) *The Doctrine of Chances*.p.253
3   Kant (1784) *Idea for a Universal History* (Introduction)

Individuals might think that marriage was their decision, but since the number of total marriages was relatively stable from year to year, Quételet claimed the individuals were determined to marry. Quételet used Auguste Comte's term "social physics," to describe his discovery of these "laws of human nature," forcing Comte to rename his work "sociologie," today's social science still has a strong bias towards finding deterministic laws of human nature.

Quételet's argument for determinism in human events is quite illogical. It appears to go something like this:

- Perfectly random, unpredictable individual events (like the throw of dice in games of chance) show statistical regularities that become more and more certain with more trials (law of large numbers and central limit theorem).
- Human events show statistical regularities.
- Therefore, human events are determined.

Quételet might more reasonably have concluded that individual human events are simply unpredictable and random. Were they determined, they might be expected to show a non-random pattern, perhaps a signature of the Determiner.

Franz Exner was not alone in defending chance long before quantum chance. In the nineteenth century in America, CHARLES SANDERS PEIRCE coined the term "tychism" for his idea that absolute chance is the first step in three steps, the second step is "ananchism" (necessity or determinism) and the third is "synechism" (continuity).

Peirce was influenced by the social statisticians, Quételet and the English THOMAS HENRY BUCKLE, by French philosophers CHARLES RENOUVIER and ALFRED FOUILLÉE, who also argued for some absolute chance, by physicists JAMES CLERK MAXWELL and Ludwig Boltzmann, but most importantly by Kant and GEORG W. F. HEGEL, who saw things arranged in philosophical triads that Peirce so loved.

Quételet and Buckle thought they had established an absolute deterministic law behind all statistical laws. Renouvier and Fouillée introduced chance or indeterminism simply to contrast it with determinism, and to discover some way, usually a dialectical argument like that of Hegel and indeed of Peirce, to reconcile the opposites.

Renouvier argues for human freedom, but nowhere explains exactly how chance might contribute to that freedom, other than negating determinism.

There is strong evidence that Maxwell may have used the mathematical equations of Quételet and Buckle's "social physics" as his model for the distribution of molecular velocities in a gas. Boltzmann also was impressed with the distributions of social statistics, and was initially convinced that individual particles must obey strict and deterministic Newtonian laws of motion.

Peirce does not explain much with his tychism, and with his view that continuity and evolutionary love is supreme, may have had serious doubts about the importance of chance. Peirce did not propose chance as directly or indirectly contributing to free will. He never mentions the ancient criticisms that we cannot accept responsibility for chance decisions. He does not really care for chance as the origin of species, preferring a more deterministic and continuous lawful development, under the guidance of his evolutionary love (his synechism and agapism). He called Darwinism a "greedy" theory. But Peirce does say clearly, well before Exner, that the observational evidence simply can not prove determinism.

Perhaps better than any other philosopher, Peirce articulated the difference between *a priori* probabilities and *a posteriori* statistics. He knew that probabilities are *a priori* theories and that statistics are *a posteriori* empirical measurements, the results of observations and experiments.

For Peirce, necessity and determinism were merely assumptions. That there is nothing necessary and logically true of the universe, Peirce learned from discussions of the work of Alexander Bain in the famous "Metaphysical Club" of the 1860's, although the ultimate source for the limits on logic was no doubt David Hume's skepticism.

It remained for WILLIAM JAMES, Peirce's close friend and his lifetime supporter, to assert that chance can provide random unpredictable alternatives from which the will can choose or "determine" one alternative. James was the first thinker to enunciate clearly a two-stage decision process, with chance in a present time of random alternatives, leading to a choice which selects one alternative and transforms an equivocal ambiguous future into an unalterable determined past. There are undetermined alternatives followed by adequately determined choices.

> "The stronghold of the determinist argument is the antipathy to the idea of chance...This notion of alternative possibility, this admission that any one of several things may come to pass is, after all, only a roundabout name for chance...
>
> What is meant by saying that my choice of which way to walk home after the lecture is ambiguous and matter of chance?...It means that both Divinity Avenue and Oxford Street are called but only one, and that one either one, shall be chosen." [4]

Chance is critically important for the question of free will because strict necessity implies just one possible future. Absolute chance means that the future is fundamentally unpredictable at the levels where chance is dominant. Chance allows alternative futures and the question becomes how the one actual present is realized from these potential alternative futures.

Of those thinkers who have considered these aspects of chance, very few besides William James have also seen the obvious parallel with biological evolution and natural selection, first microscopic quantum accidents causing variations in the gene pool and then macroscopic natural selection of the fittest genes evidenced by their reproductive success.

BERTRAND RUSSELL had said in his 1914 Lowell Lectures at Harvard that the law of causation was thought to be *a priori*, a necessity of thought, a category without which science would not be possible, although he felt that some claims for causality might be excessive, and no logical proof could be found.

In the same year, HENRI POINCARÉ was much less skeptical
> "Every phenomenon, however trifling it be, has a cause, and a mind infinitely powerful and infinitely well-informed concerning the laws of nature could have foreseen it from the beginning of the ages. If a being with such a mind existed, we could play no game of chance with him ; we should always lose. For him, in fact, the word chance would have no meaning, or rather there would be no such thing as chance." [5]

---

4   James (1897) 'The Dilemma of Determinism,' *The Will to Believe*, p.155
5   Poincaré (1914) *Science and Method*, ch. 4, Chance, p.64

We know that even in a world with microscopic chance, macroscopic objects are determined to an extraordinary degree, because large objects average over enormous numbers of quantum events which cancel out and produce macroscopic regularity. Newton's laws of motion are deterministic enough to send men to the moon and back. Though if the lunar mission had failed it might have been the consequence of a quantum event in the Apollo computers that was not correctable by their error detection and correction systems.

We call this kind of determinism "adequate determinism." Quantum uncertainty leads some philosophers to fear an undetermined world of chance, one where Chrysippus' imagined collapse into chaos would occur and reason itself would fail us.

The Discovery of Quantum Chance

The scientist Ludwig Boltzmann and the philosopher CHARLES SANDERS PEIRCE both felt the need for the fundamental existence of chance in the universe, but it was Albert Einstein in 1916 who actually discovered the microscopic source of ontological chance.

Einstein found that when light is radiated away from a material particle, each individual light quantum must go in a specific direction, even though the average over large numbers of light particles is spherically symmetric (isotropic).

Einstein saw that these quantum events are fundamentally, and we can say metaphysically, statistical.

Einstein found that the direction of the light particle (later called a photon) must be a matter of chance. He noted that ERNEST RUTHERFORD had found in 1902 that when a radioactive nucleus decays, the time of the decay appears to be completely random. Rutherford could provide only the probability of decay, the time when half the nuclei would have decayed, the so-called "half-life."

Einstein now realized that both the time and the direction of emission of a photon must be fundamentally a matter of chance.

> "It speaks in favor of the theory that the statistical law assumed for [spontaneous] emission is nothing but the Rutherford law of radioactive decay." [6]

---

6   Einstein, *Collected Papers*, vol.6, p.216

Here for the first time we have a physical and metaphysical underpinning for the concept of metaphysical possibility, which for centuries was thought to be a matter of human ignorance.

Einstein himself did not like the idea at all. The inability to predict both the time and direction of light particle emissions, said Einstein in 1917, is "a weakness in the theory..., that it leaves time and direction of elementary processes to chance (*Zufall*)."[7] It is only a weakness for Einstein because his "God does not play dice."

Besides carrying away energy $E = hv$, the light particle must also carry a momentum $p = hv/c$, Einstein reasoned. Conservation of momentum requires that the momentum of the emitted photon will cause an atom to recoil with momentum hv/c in the opposite direction. However, the standard theory of spontaneous emission of radiation is that it produces a spherical wave going out in all directions. A classical spherically symmetric wave has no preferred direction. It produces no recoil. So Einstein asked:

> "Does the molecule receive an impulse when it absorbs or emits the energy ε? For example, let us look at emission from the point of view of classical electrodynamics. When a body emits the radiation ε it suffers a recoil (momentum) ε/c if the entire amount of radiation energy is emitted in the same direction. If, however, the emission is a spatially symmetric process, e.g., a spherical wave, no recoil at all occurs. This alternative also plays a role in the quantum theory of radiation. When a molecule absorbs or emits the energy ε in the form of radiation during the transition between quantum theoretically possible states, then this elementary process can be viewed either as a completely or partially directed one in space, or also as a symmetrical (nondirected) one. *It turns out that we arrive at a theory that is free of contradictions, only if we interpret those elementary processes as completely directed processes.*" [8]

Since the direction of a photon is random, we find that it is the fundamental source for all ontological randomness in the universe. If a material particle, an electron or atom, recoils randomly whenever it interacts with radiation, we have found this is the source of Ludwig Boltzmann's "molecular disorder," the reason that mechanics is not "classical," but statistical.

---

7   Einstein (1916), quoted in Pais, *Subtle is the Lord*, p.411
8   Einstein (1917) 'On the Quantum Theory of Radiation", in Van der Waerden, *Sources of Quantum Mechanics*, p.65

With this insight we can solve the central problem in statistical physics. That problem is how macroscopic *irreversible* behavior can arise if the motions of atoms and molecules are microscopically *reversible*. Microscopic reversibility requires that the path information in each atom is preserved during collisions. We can now say that path information is destroyed in any collision that involves a photon, whether emitted or absorbed.

Our information analysis of quantum physics has discovered and explained the existence of microscopic irreversibility.

In a deterministic universe, information is conserved. Ontological chance not only destroys older information, it creates new information. It was this deep insight that led Einstein to describe quantum mechanics as a *statistical* theory, if an "incomplete" one.

This is not the "statistical" of the mathematicians and scientists (including Einstein) who hoped for an underlying determinism ensuring the macroscopic regularities.

This is quantal, ontological, and metaphysical chance. It is the chance *acausality* that Heisenberg quantified in his uncertainty principle ten years after Einstein, twenty-five years after Rutherford, and fifty years after Boltzmann' and Peirce saw a need for chance.

Sadly, for some years Einstein led the chorus of deniers who decry the chance implicit in the collapse of the wave function. A significant fraction of working physicists and perhaps most philosophers of science, especially those claiming to explore the "foundations of quantum mechanics," long for the return of classical determinism.

They all have what William James called "antipathy to chance."
> "The stronghold of the determinist argument is the antipathy to the idea of chance...This notion of alternative possibility, this admission that any one of several things may come to pass is, after all, only a roundabout name for chance..." [9]

Without metaphysical chance, there is no metaphysical possibility and the metaphysics of possibility lies at the heart of the possibility of metaphysics.

---

9   James, 'The Dilemma of Determinism.' p.155

Chapter 6

Metaphysics Problems

Change

Information is neither matter nor energy, although it needs matter to be embodied and energy to be communicated. How can abstract information explain the process of metaphysical change, specifically the change in properties over time?

Changes in various properties from place to place in space, for example density and temperature, may raise even deeper metaphysical questions, like why there is something rather than nothing. But these deep questions we set aside for now.

As most all of us know, matter and energy are conserved. This means that there is just the same total amount of matter and energy today as there was at origin of the universe. But then what accounts for all the change, the new things under the sun?

It is information, which is not conserved and has been increasing since the beginning of time, alongside the increase in disorder that we quantify as thermodynamic entropy.

What is changing is the *arrangement* of the matter into what we can call *information structures*. What is emerging is new information. What idealists and holists see is the emergence of *immaterial* information.

Living things, you and I, are dynamic growing information structures, forms through which matter and energy continuously flow. And it is information processing and biological communication that controls those flows!

Information is the modern spirit, the ghost in the machine, the mind in the body. It is the soul, and when we die, it is our information that perishes, unless the future preserves it. The matter remains.

Information is the *form* in all concrete objects as well as the content in non-existent, merely possible, thoughts and other abstract entities. And the forms of all material are constantly, if sometimes imperceptibly, changing.

This chapter on the web - metaphysicist.com/problems/change

The only things that do not change are certain abstract entities, some of which may be instantiated in or abstracted from, material objects in the physical universe.

Information philosophy goes beyond *a priori* logic and its puzzles, beyond analytic language and its paradoxes, beyond philosophical claims of necessary truths, to a contingent and constantly changing physical world that is best represented as made of dynamic, interacting information structures.

Change can be in the internal or intrinsic properties of a thing, or in its extrinsic relations to external objects, e.g., dispositional properties like coordinates. The primary view of change is a real, metaphysical change in a "thing itself." Some metaphysicians argue that this must be a change of identity. But this is wrong, because modest changes in the material substrate or the information content (shape and form, internal and external communications) do not change the essential relative identity over time of an object.

Because of motions and microscopic physical events, all material things change in time. This is the idea of the Heraclitean "flux" or Platonic "Becoming."

Such change means that the concept of "perfect or strict identity over time" is fundamentally flawed. Even in the case of a hypothetical completely inert object that could be protected from loss or gain of a single particle, its position coordinates in most space-time frames are constantly changing. All its spatial relations with the other objects in the universe are constantly changing.

Perfect identity over time is limited to unchanging ideas or concepts – Parmenidean "Being." These are abstract entities like numbers, simple universals, and logical truths.

The Eleatic followers of Parmenides, notably Zeno, invented his motion paradoxes – the Arrow, Achilles and the Tortoise – to deny change. Zeno's motion paradoxes and claims denying a plurality of beings – the bizarre idea that "all is one" – still appear in today's elementary metaphysics textbooks.

Change

Aristotle's hylomorphic theory of change argued that what persists over time is an underlying substrate (ὑποκείμενον), which he identified with matter (ὕλη). This is Aristotle's anticipation of the conservation of mass (now including energy).

But as with the puzzle of The Statue and Lump of Clay, Aristotle knew that the form (μορφή) is an equal contributor to the essence of a substance (οὐσία).

Aristotle clearly sees a statue as both its form/shape and its matter/clay.

> "The term "substance" (οὐσία) is used, if not in more, at least in four principal cases; for both the essence and the universal and the genus are held to be the substance of the particular (ἑκάστου), and fourthly the substrate (ὑποκείμενον). The substrate is that of which the rest are predicated, while it is not itself predicated of anything else. Hence we must first determine its nature, for the primary substrate (ὑποκείμενον) is considered to be in the truest sense substance.
>
> "Now in one sense we call the matter (ὕλη) the substrate; in another, the shape (μορφή); and in a third, the combination Both matter and form and their combination are said to be substrate. of the two. By matter I mean, for instance, bronze; by shape, the arrangement of the form (τὸ σχῆμα τῆς ἰδέας); and by the combination of the two, the concrete thing: the statue (ἀνδριάς). Thus if the form is prior to the matter and more truly existent, by the same argument it will also be prior to the combination." [1]

In some writing, Aristotle regards matter as individuating form. In others, it is the form that is essential. An active agent impresses the form on the matter. The matter assumes/acquires the form. The form of a cat impressed on undifferentiated matter actively gives the matter the form of a cat. The matter changes shape (μορφή).

In other cases, a passive patient is "informed," by perceiving a form. A perceiver thinking about something acquires the form without the matter. Acquisition of the form is by impressing that form onto the material brain, embedding the information as an experience that is recorded (our ERR).

---

1   Aristotle, *Metaphysics*, Book VII, § vii

Cosmic Change as the Growth of Information Structures

While we can say little about the coming into existence of the material and energy content of the universe some 13.74 billion years ago, we can show how the changing arrangement of matter over those years, together with the transformation of energy into matter and back from matter into energy, grounds the explanation for all the particular changes that we experience every day.

There could be no visible change if every new thing created was instantly destroyed and reduced to chaos. Any structure that visibly appears to be an arrangement of matter we call an information structure. Change can then be defined as a changing arrangement of the matter, a change of the information in a structure.

By information we mean a quantity that can be understood mathematically and physically. It corresponds to the common-sense meaning of information, in the sense of communicating or informing. It also corresponds to the information stored in books and computers. But it also measures the information in any physical object, like a stone or a snowflake, in a production process like a recipe or formula, and the information in biological systems, including cell and organ structures and the genetic code.

Information is mathematically related to the measure of disorder known as the thermodynamic quantity called "entropy." The information we mean is a measure of the "order" or "negative entropy," the departure of a physical system from pure chaos, from "thermodynamic equilibrium."

"Negative entropy" is simply the difference between the maximum possible entropy (where all the particles in a physical system are in a maximum state of disorder, there is no visible structure) and the actual entropy.

In a state of thermodynamic equilibrium, there is only motion of the microscopic constituent particles ("the motion we call heat"). The existence of macroscopic structures, such as the stars and planets, and their motions, is a departure from thermodynamic equilibrium. And that departure we call the "negative entropy."

The second law of thermodynamics says that the entropy (or disorder) of a closed physical system increases until it reaches a maximum, the state of thermodynamic equilibrium. It requires that the entropy of the universe is now and has always been increasing.

This established fact of increasing entropy led many scientists and philosophers to assume that the universe we have is "running down" to a "heat death." They think the universe began in a very high state of information, since the second law requires that any organization or order is susceptible to decay. The information that remains today, in their view, has always been here. There is nothing new under the sun.

But the universe is not a closed system. It is in a dynamic state of expansion that is moving away from thermodynamic equilibrium faster than entropic processes can keep up. The maximum possible entropy is increasing much faster than the actual increase in entropy. The difference between the maximum possible and actual entropy is potential information, as shown by David Layzer.[2]

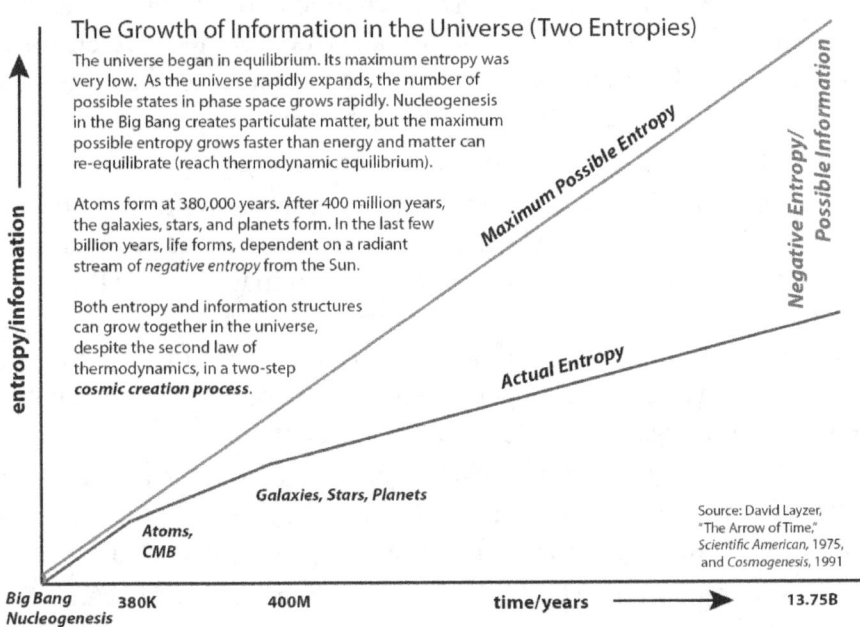

2 Layzer (1991). *Cosmogenesis: the Growth of Order in the Universe.*

Creation of information structures means that in parts of the universe the local entropy is actually going down. Creation of a low entropy system is always accompanied by radiation of entropy away from the local structures to distant parts of the universe, into the night sky for example.

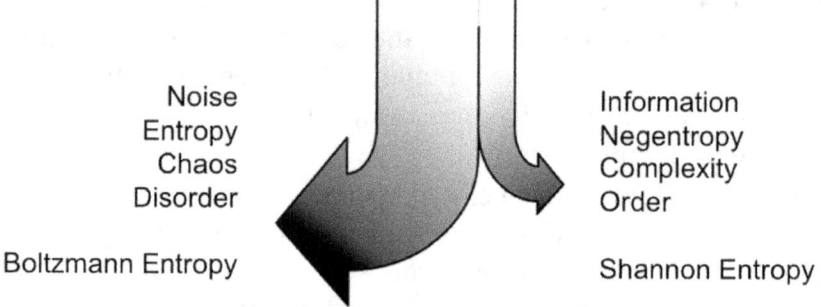

As the universe expands, both positive and negative entropy are generated. The normal thermodynamic entropy, known as the Boltzmann Entropy, is the large black arrow. The negative entropy, often called the Shannon Entropy, is a measure of the potential information content in the evolving universe.

But how does an information structure emerge?

Ex nihilo, nihil fit, said the ancients, Nothing comes from nothing. But information is no (material) thing. Information is physical, but it is not material. Information is a *property* of material. It is the form that matter can take. We can take a lump of clay and make a statue. We can thus create something (immaterial) from nothing! But we shall find that it takes a special kind of energy (free or available energy, with negative entropy) to rearrange matter.

All changes in time are rearrangements of matter and energy, even if only the translation in space of an intrinsically unchanging object from one place to another, the change we call motion.

Cosmologists know that information is being created because the universe began some thirteen billion years ago in a state of minimal information. The "Big Bang" started with just the most elementary particles and radiation. Many changes are needed to produce a galaxy with a star like our Sun shining down on life on Earth

The first changes were combinations of the simplest forms of matter. Elementary particles, quarks and gluons, combined to form protons and neutrons in the first few minutes. These later combined with electrons to change into atoms, but not for an amazingly long 380,000 years! Vast numbers of atoms became clouds of matter that gravity condensed into galaxies, stars, and planets, but that was over 400 million years after the origin.

How matter formed into information structures, from atoms to galaxies, stars, and planets, is the beginning of a story that will end with understanding how human minds emerged to understand our place in the universe.

Note that the creation of all these material structures does not in an important sense process the information that they contain.

A qualitatively different kind of information creation was when the first molecule on earth replicated itself and went on to duplicate its information exponentially. Here the prototype of life was the cause for the creation of the new information structure. Accidental errors in the duplication provided variations in replicative success. Most important, besides creating their information structures, biological systems are also information processors. Living things use information to make their changes.

The third process of information creation, and the most important to philosophy, is human creativity. Almost every philosopher since philosophy began has considered the mind as something distinct from the body. Information philosophy can now explain that distinction.

The brain, part of the material body, is a biological information processor. The mind *is* the *immaterial* information in the brain. The stuff of mind is the information being processed and the new information being created. Mental events have causal powers that can make changes in the material world. As some philosophers have speculated, *mind is the software in the brain hardware.*

Chapter 7

Coinciding Objects

Coinciding Objects

The problem of Coinciding Objects (sometimes called colocation) is whether two things can be in the same place at the same time. Common sense says that they cannot.

JOHN LOCKE described the impossibility that two things of the same kind should exist in the same place at the same time.

"ANOTHER occasion the mind often takes of comparing, is the very being of things, when, considering anything as existing at any determined time and place, we compare it with itself existing at another time, and thereon form the ideas of wherein identity and diversity. When we see anything to be in any identity place in any instant of time, we are sure (be it what it will) that it is that very thing, and not another which at that same time exists in another place, how like and undistinguishable soever it may be in all other respects: and in this consists identity, when the ideas it is attributed to vary not at all from what they were that moment wherein we consider their former existence, and to which we compare the present. For we never finding, nor conceiving it possible, that two things of the same kind should exist in the same place at the same time, we rightly conclude, that, whatever exists anywhere at any time, excludes all of the same kind, and is there itself alone." [1]

In modern metaphysics, the problem of coinciding objects should be the question of whether one mass of material – what the Greeks called substrate or ὑποκείμενον ("the underlying") – could contain the whole of two (or more) separate objects containing that same mass.

It is now common for many identity theorists to claim that the whole of one object and the whole of another can occupy just the same place at just the same time. Among them, according to MICHAEL BURKE, are RODERICK CHISHOLM, E. JONATHAN LOWE, SAUL KRIPKE, and DAVID WIGGINS.

---

[1] 'Of Identity and Diversity,' *Essay Concerning Human Understanding*, Book II, ch xxvii

This chapter on the web - metaphysicist.com/problems/colocation

But it is not clear that this was the ancient problem in debates between the Academic Skeptics and the Stoics. In modern times, multiple ancient puzzles are used to pose the problem of coinciding objects. One is the statue and the lump of clay from which it is sculpted. Another is Dion and Theon, known as the "body-minus" problem. Another is Tibbles, the Cat and a similar cat missing his tail. A third is the Stoic Chrysippus's so-called "growing argument."

All these modern claims that there can be two "coinciding objects" can be shown to be distinguishing between different aspects of a single object, in particular, the matter and form, giving them different names, and then arguing that they have different *persistence* conditions.

Aristotle's *Metaphysics* makes perhaps the earliest and clearest such distinction, using the example of a statue and its matter.

> "The term "substance" (οὐσία) is used, if not in more, at least in four principal cases; for both the essence and the universal and the genus are held to be the substance of the particular (ἑκάστου), and fourthly the substrate (ὑποκείμενον). The substrate is that of which the rest are predicated, while it is not itself predicated of anything else. Hence we must first determine its nature, for the primary substrate (ὑποκείμενον) is considered to be in the truest sense substance." [2]

Aristotle clearly sees a statue as a combination of its form/shape and its matter/clay.

> "Now in one sense we call the matter (ὕλη) the substrate; in another, the shape (μορφή); and in a third, the combination Both matter and form and their combination are said to be substrate. of the two. By matter I mean, for instance, bronze; by shape, the arrangement of the form (τὸ σχῆμα τῆς ἰδέας); and by the combination of the two, the concrete thing: the statue (ἀνδριάς). Thus if the form is prior to the matter and more truly existent, by the same argument it will also be prior to the combination." [3]

Aristotle sees no problem with the body and soul of a person being combined in one substance (οὐσία), but a hundred or so

---

2   Aristotle, *Metaphysics*, Book VII, § iii, 1-2
3   Ibid.

years after Aristotle, the Academic Skeptics attacked the Stoics, saying Stoics were making single things into dual beings, two objects in the same place at the same time, but indistinguishable. And this may have been the beginning of the modern problem.

The "two things" that bothered the Skeptics appeared first in the "growing argument" described by the later second century BCE Stoics, Posidonius and Mnesarchus, as reported by Stobaeus in the fifth century CE. What is it that grows, they asked, the material substance or the peculiar qualities of the individual? But note that this is still matter versus form. The substance (matter) does not grow. It is the individual that grows.

"The substance neither grows nor diminishes through addition or subtraction, but simply alters, just as in the case of numbers and measures. And it follows that it is in the case of peculiarly qualified individuals, such as Dion and Theon, that processes of both growth and diminution arise.

"Therefore each individual's quality actually remains from its generation to its destruction, in the case of destructible animals, plants and the like. In the case of peculiarly qualified individuals they say that there are two receptive parts, the one pertaining to the presence of the substance, the other to that of the qualified individual...

"The peculiarly qualified thing is not the same as its constituent substance. Nor on the other hand is it different from it, but is all but the same, in that the substance both is a part of it and occupies the same place as it, whereas whatever is called different from something must be separated from it and not be thought of as even part of it..." [4]

Like Aristotle, the Stoics were distinguishing the individual's "constituent substance" from the "peculiar qualifications" of the individual.

The Stoic term for "constituent substance" or substrate, following Aristotle, was ὑποκείμενον. Their term for the unique person, possibly separate from the material body, was ἴδιος ποιὸν, a particular individual "who," for example, Socrates, as opposed to κοινός ποιὸν, a general "whoness," for example, a human being.

---

4   Stobaeus, *The Hellenistic Philosophers*, Long and Sedley, v.1, p.168

But, in the vehement debates of the third century BCE, the Academic Skeptics laughed at the Stoics for seeing a dual nature in man. Their most famous puzzle was the coinciding objects of Dion and Theon (recently the puzzle of Tibbles, the Cat and a similar cat lacking a tail).

Plutarch, writing in the first century CE, accused the Stoics of "crazy arithmetic" and absurdity, that "each of us is a pair of twins, two-natured and double, joined in some parts but separate in others, two bodies sharing the same color, the same shape, the same weight, the same place,"

> "Yet this difference and distinction in us no one has marked off or discriminated, nor have we perceived that we are born double, always in flux with one part of ourselves, while remaining the same people from birth to death with the other...
>
> "If when we hear Pentheus in the tragedy say that he sees two suns and a double Thebes we say he is not seeing but mis-seeing, going crazy in his arithmetic, then when these people propose that, not one city, but all men, animals, trees, furniture, implements and clothes are double and two-natured, shall we not reject them as forcing us to misthink rather than to think?" [5]

Another early statement is Stobaeus in the first century BCE.

> "That what concerns the peculiarly qualified is not the same as what concerns the substance, Mnesarchus says is clear. For things which are the same should have the same properties. For if, for the sake of argument, someone were to mould a horse, squash it, then make a dog, it would be reasonable for us on seeing this to say that this previously did not exist but now does exist. So what is said when it comes to the qualified thing is different.
>
> "So too in general when it comes to substance, to hold that we are the same as our substances seems unconvincing. For it often comes about that the substance exists before something's generation, before Socrates' generation, say, when Socrates does not yet exist, and that after Socrates' destruction the substance remains although he no longer exists." [6]

---

5   Plutarch 'Against the Stoics on Common Conceptions,' *The Hellenistic Philosophers*, p.166-7

6   Stobaeus (I,177,21 - 179,17), *The Hellenistic Philosophers*, p.168

An Information Analysis of "Coinciding Objects"

Many of our metaphysical puzzles start with a single object, then separate it into its matter and its form, giving each of them names and declaring them to be two coinciding objects. Next we postulate a change in either the matter or the form, or both. It is of course impossible to make a change in one without the other changing, since we in fact have only one object.

But our puzzle maker asks us to focus on one and insist that the change has affected the status of only that one, usually claiming that the change has caused that one to cease to exist. This follows an ancient view that any change in material constitutes a change in identity. But the modern metaphysicist knows that all objects are always changing and that a change in identity may always preserve some information of an entity. The puzzle claims that an aspect of the object persists if the relative identity, or identity "in some respect" has not changed.

To create a paradox, we propose two axioms about identity,

Id1. Everything is identical to everything else in some respects.

Id2. Everything is different from everything else in some other respects.

We (in our minds) "pick out" one respect whose identity persists over time because of *Id1* and a second respect which changes in time because of .

We now have one object that both persists and does not persist (in different respects, of course), the very essence of a paradox. We call them different objects to create the puzzle.

For example, in the case of the statue and the clay, Mnesarchus's original version assumes someone moulds a horse, then squashes it. We are asked to pick out the horse's shape or form. The act of squashing changes that shape into another relatively amorphous shape. The object changes its identity with respect to its shape. Mnesarchus said it would be reasonable to see this sequence of events as something coming into existence and then ceasing to exist. The most obvious thing changing is the horse shape that we name "statue."

By design, there is no change in the amount of clay, so the matter is identical over time with respect to the amount of clay. The clay persists.

We now claim to have seen a difference in persistence conditions. The object *qua* clay persists. The object *qua* statue goes in and out of existence.

But this is just a way of talking about what has happened because a human observer has "picked out" two different aspects of the one object. As the statue is being smashed beyond recognition, every part of the clay must move to a new position that accommodates the change in shape of the statue. There are changes in the clay with identical information to the change in the shape of the statue. These we ignore to set up the puzzle.

In more modern versions of the statue and clay puzzle, we can make a change in the matter, for example by breaking off an arm and replacing it with a new arm made of different material but restoring the shape. We ignore the change in form, although it was obviously a drastic change until the restoration, and we focus on the clay, making the claim that the original clay has ceased to exist and new clay come into existence.

In either case, the claim to see different persistence conditions is the result of focusing on different subsets of the total information.

When identity theorists say that the whole of one object and the whole of another can occupy just the same place at just the same time, they are never talking about two objects of the same type, kind, or sort. They are always "picking out" different aspects of a single object and giving them differing existential status.

The modern problem of coinciding objects is closely related to these metaphysical problems:

- *Persistence.* Is something the same thing one second later? Some metaphysicians think an object may consist of "temporal parts," which they describe as "perduring" as different things at every instant of time. But temporarily successive objects always are identical "in some respect" and different in other respects.

- *Identity Over Time.* Different aspects of an single object may have different persistence conditions. Perdurantisists deny the possibility of identity through time. Endurantists emphasizes the subsets of total information that are unchanging over time.
- *Constitution.* For those metaphysicians who think that material constitution is identity, there is a doubt that Dion can survive the loss of his foot. Chrysippus's so-called "growing argument" was designed to show that Dion survives, despite Skeptic claims.
- *Composition.* If we remove something inessential (say one atom, or one plank from the Ship of Theseus), do we have the same thing? Or are some "proper parts" mereologically essential to the identity of the whole?

Composition

Composition

Debates about the relation of parts to wholes is a major part of modern metaphysics. Many puzzles have to do with different persistence conditions of the "parts" of a composite whole.

Mereological universalism or extensional mereology is an abstract idea, defined in 1937 by Stanislaw Leśniewski and later by Henry Leonard and Nelson Goodman (1940). It claims that any collection of things, for example the members of a set in symbolic logic, can be considered as the parts of a whole, a "fusion" or "mereological sum," and thus can *compose* an object. Critics of this idea says that such arbitrary collections are just "scattered objects." A mind-independent causal connection between objects is needed for them to be integral "parts."

Mereological essentialism is RODERICK CHISHOLM's radical idea that every whole has its parts necessarily and in every possible world. But this goes too far. No physical object can maintain its parts indefinitely and freeze its identity and information content over time. We can frame this as a third axiom of identity

Id3. *Everything is identical to itself in all respects at each instant of time, but different in some respects from itself at any other time.*[1]

Mereological nihilists, such as PETER VAN INWAGEN and the early PETER UNGER, denied the existence of composites, seeing them as simples (partless entities) arranged to look like a composite object. For them, a table is "simples arranged table-wise."

Van Inwagen made an exception for living objects. Surprisingly, he based the composite nature of biological entities on the Cartesian dualist view that humans are thinking beings. Van Inwagen then could see no obvious demarcation level at which even the simplest living things should not be treated as composite objects.

Information philosophy and metaphysics ask who or what is doing the arranging? Information provides a more fundamental reason than van Inwagen's for treating living things as integrated composites and not simply mereological sums of scattered objects.

---

1   See chapter 7, p.59 for our first two axioms of identity.

Information analysis extends a true composite nature to artifacts and to groupings of living things because they share a teleonomic property – a purpose. And it shows how some "proper parts" of these composites can have a holistic relation with their own parts, enforcing transitivity of part/whole relations.

A process that makes a composite object an integrated whole we call *teleonomic* (following Colin Pittendrigh, Jacques Monod, and Ernst Mayr) to distinguish it from a teleological cause with a "telos" that pre-existed life. We show that teleonomy is the explanatory force behind van Inwagen's "arrangement" of simple parts and that it applies to human artifacts like tables.

Biological parts, which we can call *biomers*, are communicating systems that share information via biological messaging with other parts of their wholes, and in many cases communicate with other living and non-living parts of their environments. These communications function to maintain the biological integrity (or identity) of the organism and control its growth. The teleonomy of artifacts like tables and statues is imposed by their creators.

Biocommunications are messages transferring information, for example inside the simplest single-cell organisms. For the first few billion years of life, single cells were the only living things, and they still dominate our planet. Messages between them are the direct ancestors of messages between cells in multicellular organisms. And they have evolved to become all human communications, including the puzzles and problems of metaphysics. A straight line of evolution goes from the first biological message to the contents of this book as you read it.

Like many metaphysical problems, composition arose in the quarrels between Stoics and Academic Skeptics that generated several ancient puzzles still debated today. But it has roots in Aristotle's definition of the essence (οὐσία), the unchanging "Being" of an object. We will show that Aristotle's essentialism has a biological basis that is best understood today as a biomereological essentialism. It goes beyond mereological sums of scattered objects because of the teleonomy shared between the parts, whether living or dead, of a biomeric whole.

First, back to Aristotle's definitions of terms…

> The term "substance" (οὐσία) is used, if not in more, at least in four principal cases; for both the essence (εἶναι), and the universal (καθόλου) and the genus (γένος) are held to be the substance of the particular (ἑκάστου), and fourthly the substrate (ὑποκείμενον). The substrate is that of which the rest are predicated, while it is not itself predicated of anything else. Hence we must first determine its nature, for the primary substrate (ὑποκείμενον) is considered to be in the truest sense substance.

Aristotle clearly sees a statue as both its form/shape and its matter/clay.

> Both matter and form and their combination are said to be substance (οὐσία). Now in one sense we call the matter (ὕλη) the substrate; in another, the shape (μορφή); and in a third, the combination of the two. By matter I mean, for instance, bronze; by shape, the arrangement of the form (τὸ σχῆμα τῆς ἰδέας); and by the combination of the two, the concrete thing: the statue (ἀνδριάς). Thus if the form is prior to the matter and more truly existent, by the same argument it will also be prior to the combination.[2]

The essence of an object, the "kind" or "sort" of object that it "is", its "constitution," its "identity," includes those "proper" parts of the object without which it would cease to be that sort or kind. Without a single essential part, it loses its absolute identity.

While this is strictly "true," for all practical purposes most objects retain the overwhelming fraction of the information that describes them from moment to moment, so that information philosophy offers a new and quantitative measure of "sameness" to traditional philosophy, a measure that is difficult or impossible to describe in ordinary language.

Nevertheless, since even the smallest change in time does make an entity at $t + \Delta t$ different from what it was at t, this has given rise to the idea of "temporal parts."

---

[2] Aristotle, *Metaphysics*, Book VII, § iii (

Temporal Parts

Philosophers and theologians have for many years argued for distinct temporal parts, with the idea that each new part is a completely new creation *ex nihilo*. Even modern physicists (e.g., HUGH EVERETT III) talk as if parallel universes are brought into existence at an instant by quantum experiments that collapse the wave function.

DAVID LEWIS, who claims there are many possible worlds, is a proponent of many temporal parts. His theory of "perdurance" asserts that the persistence through time of an object is as a series of completely distinct entities, one for every instant of time. Lewis's work implies that the entire infinite number of his possible worlds (as "real" and actual as our world, he claims), must also be entirely created anew at every instant.

While this makes for great science fiction and popularizes metaphysics, at some point attempts to understand the fundamental nature of reality must employ Occam's Razor and recognize the fundamental conservation laws of physics. If a new temporal part is created *ab initio*, why should it bear any resemblance at all to its earlier version?

It is extravagant in the extreme to suggest that all matter disappears and reappears at every instant of time. It is astonishing enough that matter can spontaneously be converted into energy and back again at a later time.

Most simple things (the elementary particles, the atoms and molecules of ordinary matter, etc.) are in stable states that exist continuously for long periods of time, and these compose larger objects that persist through "endurance," as Lewis describes the alternative to his "perdurance." Large objects are not absolutely identical to themselves at earlier instants of time, but the differences are infinitesimal in information content.

The doctrine of temporal parts ignores the physical connections between all the "simples" at one instant and at the following moment. It is as if this is an enormous version of the Zeno paradox of the arrow. The arrow cannot possibly be moving when thought frozen at an instant. The basic laws of physics describe the continuous motions of every particle. They generally show very slow changes in configuration – the organizational arrangement of the particles that constitutes abstract information about an object.

One might charitably interpret Lewis as admitting the endurance of the elementary particles (or whatever partless simples he might accept) and that perdurance is only describing the constant change in configuration, the arrangement of the simples that constitute or compose the whole. And the arrangement is information.

Then Lewis's temporal parts would be a series of self-identical objects that are not absolutely identical to their predecessors and successors, just a temporal series of highly theoretical abstract ideas, perhaps at the same level of (absurd) abstraction as his possible worlds?

Mereology

Mereology is the study of parts which compose a whole. What exactly is a part? And what constitutes a whole? For each concept, there is a strict philosophical sense, an ordinary sense, and a functional or teleonomic sense.

In the strict sense, a part is just some subset of the whole. The whole itself is sometimes called an "improper part."

In the ordinary sense, a part is distinguishable, in principle separable, from other neighboring parts of some whole. The smallest possible parts are those that have no smaller parts. In physics, these are the atoms, or today the elementary particles of matter.

In the functional sense, we can say that a part serves some purpose in the whole. This means that it has may be considered a whole in its own right, subordinate to any purpose of the whole entity. Teleonomic examples are the pedals or wheel of a bicycle, the organs of an animal body, or the organelles in a cell.

The same three-part analysis applies to the question of what composes a "whole" object.

Some philosophers (e.g., Peter Unger and Peter van Inwagen) deny that composite objects exist. This is called "mereological nihilism," though a more accurate name would be "holistic nihilism," since it is composite wholes that they deny. They do not deny the parts, which they call "simples." Van Inwagen argues, for example, that tables are just "simples arranged tablewise," where the simples are partless objects.

Note that the arrangement of parts is not material, but *immaterial* information.

The strict philosophical definition of a composite whole, especially in analytic language philosophy, is just its being picked out by a philosopher for analysis. An example might be "there is a table," or in Quine's existential quantification form, "$\exists\, x\, (x = \text{'a table'})$."

The ordinary sense of a whole is an object that is distinguishable from its neighboring objects. But such a whole may be just a part of some larger composite whole, up to the universe.

The teleonomic sense of a composite object is that it seems to have a purpose, the Greeks called it a *telos*, either intrinsic as in all living things, or extrinsic as in all artifacts, where the purpose was invented by the object's creator, or compositor.

The most important example of a teleonomic process is of course biology. Every biological organism starts with a first cell that contains all the information needed to accomplish its "purpose," to grow into a fully developed individual, and, for some, to procreate others of its kind.

By contrast, when a philosopher picks out an arbitrary part of something, declaring it to be a whole something for philosophical purposes, perhaps naming it, the teleonomy is simply the philosopher's intention to analyze it further as a composite object.

For example, something that has no natural or artifactual basis, that does not "carve nature at the joints," as Plato described it, that arbitrarily and violently divides the otherwise indivisible, is a perfectly valid "idea," an abstract entity. This notion that anything goes for the philosopher to select as a composite whole is known as "mereological universalism."

The combination of arbitrary objects is called a "mereological sum." A frequent example is a combination of the Statue of Liberty and the Eiffel Tower, although there is a strong teleonomic component to this mereological sum as they are both part of the oeuvre of the great engineer Alexandre-Gustave Eiffel. Remember our first axiom that everything is identical to anything else "in some respect." Here two respects are Eiffel and built in France.

Mereological Essentialism

Aristotle knew that most living things can survive the loss of various parts (limbs, for example), but not others (the head). By analogy, he thought that other objects (and even concepts) could have parts (or properties) that are essential to its definition and other properties or qualities that are merely accidental.

Mereological essentialism is the study of those essential parts.

At his presidential address to the twenty-fourth annual meeting of the Metaphysical Society of America in 1973, ROD CHISHOLM defined mereological essentialism as the idea that if some object has parts, then those parts are essential, metaphysically necessary, to the particular object..

> "I shall consider a philosophical puzzle pertaining to the concepts of whole and part. The proper solution, I believe, will throw light upon some of the most important questions of metaphysics.
>
> The puzzle pertains to what I shall call the principle of mereological essentialism. The principle may be formulated by saying that, for any whole x, if x has y as one of its parts then y is part of x in every possible world in which x exists. The principle may also be put by saying that every whole has the parts that it has necessarily, or by saying that if y is part of x then the property of having y as one of its parts is essential to x. If the principle is true, then if y is ever part of x, y will be part of x as long as x exists." [3]

Chisholm draws three important conclusions.

(A1) If x is a part of y and y is a part of z, then x is a part of z (this is the transitivity of parthood).

(A2) If x is a part of y, then y is not a part of x (the whole is an improper part of itself).

(A3) If x is a part of y, then y is such that in every possible world in which y exists x is a part of y (can we explain this?).[4]

---

3 Chisholm (1973) 'Parts as essential to their wholes. *The Review of Metaphysics*, 26: p.582.
4 *ibid.*, p.587

For Aristotle, and in ordinary use, not every part of a whole is a necessary part (let alone in all possible worlds). How does Chisholm defend such an extreme view as his A3? We can speculate that he assumes that the essential nature of something must preserve its identity, so that A3 can be rewritten

(A3') If x is a part of y, then y is an essential, that is a necessary, part of y needed to maintain its identity.

Much of the verbal quibbling in metaphysical disputes is about objects that are defined by language conventions as opposed to objects that are "natural kinds".

Mereological universalism is the idea that an arbitrary collection of objects or parts of objects can be considered a conceptual whole – a "mereological sum" – for some purpose or other (mostly to provoke an empty debate with other metaphysicians).

Modern metaphysics examines the relations of parts to whole, whole to parts, and parts to parts within a whole using the abstract axioms of set theory, a vital part of analytic language philosophy today. Because a set can be made up of any list of things, whether they have any physical integrity or even any conceivable connections, other than their membership in the arbitrary set. Consider the "whole" made up of the Eiffel Tower and the Statue of Liberty!

Mereology is a venerable subject. The Greeks worried about part/whole questions, usually in the context of the persistence of an object when a part is removed and the question of an object's identity. Is the Ship of Theseus the same ship when some of the planks have been replaced? Does Dion survive the removal of his foot?

The idea that an arbitrary collection of things, a "mereological sum," can be considered a whole, does violence to our common sense notion of a whole object. It is an extreme example of the arbitrary connection between words and objects that is the bane of analytic language philosophy. "When I use a word," Humpty Dumpty said, in rather a scornful tone, "it means just what I choose it to mean—neither more nor less."

Mereological universalism also leads to the idea that there are many ways to compose a complex material whole out of a vague collection of simple objects. This is what Peter Unger called the *Problem of the Many*.[5]

It led Peter van Inwagen to his position of mereological nihilism, that there are no composite wholes. Van Inwagen says there are no tables, only simples arranged table-wise. The "arrangement" is the information in the table. When we can identify the origin of that information, we have the deep metaphysical reason for it essence. Aristotle called the arrangement "the scheme of the ideas."

> By matter I mean, for instance, bronze; by shape, the arrangement of the form (τὸ σχῆμα τῆς ἰδέας); and by the combination of the two, the concrete thing: the statue (ἀνδριάς).[6]

Van Inwagen makes an exception of living things, and Unger has abandoned his own form of nihilism in recent years. Both Unger and van Inwagen now accept the idea that they exist.

Van Inwagen's says that his argument that living beings are composite objects is based on the Cartesian "cogito," I think, therefore I am. He proposes,

> "(∃y the xs compose y) if and only if the activity of the xs constitutes a life.
>
> If this answer is correct, then there are living organisms: They are the objects whose lives are constituted by the activities of simples, and, perhaps, by the activities of subordinate organisms such as cells; they are the objects that have proper parts. Therefore, if there are no organisms, then, since there are lives, the Proposed Answer is wrong. In Section 12 I gave reasons for supposing that there were living organisms. That is, I gave reasons that I intended to be available to the philosopher who, like me, thinks that there are no visible inanimate objects. (Most philosophers, unless they are Nihilists or general skeptics, will scarcely want reasons for believing in organisms.) I have argued that situations apparently involving tables and chairs and all the other inanimate furniture of the world are to be understood as involving only simples. There are no chairs, I maintain, but only

---

5   See chapter 30.
6   Aristotle, *Metaphysics*, Book VII, § vii

simples arranged chairwise. My "reasons for believing in organisms," therefore, are reasons for stopping where I do and not going on to maintain that there are no organisms but are only simples arranged organically. My argument for the existence of organisms, it will be remembered, involved in an essential way the proposition that I exist." [7]

DAVID WIGGINS and PETER GEACH debated the problems of absolute and relative identity over several years and one version of their argument used the ancient puzzle of Dion and Theon, as extended by Geach to a modern puzzle called Tibbles, the Cat.

Their argument can be analyzed in information terms as what *constitutes* a material object, as we discuss in the next chapter.

Biomereological Essentialism

Information philosophy provides a much deeper reason for biological organisms being "composite objects" and as having "proper parts" that are themselves composites and not merely the "simples" of van Inwagen and other mereological nihilists. These biomeric parts are created and maintained by anti-entropic processes that distribute matter and energy to all the vital parts using a biological messaging system to control the distribution of biological materials and free energy. There is a "telos" (or Aristotelian "entelechy," loosely translated as "having the final cause within") implemented by messaging between all the vital parts. We call this *teleonomy*, following the suggestions of COLIN PITTENDRIGH and JACQUES MONOD.

But teleonomy, which depends on the communication of abstract messages between the biomers, is not possible in a materialist metaphysics that denies the existence of immaterial ideas.

We should distinguish ordinary biomeric parts that can fail and be replaced from those that cannot be replaced. These *vital* biomers are essential in a stronger sense. Without them, the teleonomy of the whole is destroyed. The organism decays to smaller living things and possibly all the way to dead material ("dust to dust").

---

7   Van Inwagen (1990b), *Material Beings*, p.213

Composition as Holism and Emergence

The phrase "the whole is greater than the sum of its parts" serves as a slogan for holists and gestaltists. Mereological nihilists deny the existence of such "wholes." The "whole" or "gestalt" is best seen as the immaterial information structure of the composite object. Holists, and gestaltists think such structures are *emergent*. We agree, what emerges is an increase of immaterial information, what van Inwagen recognizes as the "arrangement" of the simple constituent objects.

Information emerges because it is not conserved, as are matter and energy. Information has been increasing since the beginning of time. Everything emergent is part of that new information. Living things are dynamic and growing information structures. Van Inwagen implicitly recognizes them as composite wholes. They are forms through which matter and energy continuously flow, powered by negative entropy from the sun and managed by information communications between their vital parts. As they grow, their information increases and genuine new capabilities emerge.[8]

And we find that information in living things (ideas, thoughts, intentions, purposes) can exert *causal control* over the material world. ROGER SPERRY famously used as an example of downward causation in the mind as similar to the way "a wheel rolling downhill carries atoms and molecules... caught up and overpowered by the higher properties of the whole."[9]

Composites exert *downward causation* over their parts. This is the solution to Descartes' mind-body problem as well as the free will problem, which very simply depends on the possibility of choosing between different actions.

---

8   See the growing argument, chapter 27.
9   Sperry (1969) 'A Modified Concept of Consciousness,' *Psychological Review*, 76, 6, p. 533

Problems

- Abstract Entities
- Being and Becoming
- Co[n]
- Chance
- Coinciding Objects
- Free Will
- God and
- Constitution
- Individuation
- Mind-Bo[dy]
- Identity
- Necessity or Contingen[cy]
- Modality
- Space
- Possibility and Actuality
- Wa[...]
- Vagueness
- Universals
- Can Information Ph[ysics...]

Constitution

Does the material constitution of an object determine its identity? Metaphysicians ask "Is constitution identity?"

Material particles (e.g., atoms) alone, what PETER VAN INWAGEN describes as partless "simples," are nothing more than a "mereological sum." They do not "compose" an integrated "whole" unless we know something about the teleonomic processes that create and maintain the object, as we saw in the previous chapter.

An eliminative materialist metaphysics that ignores immaterial information condemns metaphysicians to doing philosophy with one hand tied behind their backs.

Information philosophy says that we must know something about the abstract form of an object. Without specific information about the arrangement and organization of the material particles, and in the case of living things any information that is being communicated inside the organism and between organisms, we know little about the object's internal "form."

It is the matter plus the form that informs us about an object's identity. In general, we cannot have matter without form. But this raises the problem of recognizing a dualist idealism that has as much reality as pure materialism.

Given a lump of material, it is the form as a function of time that allows us to study change and the object's persistence conditions over time.

It is arguably the colocation[1] of form and matter that has generated several of the ancient puzzles that are still plaguing analytic language metaphysicians, problems like the Statue and Lump of Clay, the Ship of Theseus, the Problem of the Many, and Dion and Theon (a/k/a Tibbles the Cat).

Is Constitution Identity?

This is the argument that the constitutive material alone (the simple material particles) establishes an object's identity. This

---

1 See chapter 7.

would be reasonable if the complete arrangement of the particles (the form, the total information about the material) is included.

A materialist metaphysics asks questions about the underlying substrate that constitutes all the objects in the universe. Unfortunately, most modern philosophers think that the material substrate is all there is. JAEGWON KIM thinks that matter exhausts the contents of the world. To think otherwise would be to posit "entities other than material substances, such as immaterial minds, or souls, outside physical space, with immaterial, non-physical properties."[2]

But clearly the form of an object – the information it contains – plays a major role in identity, if not the dominant role for identity over time. Information philosophy posits immaterial entities.

Because all material things change in time (the Heraclitean "flux" or Platonic "Becoming"), the concept of "identity over time" is fundamentally flawed. Even in the case of a hypothetical completely inert object that could be protected from loss or gain of a single particle, its position coordinates in most spacetime frames are constantly changing.

Perfect identity over time is limited to unchanging ideas or concepts – Parmenidean "Being." These are some of the abstract entities, like numbers and logical truths.

But identity over time "in some respects" is always available. Instead of *plus ça change, plus c'est la même chose*, we have *la change á tout le temps, et seulement la même chose á la même temps*.

We thus have proposed three axioms of identity:

Id1. Everything is identical to everything else in some respects.

Id2. Everything is different from everything else in some other respects.

Id3. Everything is identical to itself in all respects at each instant of time, but different in some respects from itself at any other time.

For biological entities, complete identity should include the practically inaccessible knowledge of all stored information (memories of experiences stored in the *experience recorder and*

---

2   Kim (2007) *Physicalism, or Something Near Enough*, p. 71

reproducer) and all the instantaneous communications of information between the organism's proper parts (from the cellular up to the mental level).

In his compilation of essays on metaphysical problems, *Material Constitution: A Reader*, MICHAEL REA cites several ancient puzzles, all of which he believes are puzzles of material constitution.

> There are many different kinds of puzzles about material constitution. Some involve artifacts; others involve organisms. Some show that growth, diminution, or part replacement is paradoxical; others show that even shape change is paradoxical. Some show that actual changes are paradoxical; others show that the mere possibility of change is paradoxical. But all of them present us with scenarios in which it appears that an object a and an object b share all of the same parts but are essentially related to their parts in different ways. This is what qualifies them as "puzzles about material constitution." The fundamental problem that they all raise is what I call "the problem of material constitution."
>
> It seems most reasonable to begin our discussion by looking at a few examples. We have already seen one: the Debtor's Paradox. This puzzle is also known as the Paradox of Increase or the Growing Argument since, if the debtor's argument is sound, it follows that growth—which involves the addition of particles to an organism—is impossible...I will discuss three other puzzles: the Ship of Theseus, the Body-minus Puzzle [a/k/a Dion and Theon or Tibbles, the Cat], and Allan Gibbard's Lumpl/Goliath [a/k/a Statue and the Clay] Puzzle.[3]

We agree with Rea and will separately analyze all these puzzles of material constitution in part 2 below. Many of these puzzles are analyzed by Rea as problems of identity and/or coinciding objects (the idea that two things can be in the same place at the same time).

---

3   Rea (1997) *Material Constitution: A Reader*, pp.xvi-xvii

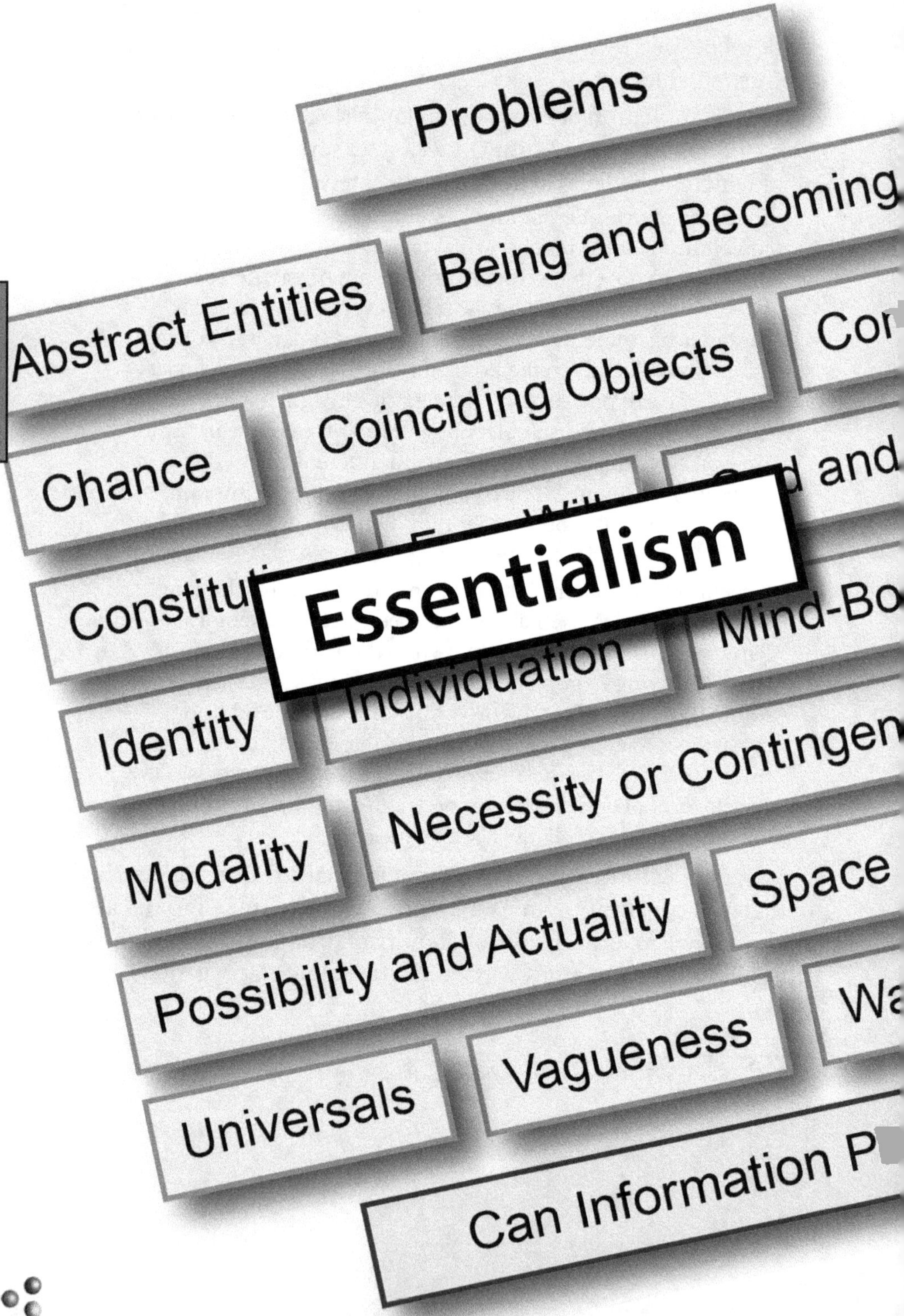

Chapter 10

Essentialism

Essentialism

Metaphysical essentialism is related to the Platonic idea that any thing has an internal essence, without which it would not be what it "is." Twentieth-century "existentialists" denied that things have an essence that precedes their existence, as PLATO believed.

Aristotle was skeptical about Plato's "Ideas" or "Forms" that a demiurge used in the creation of things, but Aristotle did accept the idea of a "telos" or purpose, his "final cause." For artifacts, the telos is put into the object by the artificer. For living things, Aristotle thought the telos was an internal property that he called *entelechy*, from *en-tel-echein* - having a telos within.

Over the centuries, some philosophers have hoped to identify various essences that are essential components of various kinds of things. In modern philosophy, there is talk of "natural kinds," which suggest that each "kind" has one or more properties that are essential to being that kind.

JOHN LOCKE was skeptical about essences in general, like the Platonic Ideas, being used to make up the essence of an individual

> "'Tis true, there is ordinarily supposed a real Constitution of the sorts of Things; and 'tis past doubt, there must be some real Constitution, on which any Collection of simple Ideas co-existing, must depend. But it being evident, that Things are ranked under Names into sorts or Species, only as they agree to certain abstract Ideas, to which we have annexed those Names, the Essence of each Genus, or Sort, comes to be nothing but that abstract Idea, which the General, or Sortal (if I may have leave so to call it from Sort, as I do General from Genus,) Name stands for. And this we shall find to be that which the word Essence imports, in its most familiar use." [1]

Intrinsic Information as Essence

In information philosophy, identity depends on the total information in an object or concept. We can "pick out" the *intrinsic* information as that which is "self-identical" in an object – the

---

1   Locke (1690) *Essay Concerning Human Understanding*, III.iii.15

"peculiar qualifications" of the individual. This suggests a precise definition of the "essence" of an object, what is "essential" about it.

A subset of the intrinsic information may be essential with respect to (*qua*) some concept of the object. As EDMUND HUSSERL emphasized, our concepts about objects depend on our intentions, our intended uses of the object, which give it different (pragmatic) meanings. We can say that an essence is the subset of an object's information that is *isomorphic* to the information in the concept. These essences are subjective, but we can define an objective essence as the total *intrinsic* information.

Two numerically distinct objects can be perfectly identical (x = x) internally, if their intrinsic information content is identical. Relational (extrinsic) information with other objects and positions in space and time is ignored. The Greeks called intrinsic information *pros heauto* or *idios poion*. ARISTOTLE and the Stoics called this the peculiar qualities of an individual. They may be loosely considered the "essence" of the individual.

The Stoics distinguished these peculiar properties from the material substrate, which they called *hupokeimenon*, the "underlying." *Extrinsic* information is found in an object's relations with other objects and space and time. The Greek terms for relations were *pros ta alla*, toward others, and *pros ti pos echon*, relatively disposed. Aristotle would have called these relative properties accidentals (*symbebekos*). They play no role in the essence.

Even two distinct objects can be considered essentially the same if they are of the same *sort* or of a *natural kind*.

Natural Kinds and Mereological Essentialism

Natural kinds may be described as sharing an essence, or being relatively identical *qua* that essence, which may be a single property or some bundle of properties.

Natural kinds are sometimes said to "carve nature at its joints," as Plato put it in the *Phaedrus*.

Essentialism has its roots in Aristotle's definition of the essence (οὐσία), the unchanging "Being" of an object. Is "Essentialism" metaphysically valid or only an analytic language claim?

The essence of an object, the "kind" or "sort" of object that it "is", its "constitution," its "identity," includes those "proper" parts of the object without which it would cease to be that sort or kind. It would lose its identity.

Mereology is the study of parts and is historically the decomposition of an entity into its components, the parts which "compose" the whole. Some of these may be "proper parts," but in what sense can we say that? Others may be merely parts that we have picked out to focus on and have given names. They may in no way be "natural" parts, kinds, or sorts.

Aristotle knew that most living things can survive the loss of various parts (limbs, for example), but not others (the head, say). By analogy, he thought that other objects (and even concepts) could have parts (or properties) that are essential to its definition and other properties or qualities that are merely accidental. Mereological essentialism should be the study of those essential parts.

As we saw in chapter 8, RODERICK CHISHOLM defined "mereological essentialism," the idea that if some object has parts, then those parts are essential, metaphysically necessary, to the particular object.

No doubt some parts are essential, in the sense that the brain or heart is essential to a human being. But surely not every part of any whole is a necessary part in all possible worlds? As Aristotle said, some parts may be accidental. And some parts may not persist as criteria of the object's "identity through time."

Chapter 11

Metaphysics

Free Will

The existence of free will depends on the existence of genuine possibility (some absence of necessity), in the sense of counterfactual situations in the past that were alternative possibilities for action. They allow us to say that we could have done otherwise.

Information philosophy has shown that ontological possibilities exist because new information has been entering the universe since its origin. Information theory shows that new information is not possible without multiple possibilities. If information were a conserved quantity, like matter and energy, the universe would be Laplacian and deterministic. The evidence from cosmological, biological, and human information growth grounds the fundamental basis for information philosophy.

Philosophical talk about possibilities today is largely found in discussions about "possible worlds." Unfortunately, the possible worlds in DAVID LEWIS's "modal realism" are all eliminative materialist and deterministic. Lewis views our "actual world" as completely deterministic. All other possible worlds, visualized by him as separate spatio-temporal domains, are equally "actual" for their inhabitants. His counterfactuals are all necessary.

> There are no genuine possibilities in Lewis's "possible worlds"!

Nevertheless, we can explain genuine free will in metaphysical terms using the possible world semantics of SAUL KRIPKE, who maintained that his semantics could be used to describe various ways our actual world might have been. Unlike many other "possible world" interpretations, Kripke accepts that empirical facts in the physical world are *contingent*, that many things might have been otherwise. Kripke's counterfactuals are genuinely different ways the world might have been.

> "I will say something briefly about 'possible worlds'. (I hope to elaborate elsewhere.) In the present monograph I argued against those misuses of the concept that regard possible worlds as something like distant planets, like our own sur-

roundings but somehow existing in a different dimension, or that lead to spurious problems of 'transworld identification'. Further, if one wishes to avoid the Weltangst and philosophical confusions that many philosophers have associated with the 'worlds' terminology, I recommended that 'possible state (or history) of the world', or 'counterfactual situation' might be better. One should even remind oneself that the 'worlds' terminology can often be replaced by modal talk—'It is possible that . . .'

'Possible worlds' are total 'ways the world might have been', or states or histories of the entire world." [1]

Following Kripke, we build a model structure $\mathcal{M}$ as an ordered triple <**G, K, R**>. **K** is the set of all "possible worlds," **G** is the "actual world," **R** is a reflexive relation on **K**, and **G** ε **K**.

If H_1, H_2, and H_3 are three possible worlds in **K**, H_1RH_2 says that H_2 is "possible relative to" or "accessible from" H_1, that every proposition true in H_2 is possible in H_1.

Indeed, the **H** worlds and the actual world **G** are all mutually accessible and each of these is possible relative to itself, since **R** is reflexive.

Now the model system $\mathcal{M}$ assigns to each atomic formula (propositional variable) P a truth-value of T or F in each world **H** ε **K**.

Let us define the worlds H_1, H_2, and H_3 as identical to the real world **G** in all respects except the following statements describing actions of a graduating college student Alice deciding on her next step.

In H_1, the proposition "Alice accepts admission to Harvard Medical School" is true, but false in other worlds, so "possible."

In H_2, the proposition "Alice accepts admission to MIT" is true.

In H_3, the proposition "Alice postpones her decision and takes a 'gap year'" is true.

At about the same time, in the actual world **K**, the statement "Alice considers graduate school" is true.

---

1   Kripke (1981) *Naming and Necessity*, p. 15, 18

Note that the abstract information that corresponds to the three possible worlds **H** is embodied physically in the matter (the neurons of Alice's brain) in the actual world and in the three possible worlds. There is no issue with the "transworld identity" of Alice as there would be with Lewis's "modal realism," because all these possible worlds are in the same spatio-temporal domain.

The metaphysical question is which of the three possible worlds becomes the new actual world, say at time t. What is the fundamental structure of reality that supports the simultaneous existence of alternative possibilities?

Just before time t, we can interpret the semantics of the model structure $\mathcal{M}$ as saying that the above statements were "merely possible" thoughts about future action in Alice's mind.

Note also that just after the decision at time t, the three possible alternatives remain in Alice's experience recorder and reproducer as memories.

Some consequences of Alice's alternative possible decisions.

In the future of world **H1**, Alice's research discovers the genetic signals used in messaging by cancer cells and cancer is eliminated. Several hundred million lives are saved (extended) in Alice's lifetime.

In the future of world **H2**, Alice engineers the miniaturization of nuclear weapons so they are small enough to be delivered by tiny drones. One is stolen from an air force base by a terrorist and flown to an enemy country where millions of lives are lost. Alice kills herself the next day.

In the future of world **H3**, a mature Alice returns to school, completes her Ph.D. in Philosophy at Princeton and writes a book titled *Free Will and Moral Responsibility*.

The Two-Stage Model of Free Will

In our possible worlds analysis of free will, two things are still not clear. First is understanding the causal processes that are involved when our agent chooses between worlds H1, H2, and H3, making one of them the new "actual world." Was the decision process causally determined? Secondly, what are the processes of thought that led to the three options "coming to mind" of the agent. Were these also determined, or was there an element of indeterminism?

The laws of nature are the same in all of our possible worlds, since they are all contained within the same spatio-temporal volume as our actual world. They include the critically important theory of quantum physics, which includes the occurrence of indeterministic events that are only statistically caused.

The two-stage model of free will is very simple. In the creative first stage the agent calls to mind familiar alternative possibilities or generates brand new possibilities, perhaps by creating new ones that depend in part on random noise events in the agent's brain (not mind). The ontological chance in the first stage ensures that actions are not determined or even pre-determined from the beginning of the universe by causal chains, as some compatibilist philosophers believe. These events bring new information into the universe.

In the deliberative second stage, the possibilities generated in the first stage are evaluated. Given enough time, each possibility is compared with the agent's reasons, motives, feelings, desires, etc. (in short, with the agent's character) and one is normally chosen. In the event that there is no obvious best decision, the agent can "think again," perhaps generating a new and better alternative. Finally, with time running out or faced with no obvious best option, the agent may just select one of the alternatives in what is called a "torn decision" by ROBERT KANE

Given the "laws of nature" and the "fixed past" just before a decision, philosophers wonder how a free agent can have any possible alternatives. This is partly because they imagine a timeline for the decision that shrinks the decision process to a single moment.

Decision

Fixed Past | Future

Collapsing the decision to a single moment between the closed fixed past and the open ambiguous future makes it difficult to see the free thoughts of the mind followed by the willed and adequately determined action of the agent in the second stage.

In our model, thoughts are freely generated. Actions are adequately determined by the agent. Thoughts are free. Actions are willed.

Notice that the two-stage model is not limited to a single step of generating alternative possibilities followed by a single step of self-determination by the will. It is better understood as a continuous process of possibilities generation, perhaps by the subconscious (parts of the brain that leave themselves open to noise) at the same time as adequately determined choices are being considered by the same brain parts, perhaps, but now averaging over any quantum events, filtering out the microscopic noisiness that might otherwise make the determination random.

In particular, note that a special kind of decision might occur when the agent finds that none of the current options are good enough for the agent's character and values to approve. The agent then might figuratively say, "Think again!"

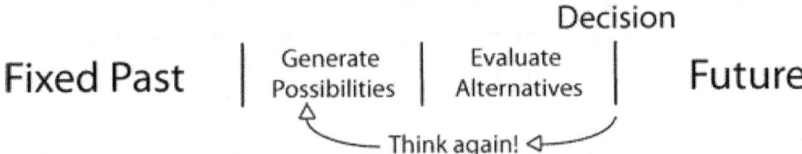

Many philosophers have puzzled how an agent could do otherwise in exactly the same circumstances. Since humans are intelligent organisms, and given our model system of "possible worlds," it is impossible that an agent is ever in exactly the same circumstances. The agent's memory (information stored in the ERR) of earlier similar experiences guarantees that.

This two-stage model makes a somewhat artificial separation between first-stage creative randomness and second-stage deliberative evaluation. These two capabilities of the mind can be going on at the same time. That can be visualized by the occasional decision to go back and think again, when the available alternatives are not good enough to satisfy the demands of the agent's character and values, or by noticing that the subconscious might be still generating possibilities while the agent is in the middle of evaluations.

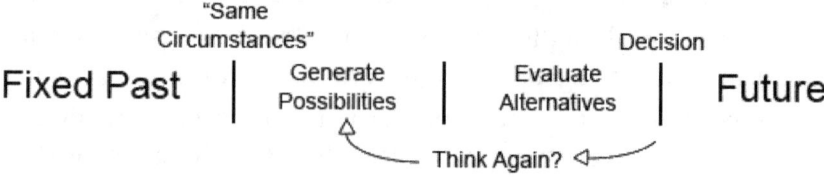

The two-stage model lies between the work of libertarians and compatibilists, in the sense that the free elements in the first stage are what the libertarian needs and the adequately determined evaluations and decisions are what the compatibilist needs for the moral responsibility of the agent. Robert Kane calls the outcomes of such torn decisions "self-forming actions," because the accumulation of such actions builds the agent's character.

Now Kane has argued that on some occasions the agent may not be able to find grounds for choosing between a prudential, self-interested choice and a moral, other-interested decision. In case of such a "torn decision" the agent may simply allow indeterminism to enter into the decision but be prepared to take responsibility for either choice.

Compatibilists have argued that any randomness in the final decision would make the agent not responsible for the decision. But Kane has nicely solved this dilemma.

Let's diagram Kane's "self-forming action" (SFA) to place it in the temporal sequence of events between the "fixed past" at the start of a decision process, and the decision itself, which marks the beginning of the future.

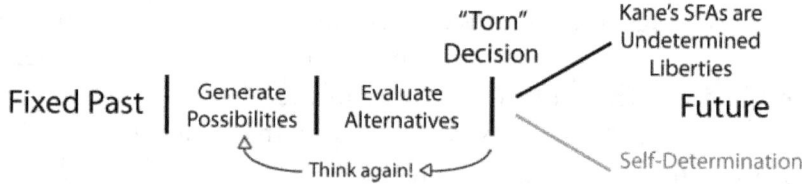

In the end, Kane's model, resolving "torn decisions" by an indeterministic choice between alternatives that are all motivated by good reasons, is an important supplement to the two-stage model. He calls this "plural rational control." We call them "undetermined liberties." They nicely complement decisions that are arrived at in an adequately determined way, which we call self-determination.

Self-determination means that the agent and only the agent "causes" the decision. There is no randomness in the choice, so we now embrace the idea of agent causation, as opposed to the idea that free will can be understood by analyzing "events."

"Free Will" in scare quotes refers to the common but mistaken notion that the adjective "free" modifies the concept "will." In particular, it indicates that the element of chance, one of the two requirements for free will is present in the determination of the will itself.

Critics of "libertarian free will" usually adopt this meaning in order to attack the idea of randomness in our decision-making process, which clearly would not help to make us morally responsible.

Unfortunately, even defenders of libertarian free will (Robert Kane, for example) continue to add indeterminism into the decision itself, making such free will "unintelligible" by their own account.

Despite their claim that they are better equipped than scientists to make conceptual distinctions and evaluate the cogency of arguments, professional philosophers have mistakenly conflated the concepts of "free" and "will." They (con)fuse them with the muddled term "free will," despite clear warnings from John Locke that this would lead to confusion.

Locke said clearly, as had some ancients like LUCRETIUS, it is not the will that is free (in the sense of undetermined), it is the mind.

Locke liked the idea of Freedom and Liberty. He thought it was inappropriate to describe the Will itself as Free. The Will is a Determination. It is the Man who is Free.

In his great *Essay Concerning Human Understanding*, Locke calls the question of Freedom of the Will unintelligible. But for Locke, it is only because the adjective "free" applies to the agent, not to the will, which is determined by the mind, and determines the action.

"I think the question is not proper, whether the will be free, but whether a man be free...

"This way of talking, nevertheless, has prevailed, and, as I guess, produced great confusion." [2]

Freedom of human action requires the randomness of absolute chance to break the causal chain of determinism, yet the conscious knowledge that we are adequately determined to be responsible for our choices and our actions.

Freedom requires some events that are not causally determined by immediately preceding events, events that are unpredictable by any agency, events involving quantum uncertainty. These random events create alternative possibilities for action.

Randomness is the "free" in free will.

In short, there must be a randomness requirement, unpredictable chance events that break the causal chain of determinism. Without this chance, our actions are simply the consequences of events in the remote past. This randomness must be located in a place and time that enhances free will, one that does not reduce it to pure chance. Randomness, in the form of creative new ideas among the alternative possibilities, is what breaks the causal chain.

(*Determinists do not like this requirement.*)

Freedom also requires an adequately determined will that chooses or selects from those alternative possibilities. There is effectively nothing uncertain about this choice.

Adequate determinism is the "will" in free will.

So there is also a determinism requirement - that our actions be adequately determined by our character and values. This requires that any randomness not be the *direct cause* of our actions.

(*Libertarians do not like this requirement.*)

Adequate determinism means that randomness in our thoughts about alternative possibilities does not *directly cause* our actions.

A random thought can lead to a "determined" action, for which we can take full responsibility.

---

2   Locke (1690) *Essay Concerning Human Understanding*, Book II, Chapter XXI, Of Power, s.21

> *We must admit indeterminism*
> *but not permit it to produce random actions*
> *as Determinists mistakenly fear.*
> *We must also limit determinism*
> *but not eliminate it*
> *as Libertarians mistakenly think necessary.*

Philosophers of logic and language are further muddled in their argument that if determinism is false, indeterminism is true. This is of course logically correct. Strict causal determinism with a causal chain of necessary events back to an Aristotelian first cause is indeed false, and modern philosophers know it, though most hold out hope that the quantum mechanical basis of such indeterminism will be disproved someday. Many analytic language philosophers simply declare themselves agnostic on the truth or falsity of determinism, missing the empirical point.

These agnostic philosophers go on to argue that the principle of bivalence requires that since determinism and indeterminism are logical contradictories, only one of them can be true. The law of the excluded middle allows no third possibility. Now since neither determinism nor indeterminism allow the kind of free will that supports moral responsibility, they claim that free will is unintelligible or an illusion. This is the *standard argument against free will*.[3]

The practical empirical situation is much more complex than such simple black and white logical linguistic thinking can comprehend. Despite quantum uncertainty, there is clearly adequate determinism in the world, enough to permit the near-perfect predictions of celestial motions, and good enough to send men to the moon and back. But this determinism is neither absolute nor required in any way by logical necessity, as Aristotle himself first argued against the determinist atomists, Democritus and Leucippus.

When we unpack the complex concept of "free will," we find the freedom is in our *thoughts*, the determination is in our willed *actions*. Self-determination is not determinism.

---

3 See Doyle, (2011) *Free Will, The Scandal in Philosophy,* chapter 4.

In our two-stage model, "free will" combines two distinct concepts. Free is found in the chance and randomness of the first stage. Will is the *adequately determined* choice in the second stage.

Our Thoughts are Free, they come to us.

Our Actions are Willed, they come from us.

Compatibilists and Determinists were right about the Will, but wrong about Freedom.

Libertarians were right about Freedom, but wrong about the Will, which is determined enough to insure moral responsibility.

Does Ontological Chance Threaten Free Will?

The modest indeterminism required for free will is not the chaotic irrational threat feared by so many philosophers and scientists since Chrysippus over 2000 years ago, since most physical and mental events are overwhelmingly "adequately determined."

There is no problem imagining that the three traditional mental faculties of reason - perception, conception, and comprehension - are all carried on with "adequate determinism" in a physical brain where quantum events and thermal noise do not interfere with normal operations.

There is also no problem imagining a role for chance in the brain in the form of quantum level noise (as well as pre-quantal thermal noise). Noise can introduce random errors into stored memories. Noise can create random associations of ideas during memory recall. Many scientists have speculated that this randomness may be driven by microscopic fluctuations that are amplified to the macroscopic level. This need not happen in some specific location in the brain. It is most likely a general property of all neurons or whichever parts of the brain are storing our memories.

We distinguish seven increasingly sophisticated ideas about the role of chance and indeterminism in the question of free will. Many libertarians have accepted the first two. Determinist and compatibilist critics of free will make the third their central attack on chance, mistaenly claiming that it denies moral responsibility.

But very few if any thinkers appear to have considered all the seven essential requirements for chance to contribute to libertarian free will.

1. Chance is important for free will because it breaks the causal chain of determinism.
2. Chance exists in the universe. Quantum mechanics is correct. Indeterminism is "true," etc.
3. But chance should not directly cause our actions. We cannot be responsible for random actions.
4. Chance can generate random (unpredictable) alternative possibilities for action or thought. But the choice or selection of one action must be adequately determined by our reasons, motives, feelings, desires, in short, by our character and values, so that we can take full responsibility for our actions. And once we choose, the connection between mind/brain and muscle control must be adequately determined to see that "our will be done."
5. Chance, in the form of noise, both quantum and thermal noise, is always present. The naive model of a single random microscopic event, amplified to affect the macroscopic brain, never made sense. Under what *ad hoc* circumstances, at what time, at what place in the brain, would it occur to affect a complex decision?
6. Although always present, chance must be overcome or suppressed by the adequately determined will when it decides to act, de-liberating the prior free options that mean "one could have done otherwise."
7. To the extent that chance is not completely suppressed by the will, the resulting choice can be considered to have an element of randomness. The agent can still take responsibility for allowing the choice to be partially or completely random, the equivalent of flipping a mental coin. We can choose to act randomly, when none of our options is clearly the "best."

Chapter 12

God and Immortality

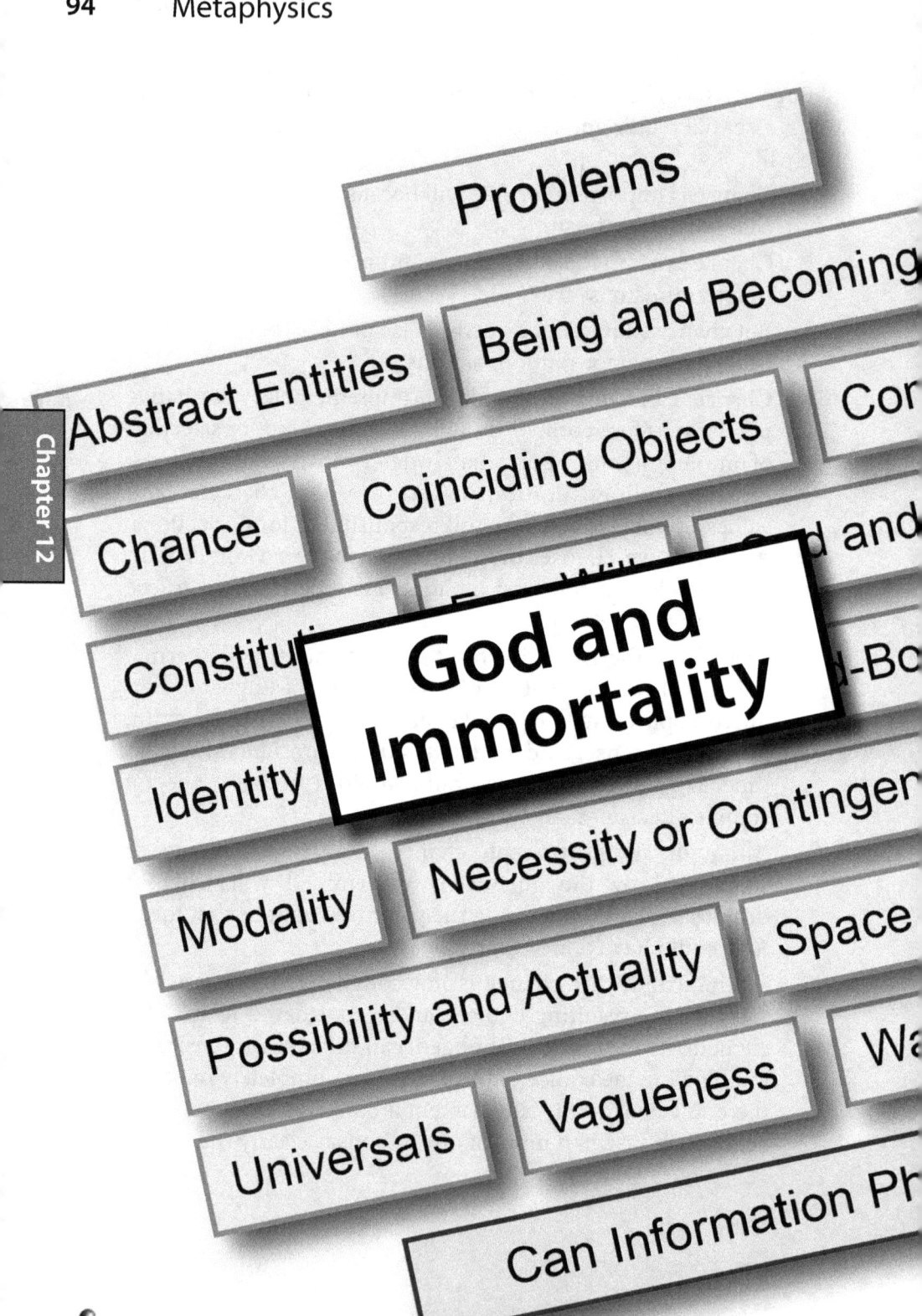

God and Immortality

Most of the world's religions have some concept of gods or a God, with some notable exceptions such as Buddhism.

Theologians claim to have discerned the essential attributes of a monotheistic God, such as omniscience (perfect foreknowledge), omnipotence (unlimited power), omnipresence (present everywhere), omnibenevolence (perfect goodness), and a necessary and eternal existence.

Information philosophy offers a simple test of the "revealed truth" of these attributes, specifically the visions by inspired thinkers that have no empirical evidence. Although these visions are in the realm of "pure ideas," we can say that if every world religion agreed completely on the attributes of God, it would increase their believability. As it is, the comparative study of religions with the incredible diversity of their claims, renders the idea of God as implausible as Santa Claus.

At the present time, arguments like these will carry little weight with the believers in a religion, most of whom have little exchange of knowledge with those of other faiths. This may be expected to change with the reach of the Internet via smartphones to most of the world's population by 2020.

In theism, God is the creator and sustainer of the universe. In deism, God is the creator, but not the sustainer of the universe, which is now assumed to be running itself following deterministic laws of motion. Open theism denies that God's foreknowledge has already determined the future. Monotheism is the belief in the existence of one God or in the oneness of God. In pantheism, God is the universe itself. Polytheists hold that there are many gods. For atheists, no gods exist.

God is sometimes conceived as an immaterial being (without a body), which information philosophy might accept, since God is quintessentially an idea, pure information. Some religions think an avatar of God has come to earth in the past. Some religions see God as a personal being, answering human supplications and

This chapter on the web - metaphysicist.com/problems/god

prayers. A God intervening in human affairs is thought to be the source of all moral norms. Logical "proofs" of God's existence are based on various of these assumed attributes.

Now that information philosophy and physics has identified the essential attributes and properties of the cosmic creation process, the problem for theologians is to reconcile their views of their gods with these new discoveries.

No Creator, But There Was/Is A Creation

Modern cosmology confirms that the universe came into existence at a definite time in the past, some 13.8 billion years ago. Although this does not need the Creator some religions want, it does confirm a creation process. Information philosophy attributes this to a *cosmic creation process*.[1] Because this process continues today (indeed human beings are co-creators of the world), deists are wrong about a creative act at the beginning followed by a mechanical clockwork universe tending to itself ever since.

Theodicy (The Problem of Evil)

The problem of evil is only a problem for monotheists who see God as omnipotent. "If God is Good, He is not God. If God is God, He is not Good." (from *J.B.*, a play by Archibald MacLeish). Our solution to the problem is a dualist world with both entropic destruction and ergodic creation. If ergodic information is an objective good, then entropic destruction of information is "the devil incarnate," as the mathematician and inventor of Cybernetics, NORBERT WIENER put it, in a most apt theological metaphor.

Are Omniscience and Omnipotence Mutually Exclusive?

The idea of God as an omniscient and omnipotent being has an internal logical contradiction that is rarely discussed by the theologians. If such a being had perfect knowledge of the future, like errors, who knows the positions, velocities, and forces for all the particles, such a God would be perfectly impotent, because the future is already determined. If God had the power to change even one thing about the future, his presumed perfect knowledge

---

1 See appendix F of Doyle (2016) *Great Problems of Philosophy and Physics*..

would have been imperfect. Omniscience entails impotence. Omnipotence some ignorance. Prayer is useless.

Albert Einstein's discovery of ontological chance poses an even greater threat to the omniscience of God and the idea of foreknowledge. The inventors of probability always regarded chance as atheistic. The use of statistics was simply to make estimates of outcomes of many independent events when detailed knowledge of those events was not possible because of human ignorance. Ontological chance means that even God cannot know some things.

For example, in quantum physics, if knowledge exists of which slot a particle goes through in a two-slit experiment, the outcome of the experiment will differ. The characteristic interference caused by the wave function is different for one slit open.

The Ergod

There is absolutely nothing supernatural about the cosmic creation process, but it is the source of support for human life. Many theologically-minded thinkers have long assumed that life and mind were given to humanity by a divine providence. The main product of the cosmic creation process is all the negative entropy in the universe. While thermodynamics calls it "negative," information philosophy sees it as the ultimate positive and deserving of a better name. So we call it Ergo, which etymologically suggests a fundamental kind of energy ("erg" zero), e.g., the "Gibbs free energy," G_0, that is available to do work because it has low entropy.

We co-opted the technical term "ergodic" from statistical mechanics as a replacement for anti-entropic, and because it very suggestively contained our neologism "ergod."

An anthropomorphization (or theomorphization) of the process that creates all the energy with low entropy that we call Ergo has a number of beneficial consequences. Most all human cultures look for the source of their existence in something "higher" than their mundane existence. This intuition of a cosmic force, a providence that deserves reverence, is validated in part by the discovery of what we provocatively call "Ergod," as the source of all life.

Such an Ergod has the power to resist the terrible and universal Second Law of Thermodynamics, which commands the increase of chaos and entropy (disorder).

Without violating that inviolable Second Law overall, the Ergod reduces the entropy locally, creating pockets of cosmos and negative entropy (order and information-rich structures). All human life, and any possible extraterrestrial life, lives in one of these pockets.

Note that the opposition of Ergod and Entropy, of Ergodic processes and Entropic processes, coincides with the ancient Zarathustrian image of a battle between the forces of light (*Ahura Mazda*) and darkness (*Angra Manyu*), of good and evil, of heaven and hell. Many religions have variations on this dualist theme, and the three major Western religions all share the same Biblical source, probably incorporated into Judaism during the Babylonian exile.

The Ergod is "present" and we can say enthusiastically is "in us." The Ergod's work is to create new information, so when we create and share information we are doing the Ergod's work.

The Problem of Immortality

The two basic kinds of immortality available today may not satisfy those looking for an "afterlife," but they are both very real and important, and there is a medical technology solution visible on the horizon that should satisfy many persons.

The first is least satisfying - partial immortality of your genes through children. This is of no significance to the childless.

A second kind of immortality will result from a solution to the problem of aging, almost certainly from stem cell research, which should allow vital organ replacement, and from a cure for runaway cancer cells, a devastating entropic force.

This should satisfy even Woody Allen, who famously said,

"I don't want to achieve immortality through my work. I want to achieve it through not dying."

The third is the ancient notion of fame or kleos (κλέος) among the Greeks. When Homer sang of Achilles and Odysseus, it was to give them undying fame, which they have today among so many literate persons.

This kind we call "information immortality." It is more realizable than ever with the development of world-wide literacy through print and now through the world-wide web, which makes the Information Philosopher and Metaphysicist websites available anywhere. In five years time, a majority of the world's population will be carrying a smartphone and thus able to read this work online.

The great Wikipedia will be capable of having something about everyone who has made a contribution to human knowledge.

If we don't remember the past, we don't deserve to be remembered by the future.

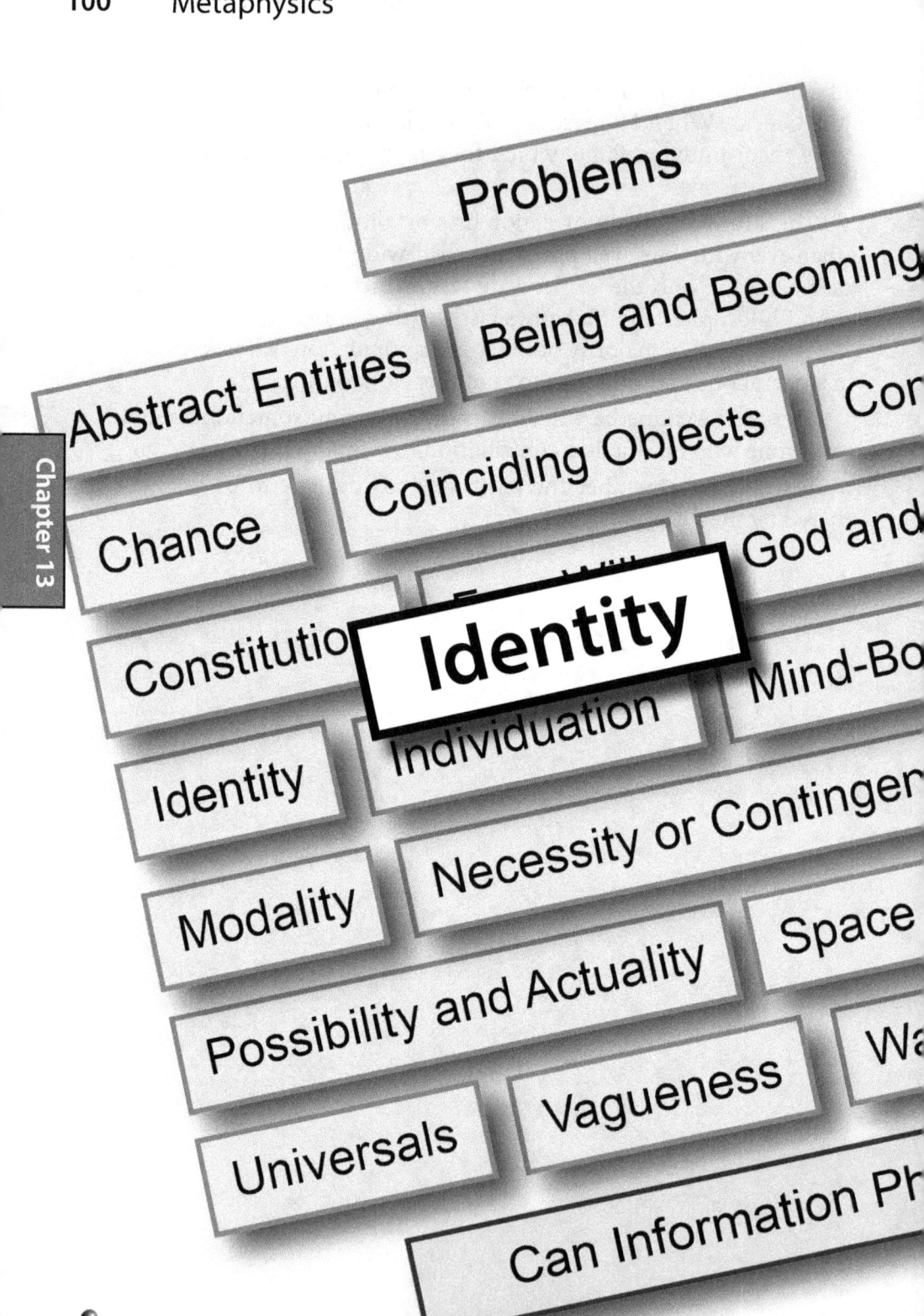

Identity

Information Identity

In information philosophy, identity depends on the *total information* in an object or concept.

We distinguish the *intrinsic* information inside the object (or concept) from any relational information with respect to other objects that we call *extrinsic* or external information. We can "pick out" the intrinsic information as that which is "self-identical" in an object. The Greeks called this the πρὸς ἑαυτο - self-relation. or ἴδιος ποιὸν, "peculiar qualifications" of the individual.

Self-identity, then, is the simple fact that the *intrinsic* information and the *extrinsic* relational or dispositional information are unique to this single object. No other object can have the same disposition relative to other objects. This is an absolute kind of identity. Some metaphysicians say that such identity is logically necessary. Some say self-identity is the only identity, but we can now support philosophers who argue for a *relative identity*.

To visualize our concept of information identity, imagine putting yourself in the position of an object. Look out at the world from its vantage point. No other object has that same view, that same relation with the objects around you, especially its relation with you. Now another object could have intrinsic information identicality. We will identify a very large number of objects and concepts in the world that are intrinsically identical, including natural and artifactual kinds, which we may call digital kinds, since they are identical, bit for bit. This is *relative identity*.

A Criterion for Identity

After accepting the fundamental fact that nothing is perfectly identical to anything but itself, the criterion for *relative identity*, for identical "in some respect," or *qua* that respect, is that some subset of the information in two different things must be the same information, bit for bit.

This chapter on the web - metaphysicist.com/problems/identity

Relative identity means that a can be the same *I* as *b*, but not the same *E* as *b*, where *I* is the sum of all the *intrinsic* properties and relations - internal self-relations between an object's different parts. For physical objects, these could be within some physical boundary, the borderlines subject to conditions of *vagueness*. In a biological entity, intrinsic information includes the vast communications going on inside and between the cells, which makes it much more than a mereological sum of its material parts.

The *E* for an object is the sum of *extrinsic* relations an object has with things outside, including its disposition in space and time.

Mathematically, $\int_i F(x) = \int_i G(x)$, but $\int_e F(x) \neq \int_e G(x)$, which says that $F(x)$ and $G(x)$ are identical over their intrinsic domains (i) but differ over their extrinsic domains (e).

Set theoretically, in classical propositional calculus, we can say that I_a is the set of intrinsic properties and relations that can be predicated in propositions about an object a. E_a is the set of extrinsic relations. We can now describe why *absolute* identity is limited to *self-identity*.

If $I_a + E_a = I_b + E_b$, then a and b are one and the same object.

And, if $Ia = Ib$, then a and b are relatively identical, *qua* their information content.

Note that while self-identity is reflexive, symmetric, and an equivalence self-relation, relative identity is often none of these. This is because, unlike MAX BLACK's identical spheres, SAUL KRIPKE's natural kinds, and our many digital clones, some part of the information in a and b may be identical, but the information that is not identical may also differ in quantity. We can say that if *aRb* is 60% identical, *bRa* may be only 10% identical.

The application of this criterion is the quantitative analysis, the quantification, of the total information in and about both objects.

Extensional *quantification* over things in analytic language philosophy is about their set membership, which is dependent on language references to the properties of objects.

By contrast, quantification in information philosophy is a calculation of the total information content in the entities, in principle free of language ambiguities, but in practice, very difficult.

A Criterion for Essence

Information identity suggests a possible definition of the "*essence*" of an object, what is "*essential*" about it. Furthermore, if two objects are considered "essentially" the same, we can pick out the subset of information that corresponds to that "essence."

A subset of the intrinsic information may be essential with respect to (*qua*) some concept of the object. As EDMUND HUSSERL emphasized, our concepts about objects depend on our intentions, our intended uses of the object, which give it different (pragmatic) meanings. We can say that an essence is the subset of an object's information that is isomorphic to the information in the concept.

What we call a "concept" about a material object is usually some subset of the information in the object, accurate to the extent that the concept is isomorphic to that subset. By "picking out" different subsets, we can sort objects. We can compare objects, finding them similar *qua* one concept and different *qua* another concept. We can say, for example, that "a = b" *qua* color but not *qua* size.

But there are concepts that may have little to do with the intrinsic peculiar information about an object. They are concepts imposed on the object by our intended uses of it.

We must distinguish these extrinsic essences – our external ideas and concepts about what the object is – from the intrinsic essences that depend only on the object itself and its own purposes, if any. The essences we see in an object are subjective, but we may define an objective essence as the total intrinsic information, including internal messaging, in the object.

Husserl and GOTTLOB FREGE both pointed out that our Ideas are dependent on our personal experience. Experience constrains and amplifies our possible concepts. Two persons may get the general "sense" or "meaning" of something referred to, but Frege said the "idea" or representation (*Vorstellung*) in each mind can be very different, based on that individual's experience. Information philosophy locates the creation of meaning in the responses of the *experience recorder and reproducer* (ERR) to different stimuli.

The relation "identical to," between two numerically distinct concrete or abstract entities, is the source of logical puzzles and language games through the ages that are little more than verbal disputes. Most such disputes are easily resolved or *"dis-solved"* by paying careful attention to all the information, all the particular properties, *intrinsic* and *extrinsic*, of the two entities that may be identical *qua* some particular properties.

Background of the Problem

Identity has been a major problem in philosophy and metaphysics since the Ancients. Even Plato wondered whether two things could be identical:

> "**Socrates**. It is in your opinion, possible for the mind to regard one thing as another and not as what it is **Theaetetus**. Yes, it is.
>
> **Socrates**. Now when one's mind does this, does it not necessarily have a thought either of both things together or of one or the other of them? **Theaetetus**. Yes, it must; either of both at the same time or in succession.
>
> **Socrates**. Then whenever a man has an opinion that one thing is another, he says to himself, we believe, that the one thing is the other. **Theaetetus**. Certainly." [1]

And here is Aristotle:

> "The same" means (a) accidentally the same...For it is not true to say that every man is the same as "the cultured"; because universal predications are essential to things, but accidental predications are not so, but are made of individuals and with a single application. ...
>
> Some things are said to be "the same" in this sense, but others (b) in an essential sense, in the same number of senses as "the one" is essentially one; for things whose matter is formally or numerically one, and things whose substance is one, are said to be the same. Thus "sameness" is clearly a kind of unity in the being, either of two or more things, or of one thing treated as more

---

1   Plato, *Theaetetus*, 189D-190B

than one; as, e.g., when a thing is consistent with itself; for it is then treated as two.

Things are called "other" of which either the forms or the matter or the definition of essence is more than one; and in general "other" is used in the opposite senses to "same."

Things are called "different" which, while being in a sense the same, are "other" not only numerically, but formally or generically or analogically; also things whose genus is not the same; and contraries; and all things which contain "otherness" in their essence." [2]

The fundamental notion of *identity* refers only to the substance and the bundle of *intrinsic* properties (the material substrate and the *immaterial* form) of a single entity. Literally and etymologically it is "id-entity," same entity, from Latin *idem*, "same," and *entitas*.

In Greek, self-identity is the *idios*, one's personal, private, peculiar (intrinsic) properties, separate and distinct from the (extrinsic) properties of others and one's relational properties to others. From Aristotle to the Stoics, Greek philosophers distinguished the individual's *material* substance from the *immaterial* "peculiar qualifications" of the individual. They were accused by the Academic Skeptics of seeing two things - coinciding objects[3] - where there is only one, but they were only distinguishing the form of an object from its matter.

The Stoic term for "constituent substance" or substrate, following Aristotle, was ὑποκείμενον ("the underlying"). Their term for the unique person, possibly separate from the material body, was πρὸς ἑαυτο - self-relation, or ἴδιος ποιὸν - the peculiar qualifications of a particular individual "who," for example, Socrates, as opposed to κοινός ποιὸν, a general "whoness," for example, a human being.

The Greeks also carefully distinguished relational or dispositional properties that depend on an individual's position in space and time or its causal interactions with other individuals. They called these the *pōs ti alla* or *pōs echon*, usually translated as the relatively dispositional qualifications.[4]

---

2   Aristotle, *Metaphysics*, V, ix, 1018b
3   See chapter 7.
4   Long and Sedley (1989) *The Hellenistic Philosophers*, vol 1. p.163

Ignoring this important ancient distinction between intrinsic and merely extrinsic properties (for example, a name) is the source of many confusions in modern identity theory.

Since the seventeenth century, logicians following GOTTFRIED LEIBNIZ have held that necessary truths, including *a priori* and *analytic* truths, have the unique property of being "true in all possible worlds."

Recently, identity figured prominently in discussions of possible worlds. In the 1940's, the concepts of necessity and possibility were added to symbolic logic. Surprisingly, the modal logicians claimed that if two things are identical, they are *necessarily* identical. Does the modal logic proof of the necessity of identity allow us to know something about possible worlds? This is the claim of SAUL KRIPKE and DAVID LEWIS.

It is a sad fact that the addition of modality found little evidence for the importance of possibilities, let alone contingency, which describes almost everything that is the case in our actual world. The possible worlds of Lewis (and perhaps Kripke?) appear to be *eliminatively materialist* and *determinist*, with no real *contingency*.

Is there a sense in which two numerically distinct objects can be identical? Can one of these be in another possible world, what Lewis calls a *counterpart* object? Metaphysicians puzzle over this and a related question, can two things be in the very same place at the same time as coinciding objects? Many metaphysical puzzles and paradoxes start with this flawed assumption.

With information as our analytic tool, we can show that two things that share every property, *intrinsic* internal properties and *extrinsic* external relations with all the other objects in the world, including their positions in space and time, can only be perfectly identical if they are *actually one and the same object*. It seems fine to say that any thing is necessarily itself. We can also show that two things sharing intrinsic internal properties are *relatively* identical.

Leibniz and Gottlob Frege both said clearly that two objects claiming to be identical are one object under two names. A large fraction of the metaphysical literature still ponders this question, (e.g., Hesperus and Phosphorus as two names for Venus).

Absolute identity is simply the relation that any thing has with itself. *Everything is identical to itself.* Anything else is merely "*relative identity*," identical in some respect (*qua*).

Self-identity is a monadic property that applies only to the object itself. Many modal logicians (starting with RUTH BARCAN MARCUS, DAVID WIGGINS, and SAUL KRIPKE) mistakenly thought that given two "identical" objects x and y, x's property of being equal to x (x = x) can be a property of y (= x). Information philosophy shows this is only the case if x and y are the same object. Numerically distinct x and y can only have a *relative* identity.

LUDWIG WITTGENSTEIN described this in *Tractatus* 5.5303,
"Roughly speaking: to say of two things that they are identical is nonsense, and to say of one thing that it is identical with itself is to say nothing."

Leibniz

Most of the metaphysical problems of identity, and especially recent claims about the necessity of identity, can be traced back to the great rationalist philosopher GOTTFRIED LEIBNIZ, who argued for the replacement of ordinary language with a *lingua characterica*, an ambiguity-free set of terms that would eliminate philosophical puzzles and paradoxes. BERTRAND RUSSELL, Ludwig Wittgenstein, and RUDOLF CARNAP all believed in this Leibnizian dream of ambiguity-free, logically true, facts about the world that may be true in all possible worlds.

Unfortunately, fundamental limits on logic and language such as the Gödel and Russell paradoxes have prevented Leibniz's ideal ambiguity-free language, but many modern paradoxes, including questions about identity and necessity, are resolvable in terms of information, as we shall see.

Leibniz defined an "axiom of identity" as "everything is identical to itself." He called it a "primary truth." He said "There are no two individuals indiscernible from one another." This is sometimes called Leibniz's Law, the *Identity of Indiscernibles*. "To suppose two things indiscernible is to suppose the same thing under two names," thus introducing some puzzles about naming that have caused massive confusion in language philosophy and metaphysics for the past seven decades, notably in the work of WILLARD VAN ORMAN QUINE.

Leibniz's Laws

More than any other philosopher, Leibniz enunciated clear principles about identity, including his *Identity of Indiscernibles*. If we can see no differences between things, they may be identical. This is an empirical fact, and must be tested empirically, as Leibniz knew.

But once again, whenever we are talking about two things, that there is a difference between them, a discernible difference, is transparently obvious. Two things are numerically distinct even if they have identical internal information.

Leibniz also described a corollary or converse, the *Indiscernibility of Identicals*.[5] But this idea is necessarily true, if such things as numerically distinct identical objects exist. We shall show that such things have only a *relative* identity, identity in some respects.

Leibniz anticipated the best modern efforts of analytical language philosophers like Frege's distinction between sense (meaning) and reference and Saul Kripke's odd idea that names are metaphysically necessary,[6] when we know well that words are arbitrary symbols.

Leibniz also gave us a *principle of substitutability* - "things are identical if they can be substituted for one another everywhere with no change in truth value."

Leibniz wrote:

"It is not true that two substances resemble each other entirely and differ in number alone.[7]

Indeed, every monad must be different from every other, For there are never in nature two beings which are precisely alike, and in which it is not possible to find some difference.[8]

There are no two individuals indiscernible from one another... Two drops of water or milk looked at under the microscope will be found to be discernible.

To suppose two things indiscernible is to suppose the same thing under two names." [9]

---

5   so named by Quine (1943) "Notes on Existence and Necessity."
6   Kripke (1981) *Naming and Necessity,*
7   'Discourses on Metaphysics,' §9, in *Leibniz: Philosophical Writings*, p.19.
8   'Monadology,' §9, in *Leibniz: Philosophical Writings*, p.180
9   'Correspondence with Clarke," in *Leibniz: Philosophical Writings*, p.216

Frege

Gottlob Frege implemented Leibniz's program of a purely logical language in which statements or sentences with subjects and predicates are replaced with propositional functions, in which a term can be replaced by a variable. In modern terminology, the sentence Socrates is mortal can be replaced, setting the subject Socrates = x, and the predicate "is mortal" with F. "x is F" is replaced by the propositional function Fx, which is read "x is F," or "x F's."

Frege developed a calculus of these propositional functions, in which they are evaluated for their truth-functionality, using the formalism of Boole's two-valued logic. Frege also introduced quantification theory, replacing Aristotle's expression "for all" with a universal quantification operator, now written $\forall x$ or (x).

Frege repeated Leibniz's idea about identity and developed Leibniz's suggestion of one thing under two names, two distinct references. Where Leibniz had said, "To suppose two things indiscernible is to suppose the same thing under two names," Frege suggested that two names referring to the same thing can be in some respect "identical" because the thing they refer to is identical to itself.

> "A relation would thereby be expressed of a thing to itself, and indeed one in which each thing stands to itself but to no other thing. What is intended to be said by a = b seems to be that the signs or names "a" and "b" designate the same thing, so that those signs themselves would be under discussion; a relation between them would be asserted... It would be mediated by the connection of each of the two signs with the same designated thing.
>
> "If we found "a = a" and "a = b" to have different cognitive values, the explanation is that for the purpose of knowledge, the sense of the sentence, viz., the thought expressed by it, is no less relevant than its referent, i.e., its truth value. If now a = b, then indeed the referent of "b" is the same as that of "a," and hence the truth value of "a = b" is the same as that of "a = a." In spite of this, the sense of "b" may differ from that of "a," and thereby the sense expressed in "a = b" differs from that of "a=a." In that case the two sentences do not have the same cognitive value." [10]

---

10   Frege (1892) *Sense and Reference*, trans. P.Geach and M.Black (1952), p.230

Names and Reference

Although Frege was very clear, generations of philosophers have obscured his clarity by puzzling over different names and/or descriptions *referring* to the same thing that may lead to logical contradictions – starting with Frege's original example of the Morning Star and Evening Star as names that refer to the planet Venus. Do these names have differing cognitive value? Yes. Can they be defined *qua* references to uniquely pick out Venus. Yes. Is identity a relation? No. But the names are relations, words that are references to the objects. And words put us back into the *ambiguous* realm of language.

Over a hundred years of confusion in logic and language consisted of finding two expressions that can be claimed in some sense to be identical, but upon *substitution* in another statement, they do not preserve the truth value of the statement. Besides Frege, and a few examples from BERTRAND RUSSELL ("Scott" and "the author of Waverly." "bachelor" and "unmarried man"), Willard Van Orman Quine was the most prolific generator of substitution paradoxes ("9" and "the number of planets," "Giorgione" and "Barbarelli," "Cicero" and "Tully," and others).

Just as information philosophy shows how to pick out information in an object or concept that constitutes the "peculiar qualifications" that individuate it, so we can pick out the information in two designating references that provide what Quine called "purely designative references." Where Quine picks out information that leads to contradictions and paradoxes (he calls this "referential opacity"), we can "qualify" the information, the "sense" or meaning needed to make them referentially transparent when treated "intensionally."

Frege pointed out that the reference (a name) may not be the general "sense" that a person educated in the customary knowledge of their community may have in mind. Nor is this general sense the specific idea or representation that will actually come to mind. That will be different and dependent on the person's experiences.

Identity

Peirce

Peirce wrote on identity some time in the late nineteenth century, already including Frege's quantization and suggesting notation to express the identity of "second-intention" relations.

His papers did not appear until two decades after his death.

"§4. SECOND-INTENTIONAL LOGIC

398. Let us now consider the logic of terms taken in collective senses. Our notation, so far as we have developed it, does not show us even how to express that two indices, i and j, denote one and the same thing. We may adopt a special token of second intention, say 1, to express identity, and may write 1^*_{ij}. But this relation of identity has peculiar properties. The first is that if i and j are identical, whatever is true of i is true of j. This may be written

$$\Pi_i \Pi_j \{1^*_{ij} + x_i + x_j\}.$$

The use of the general index of a token, x, here, shows that the formula is iconical. The other property is that if everything which is true of i is true of y, then i and j are identical. This is most naturally written as follows: Let the token, q, signify the relation of a quality, character, fact, or predicate to its subject. Then the property we desire to express is

$$\Pi_i \Pi_j \Sigma_k (1_{ij} + q^*_{ki} q_{kj}).$$

And identity is defined thus

$$1_{ij} = \Pi_k (q_{ki} q_{kj} + q^*_{ki} q^*_{kj}) \bullet$$

That is, to say that things are identical is to say that every predicate is true of both or false of both. It may seem circuitous to introduce the idea of a quality to express identity; but that impression will be modified by reflecting that $q_{ki} q_{jk}$, merely means that i and j are both within the class or collection k. If we please, we can dispense with the token q, by using the index of a token and by referring to this in the Quantifier just as subjacent indices are referred to. That is to say, we may write

$$1_{ij} = \Pi x (x_i x_j + x^*_i x^*_j)."\ [11]$$

Here we see Leibniz's Law, just as it is presented in the *Principia Mathematica*

---

[11]   Peirce (1885) 'Exact Logic', *Collected Papers*, (1933) vol.III, p.233

Peirce also commented briefly on Leibniz's principle of the Identity of Indiscernibles.

> "They are like two ideal rain drops, distinct but not different. Leibniz's "principle of indiscernibles" is all nonsense. No doubt, all things differ; but there is no logical necessity for it. To say there is, is a logical error going to the root of metaphysics; but it was an odd hodge-podge, Leibniz's metaphysics, containing a little to suit every taste." [12]

Principia Mathematica

It is in Bertrand Russell's *Principia Mathematica* that we first encounter identity theory written in symbolic logic terminology, using the mathematical sign of equality.

Part I, Mathematical Logic

Section B, Theory of Apparent Variables

*13. IDENTITY

The propositional function "x is identical with y" will be written "x = y." We shall find that this use of the sign of equality covers all the common uses of equality that occur in mathematics. The definition is as follows:

*13.01. $x = y . = : (\varphi) : \varphi ! x . \supset . \varphi ! y$ Df" [13]

Russell does not mention Leibniz or Frege.

If we read this equality left to right as a conditional, it is Leibniz's Law – the Identity of Indiscernibles, which is a tautology, analytically true. If two things are identical, they share every property. Sharing every intrinsic and extrinsic property is only possible for a thing itself.

If we read it right to left, it is the converse of Leibniz's Law – the Indiscernibilty of Identicals (this converse name suggested by Quine in 1943). This is best understood as a hypothetical and synthetic statement, its validity to be determined empirically. If we discover two things that share every property, they are identical. Leibniz was emphatic that this is not possible for numerically distinct objects. This at most is *relative identity*.

> "This definition states that x and y are to be called identical when every predicative function satisfied by x is also satisfied by y. We cannot state that every function satisfied by x is to be satisfied by

---

12   Peirce (1902) 'The Simplest Mathematics,' *Collected Papers. Vol.4* , (1933), p.251

13   Russell (1927) *Principia Mathematica*, Vol. 1, Second Edition, p.176

Identity 113

y, because x satisfies functions of various orders, and these cannot all be covered by one apparent variable. But in virtue of the axiom of reducibility it follows that, if x = y and x satisfies ψx, where ψ is any function, predicative or non-predicative, then y also satisfies ψy (cf. *13.101., below). Hence in effect the definition is as powerful as it would be if it could be extended to cover all functions of x...

The propositions of the present number are constantly referred to. Most of them are self-evident, and the proofs offer no difficulty. The most important of the propositions of this number are the following:

*13.101. ⊢ : x = y . ⊃ . ψx ⊃ ψy

I.e. if x and y are identical, any property of x is a property of y.

*13.12. ⊢ : x = y . ⊃. ψx ⊃ ψy

This includes *13.101 together with the fact that if x and y are identical any property of y is a property of x.

*13.15.16.17. which state that identity is reflexive, symmetrical and transitive." [14]

Wittgenstein

Wittgenstein also does not mention Leibniz in his section on identity in the *Tractatus*, but the substance of Leibniz's Law is in his 5.5302.

> 5.53 Identity of the object I express by identity of the sign and not by means of a sign of identity. Difference of the objects by difference of the signs.
>
> 5.5301 That identity is not a relation between objects is obvious. This becomes very clear if, for example, one considers the proposition "(x) : fx . HOOK . x = a". What this proposition says is simply that only a satisfies the function f, and not that only such things satisfy the function f which have a certain relation to a.
> One could of course say that in fact only a has this relation to a, but in order to express this we should need the sign of identity itself.
>
> 5.5302 Russell's definition of "=" won't do; because according to it one cannot say that two objects have all their properties in common. (Even if this proposition is never true, it is nevertheless significant.)

---

14   Ibid.

5.5303 Roughly speaking: to say of two things that they are identical is nonsense, and to say of one thing that it is identical with itself is to say nothing.

5.532 And analogously: not "(EXISTS x, y) . f(x, y) . x=y", but "(EXISTS x) . f(x, x)"; and not
"(EXISTS x, y) . f(x, y) . ~x=y", but "(EXISTS x, y) . f(x, y)".
Therefore instead of Russell's "(EXISTS x, y) . f(x, y)" : "(EXISTS x, y) . f(x, y) .v. (EXISTS x) . f(x, x)".)

5.533 The identity sign is therefore not an essential constituent of logical notation.

5.534 And we see that the apparent propositions like: "a=a", "a=b . b=c . HOOK a=c", "(x) . x=x". "(EXISTS x) . x=a", etc. cannot be written in a correct logical notation at all.

5.535 So all problems disappear which are connected with such pseudo-propositions.

This is the place to solve all the problems which arise through Russell's "Axiom of Infinity".

What the axiom of infinity is meant to say would be expressed in language by the fact that there is an infinite number of names with different meanings.[15]

Frank Ramsey on Identity

FRANK RAMSEY criticized the section on identity in *Principia Mathematica*, He too uses Leibniz's Law.

> "The third serious defect in Principia Mathematica is the treatment of identity. It should be explained that what is meant is numerical identity, identity in the sense of counting as one, not as two. Of this the following definition is given:
>
> '$x = y . = : (\varphi) : \varphi ! x . \supset . \varphi ! y :$ Df. ' [Cf., Principia Mathematica, 13.01]
>
> That is, two things are identical if they have all their elementary properties in common...
>
> The real objection to this definition of identity is the same as that urged above against defining classes as definable classes: that it is a misinterpretation in that it does not define the meaning with which the symbol for identity is actually used.

---

15   Wittgenstein (1922) *Tractatus Logico-Philosphicus*, section 5.53

This can be easily seen in the following way: the definition makes it self-contradictory for two things to have all their elementary properties in common. Yet this is really perfectly possible, even if, in fact, it never happens. Take two things, a and b. Then there is nothing self-contradictory in a having any self-consistent set of elementary properties, nor in b having this set, nor therefore, obviously, in both a and b having them, nor therefore in a and b having all their elementary properties in common. Hence, since this is logically possible, it is essential to have a symbolism which allows us to consider this possibility and does not exclude it by definition.

It is futile to raise the objection that it is not possible to distinguish two things which have all their properties in common, since to give them different names would imply that they had the different properties of having those names. For although this is perfectly true—that is to say, I cannot, for the reason given, know of any two particular indistinguishable things—yet I can perfectly well consider the possibility, or even know that there are two indistinguishable things without knowing which they are." [16]

For distinct objects to be identical in Ramsey's sense, we would have to ignore relational properties and positional properties, and focus only on intrinsic properties.

Is an object's name a property? It is certainly not intrinsic, essential or even a peculiar quality, in Aristotle's and the Stoics' sense.

Leibniz's Law about the *identity of indiscernibles* is not enough. Some properties that differ might not be discernible, as he knew.

Willard Van Orman Quine on Identity

WILLARD VAN ORMAN QUINE commented on identity in his 1940 book *Mathematical Logic*, explaining it in terms of class membership.

"WE TURN now to the problem of so defining '$x = y$', in terms of '$\in$' and our other primitives, that it will carry the intended sense 'x and y are the same object'. In the trivial case where y is not a class, indeed, $x \in y$ if and only if $x = y$ in this sense (cf. § 22); but our problem remains, since '$x \in y$' diverges in meaning from '$x = y$' in case y is a class. We must find a formula, composed of 'x'

---

16   Ramsey (1926) *The Foundation of Mathematics*, p.29 in the 1960 edition

and ' y ' by means of '∈' and our other primitives, which will be true just in case x and y are the same object — whether a class or a non-class. The requirement is met by:

(1) $(z)(z \in x . = . z \in y)$

when x and y are classes, since classes are the same when their members are the same (cf. § 22). Moreover, (1) continues to meet the requirement when x and y are not classes. For, in this case 'z ∈ x' and 'z ∈ y ' identify z with x and with y; and (1) as a whole then says that whatever is the same as x is the same as y, thus identifying x and y. Both where x and y are classes and where they are not, therefore, (1) meets our requirements; (1) is true if and only if x and y are the same. We are thus led to introduce 'x = y' as an abbreviation of (1)…

Variables and abstracts will be spoken of collectively as terms. Now let us supplement our Greek-letter conventions to this extent: just as we use ' φ ', ' ψ ', and 'χ', to refer to any formulae, and ' α ', ' β ', ' γ ', and ' δ ' to refer to any variables, so let us use 'ζ ', ' η ', and ' θ ' (along with their accented and subscripted variants) to refer in general to any terms. With help of this convention we can express the general definition of identity as follows, for application to variables and abstracts indifferently:

D10. ⌐$(\zeta = \eta)$⌐ for ⌐$(\alpha) (\alpha \in \zeta . = . \alpha \in \eta)$⌐." [17]

In 1943, a few years before Ruth C. Barcan introduced her two new modal operators, ◊ for possibility, and □ for necessity (the square was suggested by her thesis adviser, Frederic B. Fitch), Quine published an important paper on existence and necessity.

Here is the converse of Leibniz's Law, first given its converse name here by Quine:

"One of the fundamental principles governing identity is that of substitutivity - or, as it might well be called, that of indiscernibility of identicals. It provides that, given a true statement of identity, one of its two terms may be substituted for the other in any true statement and the result will be true. It is easy to find cases contrary to this principle. For example, the statements:

(1) Giorgione = Barbarelli,

2) Giorgione was so-called because of his size

are true; however, replacement of the name 'Giorgione' by the

---

[17] Quine (1951) §25 'Identity,' *Mathematical Logic*, p.134 in the 1951 edition.

name 'Barbarelli' turns (2) into the falsehood:
Barbarelli was so-called because of his size." [18]

Frege had warned about the confusion possible between the bare denotation or name and the sense intended by the speaker and interpreted by the listener. C. I. LEWIS said we need to consult the intension, the meaning, to draw the right logical conclusions. Lewis felt Quine's extensionality, based on set membership, is not enough.

The proper resolution of this word quibble and quasi-paradox is to take the intension of "Barbarelli" as a second name for the same thing named by "Giorgione" - "big George." Barbarelli, *qua* Giorgione, was so-called because of his size.

In his brief discussion of necessity, Quine, following RUDOLF CARNAP, said

> "Among the various possible senses of the vague adverb 'necessarily', we can single out one - the sense of *analytic* necessity - according to the following criterion: the result of applying 'necessarily' to a statement is true if, and only if, the original statement is analytic.
>
> (16) Necessarily no spinster is married,
>
> for example, is equivalent to:
>
> (17) 'No spinster is married' is analytic,
>
> and is therefore true."

Quine concludes that the notion of necessity may simply not be susceptible to quantification, and insists extensionality is the best approach, because there is no need for intensionality in mathematics!

> The effect of these considerations is rather to raise questions than to answer them. The one important result is the recognition that any intensional mode of statement composition, whether based on some notion of "necessity" or, for example, on a notion of "probability" (as in Reichenbach's system), must be carefully examined in relation to its susceptibility to quantification. Perhaps the only useful modes of statement composition susceptible to quantification are the extensional ones, reducible to '-' and '.'. Up to now there is no clear example to the contrary. It is known, in particular, that no intensional mode of statement composition is needed in mathematics.[19]

---

18   Quine (1943) 'Notes on Existence and Necessity,' p.113
19   *Ibid.* p.124-5

Immediately after Barcan's 1946 paper, Quine said there would be problems interpreting *quantified modal logic*. Quine himself was the source of most of those problems.

He clearly distinguished *a priori*, *analytic*, and *necessary* truths. The first include only logical signs, the second uses words and the semantics of symbolic logic. Necessity he calls modal and interprets it in terms of analyticity.

"All true statements which (like '(x) (x = x)') contain only logical signs are naturally to be classified as logically true. But there are also other logically true statements (e. g. 'Socrates is mortal ⊃ Socrates is mortal'). which contain extra-logical signs...

The class of analytic statements is broader than that of logical truths, for it contains in addition such statements as 'No bachelor is married.' ...

What is rather in point, I think, is a relation of synonymy, or sameness of meaning, which holds between expressions of real language (though there be no standard hierarchy of definitions. In terms of synonym) and logical truth we could define analyticity: a statement is analytic if by putting synonyms for synonyms (e.g. 'man not married' for 'bachelor') it can be turned into a logical truth.

The particular synonymy relation wanted is one of several which have about equal right to the name "synonymy" and are all describable as "sameness of meaning" - in varying senses of "meaning." Synonymy of the kind which renders expressions interchangeable without violence to indirect quotation, for example...

We need consider only the mode of logical necessity, symbolized by ' □ '; for the other modal ideas (possibility, impossibility, and the strict conditional and biconditional) are expressible in terms of necessity in obvious fashion. Now ' □ ' is not quite interchangeable with 'is analytic,' for this reason: the former attaches to a statement (as ' ~ ' does) to form a statement containing the original statement, whereas 'is analytic' (like 'is true,' 'is false') attaches to the name of a statement to form a statement about the named statement. Grammatically '□' is an adverb; 'is analytic' is a verb...

However, '□' can be explained in terms of analyticity as follows:

(i) The result of prefixing ' □ ' to any statement is true if and only if the statement is analytic." [20]

Quine spent the next several years publishing examples of failure of this substititivity of synonyms which change meaning.

Quine uses the new necessity symbol, '□ ', suggested by Ruth Barcan's thesis adviser at Yale, F. B. Fitch, and introduced in 1946.

Max Black

In the same year that he and PETER GEACH translated Frege's *Sinn und Bedeutung* (1952), Black wrote an amusing dialogue questioning an identity that allows a = b and his opponent suggested two spheres in otherwise empty space could be identical. He wrote:

> "B. Then this is a poor way of stating your conclusion. If a and b are identical, there is just one thing having the two names ' a' and ' b '; and in that case it is absurd to say that a and b are two. Conversely, once you have supposed there are two things having all their properties in common, you can't without contradicting yourself say that they are " identical ".
>
> A. I can't believe you were really misled. I simply meant to say it is logically impossible for two things to have all their properties in common.
>
> I showed that a must have at least two properties-the property of being identical with a, and the property of being different from b - neither of which can be a property of b. Doesn't this prove the principle of Identity of Indiscernibles ?
>
> B. Perhaps you have proved something. If so, the nature of your proof should show us exactly what you have proved. If you want to call " being identical with a " a " property " I suppose I can't prevent you. But you must then accept the consequences of this way of talking. All you mean when you say " a has the property of being identical with a " is that a is a. And all you mean when you say " b does not have the property of being identical with a " is that b is not a. So what you have "proved " is that a is a and b is not a, that is to say, b and a are different. Similarly, when you said that a, but not b, had the property of being different from b, you were simply saying that a and b were different...
>
> Isn't it logically possible that the universe should have contained nothing but two exactly similar spheres ? We might suppose that

---

20   Quine (1947) 'The Problem of Interpreting Modal Logic,' *Journal of Symbolic Logic* (1947) 12 (2) pp.43, 45

each was made of chemically pure iron, had a diameter of one mile, that they had the same temperature, colour, and so on, and that nothing else existed." [21]

Black says that b cannot have the self-identical property of " = a." Yet we will find this in many modern arguments (e.g., Wiggins, Kripke) Black's spheres could of course have identical *intrinsic* information. We just need to ignore their coordinates and relations to each other and say they are relatively identical.

Ruth Barcan Marcus

In 1947, Ruth C. Barcan (later *Ruth Barcan Marcus*) wrote an article on "The Identity of Individuals." It was the first assertion of the so-called "necessity of identity." Her work was written in the dense expressions of symbolic logic, with little explanation. We present it here for historical completeness,

2.33*. ⊢ $(\beta_1 I(\beta_2) \equiv (\beta_1 I_m(\beta_2))$.

$((\beta_1 1_m(\beta_2)\ (\beta_1 I(\beta_1)))$ hook $(\beta_1 1(\beta_2))$ 2.21, 2.3, subst, *14.26*

$(\beta_1 I_m(\beta_2))$ hook $(\beta_1 I(\beta_2))$ 2.6, 2.32*, subst, adj, *18.61*, mod pon

$(\beta_1 I(\beta_2) \equiv (\beta_1 I_m(\beta_2))$ *18.42*, 2.23, subst, adj, def

Five years later, Marcus's thesis adviser, Frederic B. Fitch, published his book, *Symbolic Logic*, which contained the simplest proof ever of the necessity of identity, by the simple mathematical *substitution* of b for a in the necessity of self-identity statement (2).

23.4

(1) a = b,

(2) □ [a = a],

then (3) □ [a = b], by identity elimination. [22]

Clearly this is *mathematically* and *logically* sound. Fitch substitutes b from (1), for a in the modal context of (2). This would be fine if these are just mathematical equations. But as Barcan Marcus knew very well from C. I. Lewis's work on strict implication, substitutivity in statements also requires that the substitution is intensionally meaningful. In the sense that b is actually just a, substituting b is equivalent to keeping a there, as a tautology, something with no new information. To be informative and prove the necessary truth of the

---

21   Black (1952) 'The Identity of Indiscernibles,' *Mind*, 61(242), p.154
22   Fitch (1952) *Symbolic Logic*, p.164

new statement, we must know more about b, for example, that the *intrinsic* information in b is identical to that of a. And of course this is at best *relative identity* for numerically distinct objects.

Fourteen years after her original identity article, Marcus presented her work at a 1961 colloquium at Boston University attended by Quine and Kripke.

Marcus reprised the proof of her claim about the necessity of identity. She explicitly added Leibniz's Law relating identicals to indiscernibles to her argument.

"$(x)(y) (x = y) \supset \Box (x = y)$

In a formalized language, those symbols which name things will be those for which it is meaningful to assert that *I* holds between them, where ' *I* ' names the identity relation... If 'x' and 'y' are individual names then

(1) $x \, I \, y$

Where identity is defined rather than taken as primitive, it is customary to define it in terms of indiscernibility, one form of which is

(2) $x \, Ind \, y =_{df} (\varphi)(\varphi x \, eq \, \varphi y)$

(3) $x \, eq \, y = x \, I \, y$." [23]

Statement (2) is Leibniz's Law, the indiscernibility of x from y, by definition means that for every property φ, both x and y have that same property, $\varphi x \, eq \, \varphi y$.

David Wiggins

DAVID WIGGINS and Peter Geach debated back and forth about the idea of *"relative identity"* for many years after Geach first suggested it in 1962. Wiggins also speculated about the so-called *necessity of identity*, which was first argued by Marcus back in 1947.

As we saw, Ruth Barcan Marcus published her original proof of the *necessity of identity* in 1947 and repeated her argument at a 1961 Boston University colloquium. Whether Wiggins knew of Marcus 1961 is not clear. He should have known of her 1947, through Quine's criticisms, perhaps. Wiggins work is similar to her 1961 derivation (which uses Leibniz's Law). Wiggins gives no credit to Marcus, a pattern in the literature for the next few decades still seen today.

---

23 Marcus (1961) 'Modalities and Intensional Languages,' *Synthése*, 13(4), p.305

Saul Kripke clearly modeled much of his derivation after Wiggins, especially his criticism of the derivation as "paradoxical". Kripke gives no credit to Marcus and only indirectly to Wiggins for the specific steps in his argument And we know Kripke heard Marcus present at the 1961 colloquium.

In the two columns on the right, we compare Kripke's somewhat abbreviated derivation of the necessity of identity with Wiggins' longer and somewhat skeptical account. Wiggins suspected that what can be shown is not "x = y," but merely the tautology "y = y."

> The derivation of (2) itself, via x's predicate ' (= x)', might be blocked by insisting that when expressions for properties are formed by subtraction of a constant or free variable, then every occurrence of that constant or free variable must be subtracted. '(a = a)' would then yield ' (=)', and (2) could not be derived by using ' (= x) '. One would only get the impotent
>
> (2') $(x = y) \supset (x = x. \supset . y = y)$.[24]

Wiggins predicates the property "= x" of y. Kripke writes this as "x = y," logically equivalent, but intensionally predicating "= y" of x!

Wiggins' note (3) is almost Kripke's (3), but with intensional "y = x." Wiggins needs one more step. His (4) is Kripke's (3).

Saul Kripke on Identity

Kripke only indirectly cites Wiggins as the source of his argument. Just after his exposition, Kripke quotes Wiggins as saying in his 1965 "Identity-Statements"

> "Now there undoubtedly exist contingent identity-statements. Let a = b be one of them. From its simple truth and (5) [= (4) above] we can derive '□ (a = b)'. But how then can there be any contingent identity statements?" [25]

The short answer is there cannot, if we are discussing numerically distinct material objects. Kripke goes on to describe the argument about b sharing the property " = a" of being identical to a, which information philosophy reads as merely self-identity.

---

24 Wiggins (1965) 'Identity Statements,' *Analytical Philosophy*, pp.40-41
25 Kripke (1971) 'Identity and Necessity,' in Munitz, Milton, *Identity and individuation..* p. 136

Identity

Wiggins (1965)

The connexion of what I am going to say with modal calculi can be indicated in the following way. It would seem to be a necessary truth that if a = b then whatever is truly ascribable to a is truly ascribable to b and vice versa (Leibniz's Law). This amounts to the principle

(1) $(x)(y)((x = y) \supset (\varphi)(\varphi x \supset \varphi y))$

Suppose that identity-statements are ascriptions or predications.! Then the predicate variable in (1) will apparently range over properties like that expressed by '(= a)' and we shall get as consequence of (1)

(2) $(x) (y) ((x = y) \supset (x = x \,.\, \supset\, . \,y = x))$

There is nothing puzzling about this. But if (as many modal logicians believe), there exist de re modalities of the form

$\Box (\varphi a)$ (i.e., necessarily (φa)),

then something less innocent follows. If '(= a)' expresses property, then '$\Box$ (a=a)', if this too is about the object a, also ascribes something to a, namely the property $\Box$ (= a). For on a naive and pre-theoretical view of properties, you will reach an expression for a property whenever you subtract a noun-expression with material occurrence (something like ' a ' in this case) from a simple declarative sentence. The property

$\Box$ (= a) then falls within the range of the predicate variable in Leibniz's Law (understood in this intuitive way) and we get

(3) $(x) (y) (x = y \supset (\Box (x = x) \,.\, \supset\, . \,\Box (y = x)))$

Hence, reversing the antecedents,

(4) $(x) (y) (\,\Box (x = x) \,.\, \supset\, . \,(x = y) \supset \Box (x = y))$

But $(x) (\Box (x=x))$' is a necessary truth, so we can drop this antecedent and reach

(5) $(x)(y)((x = y) \,.\, \supset\, . \,\Box (x = y))$

Kripke (1971)

First, the law of the substitutivity of identity says that, for any objects x and y, if x is identical to y, then if x has a certain property F, so does y:

(1) $(x)(y) [(x = y) \supset (Fx \supset Fy)]$

{Note Kripke left out Wiggins' universal quantifier (F) - for all properties.}

On the other hand, every object surely is necessarily self-identical:

(2) $(x) \Box (x = x)$

But

(3) $(x)(y) (x = y) \supset [\Box(x = x) \supset \Box (x = y)]$

is a substitution instance of (1), the substitutivity law. From (2) and (3), we can conclude that, for every x and y, if x equals y, then, it is necessary that x equals y:

(4) $(x)(y) ((x = y) \supset \Box(x=y))$

This is because the clause $\Box(x = x)$ of the conditional drops out because it is known to be true.

Compare the simplicity and clarity of Marcus' thesis adviser...

Fitch (1952)

(1) a = b,
(2) $\Box [a = a]$,
then (3) $\Box [a = b]$,
by identity elimination.

"If x and y are the same things and we can talk about modal properties of an object at all, that is, in the usual parlance, we can speak of modality *de re* and an object necessarily having certain properties as such, then formula (1), I think, has to hold. Where x is any property at all, including a property involving modal operators, and if x and y are the same object and x had a certain property F, then y has to have the same property F. And this is so even if the property F is itself of the form of necessarily having some other property G, in particular that of necessarily being identical to a certain object. [viz., = x]

Well, I will not discuss the formula (4) itself because by itself it does not assert, of any particular true statement of identity, that it is necessary. It does not say anything about statements at all. It says for every object x and object y, if x and y are the same object, then it is necessary that x and y are the same object. And this, I think, if we think about it (anyway, if someone does not think so, I will not argue for it here), really amounts to something very little different from the statement (2). Since x, by definition of identity, is the only object identical with x, "(y)(y = x ⊃ Fy)" seems to me to be little more than a garrulous way of saying 'Fx' and thus (x) (y)(y = x ⊃ Fx) says the same as (x) Fx no matter what 'F' is — in particular, even if 'F' stands for the property of necessary identity with x. So if x has this property (of necessary identity with x), trivially everything identical with x has it, as (4) asserts. But, from statement (4) one may apparently be able to deduce various particular statements of identity must be necessary and this is then supposed to be a very paradoxical consequence." [26]

The indiscernibility of identicals claims that if x = y, then x and y must share all their properties, otherwise there would be a discernible difference. Now Kripke argues that one of the properties of x is that x = x, so if y shares the property of '= x,' we can say that y = x. Then, necessarily, x = y. But this is nonsense for distinct objects.

Two distinct things, x and y, cannot be identical, because there is some difference in *extrinsic* external information between them. Instead of claiming that y has x's property of being identical to x ("= x"), we can say only that y has x's property of being *self-identical*, thus y = y. Wiggins calls this result "impotent." Then x and y remain distinct in at least this *intrinsic* property as well as in *extrinsic* properties like their distinct positions in space.

26   Kripke (1971) 'Identity and Necessity,' p. 137-138

Peter Geach on Relative Identity

PETER GEACH proposed the relativity of identity in 1962 and debated for years with David Wiggins about it.

For Geach and Wiggins, relative identity means "x is the same F as y," but "x may not be the same G as y." Wiggins argued against this idea of relative identity, but accepted what he called a sortal-dependent identity, "x is the same F as y." Geach called this a "criterion of identity."

> "I had here best interject a note on how I mean this term "criterion of identity". I maintain that it makes no sense to judge whether x and y are 'the same', or whether x remains 'the same', unless we add or understand some general term—"the same F". That in accordance with which we thus judge as to the identity, I call a criterion of identity; this agrees with the etymology of "criterion". Frege sees clearly that "one" cannot significantly stand as a predicate of objects unless it is (at least understood as) attached to a general term; I am surprised he did not see that the like holds for the closely allied expression 'the same'." [27]

In his 1967 article "Identity," in the *Review of Metaphysics*, Geach wrote

> "I am arguing for the thesis that identity is relative. When one says "x is identical with y", this, I hold, is an incomplete expression; it is short for "x is the same A as y", where "A" represents some count noun understood from the context of utterance—or else, it is just a vague expression of a half-formed thought. Frege emphasized that "x is one" is an incomplete way of saying "x is one A, a single A", or else has no clear sense; since the connection of the concepts one and identity comes out just as much in the German "ein und dasselbe" as in the English "one and the same", it has always surprised me that Frege did not similarly maintain the parallel doctrine of relativized identity, which I have just briefly stated. On the contrary, Frege actually enunciated with all vigour a doctrine that identity cannot be relativized: "Identity is a relation given to us in such a specific form that it is inconceivable that various forms of it should occur" (*Grundgesetze*, Vol. II, p. 254)." [28]

---

27   Geach (1962) *Reference and Generality*, p.39; 1980, p.63
28   Geach (1967) 'Identity ', *Review of Metaphysics*, in *Logic Matters*, 1972, p.238-

David Lewis

DAVID LEWIS, the modern metaphysician who built on Leibniz' possible worlds to give us his theory of "modal realism," is just as clear as Leibniz on the problem of identity.

> "[W]e should not suppose that we have here any problem about identity. We never have. Identity is utterly simple and unproblematic. Everything is identical to itself; nothing is ever identical to anything else except itself. There is never any problem about what makes something identical to itself, nothing can ever fail to be. And there is never any problem about what makes two things identical; two things never can be identical." [29]

Except, says an information philosopher, "in some respects," in which case we have *relative identity*.

Relative Identity

The concept of relative identity, identical in some respect, identical *qua*, is a property of so-called "interchangeable parts." They can be substituted for one another. The concept of substitutability is an essential concept in mathematics, in symbolic logic, and to some extent in language, where it has generated much confusion. The fundamental ambiguity and polysemy of language, which generates its metaphorical power, means that one word or phrase is never perfectly substitutable for another.

After accepting the fundamental fact that nothing is perfectly identical to anything but itself, the criterion for relative identity, for identical "in some respect," or *qua* that respect, is that some subset of the information in two different things must be the same information, bit for bit.

We defined I as the sum of all the intrinsic properties and relations - internal self-relations between an object's different parts. And we defined E for an object as the sum of extrinsic relations an object has with things outside, including its disposition in space and time.

Relative identity means that a can be the same I as b, but not the same E as b, For physical objects, these could be within some physical boundary, subject to conditions of vagueness. In a biologi-

---

29   Lewis (1986) 'Counterparts or Double Lives,' *On the Plurality of Worlds*, p.192.

cal entity, it includes the vast teleonomic communications going on inside and between the cells, which makes it much more than a mereological sum of its parts.

Set theoretically, in classical propositional calculus, we can say that Ia is the set of *intrinsic* properties and relations that can be predicated in propositions about an object a. Ea is the set of *extrinsic* relations. We can now describe why absolute identity is limited to self-identity.

If $Ia + Ea = Ib + Eb$, then a and b are one and the same object.

And, if $Ia = Ib$, then a and b are relatively identical, *qua* their information content.

Metaphysicians like the notion of kinds or sorts, or even tropes, which are *abstract entities* that can be used as particular properties. All three of these can be redescribed in information terms. To be of such-and-such a sort, for example, would be to contain the information characteristic of that sort. Numerically distinct entities can then be identical in respect of being of the same sort – identical *qua* that sort.

Seeing the relative identity between two things is something done by minds. This is a mind's ability to "pick out" the resemblances. The metaphysicist emphasizes resemblances that are mind-independent properties in the objects themselves. But concepts especially are always initially invented by humans and must be scrutinized for the genetic fallacy.

When information philosophy claims we have knowledge of something (in a mind), it is the claim that what is in the mind is relatively identical to some of the information in the thing. This idea has been criticized as the "picture theory of meaning." Consider Wittgenstein,

"A picture is a model of reality.
There must be something identical in a picture and what it depicts, to enable the one to be a picture of the other at all." [30]

The *experience recorder and reproducer* (ERR) explains the indirect way in which this happens. The perception of an object is

---

30   Wittgenstein (1922) *Tractatus Logico-Philosphicus*, 2.12, 2.161

encoded in the brain as an experience. When the reproducer "plays back" the experience, the neurons that were "wired together" during earlier experiences now "fire together" and the brain presents (re-presents) to the mind parts of the original perception. The "decoding" process may activate any or all of the original sensations of the experience, together with any emotions recorded.

This does not mean that the information stored in the neurons is directly isomorphic to some of the information in the thing itself. Very little in the brain "resembles" the world. Exceptions are mappings of our sensorimotor apparatus, and in some animals, maps of their environment. What the ERR means is that the mind re-experiences some subset of the original experiences. This is actually very close to Wittgenstein's "picture." The "mind's eye" sees before it a "representation." ARTHUR SCHOPENHAUER called it a *Vorstellung*.

There is of course an implicit complicated mapping between neurons and the organs of sensation, somewhat analogous to the complex mapping of bits in a DVD to the colored pixels of a video monitor. But the ERR model goes well beyond a visual picture, since the body experiences a subset of the feelings that were recorded along with the original experience.

Minds not only pick out relative identity, they also see differences, so we have this apparent contradiction as first enunciated by CHARLES SANDERS PEIRCE:

"Everything is both similar and dissimilar to everything else,"[31]

We unpack Peirce in our three axioms as follows...

Id1. Everything is identical to everything else in some respects.

Id2. Everything is different from everything else in some other respects.

Id3. Everything is identical to itself in all respects at each instant of time, but different in some respects from itself at any other time.

We can rewrite these axioms in terms of information philosophy

I1. Any two things have some information in common.

I2. Any two things have some different information.

I3. The identity of anything over time is changing because the information in it (and about it) is changing with time.

---

31   Peirce. *Collected Papers* Vol. I, Principles of Philosophy, 1.566

These three observations might be called information axioms. Armed with them, we are in a position to "dis-solve" or deconstruct some of the most famous metaphysical puzzles and paradoxes.

Now I3 requires the metaphysical possibility that information can change with time. The cosmological observation of astronomical objects provides convincing evidence of increases in the total information with time, as does biological evolution.

DAVID HUME argued that there are only three basic relations between things, contiguity, causality, and resemblance. We can see the first as how things or events are arranged in space, the second as to how they follow one another in time, the third as similarities in their form. Information philosophy condenses these three to information in space and time.

A = A

The mathematical expression "A equals A" (notice there are two distinct A's) is an empty tautology. Its usefulness comes from other equivalences, such as the equation "A = B." Whenever A appears, we may substitute B.

A and B are substitutable, interchangeable parts, for some practical purpose, like logic, mathematics, or engineering.

But, when we think and speak carefully, neither in metaphysics nor in ordinary language do we unconditionally accept the statement "A is identical to B."

Indeed, we see that the expressions "A = A" or "A is A" are not at all innocently true, since there are manifold differences between the two A's, their positions in space, their ink particles on the paper they are printed on, the pixels on your computer screen, etc.

It is the immaterial information content of "A," abstracted from concrete examples of letters, that has a self-identical property, but only in the realm of information and abstract entities. Any single concrete example of an "A" has the property of self-identity, but only in the realm of material, and then only for an instant of time, because everything in the material realm is constantly changing.

Analytical language philosophers, puzzling over statements like "A is B," say that the identity of the two symbols is because they refer to the same thing. Much philosophical ink has been spilled puzzling over Frege's observation that "the morning star is the evening star."

The total meaningful content of this sentence is not limited to the banal point that two names or designators ("Phosphorus" and "Hesperus") are references (Frege's *Bedeutung*) to the one planet Venus (a concrete entity). We might call this property "referential identity."

While the statement "the morning star is the morning star" is considered analytically true (like "A is A"), the two terms in the statement have different meanings or senses (Frege's *Sinn*).

Information philosophers agree that the meanings of the referring terms contain much more knowledge than just the information in the planet itself. Both terms tell us where Venus is in the sky, where it is compared to the Sun along the ecliptic, when to look for it, etc. But this additional (and differing) information makes paradoxical even analytic linguistic identity.

Indeed the paradox of all analytic philosophy (that all analysis is either trivial of false) can be seen in the fact that all analytic statements are tautologies. If the expression to be analyzed (the *analysandum*) and the analyzing expression (the *analysans*) contain identical information, then the analysis is trivial.

If the *analysandum* and *analysans* do not contain the same information, the analysis is false. WILLARD VAN ORMAN QUINE threw up his hands and declared (correctly) that all knowledge must be synthetic *a posteriori* (based on experience).

Identity through Time

Because all material things change in time (the Heraclitean "flux"), "identity over time" is fundamentally impossible. Even in the case of a hypothetical completely inert object that could be protected from loss or gain of a single atom, its external dispositional relations (e.g., position coordinates in most spacetime frames) are constantly changing, and these are fundamental "properties", in both classical Aristotelian and modern Kantian categories.

If we identify the essence of something as the total information that makes it identical with itself, then all that information is essential. Several puzzling metaphysical facts follow that do violence to our ordinary way of talking about essence and identity.

Aristotle's distinction between essence or Being (τὸ ὄν) and accident (συμβεβεκός) surely did not make every property or quality of an entity essential. But modern metaphysicians do argue for a number of "essentialisms." We shall see that they are mostly the result of the metaphysicians' definitions. They are in no way "true at any world" in the sense of a "mind-independent" external world, let alone facts in our world, except for their arbitrary definitions.

Changes in Time

However imperceptibly, every concrete material thing changes both its matter and form with time. The Heraclitean river changes its water constantly at any particular place. Living things change their material elements very rapidly as they ingest low-entropy, high information food and excrete higher-entropy, lower information matter.

It is only immaterial abstract entities that do not change. They have Parmenidean "Being."

Something that changes in time cannot be perfectly identical to what it was in the past. If it were identical, there would be no change. This gives rise to several metaphysical problems that involve different persistence conditions for different properties of an entity.

Information philosophy shows the way out of this apparent paradox by distinguishing the part or parts of information that are changing from any part which is constant. We can then say that an entity is identical to its earlier self "with respect to" (or "qua"") the unchanged information.

What emerges is the concept of a relative or partial identity over time, accompanied by partial or relative differences in the object.

We have seen that change can be in the intrinsic or internal properties of a thing, or in its extrinsic relations to external objects, its dispositional properties such as its coordinates. The primary view of change is a real, metaphysical change in a "thing itself." Some metaphysicians argue that this must be a change of identity.

The conservation of matter and energy requires that there cannot be complete destruction of an entity and creation of a new entity from nothing. But identity never changes completely, because modest changes in the material substrate or the information content (shape and form, internal and external relations and communications) do not invalidate an essential relative identity over time of any object.

Because of motion and microscopic physical events, all material things change in time. Change in time means that the concept of "perfect or strict identity over time" is fundamentally flawed. Even in the case of a hypothetical completely inert object that could be protected from loss or gain of a single particle, its position coordinates in most spacetime frames are constantly changing. All the other objects in the universe are changing their spatial relations with the object.

Personal Identity

Apart from the obvious fact that every person (individual) is different from every other person, which has been confirmed by the latest understanding of all biological organisms, even an individual person is not perfectly identical to her or his self over time.

If persons were perfectly identical to themselves over time, they would not experience growth, one of the defining, therefore essential, characteristics of living things. Moreover, some metaphysicians who claim that material constitution is identity maintain that even the loss or gain of a tiny bit of matter destroys an individual and replaces that individual with another. This is a flawed idea put forward by the ancient Skeptics still taught in modern metaphysics.[32]

Identity and Biology

Since the creation of information and its communication is the outstanding characteristic of life, biological information is perhaps the best way to explain the relative identity, the persistence of living things through time, *qua* person, for example. An information-based metaphysics can help solve the problem of personal identity. The genetic code (DNA) remains essentially constant through the life of an individual and should be mentioned first as a uniquely "identifying" piece of information.

Besides this "Evo" element, there is information that is created and preserved during an individual's growth and development (the

---

32   See chapter 27 on the growing argument.

"Devo" element). For higher organisms especially, this is its ability to record its past experiences and play them back as a guide to present actions. The experience recorder and reproducer (ERR) is a central component of consciousness and memory. This is the psychological argument for the persistence of personal identity.

Vague Identity

The primary source of vagueness in philosophy has been vagueness in the language terms used to identify an object, which lack the information content or depth to match the information depth in typical physical objects, let alone living things.

Ontological vagueness in the position of things themselves is introduced by the uncertainty principle of quantum mechanics.

There is a deep metaphysical connection between vagueness and possibilities. An object or event that has more than one possible future can be said to be vague not in the usual spatial sense or mereological sense, but in the temporal sense.

The bit-by-bit nature of digital information introduces vagueness in the representation of analog (continuous) objects, if there are any. Whether the nature of fundamental reality shows matter to be analog or digital, fields or particles, is a deep metaphysical question.

Individuation

Since at least the time of Aristotle, philosophers have debated what it is that constitutes an individual person or thing. What makes it a unity, numerically one? What distinguishes it from everything else?

Individuation is related to the metaphysical problems of constitution, composition, colocation, essentialism, and identity.

Given two equal amounts of matter, they are distinguished by their shape or form. Given two things with identical form, they are individuated by being embodied in different material.

The History of Individuation

It was the general opinion of scholars for many centuries that Aristotle claimed that matter (*hyle*) is what individuates a form or essence. Aristotle was openly skeptical about the independent existence of his mentor Plato's Ideas in the Theory of Forms (*eidoi*). But many commentators in the past several decades have shown that Aristotle ultimately came around to believe that an *immaterial* Parmenidean "being" or "essence" (*einai*) is also involved.[1]

Although a few scholars argue for form *instead of* matter, information philosophy and modern biology show that both form ("information") and matter ("stuff") are always needed.

In his metaphysics, Aristotle sought to understand "being *qua* being." Can there be a form without matter? Surely form without matter is empty and invisible, merely conceivable. Matter without form is impossible, but if some material is merely formless or shapeless, it contains no valuable information.

Information philosophy notes that information is neither matter nor energy, though it needs matter to be embodied and energy to be communicated. Unlike matter-energy, information can be created and destroyed. The material universe creates it by rearranging the material. The biological world creates it and

---

[1] Lukasiewicz, Anscombe and Popper (1953), Lloyd (1970), Regis (1976), Cohen (1984), Whiting (1986).

utilizes it. Above all, human minds create, process, and preserve information, the sum of human knowledge that distinguishes humanity from all other biological species and that provides the extraordinary power humans have over our planet.

Information is the modern spirit, the ghost in the machine, the mind in the body. It is the soul, and when we die, it is our information that perishes. The matter remains.

Aristotle's speculations about the mother (*mater*) providing formless matter for a child and the father (*pater*) providing the form (*pattern*) in his seed (σπερμα) show that Aristotle knew both matter and form are needed to create an individual. At *Metaphysics* 1033b, he says, everything must "be partly one thing and partly another; I mean partly matter (*hyle*) and partly form (*eidos*)."

It is tempting to associate matter with Aristotle's material cause and form with his formal cause. We know he sometimes claimed one and sometimes the other as individuating, but everything consists of both.

At *Metaphysics* 1034a, Aristotle says Callias and Socrates are identical in form (man), but different because their matter is different. But at Metaphysics 1041b 8, he says, "Thus what we seek is the cause (i.e., the form) in virtue of which the matter is a definite thing; and this is the substance (*ousia*) of a thing.

Ancient religions described *immaterial* souls coming to earth to become embodied as material individuals. Did they bring a personal identity with them? Scholastics argued that all angels, who are not material, cannot be easily differentiated. They could all be colocated in the same place at the same time, on the head of a pin, for example.

Was Socrates' soul, before his instantiation in material, already Socrates? We have clear evidence that some Greeks thought not. Others wanted the immortal soul of Socrates to survive death. Consider this passage from Stobaeus:

> So too in general when it comes to substance, to hold that we are the same as our substances seems unconvincing. For it often comes about that the substance exists before something's generation, before Socrates' generation, say, when Socrates

does not yet exist, and that after Socrates' destruction the substance remains although he no longer exists.²

Aristotle, though he was critical of the Platonic forms (*eidos* or ideas), noted the importance of form as completing the individual. He notoriously used the term we usually translate as "substance" (*ousia*) in conflicting ways, sometimes talking of form as an essence (*einai* or being) and as a "primary substance," (*proten ousian*) for example,

by "form" I mean the essence of each thing, and its primary substance

εἶδος δὲ λέγω τὸ τί ἦν εἶναι ἑκάστου καὶ τὴν πρώτην οὐσίαν³

Stoics, like Chrysippus, argued that matter is the basic "underlying substrate" (υποκειμενον). That which identifies a "peculiarly qualified individual" (ιδιοσ ποιον) is a unique bundle of qualities or properties that come with the *pneuma*, a combination of air and fire that is approximately the earlier Greek soul (*psyche*).

Academic Skeptics mocked the Stoics as seeing two things as "colocated," occupying the same place at the same time. The paradox of the lump of clay and the statue was a prominent example. This puzzle can be resolved by noticing that the two things are simply matter and form, which are always colocated even if a particular form might appear to be "formless."

The Roman philosopher Boethius said in his *Isagoge* that numerically distinct individuals differ only in accidental properties.

Ea vero quae individuae sunt et solo numero discrepunt, solis accidentibus distant

The early medieval philosopher AVICENNA (*Ibn Sinna*) used the concept of a "determinate individual" which suggests the Stoic concept of "peculiar qualifications," but it was translated into Latin as *signatum*, which suggest an entity with a name.

The later AVERROES (*Ibn Rushd*) compared individuation to the process where a sculptor creates a statue from the otherwise indeterminate shape of a block of marble.

---

2   Stobaeus *The Hellenistic Philosophers*, Long and Sedley, v.1, p.168
3   Aristotle. *Metaphysics*, VII, vii, 1032b

The scholastic discussions of individuation by THOMAS AQUINAS followed Aristotle, making matter the principle of individuation, but he deliberated between Averroes and Avicenna. He first supported Averroes and his *signatum*, understood as the acquisition by matter of determinate dimensions. But later Aquinas also accepted Avicenna's arguments about dimensions, which today we might see as an emphasis on the form.

JOHN DUNS SCOTUS had a distinctly empiricist attitude compared to the rationalism of his older contemporary Aquinas. From two material things with identical form, a universal can be abstracted that he called *quiddity* or "whatness." Any aspects of a thing that makes it particular, he called *haecceity*, its "thisness."

WILLIAM OF OCCAM was a nominalist who regarded the question of individuation meaningless, since for him individual things were the only reality. Ideas like species were only concepts in minds.

The principle of individuation of the last great Scholastic, FRANCISCO SUÁREZ, included both matter and form, the *total* of information in an entity, as we would say in information philosophy.

The Process of Individuation

Given one lump of undifferentiated matter, breaking it in two by sculpting it into distinct forms, would appear to create two individuals. In this case, form would appear to be the operating principle of individuation.

Like most problems in metaphysics, individuation has been analyzed and debated with close attention to words and concepts.

Information philosophy identifies abstract immaterial form as the information needed to specify exactly how to create an identical copy of a thing. In standard usage, the word form refers to an outer two-dimensional surface, that part of something that is most easily perceived. But information philosophy also needs information about the internal material parts - the elementary particles, the atoms, the molecules, etc., their instantaneous positions over time, their interactions with each other, and, in the case of living things, the communications of their component parts with one another and with other beings.

For *abstract entities* that contain no material substance, we can ask what could individuate them - two circles with the same radius, for example. If they are located at different places in space, that would work. But does this require their material embodiment, as ink on paper, for example?

What about a circle that is in a single place, should we distinguish its temporal parts diachronically and ask whether the circle at *t=0* is the same circle at *t=1*? This is a metaphysical problem known as persistence.[4]

The Biology of Individuation

Although metaphysicians rarely look to what is going on scientifically, a metaphysicist looks at the powerful connection between matter and its embodied information that explains a biological individual.

For example, we now know that every organism, even the simplest single-cell bacteria, archaea, and eukaryotes are unique individuals.

From the very earliest proto-life forms that could duplicate themselves, only some duplicates were exact replicas. As JACQUES MONOD pointed out, perfect reproductive invariance would proliferate a species, but without a modest number of random variations, there would be no evolution.

Perfect copies would be identical, differing only in their physical locations. A variation in their information content produces two intrinsically different individuals.

The most complex organisms, eukaryotic cells and multicellular organisms, use the deliberate randomization of chromosomes in sexual reproduction to produce essential variety in the gene pool. Even when a cell divides to produce two individuals that are genetically alike, the development process introduces variations that are not inheritable, but that ensure adults are unique individuals, because their information content differs.

---

4 See chapter 18.

The *principle of individuation* in biology is a combination of genetic and epigenetic differences in the information content of individuals. It is the form that differentiates them, not the specific material they are made of. We are different individuals because of chance events, from our first zygote stage to our last breath, that change our information content. Here the change is growth and decline, with a high degree of preservation of the vital information. In higher organisms, what is preserved is learned information - recordings of experiences.

The material content of any organism also is in a state of continuous change, as food (matter with low entropy and high free energy) moves through an organism. It is the comparatively stable, but constantly growing, information content embodied in the material that we recognize as the essence of an organism.

Very few cells in a multicellular organism have lifetimes close to the life on an individual. In humans, some neurons and egg cells that do not reproduce can last a lifetime, sperm cells last only a few days, skin cells a few weeks, red blood cells a few months, and white blood cells a year or so. The stem cells that form new blood cells and form the rapidly shed epithelial cells in skin and the gastrointestinal tract can themselves last a lifetime.

On average, all the material at the atomic and molecular level in a human body is replaced every seven or eight years, yet we persist as the same person over our lifetime. What philosophers of mind describe as the continuity of memory or consciousness, information philosophy sees as the stored information in the ERR (experience recorder and reproducer).

Individuation and Quantum Mechanics

We saw in the last chapter that no two distinct things can have the perfect identity that made the question of individuation so serious a problem for the ancients.

But it turns out that modern physics has discovered properties of elementary particles that again raise what appear to be metaphysical questions about what we can regard as individuals.

Specifically, quantum physics finds that two particles (electrons, for example) can be so identical that we cannot tell which is which. They are "indistinguishable" in a way that affects their statistical properties.

They are loosely called "identical particles," but this contradicts our notion of "self-identity." "Two" classical particles that are "self-identical" must be just one particle.

All electrons are indistinguishable and identical in the sense that interchanging them does not create a new quantum state. In classical statistical mechanics, we count the number of possible distributions of the system as the number of ways that we can arrange the particles, the ways we can distribute them among volumes in phase space, a combination of ordinary configuration space and momentum space.

If we have two particles 1 and 2 and two volumes a and b, with distinguishable particles, we have two states we can call ab and ba. With indistinguishable elementary particles, in quantum mechanics these are counted as just one quantum state, giving rise to what are called Bose-Einstein statistics and Fermi-Dirac statistics.

What we called the extrinsic or relational properties of objects become very puzzling, because we cannot say that one quantum particle is "here" and the other "there." Either particle may be found anywhere the value of the probability amplitude is non-zero.

The intuitive metaphysics of individuation apparently does not apply in the microscopic quantum world, as was first discovered by ALBERT EINSTEIN in 1924, just one of the many non-intuitive aspects of quantum mechanics that he discovered.

Chapter 15

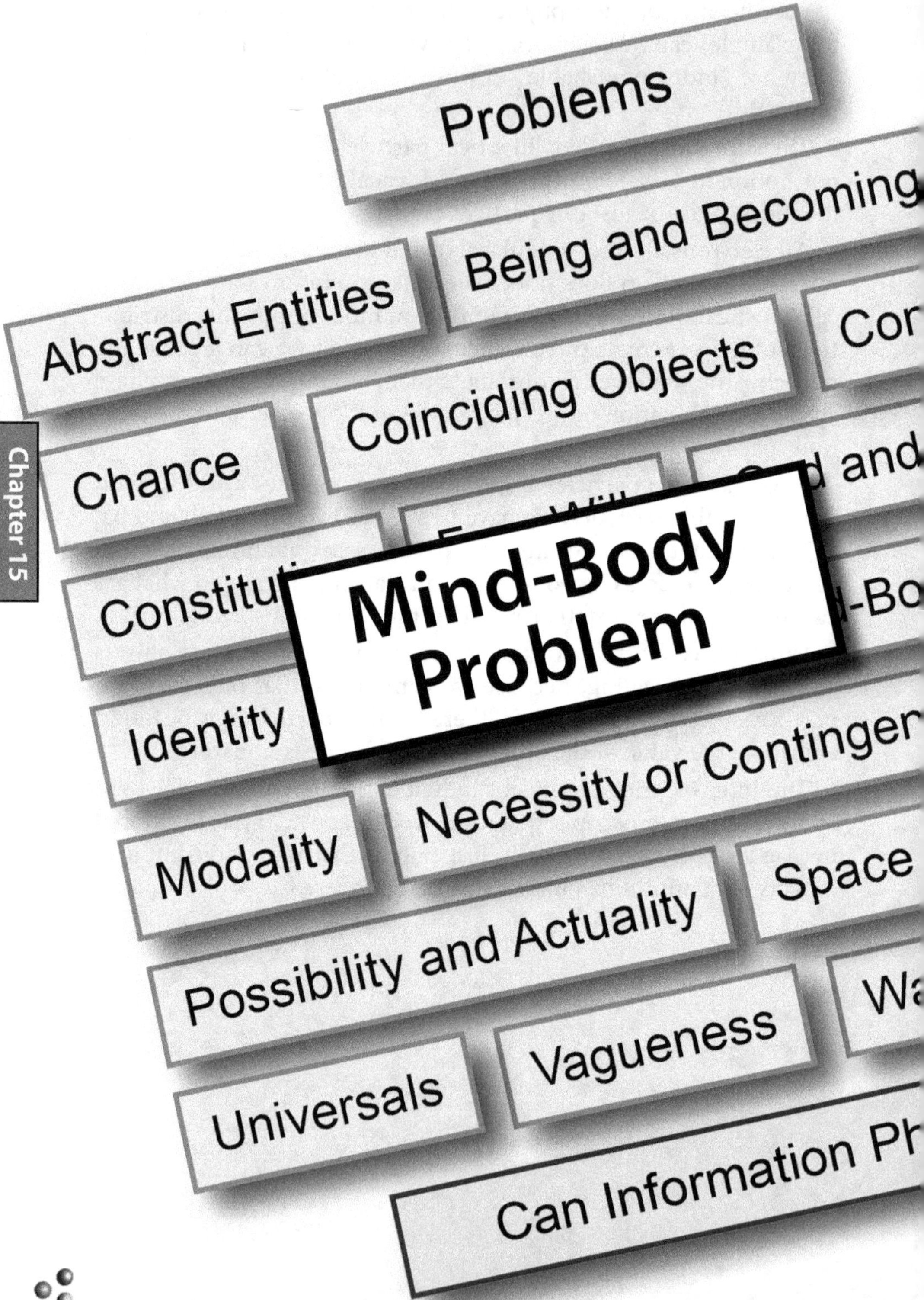
Problems
Being and Becoming
Abstract Entities
Coinciding Objects
Chance
Mind-Body Problem
Identity
Modality
Possibility and Actuality
Space
Universals
Vagueness

Mind-Body Problem

Information philosophy views the mind as the *immaterial* information in the brain, which is seen as a biological information processor. *Mind is software in the brain's hardware.*

The "stuff" of mind is pure information. Information is neither matter nor energy, though it needs matter for its embodiment and energy for its communication.

In traditional philosophy, mind and body form one of the classic *dualisms*, like *idealism* versus *materialism*, the problem of the one (monism) or the many (pluralism), the distinction between essence and existence, between universals and particulars, and between the eternal and the ephemeral.

When mind and body are viewed today as a dualism, the emphasis is on the mind, that is to say the information, being fundamentally different from the material brain. Since the universe is continuously creating new information, by rearranging existing matter, this is an important and understandable difference. Matter (and energy) is conserved, a constant of the universe. Information is not conserved, it is the source of genuine novelty over time.

Mind in a mind-body dualism coincides with Plato's "ideas" as pure form. Its ontology is different from that of matter. The ancients asked about the existential status of Platonic Ideas. On the other hand, monists can see the mind-body distinction as pure physicalism, since information embodied in matter corresponds to a mere reorganization of the matter. This was Aristotle's more practical view. For him, Plato's Ideas were mere abstractions generalized from many existent particulars.

Mind-body as a "problem" is generally traced to René Descartes, who asked how the *immaterial* mind (or soul) could influence the material body. Would not the interaction between the two have to partake somehow of the character of both? Descartes famously identified the tiny pineal gland as the point of contact between mind and body.

This chapter on the web - metaphysicist.com/problems/mind-body

Descartes made the mind the locus of freedom. For him, the body is a mechanical system of tiny fibres causing movements in the brain (the afferent sensations), which then can pull on other fibres to activate the muscles (the efferent nerve impulses). This is the basis of stimulus and response theory in modern physiology (sometimes called reflexology).

The popular idea of animals as machines included the notion that man too is a machine - the body obeying strictly deterministic causal law. But man may have a soul or spirit that is exempt from determinism and thus from what is known today as "causal closure." But how can the mind both cause something physical to happen and yet itself be exempt from lower-level causal chains?

The Problem of Mental Causation

Philosophers who accept the idea that all laws of nature are deterministic and that the world is causally closed still cannot understand how an *immaterial* mind can be the cause of an action. On this view, every physical event is reducible to the microscopic motions of physical particles. The laws of biology are reducible to those of physics and chemistry. The mind is reducible to the brain, with no remainder.

For these philosophers of mind, essentially no progress has been made on the problem of mental causation since Descartes. "Reductionists" who accept "causal closure" think that every brain event must have been determined by causes coming "bottom-up" from the brain's atoms and molecules. Any additional mental cause would be extraneous, according to JAEGWON KIM.

Since the early twentieth century, quantum mechanics adds the possibility that some physical processes are indeterministic, but random quantum-mechanical events have generally been thought to be unhelpful by philosophers of mind. They think adding indeterminism to mental events would only make our actions random and our desires the product of pure chance. If our willed actions are not determined by anything, they say, we are neither morally responsible nor truly free. Whether mental events are reducible to physical events, or whether mental events can be physical events without such a reduction, the interposition of indeterministic quantum processes apparently adds no explanatory power. And of course if mental events are epiphenomenal, they are not causally related to bodily actions. Epiphenomenal access to quantum physics would not help.

Mental causation is a special case of the more general problem of downward causation, for example the downward control of the motions of a cell's atoms and molecules by supervening biological macromolecules. Is the molecular biology of a cell reducible to the laws governing the motions of its component molecules, or are there emergent laws governing motions at the cellular level, still different laws at the organ level, at the organism level up to the mental level?

Emergent properties or laws at the higher levels of a physical-chemical-based biological system would have to prevent those higher levels from being reduced to the properties and laws of the base physical level? These emergent properties are not a new kind of "stuff," but they are nevertheless often described as an emergent dualism, specifically a property dualism.

Is it illogical to deny reductionist ideas of bottom-up causation (because of indeterministic quantum noise) and yet to defend adequately determined downward causation (because quantum effects are averaged out by macroscopic objects)? The arguments are subtle and depend on the complementary roles of determinism (Schrödinger evolution of the wave function) and indeterminism (wave-function collapse) in quantum physics.

Perhaps the most critically important emergent law of all is the abstract idea of determinism itself. Determinism in the macroscopic world emerges from the indeterministic microscopic quantum world by averaging over vast numbers of atoms and molecules. Even before quantum mechanics, LUDWIG BOLTZMANN knew that the macroscopic gas laws were only adequately determined by the average motions of extremely large numbers of molecules. He thought that significant fluctuations away from thermodynamic equilibrium are statistically quite possible.

Mind as an Experience Recorder and Reproducer

Our specific mind model grows out of the question of what sort of "mind" would provide the greatest survival value for the lowest (or the first) organisms that evolved mind-like capabilities.

We propose a primitive mind that can "play back" experiences, reproducing the entire complex of the sensations experienced, together with the emotional response to the original experience (pleasure, pain, fear, etc.).

Our *experience recorder and reproducer* (ERR) model for the mind stands in contrast to the popular cognitive science or "computational" model of a mind as a digital computer with a "central processor" or even "parallel processors." No algorithms or stored programs are needed for the ERR model.

The physically realizable equivalent is a non-linear random-access data recorder, where data is stored using "content-addressable" memory (the memory address - a string of bits in a digital computer - is the data content itself).

Much simpler than a computer with stored algorithms, a better technological metaphor for ERR might be a multi-channel, multi-track analog video and sound recorder, enhanced with the ability to record smells, tastes, touches, and most important, feelings. Imagine one channel for each sense, one track for each neuron. But of course machines currently cannot smell or taste and have no feelings so could not reproduce them (although Gerald Edelman's neural network learning computers have some reward/punishment systems designed in).

The biological basis is very straightforward. We assume that neurons wire together (strengthening synapses) during an organism's experiences, in multiple sensory and limbic systems. Later firing of even a part of those wired-together neurons can stimulate firing of all or part of the original complex, thus "playing back" the original experience (including the reaction to the experience and whether it was a useful reaction).

Related experiences are likely stored nearby (in the many "dimensions" of visual cortex, hearing pathways, olfactory nerves, etc., etc., plus the amygdala).

The ERR model might then explain the philosophical notion of association of ideas. If it is neighboring neurons that fire, they will likely be closely related in some way (since they were stored based on the fundamental pattern of information in the original experience). Similar experiences are likely stored in adjacent neurons. Note that a particular smell could cause the recall of experiences where that smell was present, and similarly for other senses.

Neuroscientists are investigating how diverse signals from multiple pathways can be unified in the brain. We offer no specific insight into this "binding" problem. Nor can we shed much light on the question of philosophical "meaning" of any given information structure, beyond the obvious relevance (survival value) for the organism of remembering past experiences.

In modern times some philosophers and scientists have proposed interactionist models and have also attempted to locate specific parts of the brain, for example at the synapses between neurons, where quantum effects might be important. The neuroscientist JOHN ECCLES and philosopher KARL POPPER considered such interactionist models in their articles and books over many years.

All the attempts to use the mysterious properties of quantum mechanics to explain the mysterious problems of consciousness and psycho-physical relations between mind and body have been just that, explaining one mystery with another mystery.

Many philosophers, most psychologists, and most neuroscientists, *identify* the mind with the brain.

Information philosophy identifies the (immaterial) mind with the incredible biological information processing going on in the brain. This processing operates on two levels.

At the macroscopic level, the mind/brain is adequately determined to make its decisions and resulting actions in ways that are causally connected with the agent's character and values. It is everything that determinist or compatibilist philosopher expects it to be.

At the microscopic level, the mind/brain leaves itself open to significant thermal and quantal noise in its retrieval of past experiences. This noise generates creative and unpredictable alternative possibilities for thought and action. This is our best hope for a measure of freedom from the causal chains of predeterminism.

Our mind/brain model emphasizes the abstract information content of the mind. Information is neither matter nor energy, yet it needs matter for its concrete embodiment and energy for its communication. Information is the modern spirit, the ghost in the machine.

Because it is embodied in the brain, this mind can control the actions of a body that is macroscopic and is normally unaffected by its own quantum level uncertainty (excepting when we want to be creative and unpredictable).

Thus our mind/body model explains how a relatively immaterial, "free," unpredictable, and creative mind can control the adequately determined material body through the self-determinative and responsible actions selected by the will from an agenda of alternative possibilities.

Moreover, some "mental events" are large enough information structures to be adequately determined, these mental events can act causally on lower biological and physical levels in the hierarchy, in particular, the mind can move the body and all its contained physical particles, thus solving the mind-body problem.

A specific example of the mind causing an action, while not itself being caused by antecedent events is the following. Faced with a decision of what to do next, the mind considers several possible alternatives, at least some of which are creatively invented based on random ideas that just "come to mind." Other possible alternatives might be familiar options, even habits, that have frequently been done in earlier similar situations.

All these mental alternatives show up as "neural correlates of consciousness" - brain neurons firing. When the alternatives are evaluated and one is selected, the selected action results in still other neurons firing, some of which connect to the motor cortex that signals muscles to move the body.

Apart from the occasional indeterministic generation of creative new alternative ideas, the "free creations of the human mind," as Albert Einstein called them, this whole causal process is adequately determined and it is downwardly causal. Mental events, pure ideas, abstract thoughts, immaterial information, are the causes of physical body events.

Consciousness a Property of Mind

Consciousness can be defined in information terms as a property of an entity that reacts to the information (particularly to changes in the information) in its environment, including its own body.

Considering the mind as the information in the brain, we can define this as *information consciousness*. It is information in the environment that is being communicated as information to the mind.

Thus an animal in a deep sleep is not conscious, because it ignores changes in its environment. And robots may be conscious in our sense. Even the lowliest control system using negative feedback (a thermostat, for example) is in a minimal sense conscious of (aware of, exchanging information about) changes in its environment.

Where Donald Hebb famously argued that "neurons that fire together wire together," our experience recorder and reproducer ERR model simply assumes that "neurons that have been wired together will fire together."

Being conscious of an experience is this secondary firing of neurons playing back associated experiences. If there are no secondary firings of associated experiences, we suggest that the mind is not aware of any *meaning* in the experience.

Of course, some experiences may initiate secondary firings that are built-in as instincts acquired genetically. Many animals thus "know" the "meanings" of many experiences at the first occurrence. Human knowledge can be understood as the number of associated experiences played back by the ERR. Human intelligence may then be the mind's ability to focus attention on the most relevant of all the past experiences that are playing back subconsciously in what William James called a "blooming, buzzing confusion."

Modality

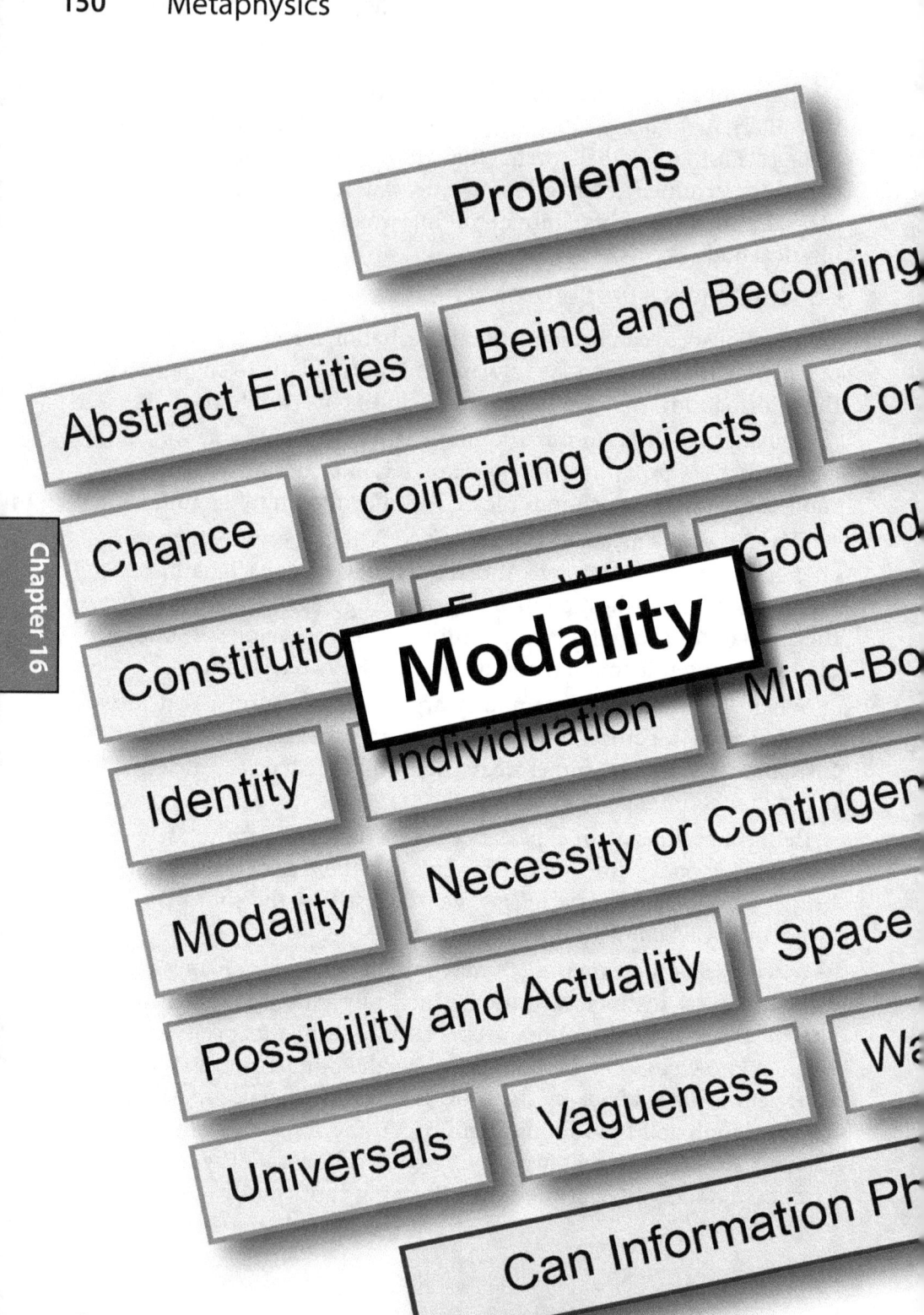

Modality

Logic is an *abstract* human invention, a formal system of ideas much like mathematics, or purely theoretical physics. It is a kind of language, another human invention. Although we can see language as arguably the latest natural evolution of a biological communication system that uses arbitrary symbols for messages in and between all organisms, logic and mathematics are purely the products of rational human minds.

There is nothing material about logic. It is purely abstract and *immaterial* information. Its application to the material world is fraught with danger. A purely materialistic metaphysics cannot understand the fundamental nature of physical reality, cannot understand metaphysics, without including *immaterial* forms, the "Ideas" of PLATO.

Where symbols in ordinary language are notoriously ambiguous, logic is an attempt to formalize the allowed terms, the rules by which they are assembled into statements, and the principles for deductively reasoning from some statements (premises) to others (conclusions), such that true premises lead to true (valid) conclusions.

It was the vision of the great rationalist philosopher GOTTFRIED LEIBNIZ that we could develop an ambiguity-free language for logic and mathematics. That dream was pursued by BERTRAND RUSSELL, LUDWIG WITTGENSTEIN, RUDOLF CARNAP, and others.

Their logical truth-functional analyses are severely limited by the principle of bivalence, the excluded middle, that the only possible values are true and false. But the world is not limited to truth and falsity and attempts to develop three-valued or many-valued logics have largely failed.

Modal logic is the analysis and qualification of statements or propositions as asserting or denying necessity, possibility, impossibility, and, most problematic, *contingency*.

The use of "necessity" and "impossibility" to describe the physical world should be guarded and understood to describe events or "states of affairs" that have extremely high or low probability. The term certainty, when used about knowledge of the physical world, normally represents only extremely high probability.

Possibility and contingency are not easily constrained to the binary values of true and false. To begin with, possibility is normally understood to include necessity. If something is necessary, it is *a fortiori* possible. Contingency is then defined as the subset of possibility that excludes necessity.

The modal operators are a box '□' for necessity and a diamond '◊' for possibility. Impossibility is the negation of possibility, ¬◊, and contingency must negate necessity and also negate impossibility, so it is the logical conjunction of "not necessity" and "possibility" (¬□ ∧ ◊).

Mathematically, contingency is a continuum of values between impossibility and necessity, the open interval between 0 and 1 that represents all the probabilities (excluding the certainties). It is the negation of the logical disjunction of necessity and impossibility, neither necessary nor impossible. (¬ (□ ∨ ¬◊)).

But physically, contingency is the closed interval, including the endpoints of necessity (1) and impossibility (0). Theoretical physics today is often described as probabilistic and statistical, which is sometimes misunderstood to exclude perfect certainties like 0 and 1, but this is not the case. Even quantum physics, the basis of ontological chance in the universe, sometimes predicts certain outcomes, as explained by PAUL DIRAC.[1]

With its four modes, necessity, possibility, impossibility, and contingency, modal analyses simply contain more than can be confined to two-valued truth-functions, whether in logic, usually called *a priori* truths, or language analysis, usually called *analytic* truths, nor in supposed metaphysical truths.

Truth is a binary relation of ideas, true or false. Facts of the matter have a continuous value somewhere between 0 and 1, with plus or minus estimates of the standard deviation of probable errors around that value.

---

1 Dirac (1930) *The Principles of Quantum Mechanics*, chapter 1..

In analytic language philosophy, we need more than the "truth" of statements and propositions with their apparent claims about "necessary" facts in the world. The logical empiricists equate necessity in the first-order logic of their "object language" with analyticity in their higher-order "metalanguage" of propositional functions.

Although we distinguish the *a priori* truths of logic from the analytic truths of language philosophy, many such "truths" were discovered long before modern methods were invented to demonstrate their "proofs." In that sense, knowledge is usually discovered *a posteriori* and ultimately all knowledge is synthetic in the Kantian sense.

All facts about the world are (necessarily?) empirical and *a posteriori*, and thus contingent, so it is best to restrict the use of the concept "truth" to logic and to analytic discourse about statements and propositions. Truth is an appropriate concept in "ideal" formal systems like philosophical logic and mathematics where the extremes of necessity and impossibility are defined parts of the system. But the world itself cannot be confined to a Procrustean bed of true and false.

We therefore conclude that the logical empiricist's idea that the laws of nature can be described with linguistic statements or logical propositions is simply wrong. This is particularly the case for the laws of modern physics, which are now irreducibly probabilistic in view of the indeterministic nature of quantum mechanics, the uncertainty principle, etc.

The "evidence" that "verifies" or validates a physical theory is gathered from a very large number of experiments. No single measurement can establish a fact in the way that a single valid argument can assert the "truth" of an analytic statement. The large number of measurements means that physical evidence is statistical. Indeed, physical theories make predictions that are probabilities. Theories are confirmed when the *a priori* probabilities match the *a posteriori* statistics.

Probability is a theory. Statistics are the results of experiments.

Information philosophy considers claims such as "If P, then P is true" to be redundant, adding no information to the (true) assertion of the statement or proposition "P." Further redundancies are equally vacuous, such as "If P is true, then P is necessarily true" and "If P is true, then P is necessarily true in all possible worlds."

Logically necessary and analytic statements are tautological and carry no new information. This is the *paradox of analyticity*. The statement "A is A" tells us nothing. The statement "A is B" is informative.

Adding "is true" and the like add no new information. They cannot change the fundamental nature of a statement. For example, they cannot change a contingent statement into a necessary one. Consider the statement "A is contingently B." Prepending the necessity operator, "Necessarily, A is contingently B," changes nothing.

We adopt Ludwig Wittgenstein's terminology from "The world is all that is the case." In fact, that is to say in the empirical world, any fact F is at best probably "the case," with the probability approaching certainty in cases that are adequately determined. And, in any case, any past F was contingent and could possibly have been *otherwise*. The idea of a "possible world" is best understood as a way this actual world might have been.

There is, "in fact," only one actual world, the one that is the case. The original purpose of the invention of the idea that there are "possible worlds" – abstract entities – was to provide metaphysicians with other ways of talking about possibilities unrealized in our actual world.[2]

The "sample space" of modern probability theory and the "phase space" of statistical physics are spaces for possible worlds. The 36 ways that two dice can be thrown, the 64 squares where a pawn can be located on a chessboard, the coarse-grained cells for gas particles in position-momentum space, and the minimum uncertainty volumes $\Delta p \, \Delta x = \hbar$ of quantum physics, all can be used to describe possible worlds, how worlds can be, and thus how our world might be.

---

2 Kripke (1981), *Naming and Necessity*, p.19.

Information philosophy maintains that ontologically real possibilities "exist" or subsist as ideas, as pure abstract information, at the present time, alongside "actual" material objects. The ontological or existential status of ideas has always been a controversial question in metaphysics. The exact status of their "existence", asymmetrical in the past and future, is controversial.

Actual Possibles and Possible Possibles

Possibilities in the past may be described as having been "actual possibles." Possibilities in the future are merely "possible possibles."

Possibilities in the past, for example the past alternatives for human actions or the past outcomes of experiments in probabilistic quantum physics, were mostly "roads not taken" and were condemned to "non-being," as the existentialists described it. But they were actual as possibilities in the more distant past that were never "really" actualized. Thus, we can say they were at one time, that they once "existed" as, "actual possibles."

The existence of alternative possibilities in the future raises the famous problem of future contingency, which, since Aristotle's *De Interpretatione*, has called into question the principle of bivalence (either P or not-P), since statements about the future may be (now) neither true nor false. P and not-P are (now) possible possibles about future actuals.

But what can be said about the existential status of these future alternative possibilities in the present time? What can "actual possibles" mean metaphysically? We shall show that possibilities are ideas, abstract entities, which from the time they are embodied in a physical system or in a human mind become "actual possibles." At later times, we are justified in describing them as past "actual possibles" that were never actualized.

Whenever one of many actual possibles is actualized, it does not mean that alternatives that existed as abstract entities at that moment are no longer possibly actualizable in the future. Unless they are forgotten, they remain as "actual possibles" for future use.

We can now describe the many possible worlds that exist within our actual world. They are ways our actual world may be.

If you see a connection between quantum chance and "free" human decisions, there is one, but it does not make our decisions random. Information philosophy provides two examples of future "possible possibles" that are transformed when one is actualized into past "actual possibles." One comes from the world of quantum physics (the source of ontological chance), the other from the human mind when evaluating alternatives and making a decision.

The Many Possible Worlds in Our Actual World

We distinguish three kinds of information structures and processes in our world, the physical, the biological, and the particularly human and mental. All such processing systems can have multiple possibilities for the next step in their processes. These possibilities are abstract bits of information ("ideas") that must be embodied physically to be available as "actual possibles."

At the physical level, quantum events that are amplified to the macroscopic world start new causal chains in "adequately determined" physical processes.

Biological possibilities include sexual selection, where chromosomes for the zygote are randomly selected from the sperm and egg, as a genuinely new individual is created and novel information enters the universe.

For human beings, possibilities are ideas in minds about what to do next. Many of these ideas are constantly available in the normal repertoire of behaviors. That one is chosen over others does not remove the others from future actualization. They remain as "actual possibles" unless they are forgotten. Human minds also create genuinely new information, like that created in biological evolution, when they mentally consider an idea never before thought as an "actual possible."

Although our metaphysically actual possibles are not as numerous as the plurality of worlds of DAVID LEWIS or the many worlds of HUGH EVERETT III, they are plentiful enough. With ten billion humans, millions of other species, some with trillions of individuals that have behavioral repertoires, the numbers of possibilities being actualized in the world each instant is truly vast.

There are many ways that our world may be. It is thus very strange that modal logicians, especially those who are necessitists, assume our actual world has only one way to be and all possibilities are found in worlds that are physically inaccessible, though modally accessible.

Necessity of Identity and the Limits of Necessitism

DAVID WIGGINS and SAUL KRIPKE claimed that the proof of the necessity of identity appeared to make contingent identity impossible. Wiggins also argued against PETER GEACH's idea of *relative identity*.

An information analysis of identity limits perfect and total identity to cases of self-identity, which includes an object's intrinsic internal information and the extrinsic information in dispositional relations of one object to others and to space and time. We can say that any object is absolutely identical to itself. We can also say that some objects are relatively identical if their "identity" is limited to their intrinsic internal information. We then discover a large number of relatively identical objects, both concrete and abstract, including some of those claimed as "natural kinds" by Kripke and HILARY PUTNAM, for example, atoms of gold and molecules of water (H_2O)

Kripke claims that things which we describe as informationally intrinsically identical, are metaphysically *necessary a posteriori*. The domain of things that are intrinsic information identicals is much larger, including both natural and artifactual "digital clones," whether embodied or so-called "non-existent" abstract entities.

It was the claim for the necessity of identity that led to the leading modal systems including a "rule of necessitation," that if P, then necessarily P. (P ⊃ □ P) We should examine this claim carefully. If correct, it may only be a tautological or analytical statement about a universe of discourse, with no significance for the physical world. By contrast, our claim for intrinsic information identicals is a metaphysical and ontological claim about the fundamental nature of reality as including digital clones.

The first proof of the necessity of identity, by RUTH BARCAN MARCUS, was little more than the substitutivity of identicals, which may be seen as begging the question of that identity! It is best seen in the simple proof by her thesis adviser, Frederic B. Fitch,

23.4

(1) a = b,

(2) □[a = a],

then (3) □[a = b], by identity elimination.[3]

Clearly this is mathematically and logically sound. Fitch substitutes b from (1), for a in the modal context of (2). This would be fine if these are just equations. But substitutivity in statements also requires that the substitution is intensionally meaningful. In the sense that b is actually just a, substituting b is equivalent to keeping a there, as a tautology, something with no new information. To be informative and prove the necessary truth of the new statement, we must know more about b, for example, that its intrinsic information is identical to that of a.

Most earlier identity claims showed only that a and b were references (names) for the same thing, Frege's Morning Star and Evening Star for example. But this is a new claim, that numerically distinct things are identical – in some respect.

Those earlier claims often referred to Leibniz's Law, the *Identity of Indiscernibles*. Marcus in 1961, Wiggins in 1965, and Kripke in 1971 all added Leibniz's Law, usually without specifically mentioning Leibniz. But none of these changed the fact that contingent identities are merely possible, that substitution of b for a is valid if and only if you already know that a and b are intrinsic information identicals, and that such knowledge, gained *a posteriori*, is in no way made metaphysically necessary by substituting into the modal context of necessity. Wiggins offered a definitive argument,

> "If a and b refer to the same object, it is already a perfect and absolute self-identity. Calling the identity necessary adds nothing more than "is true" or "necessarily true in all possible worlds." [4]

---

3 Fitch (1952) *Symbolic Logic*, p.164
4 Wiggins (1980) *Sameness and Substance*, p.21

Modal Realism and Possible Worlds

It is critical to note that the metaphysicians proposing possible worlds are for the most part materialists and determinists who do not believe in the existence of ontological possibilities in our world.

They are mostly actualists who say that the only 'possibilities' have always been whatever it was that has actually happened. This is DANIEL DENNETT's position, for example, not far from the original actualist, DIODORUS CRONUS.

Moreover, their infinite numbers of worlds, e.g., DAVID LEWIS's modal realism and possible worlds, are governed by deterministic laws of nature. This means that there are also no real possibilities in any of their possible worlds, only actualities there as well.

Now this is quite ironic, since the invention of possible worlds was proposed as a superior way of talking about counterfactual possibilities in our world.

Since information philosophy defends the existence of alternative possibilities leading to different futures, we can adopt a form of modal discourse to describe these possibilities as possible future worlds for our to-be-actualized world.

Saul Kripke recommended that his "possible worlds" are best regarded as "possible states (or histories) of the world," or just "counterfactual situations," or simply "ways the world might have been."

Kripke appears to endorse the idea of alternative possibilities, that things could have been otherwise.

But there are Lewisian worlds in which your "counterpart" is a butcher, baker, candlestick maker, and every other known occupation. There are possible worlds in which your counterpart eats every possible breakfast food, drives every possible car, and lives in every block on every street in every city or town in the entire word.

This extravagance is of course part of Lewis's appeal. It makes Hugh Everett III's "many worlds" of quantum mechanics (which split the universe in two when a physicist makes a quantum measurement) minuscule, indeed quite parsimonious, by comparison.

Chapter 17

Necessity

Necessity (or Contingency)

Physical necessity is the ancient idea that everything that has ever happened and ever will happen is necessary, and can not be otherwise. It is also known as actualism. The only thing that can possibly happen is what actually happens.

Necessity is often opposed to chance and contingency. In a necessary world there is no chance. Everything that happens is necessitated, determined by the laws of nature. There is only one possible (necessary?) future.

The great atomist LEUCIPPUS stated the first dogma of determinism, an absolute necessity.

> "Nothing occurs at random, but everything for a reason and by necessity."

Contingency is the idea that many things or events are neither necessary nor impossible. Possibility is normally understood to include necessity. If something is necessary, it is *a fortiori* possible. Contingency must be defined as the subset of possibility that excludes necessity.

Information philosophy claims that there is no physical necessity. The world is irreducibly contingent. Necessity is a logical concept, an idea that is an important part of a formal logical or mathematical system that is a human invention.

Like certainty, analyticity, and the *a priori*, necessity and necessary truths are useful concepts for logicians and mathematicians, but not for a metaphysicist exploring the fundamental nature of reality, which includes irreducible contingency.

The Logical Necessity of the Analytic and the *A Priori*

Consider the simple analytically true proposition, "A is A." Or perhaps the logical and mathematical statement that "1 = 1."

Most philosophers cannot imagine denying these true statements. But information philosophy now puts them in the correct historical perspective of new information creation and human knowledge acquisition. Both these facts became known long

This chapter on the web - metaphysicist.com/problems/necessity before humans developed the logical and mathematical apparatus needed to declare them *a priori* and analytic.

WILLARD VAN ORMAN QUINE's claim that all knowledge is synthetic is correct from this perspective. And since nothing in the world was pre-determined to happen, the acquisition of this knowledge was ultimately *contingent*.

We may consider some knowledge to be *synthetic a priori* (IMMANUEL KANT) or *necessary a posteriori* (SAUL KRIPKE) if we find such descriptions useful, but neither is metaphysically true.

Of course truth itself is another human invention. So we should probably say metaphysically valid, where validity is defined as a procedure within our axiomatic metaphysical apparatus.

Information metaphysics begins by establishing the meaning of intrinsic information identicals, so we can provide an axiomatic ground for "A is A" and "1 = 1," which are usually considered fundamental laws of thought.[1]

The Logical Necessity of Necessity

GOTTFRIED LEIBNIZ gave us perhaps the best definition of logical necessity in his discussion of necessary and contingent truths. Beyond the *a priori* and analytic, this is metaphysical necessity.

> "An affirmative truth is one whose predicate is in the subject; and so in every true affirmative proposition, necessary or contingent, universal or particular, the notion of the predicate is in some way contained in the notion of the subject
>
> An absolutely necessary proposition is one which can be resolved into identical propositions, or, whose opposite implies a contradiction... This type of necessity, therefore, I call metaphysical or geometrical. That which lacks such necessity I call contingent, but that which implies a contradiction, or whose opposite is necessary, is called impossible. The rest are called possible.
>
> In the case of a contingent truth, even though the predicate is really in the subject, yet one never arrives at a demonstration or an identity, even though the resolution of each term is continued indefinitely..."[2]

---

1   See chapter 13 on Identity
2   Leibniz. 'Necessary and contingent truths' *Leibniz: Philosophical Writings* (1973).

First, we should note that Leibniz's definitions refer to propositions and predicates. In this respect, he is the original logical and analytic language philosopher. He shared the dream of BERTRAND RUSSELL, LUDWIG WITTGENSTEIN, and RUDOLF CARNAP, that all our knowledge of the world could be represented in propositions, or "logical atoms," as Russell and Wittgenstein called them, "atomic sentences" written in symbolic logic

Secondly, Leibniz's truths are always tautological, as Wittgenstein emphasized. They are of the form, "A is A," propositions "which can be resolved into identical propositions." Their truth ultimately lies in the identity of the subject with the predicate.

Note that Leibniz's "absolutely necessary" compares to modern modal logic axioms that define not only necessity, but the necessity of necessity, like the axiom that extends the model system M to become C.I. LEWIS's S4, necessarily A implies necessarily necessarily A!

$\Box A \supset \Box \Box A$

The analytic philosopher Arthur Pap gave a clear account of the "necessity of necessity" argument in 1958. He asked the fundamental question "Are Necessary Propositions Necessarily Necessary?" Any contingency of truth must be denied. Necessary truths are independent of the physical world, outside space and time.

> "The question whether "it is necessary that p" is, if true, itself a necessary proposition is of fundamental importance for the problem of explicating the concept of necessary truth, since it is likely that any philosopher who answers it affirmatively will adopt the necessity of the necessity of p as a criterion of adequacy for proposed explications of necessary truth. He will, in other words, reject any explication which entails the contingency of such modal propositions as failing to explicate the explicandum he has in mind. The same holds, of course, for the concept of logical truth: since all logical truths are necessary truths (whether or not the converse of this proposition be true also), any criterion of adequacy for explications of "necessary truth" is at the same time a criterion of adequacy for explications of "logical truth." This question cannot be decided by formal reasoning within an uninterpreted system

of modal logic, containing the usual explicit definition of "necessary" in terms of "possible": p is necessary = not-p is not possible. Indeed, an uninterpreted system of modal logic can be constructed without even raising the question of the necessity of the necessity of p; thus there is no postulate or theorem in Lewis' system S2 that bears on the question, nor is the question informally discussed in the metalanguage. In Appendix II to Lewis and Langford's Symbolic Logic (New York and London, 1932) it is pointed out that Lewis' system of strict implication "leaves undetermined certain properties of the modal functions, ◊ p, ~ ◊ p, ◊ ~ p, and ~ ◊ ~ p." Accordingly "Np hook NNp," as well as "Np ⊃ NNp" (N . . . = it is necessary that . . .). is both independent of and consistent with the axioms of the system, and whether an axiom of modal iteration, e.g. "what is possibly possible, is possible" (which can be shown to be equivalent to "what is necessary, is necessarily necessary") should be adopted must be decided by extrasystematic considerations based on interpretation of the modal functions. Now, let us refer to the thesis that necessary propositions are necessarily necessary henceforth as the "NN thesis." What appears to be the strongest argument in favor of the NN thesis is based on the semantic assumption that "necessary" as predicated of propositions is a time-independent predicate, where a "time-independent" predicate is defined as a predicate P such that sentences of the form "x is P at time t" are meaningless.[3]

In the latest systems of modal logic (S5 and K), there are reduction theorems that show *iterated* modalities of any degree (NN, NNN, NNNN, etc.) can be reduced to first degree.[4] So we can point out that all such additions of "necessarily" add no strength to an analytical statement that is tautologically true. Nor do additions of "is true," "in all possible worlds," etc. add anything.

As David Wiggins, a champion of identity said clearly, "Calling the identity necessary adds nothing more than "is true" or "necessarily true in all possible worlds."

---

3   Pap (1958) 'The Linguistic Theory of Logical Necessity,' *Semantics and Necessary Truth*, p.120

4   Hughes and Cresswell (1996), *New Introduction to Modal Logic*, p. 98

Consider P, the proposition that A = A. A is A, A is identical to A, etc.

We can assert P.

Do any of these *iterated modality* statements add anything?

It is true that P.

It is necessarily true that P.

P is true in all possible worlds.

P is necessarily true in all possible worlds.

The Necessity of Identity

In the physical and the logical worlds, no entity can fail to be identical to itself. *The only strict identity is self-identity.* So we can speak loosely of the necessity of identity. But is this a tautology, empty of meaning, like A = A?

In recent years, modal logicians claim to prove the "necessity of identity" using the converse of Leibniz's Law – the "Identity of Indiscernibles." [5]

What WILLARD VAN ORMAN QUINE called the indiscernibility of identicals claims that if x = y, then x and y must share all their properties, otherwise there would be a discernible difference. Now one of the properties of x is that x = x, so if y shares that property "= x" of x, we can say y = x. Necessarily, x = y. QED.

Our rule that the only identity is self-identity becomes in information philosophy that two distinct things, x and y, cannot be identical because there is some difference in information between them. Instead of claiming that y has x's property of being identical to x, we can say only that y has x's property of being self-identical, thus y = y..

The necessity of identity in symbolic logic is

(x)(y) (x=y) ⊃ □ (x=y)

Despite many such arguments in the philosophical literature over the past forty or fifty years, this is a flawed argument. Numerically distinct objects can only be identical "in some respect," if they share qualities which we can selectively "pick out". We can say that a red house and a blue house are identical *qua* house. But they are quite different *qua* color.

---

5   See chapter 13.

Here is Saul Kripke's argument against the possibility of *contingent* identity statements:

> First, the law of the substitutivity of identity says that, for any objects x and y, if x is identical to y, then if x has a certain property F, so does y:
>
> (1) (x)(y) [(x = y) ⊃ (Fx ⊃Fy)]
>
> [Note that Kripke omits the critically important universal quantifier (F), "for all F."]
>
> On the other hand, every object surely is necessarily self-identical:
>
> (2) (x) □(x = x)
>
> But
>
> (3) (x)(y) (x = y) ⊃[□(x = x) ⊃ □ (x = y)]
>
> is a substitution instance of (1), the substitutivity law. From (2) and (3), we can conclude that, for every x and y, if x equals y, then, it is necessary that x equals y:
>
> (4) (x)(y) ((x = y) ⊃ □(x=y))
>
> This is because the clause □(x = x) of the conditional drops out because it is known to be true.

This is an argument which has been stated many times in recent philosophy. Its conclusion, however, has often been regarded as highly paradoxical. For example, David Wiggins, in his paper, "Identity-Statements," says,

> Now there undoubtedly exist contingent identity statements. Let a = b be one of them. From its simple truth and (5) [= (4) above] we can derive '□{a = b}'. But how then can there be any contingent identity statements? [6]

Where are Kripke's errors? We must unpack his "indiscernibility of identicals." Instead of (x)(y) [(x = y) ⊃ (Fx ⊃ Fy)], we must say that we can clearly discern differences between x and y, their names and their numerical distinctness, unless we are merely talking about a single object using two different names. For example, Hesperus = Phosphorus *qua* names referring to the planet Venus.

---

6   Kripke (1971) 'Identity and Necessity,' in Munitz, M., *Identity and Individuation*. p. 136

Separating Necessity from Analyticity and A Prioricity

Kripke is well known both for his "metaphysical necessity" and the "necessary *a posteriori*."

Broadly speaking, modern philosophy has been a search for truth, for *a priori*, analytic, certain, necessary, and provable truth. For many philosophers, *a priori*, analytic, and necessary, have been more or less synonymous.

But all these concepts are mere ideas, invented by humans, some aspects of which have been discovered to be independent of the minds that invented them, notably formal logic and mathematics. Logic and mathematics are systems of thought, inside which the concept of demonstrable (apodeictic) truth is useful, but with limits set by KURT GÖDEL's incompleteness theorem. The truths of logic and mathematics appear to exist "outside of space and time." We call them *a priori* because their proofs are independent of experience, although they were initially abstracted empirically from concrete human experiences.

Analyticity is the idea that some statements, some propositions in the form of sentences, can be true by the definitions or meanings of the words in the sentences. This is correct, though limited by verbal difficulties such as Russell's paradox and numerous other puzzles and paradoxes. Analytic language philosophers claim to connect our words with objects, material things, and thereby tell us something about the world. Some modal logicians, inspired by Kripke, claim that words that are names of things are necessary *a posteriori*, "true in all possible worlds." But this is nonsense, because we invented all those words and worlds. They are mere ideas.

Perhaps the deepest of all these philosophical ideas is necessity. Information philosophy can now tell us that there is no such thing as absolute necessity. There is of course an adequate determinism in the macroscopic world that explains the appearance of deterministic laws of nature, of cause and effect, for example. This is because macroscopic objects consist of vast numbers of atoms and their individual random quantum events average out. But there is no metaphysical necessity. At the fundamental microscopic level of material reality, there is an irreducible contingency and indeterminacy.

Everything that we know, everything we can say, is fundamentally empirical, based on factual evidence, the analysis of experiences that have been recorded in human minds.

As ALBERT EINSTEIN put it,
"Pure logical thinking can give us no knowledge whatsoever of the world of experience; all knowledge about reality begins with experience and terminates in it." [7]

So information philosophy is not what we can logically know about the world, nor what we can analytically say about the world, nor what is necessarily the case in the world. There is nothing that is the case that is necessary and perfectly determined by logic, by language, or by the physical laws of nature. Our world and its future are open and contingent, with actualizable possibilities that are the source of human freedom.

For the most part, philosophers and scientists do not believe in possibilities, despite their invented "possible worlds," which are on inspection merely multiple "actual worlds." This is because they cannot accept the idea of ontological chance. They hope to show that the appearance of chance is the result of human ignorance, that chance is merely an epistemic phenomenon.

Now chance, like truth, is just another idea, just some more information. But what an idea! In a self-referential virtuous circle, it turns out that without the real possibilities that result from ontological chance, there can be no new information. Information philosophy offers cosmological and biological evidence for the creation of new information in the universe. So it follows that chance is real, fortunately something that we can keep under control. We are biological beings that have evolved, thanks to chance, from primitive single-cell communicating information structures to multi-cellular organisms whose defining aspect is the creation and communication of information.

The theory of communication of information is the foundation of our "information age." To understand how we know things is to understand how knowledge represents the material world of "information structures" in the mental world of immaterial ideas.

---

7 Einstein (1933) 'On the Method of Theoretical Physics,' (The Herbert Spencer Lecture) *Philosophy of Science*, Vol. 1, No. 2 (Apr., 1934), p. 165

All knowledge starts with the recording of experiences in minds. The experiences of thinking, perceiving, knowing, feeling, desiring, deciding, and acting may be bracketed by philosophers as "mental" phenomena, but they are no less real than other "physical" phenomena. They are themselves physical phenomena.

They are just not material things.

Information philosophy defines human knowledge as immaterial information in a mind, or embodied in an external artifact that is an information structure (e.g., a book), part of the sum of all human knowledge. Information in the mind about something in the external world is a proper subset of the information in the external object. It is isomorphic to a small part of the total information in or about the object. The information in living things, artifacts, and especially machines, consists of much more than the material components and their arrangement (positions over time). It also consists of all the information processing (e.g., messaging) that goes on inside the thing as it realizes its entelechy or telos, its internal or external purpose.

All science begins with information gathered from experimental observations, which are mental phenomena. Observations are experiences recorded in minds. So all knowledge of the physical world rests on the mental. All scientific knowledge is information shared among the minds of a community of inquirers. As such, science is a collection of thoughts in thinkers, immaterial and mental, some might say funda*mental*. Recall Descartes' argument that the experience of thinking is that which for him is the most certain.

The Master Argument for the Actual World

Aristotle's logic defended the logical necessity that only one of two contradictory statements can be true, and the other false. DIODORUS CRONUS developed his Master Argument to show that only one answer to a question about a future event can be true. This led to the Megarian idea of actualism. There is no future contingency and only one possible future.

Diodorus' paradox was the result of the principle of bivalence or the law of the excluded middle. Only one of two logically contradictory statements can be necessarily true. ARISTOTLE solved the paradox by saying that the truth of statements about the future is contingent on the actual future, as follows,

"A sea battle must either take place tomorrow or not,
but it is not necessary that it should take place tomorrow,
neither is it necessary that it should not take place,
yet it is necessary that it either should or should not
take place to-morrow." [8]

The major founder of Stoicism, CHRYSIPPUS, took the edge off strict necessity. Like DEMOCRITUS, Aristotle, and EPICURUS before him, Chrysippus wanted to strengthen the argument for moral responsibility, in particular defending it from Aristotle's and Epicurus's indeterminate chance causes. Whereas the past is unchangeable, Chrysippus argued that some future events that are possible do not occur by necessity from past external factors alone, but might depend on us. We have a choice to assent or not to assent to an action.

Later, Leibniz distinguished two forms of necessity, necessary necessity and contingent necessity. This basically distinguished logical necessity from physical (or empirical) necessity.

Necessity and Free Will

The eighteenth century debates about free will and determinism were called freedom and necessity. Deniers of free will were called "necessitarians."

Many thinkers distinguished a moral necessity from physical necessity. Moral necessity describes the will being (self-) determined by an agent's reasons and motives. Extreme libertarians insisted that the will cannot be "determined" by reasons, thinking this implies pre-determinism, which it does not.

In two-stage models of free will, chance or indeterminism in the generation of alternative possibilities for action breaks the causal chain of determinism. Actions are not directly determined by reasons or motives, but by an agent evaluating those possibilities in the light of reasons and motives.

---

8   Aristotle. *De Interpretatione* IX, 19 a 30

The thinking agent generates new ideas and chooses to act on one of them. Thoughts are free. Actions are willed. Free and Will are two temporal stages in the process of free will.

Chance is regarded as inconsistent with logical determinism and with any limits on causal, physical or mechanical determinism.

Despite abundant evidence to the contrary, many philosophers deny that chance exists. If a single event is determined by chance, then indeterminism would be true, they say, and undermine the very possibility of certain knowledge. Some go to the extreme of saying that chance would make the state of the world totally independent of any earlier states, which is nonsense, but it shows how anxious they are about chance.

The core idea of determinism is closely related to the idea of causality. Indeterminism for some is simply an event without a cause. But we can have an adequate causality without the strict determinism that implies complete predictability of events and only one possible future.

An example of an event that is not strictly caused is one that depends on chance, like the flip of a coin. If the outcome is only probable, not certain, then the event can be said to have been caused by the coin flip, but the head or tails result was not predictable. So this causality, which recognizes prior events as causes, is undetermined and the result of chance alone.

Events are caused by a combination of caused and uncaused prior events, but not completely pre-determined by events earlier in the causal chain, which has been broken by the uncaused causes.

Despite DAVID HUME's critical attack on the logical necessity of causes, many philosophers embrace causality strongly. Some even connect it to the very possibility of logic and reason. And Hume himself strongly, if inconsistently, believed in necessity while denying causality. He said "'tis impossible to admit any medium betwixt chance and necessity." [9]

Even in a world with chance, macroscopic objects are determined to an extraordinary degree. This is the basis for an adequate physical causality.

---

9   Hume (1739) *Treatise on Human Nature*, Book I, Part I, Section XIV, p.171

We call this kind of determinism (determined but not pre-determined) "adequate determinism." This determinism is adequate enough for us to predict eclipses for the next thousand years or more with extraordinary precision. Newton's laws of motion are deterministic enough to send men to the moon and back.

The presence of quantum uncertainty leads some philosophers to call the world undetermined. But indeterminism is misleading, with strong negative connotations, when most events are overwhelmingly "adequately determined." The neural system is robust enough to insure that mental decisions are reliably transmitted to our limbs. Our actions are determined by our thoughts and our choices. But our thoughts themselves are free. This simply means that our actions were not pre-determined from before we began thinking about our options.

No Logical Necessity in the Material World

We conclude with the metaphysical position that necessity is merely an idea. It is a valuable idea in the world of thought, in logic and in mathematics especially. But it does not bind events in the material world, which we find to be metaphysically contingent.

Many modern metaphysicians have become strong necessitarians. Symbolic logic and modal logic are powerful tools for reasoning. They are applicable to metaphysical questions about abstract entities and non-existent objects.

Necessitist philosophers deny the contingency of what there is, asserting the necessity of all that exists, perhaps allowing contingency of how things are arranged. This conforms to the idea that matter (with energy) are conserved quantities, where their information content is variable and growing. But the metaphysicians' insistence that the question of necessity versus contingency can only be settled by theoretical enquiry is mistaken.[10]

---

10   Williamson (2013). *Modal Logic as Metaphysics*, chapter 1.

Necessitism

We can accept a necessitist analysis of some limited set of propositions. The leading proponent of necessitism is TIMOTHY WILLIAMSON, who describes his work as follows.

> "Necessitism is the view that necessarily everything is necessarily something; contingentism is the negation of necessitism. The dispute between them is reminiscent of, but clearer than, the more familiar one between possibilism and actualism. A mapping often used to 'translate' actualist discourse into possibilist discourse is adapted to map every sentence of a first-order modal language to a sentence the contingentist (but not the necessitist) may regard as equivalent to it but which is neutral in the dispute. This mapping enables the necessitist to extract a 'cash value' from what the contingentist says." [11]

Modal logicians like RUDOLF CARNAP and WILLARD VAN ORMAN QUINE thought their work in logical positivism and logical empiricism had applications to the world. Quine's idea of "naturalizing epistemology" was an attempt to add the scientific method of experimental evidence to what was otherwise an "internalist" approach to the justification of knowledge.

As long as we limit necessitism to a select set of sentences in a language, we can accept the elimination of anything contingent in such a formal mathematical "model system."

But attempts to apply concepts from a model system, inside which everything has a necessary relationship to everything else, to the external world is fraught with danger.

---

[11] Williamson (2010) 'Necessitism, Contingentism and Plural Quantification,' *Mind*, 2010, 119, pp.657-748

Persistence

Persistence is the metaphysical question of whether and how things persist over time. Things include concrete material objects from natural to artifactual to biological entities, as well as pure abstract objects like concepts and ideas that may be "universals."

Persistence is related to the ancient Academic Skeptic argument about growth, that even the smallest material change destroys an entity and another entity appears. In this case, a change in the instant of time also destroys every material object, followed instantaneously by the creation of an almost "identical" object.

The Academic Skeptics argued that an individual cannot survive material change. When any material is subtracted or added, the entity ceases to exist and a new numerically distinct individual comes into existence. By contrast, the Stoics saw the identity of an individual as its immaterial bundle of properties or qualities that they called the "peculiarly qualified individual" or ἰδίος ποιὸν.

The Stoics were following ARISTOTLE. Like him, they called the material substance or substrate ὑποκείμενον (or "the underlying"). They believed the material substrate is "transformed" when matter is lost or gained. The Stoics suggested these changes should be called "generation (γενέσεις) and destruction (φθορὰς)." They said it is wrong to call material changes "growth (αὐξήσεις) and decay (φθίσεις)." These terms were already present in Aristotle, who said that the form, as essence, is not generated. He said that generation and destruction are material changes that do not persist. The Stoics argued that the peculiarly qualified individual does persist. Aristotle had commented on his use of words about persistence:

> "It is therefore obvious that the form (or whatever we should call the shape in the sensible thing) is not generated—generation does not apply to it—nor is the essence generated; for this is that which is induced in something else either by art or by nature or by potency. But we do cause a bronze sphere to be, for we produce it from bronze and a sphere; we induce the form into this particular matter, and the result is a bronze sphere...

> For if we consider the matter carefully, we should not even say without qualification that a statue is generated from wood, or a house from bricks; because that from which a thing is generated should not persist, but be changed. This, then, is why we speak in this way." [1]

In his work *On Common Conceptions*, Plutarch describes CHRYSIPPUS' "Growing Argument" as discovering what it is that persists.

> "The argument about growth is an old one, for, as Chrysippus says, it is propounded by Epicharmus. Yet when the Academics hold that the puzzle is not altogether easy or straightforward, these people [sc. the Stoics] have laid many charges against them and denounced them as destroying our preconceptions and contravening our conceptions. Yet they themselves not only fail to save our conceptions but also pervert sense-perception. (2) For the argument is a simple one and these people grant its premises: a all particular substances are in flux and motion, releasing some things from themselves and receiving others which reach them from elsewhere; b the numbers or quantities which these are added to or subtracted from do not remain the same but become different as the aforementioned arrivals and departures cause the substance to be transformed; c the prevailing convention is wrong to call these processes of growth and decay: rather they should be called generation and destruction, since they transform the thing from what it is into something else, whereas growing and diminishing are affections of a body which serves as substrate and persists." [2]

In one of his plays, EPICHARMUS introduced the "debtor's paradox," in which a lender trying to collect on his loan was told that his growth and change meant that he was no longer the person to whom the loan was made. The debtor at that earlier time had not persisted. When the lender strikes the debtor and the debtor threatens a lawsuit, the lender says the person who struck the debtor no longer exists, so he, the current version of the lender, is not responsible! Even the lender does not persist!

---

1   Aristotle, *Metaphysics*, Book VII, § vii & viii
2   Plutarch. *The Hellenistic Philosophers*, Long and Sedley, v.1, p.166

Perdurance

The basic definition of persistence is to show how and why an object is the same object at different times. Although this may seem trivially obvious for ordinary objects, information philosophy shows that there is strictly no such thing as perfect identity over time. The "same" object at two different times contains different information (minimally, its time coordinate in four-dimensional space-time has changed). Metaphysicians say it is better considered as two objects that are not absolutely identical.

The great Anglo-American philosopher ALFRED NORTH WHITEHEAD attributed the continued existence of objects from moment to moment to the intervention of God. Without a kind of continuous creation of every entity, things would fall apart. This notion can also be traced back to the American theologian Jonathan Edwards, who thought God creates every person anew from moment to moment, and is responsible for the way the world is at every instant.

WILLARD VAN ORMAN QUINE proposed that we consider an object as existing in "stages." Quine's student, DAVID LEWIS argues that at every instant of time, every object disappears, ceases to exist, to be replaced by a very similar new entity.

Lewis proposes "temporal parts" as a solution to the problem of persistence. He calls his solution "perdurance," which he distinguishes from "endurance," in which the whole entity exists at all times. Lewis says:

> "Our question of overlap of worlds parallels the this-worldly problem of identity through time; and our problem of accidental intrinsics parallels a problem of temporary intrinsics, which is the traditional problem of change. Let us say that something persists iff, somehow or other, it exists at various times; this is the neutral word. The road parts do not exactly persist. They are intrinsically different parts. The enduring entity does persist simpliciter.
>
> Matter that disappears and reappears violates the conservation laws for matter and energy.. Something perdures iff it persists by having different temporal parts, or stages, at different times.

though no one part of it is wholly present at more than one time; whereas it endures iff it persists by being wholly present at more than one time. Perdurance corresponds to the way a road persists through space; part of it is here and part of it is there, and no part is wholly present at two different places. Endurance corresponds to the way a universal, if there are such things, would be wholly present wherever and whenever it is instantiated. Endurance involves overlap: the content of two different times has the enduring thing as a common part. Perdurance does not." [3]

In their thinking about persistence, many metaphysicians have been inspired by ALBERT EINSTEIN's theory of special relativity. The idea of a four-dimensional manifold of space and time supports the idea that the "temporal parts" of an object are as distinct from one another as its spatial parts. This raises questions about its continued identity as it moves in space and time.

"Presentists" believe that only present objects "exist," or their existence is different in kind from their past "real" and any future merely possible existence. "Eternalists" think past, present, and future existence are all the same in an Einstein-Minkowski "block universe" of space-time.

JOHN MCTAGGART described a series of events in the ordinary presentist view as an A-series of events, privileging the present and called a "tensed" theory of time. In what he called a B-series, events are described only by their temporal relation to other events, "before" or "after" or "simultaneous". In this "tenseless" view, all events are equally here and now, as is claimed for a "God's eye" view. All future events are said to be actual, an idea called "actualism."

There is no physical basis for the wild assumptions of past metaphysicians and theologians, from Jonathan Edwards to ALFRED NORTH WHITEHEAD's idea of "continuous creation," that the contents of the universe cease to exist and then reappear *de novo* at the next instant. Whitehead's "process philosophy" argues that the reappearance could not happen without the intervention of God. This notion violates one of the most fundamental of physical laws, the conservation of matter and energy.

---

3   Lewis (1986) *On the Plurality of Worlds*, p. 202

More metaphysically significant, neither temporal nor spatial "slices" carve nature at the joints. They are arbitrary mental constructions imposed on the world by philosophers that have little to do with "natural" objects, their component parts, and their time evolution.

Endurance

It is metaphysically necessarily the case, both logically and in terms of an information analysis, that everything is identical to itself. Self-identity is a necessary truth. If you exist, you do not exist necessarily, as TIMOTHY WILLIAMSON claims, but you are necessarily self-identical at each instant of time.

Despite the absence of any absolute physical necessity about what there is (ontology), information philosophy can and does embrace SAUL KRIPKE's metaphysical necessity. We take this to be his proof of the necessity of identity, first suggested by RUTH BARCAN MARCUS using Leibniz's Law of the Identity of Indiscernibles and its tautological converse, the indiscernibility of identicals.

If you exist, you are very nearly identical to yourself a moment ago. But because your information content is a strong function of time, you (t) ≠ you (t + 1). This will make the perdurantists happy, but the change in information is a tiny fraction of your total, so endurantists are closer to the truth in the problem of persistence.

Temporal Parts?

The claim that an entity ceases to exist at every instant and then is newly created at the next instant is often described as creating temporal parts analogous to spatial parts.

This analogy is severely flawed by an information analysis. Spatial parts have no essential (or accidental) properties in common. The information content can be arbitrarily different. The information content of successive "temporal parts." on the other hand, will have a high degree of identical intrinsic information.

There will of course be some properties that change with time and others that persist.

Chapter 19

Possibility

Possibility

In the "semantics of possible worlds," necessity and possibility in modal logic are variations of the universal and existential quantifiers of non-modal logic. Necessary truth is defined as "truth in all possible worlds." Possible truth is defined as "truth in some possible worlds." These abstract notions about "worlds" – sets of propositions in universes of discourse – have nothing to do with physical possibility, which depends on the existence of real *contingency*. Propositions in modal logic are required to be true or false. Contingent statements that are neither true or false are not allowed in modal logic. So much for real possibilities!

Historically, the opposition to metaphysical possibility has come from those who claim that the only possible things that can happen are the actual things that do happen. To say that things could have been otherwise is a mistake, say eliminative materialists and determinists. Those other possibilities simply never existed in the past. The only possible past was the actual past.

Similarly, there is only one possible future. Whatever will happen, will happen. The idea that many different things can happen, the reality of modality and words like "may" or "might" are used in everyday conversation, but they have no place in metaphysical reality. The only "actual" events or things are what exists. For "presentists," even the past does not exist. Everything we remember about past events is just a set of "Ideas." And philosophers have always been troubled about the ontological status of Plato's abstract "Forms," entities like the numbers, geometric figures, mythical beasts, and other fictions.

Traditionally, those who deny possibilities in this way have been called "Actualists."

In the last half-century, one might think that metaphysical possibilities have been restored with the development of modal logic. So-called modal operators like "necessarily" and "possibly" have been added to the structurally similar quantification operators "for all" and "for some." The metaphysical literature is full of talk about "possible worlds."

The most popular theory of "possible worlds" is DAVID LEWIS's "modal realism," an infinite number of worlds, each of which is just as actual (eliminative materialist and determinist) for its inhabitants as our world.

There are no genuine possibilities in Lewis's "possible worlds"! It comes as a shock to learn that every "possible world" is just as actual, for its inhabitants, as our world is for us. There are no alternative possibilities, no contingency, no things that might have been otherwise, in any of these possible worlds. Every world is as physically deterministic as our own.

Modal logicians now speak of a "rule of necessitation" at work in possible world semantics. The necessarily operator ' □ ' and the possibly operator ' ◊ ' are said to be "duals" - either one can be defined in terms of the other (□ = ~◊~, and ◊ = ~□~), so either can be primitive. But most axiomatic systems of modal logic appear to privilege necessity and de-emphasize possibility. They rarely mention contingency, except to say that the necessity of identity appears to rule out contingent identity statements.

The rule of necessitation is that "if p, then necessarily p," or p ⊃ □p. This gives rise to the idea that if anything exists, it exists necessarily. This is called "necessitism." The idea that if two things are identical, they are necessarily identical, was "proved" by RUTH BARCAN MARCUS in 1947, by her thesis adviser F.B.Fitch in 1952, and by WILLARD VAN ORMAN QUINE in 1953. DAVID WIGGINS in 1965 and SAUL KRIPKE in 1971 repeated the arguments, with little or no reference to the earlier work.

This emphasis on necessitation in possible-world semantics leads to a flawed definition of possibility that has no connection with the ordinary and technical meanings of possibility.

Modal logicians know little if anything about real possibilities and nothing at all about possible physical worlds. Their possible worlds are abstract universes of discourses, sets of propositions that are true or false. Contingent statements, that may be true or false, like statements about the future, are simply not allowed.

The modal operators □ and ◊ are designed to correspond to the universal and existential quantification operators "for all" ∀ and "for some" ∃. But the essential nature of possibility is the conjunction of contingency and necessity. Contingency is not impossible and not necessary (~~◊ ∧ ~□).

Information philosophy proposes the existence of a *metaphysical possibilism* alongside the currently popular notion of necessitism.

"Actual possibilities" exist in minds and in quantum-mechanical "possibility functions" It is what we might call "actual possibilism," the existence in our actual world of possibilities that may never become actualized, but that have a presence as abstract entities that have been embodied as ideas in minds. In addition, we include the many possibilities that occur at the microscopic level when the quantum-mechanical probability-amplitude wave function collapses, making one of its many possibilities actual.

Actual Possibles

Although there are no genuine possibilities in Lewis's "possible worlds," we can explain the existence of "actual possibles" in metaphysical terms using the possible world semantics of Kripke, who maintained that his semantics could be used to describe various ways our actual world might have been. Unlike many other "possible world" interpretations, Kripke accepts that empirical facts in the physical world are contingent, that many things might have been otherwise. Kripke's counterfactuals are genuinely different ways the actual world might have been or might become.

> "I will say something briefly about 'possible worlds'. (I hope to elaborate elsewhere.) In the present monograph I argued against those misuses of the concept that regard possible worlds as something like distant planets, like our own surroundings but somehow existing in a different dimension, or that lead to spurious problems of 'transworld identification'. Further, if one wishes to avoid the Weltangst and philosophical confusions that many philosophers have associated with the 'worlds' terminology, I recommended that 'possible state (or history) of the world', or 'counterfactual situation' might be better. One should even remind oneself that the 'worlds' terminology can often be replaced by modal talk—'It is possible that.' ... 'Possible worlds' are total 'ways the world might have been', or states or histories of the entire world." [1]

---

1   Kripke (1981) *Naming and Necessity*, p. 15, 18

Actualism

Actualism appeals to philosophers who want the world to be determined by physical laws and by theologians who want the world to be the work of an omnipotent, omniscient, and benevolent god.

Some physicists think the future is causally closed under deterministic laws of nature and the "fixed past." If the knowledge that a Laplacian "super-intelligence" has about all the motions at any instant is fixed for all time, then everything today might have been pre-determined from the earliest moments of the physical universe.

The special theory of relativity, for example, describes a four-dimensional "block universe" in which all the possible events of the future already exist alongside those of the past. It makes "fore-knowledge" of the future conceivable.

DIODORUS CRONUS dazzled his contemporaries in the fourth century BCE with sophisticated logical arguments, especially paradoxes, that "proved" there could be only one possible future.

Diodorus' "master argument" is a set of propositions designed to show that the actual is the only possible and that some true statements about the future imply that the future is already determined. This follows logically from his observation that if something in the future is not going to happen, it must have been that statements in the past that it would not happen must have been true.

Modern day "actualists" include DANIEL DENNETT, for whom determinism guarantees that the actual outcome is and always was the only possible outcome. The notion that we can change the future is absurd, says Dennett, change it from what to what?

The ancient philosophers debated the distinction between necessity and contingency (between the *a priori* and the *a posteriori*). Necessity includes events or concepts that are logically necessary and physically necessary, contingency those that are logically or physically possible. In the middle ages and the enlightenment, necessity was often contrasted with freedom. In modern times it is often contrasted with mere chance.

Causality is often confused with necessity, as if a causal chain requires a deterministic necessity. But we can imagine chains where the linked causes are statistical, and modern quantum physics tells us that all events are only statistically caused, even if for large macroscopic objects the statistical likelihood approaches near certainty for all practical purposes. The apparent deterministic nature of physical laws is only an "adequate" determinism.

In modern philosophy, modal theorists like DAVID LEWIS discuss counterfactuals that might be true in other "possible worlds." Lewis' work at Princeton may have been inspired by the work of Princeton scientist HUGH EVERETT III. Everett's interpretation of quantum mechanics replaces the "collapse" of the wave function with a "splitting" of this world into multiple worlds existing in parallel universes.

Possibilities in Quantum Mechanics

According to the Schrödinger equation of motion, the time evolution of the wave function describes a "superposition" of possible quantum states. Standard quantum mechanics says that interaction of the quantum system with other objects causes the system to collapse into one of the possible states, with probability given by the square of the "probability amplitude."

One very important kind of interaction is a measurement by an "observer."

In standard quantum theory, when a measurement is made, the quantum system is "projected" or "collapsed" or "reduced" into a single one of the system's allowed states. If the system was "prepared" in one of these "eigenstates," then the measurement will find it in that state with probability one (that is, with certainty).

However, if the system is prepared in an arbitrary state ψ_a, it can be represented as being in a linear combination of the system's basic eigenstates φ_n.

$\psi_a = \Sigma\, c_n \,|\,n>$.

where

$c_n = <\psi_a\,|\,\varphi_n>$.

The system ψ_a is said to be in "superposition" of those basic states φ_n. The probability P_n of its being found in a particular state φ_n is

$P_n = <\psi_a\,|\,\varphi_n>^2 = c_n^2$.

Shannon and Quantum Indeterminism

In his development of the mathematical theory of the communication of information, CLAUDE SHANNON showed that there can be no new information in a message unless there are multiple possible messages. If only one message is possible, there is no information in that message.

We can simplify this to define a Shannon Principle. No new information can be created in the universe unless there are multiple possibilities, only one of which can become actual.

An alternative statement of the Shannon principle is that in a deterministic system, information is conserved, unchanging with time. Classical mechanics is a conservative system that conserves not only energy and momentum but also conserves the total information. Information is a "constant of the motion" in a determinist world.

Quantum mechanics, by contrast, is *indeterministic*. It involves irreducible ontological chance.

An isolated quantum system is described by a wave function ψ which evolves - deterministically - according to the *unitary* time evolution of the linear Schrödinger equation.

$$(ih/2\pi)\, \partial\psi/\partial t = H\psi$$

The possibilities of many different outcomes evolve deterministically, but the individual actual outcomes are indeterministic.

This sounds a bit contradictory, but it is not. It is the essence of the highly non-intuitive quantum theory, which combines a deterministic "wave" aspect with an indeterministic "particle" aspect.[2]

In his 1932 *Mathematical Foundations of Quantum Mechanics*, JOHN VON NEUMANN explained that two fundamentally different processes are going on in quantum mechanics (in a temporal sequence for a given particle - not at the same time).

Process 1. A non-causal process, in which the measured electron winds up randomly in one of the possible physical states (eigenstates) of the measuring apparatus plus electron.

---

2   See chapter 23.

The probability for each eigenstate is given by the square of the coefficients c_n of the expansion of the original system state (wave function ψ) in an infinite set of wave functions φ that represent the eigenfunctions of the measuring apparatus plus electron.

$c_n = <\varphi_n | \psi>$

This is as close as we get to a description of the "motion" of the "particle" aspect of a quantum system. According to von Neumann, the particle simply shows up somewhere as a result of a measurement. These measurements are *irreversible,* he said.

Information physics says that the particle shows up whenever a new stable information structure is created, information that can be "observed" by the experimenter.

Process 1b. The information created in Von Neumann's **process 1** will only be stable if an amount of positive entropy greater than the negative entropy in the new information structure is transported away, in order to satisfy the second law of thermodynamics.

Process 2. A causal process, in which the electron wave function ψ evolves deterministically according to Schrödinger's equation of motion for the "wave"aspect. This evolution describes the motion of the probability amplitude wave ψ between measurements. The wave function exhibits interference effects. But interference is destroyed if the particle has a definite position or momentum. The particle path itself can never be observed.

Von Neumann claimed there is another major difference between these two processes. **Process 1** is thermodynamically *irreversible.* **Process 2** is in principle reversible. This confirms the fundamental connection between quantum mechanics and thermodynamics that is explainable by information physics.

Information physics establishes that process 1 may create information. It is always involved when information is created.

Process 2 is deterministic and information preserving.

The first of these processes has come to be called the "collapse of the wave function."

It gave rise to the so-called problem of measurement, because its randomness prevents it from being a part of the deterministic mathematics of **process 2**.

But isolation is an ideal that can only be approximately realized. Because the Schrödinger equation is linear, a wave function $|\psi>$ can be a linear combination (a superposition) of another set of wave functions $|\varphi_n>$,

$$|\psi> = \Sigma c_n |\varphi_n>,$$

where the c_n coefficients squared are the probabilities of finding the system in the possible state $|\varphi_n>$ as the result of an interaction with another quantum system.

$$c_n^2 = <\psi|\varphi_n>^2.$$

Quantum mechanics introduces real possibilities, each with a calculable probability of becoming an actuality, as a consequence of one quantum system interacting (for example colliding) with another quantum system. These actualizations are *irreversible*.

It is quantum interactions that lead to new information in the universe - both new information structures and information processing systems. But that new information cannot subsist unless a compensating amount of entropy is transferred away from the new information.

Even more important, it is only in cases where information persists long enough for a human being to observe it that we can properly describe the observation as a "measurement" and the human being as an "observer." So, following von Neumann's "process" terminology, we can complete his admittedly unsuccessful attempt at a theory of the measuring process by adding an anthropomorphic

Process 3 - a conscious observer recording new information in a mind. This is only possible if the local reductions in the entropy (the first in the measurement apparatus, the second in the mind) are both balanced by even greater increases in positive entropy that must be transported away from the apparatus and the mind, so the overall change in entropy can satisfy the second law of thermodynamics.

An Information Interpretation of Quantum Mechanics

Our emphasis on the importance of information suggests an "information interpretation" of quantum mechanics that eliminates the need for a conscious observer as in the "standard orthodox" Copenhagen Interpretation. An information interpretation dispenses with the need for a separate "classical" measuring apparatus.

There is only one world, the quantum world.

It is ontologically indeterministic, but epistemically deterministic, because of human ignorance. It *appears* to be deterministic.

Information physics claims there is only one world, the quantum world, and the "quantum to classical transition" occurs for any large macroscopic object with mass m that contains a large number of atoms. In this case, independent quantum events are "averaged over," the uncertainty in position and momentum of the object becomes less than the observational accuracy as

$\Delta v \, \Delta x > h / m$ and as h / m goes to zero.

The classical laws of motion, with their implicit determinism and strict causality emerge when microscopic events can be ignored.

Information philosophy interprets the wave function ψ as a "possibilities" function. With this simple change in terminology, the mysterious process of a wave function "collapsing" becomes a much more intuitive discussion of possibilities, with mathematically calculable probabilities, turning into a single actuality, faster than the speed of light.

Information physics is standard quantum physics. It accepts the Schrödinger equation of motion, the *principle of superposition*, the *axiom of measurement* (including the actual information "bits" measured), and, most important, the *projection postulate* of standard quantum mechanics (the "collapse" so many interpretations deny).

A conscious observer is not required for a projection, for the wave-function to "collapse", for one of the possibilities to become an actuality. What projection does require is an interaction between (quantum) systems that creates *irreversible* information.

In less than two decades of the mid-twentieth century, the word information was transformed from a synonym for knowledge into a mathematical, physical, and biological quantity that can be measured and studied scientifically.

In 1929, LEO SZILARD connected an increase in thermodynamic (Boltzmann) entropy with any increase in information that results from a measurement, solving the problem of "Maxwell's Demon," a thought experiment suggested by JAMES CLERK MAXWELL, in which a local reduction in entropy is possible when an intelligent being interacts with a thermodynamic system.

In the early 1940s, digital computers were invented by von Neumann, Shannon, ALAN TURING, and others. Their machines run a stored program to manipulate stored data, processing information, as biological organisms have been doing for billions of years.

Then in the late 1940s, the problem of communicating digital data signals in the presence of noise was first explored by Shannon, who developed the modern mathematical theory of the communication of information. NORBERT WIENER wrote in his 1948 book Cybernetics that "information is the negative of the quantity usually defined as entropy," and in 1949 Leon Brillouin coined the term "negentropy."

Finally, in the early 1950s, inheritable characteristics were shown by Francis Crick, James Watson, and George Gamow to be transmitted from generation to generation by information in a digital code.

Possible Worlds

> In ancient times, LUCRETIUS commented on possible worlds: "for which of these causes holds in our world it is difficult to say for certain ; but what may be done and is done through the whole universe in the various worlds made in various ways, that is what I teach, proceeding to set forth several causes which may account for the movements of the stars throughout the whole universe; one of which, however, must be that which gives force to the movement of the signs in our world also ; but which may be the true one," [3]

The sixteenth-century philosopher GIORDANO BRUNO speculated about an infinite universe, with room for unlimited numbers of other stars and their own planets.

---

3   Lucretius. *De Rerum Natura*, Book V, lines 526-533

"**Philotheo**. This is indeed what I had to add; for, having pronounced that the universe must itself be infinite because of the capacity and aptness of infinite space; on account also of the possibility and convenience of accepting the existence of innumerable worlds like to our own; it remaineth still to prove it.

I say that the universe is entirely infinite because it hath neither edge, limit, nor surfaces. But I say that the universe is not all-comprehensive infinity because each of the parts thereof that we can examine is finite and each of the innumerable worlds contained therein is finite.

Theophilo. For the solution that you seek you must realize Firstly, that since the universe is infinite and immobile, there is no need to seek the motive power thereof, Secondly, the worlds contained therein such as earths, fires and other species of body named stars are infinite in number, and all move by the internal principle which is their own soul, as we have shewn elsewhere;" [4]

GOTTFRIED LEIBNIZ famously introduced his idea of possible worlds as a proposed solution to the problem of evil.

"Metaphysical considerations also are brought up against my explanation of the moral cause of moral evil; but they will trouble me less since I have dismissed the objections derived from moral reasons, which were more impressive. These metaphysical considerations concern the nature of the possible and of the necessary; they go against my fundamental assumption that God has chosen the best of all possible worlds. There are philosophers who have maintained that there is nothing possible except that which actually happens. These are those same people who thought or could have thought that all is necessary unconditionally. Some were of this opinion because they admitted a brute and blind necessity in the cause of the existence of things: and it is these I have most reason for opposing. But there are others who are mistaken only because they misuse terms. They confuse moral necessity with metaphysical necessity: they imagine that since God cannot help acting for the best he is thus deprived of freedom, and things are endued with that necessity which philosophers and theologians endeavour to avoid." [5]

---

4   Bruno. *On the Infinite Universe and Worlds*, First Dialogue

5   Leibniz. *Theodicy*, § 168

As we have seen, the logician and philosopher Saul Kripke described various universes of discourse, collections of true and false propositions, as various "ways the world might be."

But most talk about possible worlds is the work of the analytic language philosopher DAVID LEWIS. He developed the philosophical methodology known as "modal realism" based on his claims that

> Possible worlds exist and are just as real as our world.
>
> Possible worlds are the same sort of things as our world – they differ in content, not in kind.
>
> Possible worlds cannot be reduced to something more basic – they are irreducible entities in their own right.
>
> Actuality is indexical. When we distinguish our world from other possible worlds by claiming that it alone is actual, we mean only that it is our world.
>
> Possible worlds are unified by the spatiotemporal interrelations of their parts; every world is spatiotemporally isolated from every other world.
>
> Possible worlds are causally isolated from each other.[6]

Lewis's "modal realism" implies the existence of infinitely many parallel universes, an idea similar to the many-world interpretation of quantum mechanics.

Possible worlds and modal reasoning made "counterfactual" arguments extremely popular in current philosophy. Possible worlds, especially the idea of "nearby worlds" that differ only slightly from the actual world, are used to examine the validity of modal notions such as necessity and contingency, possibility and impossibility, truth and falsity.

Lewis appears to have believed that the truth of his counterfactuals was a result of believing that for every non-contradictory statement there is a possible world in which that statement is true.

- True propositions are those that are true in the actual world.
- False propositions are those that are false in the actual world.
- Necessarily true propositions are those that are true in all possible worlds.
- Contingent propositions are those that are true in some possible worlds and false in others.

---

6   Wikipedia article on Modal Realism, accessed 11/11/2016

- Possible propositions are those that are true in at least one possible world.
- Impossible propositions are those that are true in no possible world.

Unfortunately, the modern defender of "modally real" possible worlds is a determinist who does not believe that alternative possibilities are real. Ironically, Lewis is an actualist, in every "possible" world.

And apart from his extravagant and outlandish claim that there are an infinite number of inaccessible "possible" worlds, he is also the creator of another absurd set of infinities. According to his theory of temporal parts, sometimes called four-dimensionalism, Lewis argues that at every instant of time, every individual disappears, ceases to exist, to be replaced by a very similar new entity.

He proposes temporal parts as a solution to the metaphysical problem of persistence.[7] He calls his solution "perdurance," which he distinguishes from "endurance."

Perdurance is a variation of an Academic Skeptic argument about growth, that even the smallest material change destroys an entity and another entity appears. There is no physical or metaphysical reason for this wild assumption. Nevertheless, Lewis's "counterfactual" thinking is highly popular among modern metaphysicians.

Other Possible Worlds

HUGH EVERETT III's many-worlds interpretation of quantum mechanics is an attempt to deny the random "collapse" of the wave function and preserve determinism in quantum mechanics. Everett claims that every time an experimenter makes a quantum measurement with two possible outcomes, the entire universe splits into two new universes, each with the same material content as the original, but each with a different outcome. It violates the conservation of mass/energy in the most extreme way.

The scientist DAVID LAYZER argues that since the universe is infinite there are places in the universe where any possible thing is being realized. This is a cosmologist's version of David Lewis's "possible worlds." Layzer argues that free will is a consequence of not knowing which of the many possible worlds that we are in.

---

7   See chapter 18.

Chapter 20

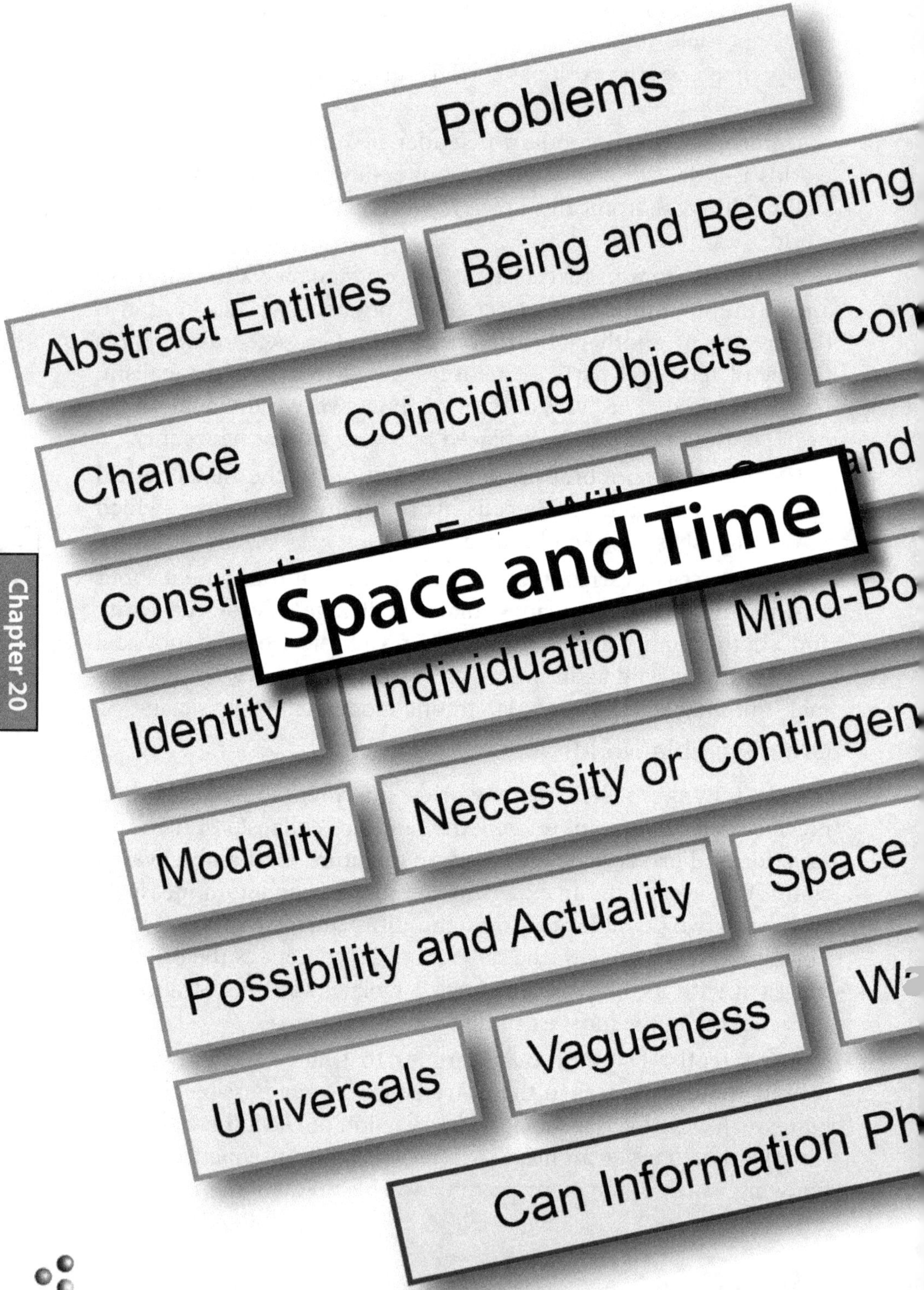
Problems
Being and Becoming
Abstract Entities
Coinciding Objects
Chance
Space and Time
Individuation
Identity
Modality
Possibility and Actuality
Space
Universals
Vagueness

Space and Time

Modern investigations into the fundamental nature of space and time have produced a number of paradoxes and puzzles that also might benefit from a careful examination of the information content in the problem. An information metaphysicist might throw new light on nonlocality, entanglement, spooky action-at-a-distance, the uncertainty principle, and even eliminate the conflict between special relativity and quantum mechanics!

Space and time form an immaterial coordinate system that allows us to keep track of material events, the positions and velocities of the fundamental particles that make up every body in the universe. As such, space and time are pure information, a set of numbers that we use to describe matter in motion.

When IMMANUEL KANT described space and time as *a priori* forms of perception, he was right that scientists and philosophers impose the four-dimensional coordinate system on the material world. But he was wrong that the coordinate geometry must therefore be a flat Euclidean space. That is an empirical and contingent fact, to be discovered *a posteriori*.

ALBERT EINSTEIN's theories of relativity have wrenched the metaphysics of space and time away from Kant's common-sense intuitive extrapolation from everyday experience.

Einstein's special relativity has shown that coordinate values in space and time depend on (are relative to) the velocity of the reference frame being used. It raises doubts about whether there is any "preferred" or "absolute" frame of reference in the universe.

And Einstein's theory of general relativity added new properties to space that depend on the overall distribution of matter. He showed that the motion of a material test particle follows a geodesic (the shortest distance between two points) through a curved space, where the curvature is produced by all the other matter in the universe.

At a deep, metaphysical level the standard view of gravitational forces acting between all material particles has been replaced by

This chapter on the web - metaphysicist.com/problems/space

geometry. The abstract immaterial curvature of space-time has the power to influence the motion of a test particle.

It is one thing to say that something as *immaterial* as space itself is just information about the world. It is another to give that immaterial information a kind of power over the material world, a power that depends entirely on the geometry of the environment.

Space and Time in Quantum Physics

For over thirty years, from his 1905 discovery of *nonlocal* phenomena in his *light-quantum hypothesis* as an explanation of the photoelectric effect, until 1935, when he showed that two particles could exhibit nonlocal effects between themselves that ERWIN SCHRÖDINGER called *entanglement*, Einstein was concerned about abstract functions of spatial coordinates that seemed to have a strange power to control the motion of material particles, a power that seemed to him to travel faster than the speed of light, violating his principle of relativity that nothing travels faster than light.

Einstein's first insight into these abstract functions may have started in 1905, but he made it quite clear at the Salzburg Congress in 1909. How exactly does the classical intensity of a light wave control the number of light particles at each point, he wondered.

The classical wave theory assumes that light from a point source travels off as a spherical wave in all directions. But in the photoelectric effect, Einstein showed that all of the energy in a light quantum is available at a single point to eject an electron.

> "The usual conception, that the energy of light is continuously distributed over the space through which it propagates, encounters very serious difficulties when one attempts to explain the photoelectric phenomena... one can conceive of the ejection of electrons by light in the following way. Energy quanta penetrate into the surface layer of the body, and their energy is transformed, at least in part, into kinetic energy of electrons. The simplest way to imagine this is that a light quantum delivers its entire energy to a single electron." [1]

Does the energy spread out as a light wave in space, then somehow collect itself at one point, moving faster than light to do so?

---

1 Einstein (1905) 'A Heuristic Viewpoint on the Production and Transformation of Light,' English translation - *American Journal of Physics*, 33, 5, 367

Einstein already in 1905 saw something *nonlocal* about the photon and saw that there is both a wave aspect and a particle aspect to electromagnetic radiation. In 1909 he emphasized the dualist aspect and described the wave-particle relationship more clearly than it is usually presented today, with all the current confusion about whether photons and electrons are waves or particles or both.

Einstein greatly expanded the 1905 light-quantum hypothesis in his presentation at the Salzburg conference in September, 1909. He argued that the interaction of radiation and matter involves elementary processes that are not reversible, providing a deep insight into the *irreversibility* of natural processes. The irreversibility of matter-radiation interactions can put microscopic statistical mechanics on a firm quantum-mechanical basis.

While *incoming* spherical waves of radiation are mathematically possible, they are not practically achievable and never seen in nature. If outgoing waves are the only ones possible, nature appears to be asymmetric in time. Einstein speculated that the continuous electromagnetic field might be made up of large numbers of discontinuous discrete light quanta - singular points in a field that superimpose collectively to create the wavelike behavior. The parts of a light wave with the greatest intensity would have the largest number of light particles.

Einstein's connection between the wave and the particle is that the wave indicates the probability of finding particles somewhere. The wave is not in any way a particle. It is an abstract field carrying information about the probability of photons in that part of space. Einstein called it a "ghost field" or "guiding field," with a most amazing power over the particles.

The probability amplitude of the wave function includes interference points where the probability of finding a particle is zero! Different null points appear when the second slit in a two-slit experiment is opened. With one slit open, particles are arriving at a given point. Opening a second slit should add more particles to that point in space. Instead it prevents any particles at all from arriving there.

Light falling at a point plus more light gives us no light!

Such is the power of a "ghost field" wave function, carrying only information about probabilities. Abstract information can influence the motions of matter and energy!

We can ask where this information comes from? Similar to the general relativity theory, we find that it is information determined by the distribution of matter nearby, namely the wall with the two slits in it and the location of the particle detection screen.

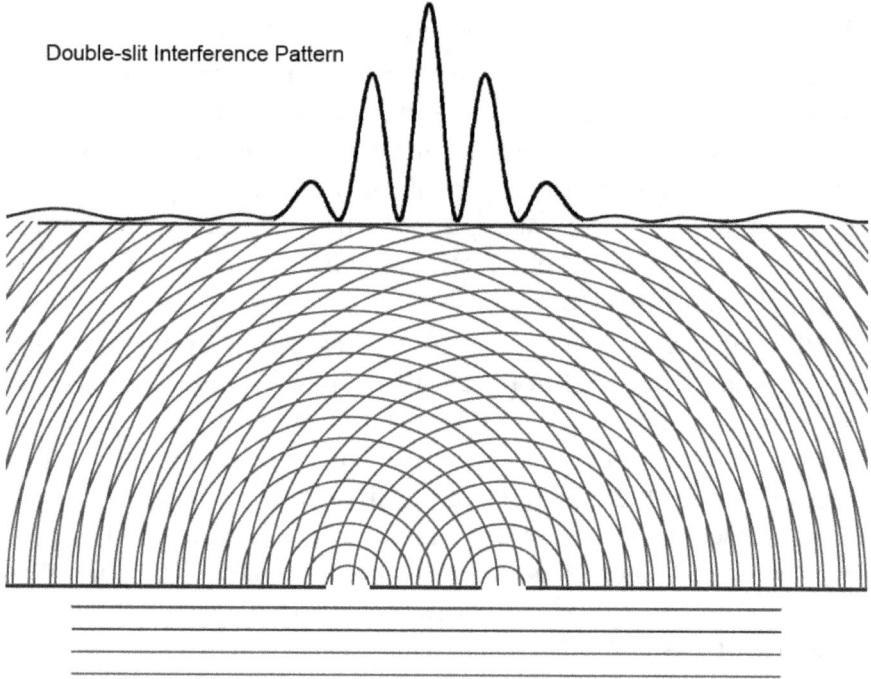

Figure 25-1. The points of constructive and destructive interference depend only on the particle wavelength and the location of the screen and the two slits.

These are the "boundary conditions" which, together with the known wavelength of the incoming monochromatic radiation, tells us the probability of finding particles everywhere, including the null points. Think of the waves above as standing waves.

Einstein might have seen that like his general relativity, the possible paths of a quantum particle are also determined by the spatial geometry. The boundary conditions and the wavelength tell us everything about where particles will be found and not found.

The locations of null points where particles are never found, are all static, given the geometry. They are not moving. The fact that water waves are moving, and his sense that the apparent waves might be matter or energy moving, led Einstein to suspect something is moving faster than light, violating his relativity principle.

But if we see the waves as pure information, mere probabilities, we may resolve a problem that remains today as the greatest problem facing interpretations of quantum mechanics, the idea that special relativity and quantum mechanics cannot be reconciled. Let us see how an information metaphysics might resolve it.

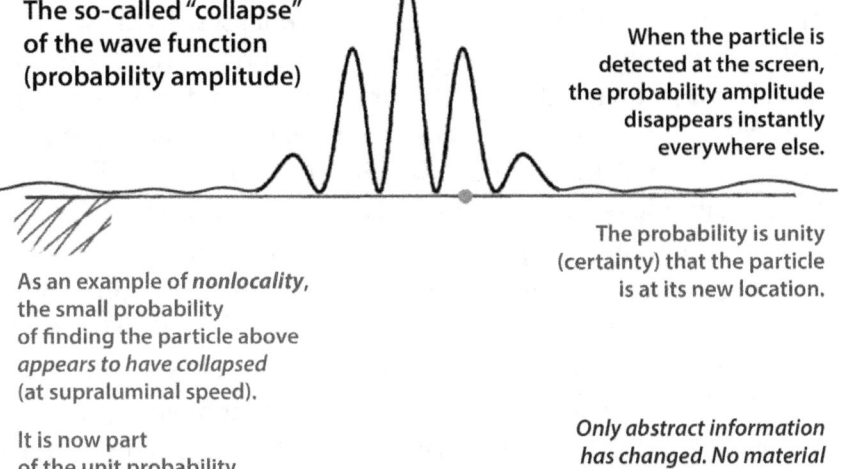

Figure 25-2. The appearance of a "collapse" is because the non-zero values of probability amplitude disappear instantly except where a particle is located.

First we must understand why Einstein thought that something might be moving faster than the speed of light. Then we must show that values of the probability amplitude wave function are static in space. Nothing other than the particles is moving at any speed, let alone faster than light.

Although he had been concerned about this for over two decades, it was at the fifth Solvay conference in 1927 that Einstein went to a blackboard and drew the essential problem shown in the above figure. He clearly says that the square of the wave function $|\psi|^2$ gives us the probability of finding a particle somewhere on the screen.

But Einstein oddly fears some kind of action-at-a-distance is preventing that probability from producing an action elsewhere. He says that "implies to my mind a contradiction with the postulate of relativity."[2] As WERNER HEISENBERG described Einstein's 1927 concern, the experimental detection of the particle at one point exerts a kind of action (reduction of the wave packet) at a distant point.[3] How does the tiny remnant of probability on the left side of the screen "collapse" to the position where the particle is found?

The simple answer is that nothing really "collapses," in the sense of an object like a balloon collapsing, because the probability waves and their null points do not move. There is just an instantaneous change in the probabilities, which happens whenever one possibility among many becomes actualized. That possibility becomes probability one. Other possibilities disappear instantly. Their probabilities become zero, but not because any probabilities move anywhere.

So "collapse" of the wave function is that non-zero probabilities go to zero everywhere, except the point where the particle is found. *Immaterial* information has *changed* everywhere, but not "*moved*."

If nothing but information changes, if no matter or energy moves, then there is no violation of the principle of relativity, and no conflict between relativity and quantum mechanics!

Nonlocality and Entanglement

Since 1905 Einstein had puzzled over information at one place instantly providing information about a distant place. He dramatized this as "spooky action-at-a-distance" in the 1935 Einstein-Podolsky-Rosen thought experiment with two "entangled" particles.

Einstein's simplest such concern was the case of two electrons that are fired apart from a central point with equal velocities, starting at rest so the total momentum is zero. If we measure electron 1 at a certain point, then we immediately have the information that electron 2 is an equal distance away on the other side of the center.

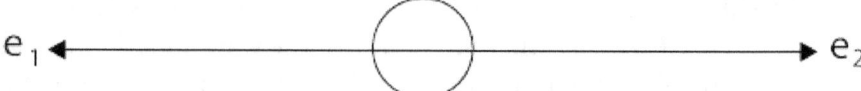

Figure 25-3. Particles separate symmetrically from the center.

---

2   Einstein (1927) *Quantum Theory at the Crossroads: Reconsidering the 1927 Solvay Conference*, G. Bacciagaluppi and A. Valentini, 2009. p.442

3   Heisenberg (1930) *The Physical Principles of the Quantum Theory*, p.39

We have information or knowledge about the second electron's position, not because we are measuring it directly. We are *calculating* its position using the *principle* of the conservation of momentum.

This metaphysical information analysis will be our basis for explaining the EPR "paradox," which is actually not a paradox, because there is really no action-at-a-distance in the sense of matter or energy or even information *moving* from one place to another! It might better be called *"knowledge-at-a-distance."*

Einstein and his colleagues hoped to show that quantum theory could not describe certain intuitive "elements of reality" and thus is *incomplete*. They said that, as far as it goes, quantum mechanics is correct, just not "complete." Einstein was correct that quantum theory is "incomplete" relative to classical physics, which has twice as many dynamical variables that can be known with arbitrary precision. The "complete" information of classical physics gives us the instantaneous position and momentum of every particle in space and time, so we have complete path information. Quantum mechanics does not give us that path information.

For NIELS BOHR and others to deny the incompleteness of quantum mechanics was to play word games, which infuriated Einstein.

Einstein was also correct that indeterminacy makes quantum theory an irreducibly discontinuous and statistical theory. Its predictions and highly accurate experimental results are statistical in that they depend on an ensemble of identical experiments, not on any individual experiment. Einstein wanted physics to be a continuous field theory like relativity, in which all physical variables are completely and locally determined by the four-dimensional field of space-time in his theories of relativity. In classical physics we can have complete path information. In quantum physics we cannot.

Visualizing Entanglement

ERWIN SCHRÖDINGER said that his "wave mechanics" provided more "visualizability" (*Anschaulichkeit*) than the "damned quantum jumps" of the Copenhagen school, as he called them. He was right. We can use his wave function to visualize EPR.

But we must focus on the probability amplitude wave function of the "entangled" two-particle state. We must not attempt to describe the paths or locations of independent particles - at least until after some measurement has been made. We must also keep in mind the conservation laws that Einstein used to describe nonlocal behavior in the first place. Then we can see that the "mystery" of nonlocality for two particles is primarily the same mystery as the single-particle collapse of the wave function. But there is an extra mystery, one we might call an "enigma," that results from the *nonseparability* of identical indistinguishable particles.

RICHARD FEYNMAN said there is only one mystery in quantum mechanics (the superposition of multiple states, the probabilities of collapse into one state, and the consequent statistical outcomes).

> "We choose to examine a phenomenon which is impossible, absolutely impossible, to explain in any classical way, and which has in it the heart of quantum mechanics. In reality, it contains the only mystery. We cannot make the mystery go away by "explaining" how it works. We will just tell you how it works. In telling you how it works we will have told you about the basic peculiarities of all quantum mechanics." [4]

The additional enigma in two-particle nonlocality is that two indistinguishable and nonseparable particles appear simultaneously (in their original interaction frame) when their joint wave function "collapses." There are two particles but only one wave function.

In the time evolution of an entangled two-particle state according to the Schrödinger equation, we can visualize it - as we visualize the single-particle wave function - as collapsing when a measurement is made. Probabilities go to zero except at the particles' two locations.

Quantum theory describes the two electrons as in a superposition of electron spin up states (+) and spin down states (-),

$| \psi > = 1/\sqrt{2}) | + - > - 1/\sqrt{2}) | - + >$

What this means is that when we square the probability amplitude there is a 1/2 chance electron 1 is spin up and electron 2 is spin down. It is equally probable that 1 is down and 2 is up. We simply cannot know. The discontinuous "quantum jump" is also described as the "reduction of the wave packet." This is apt in the two-particle

---

[4] Feynman (1964) *The Feynman Lectures on Physics*, vol III, p.1-1

case, where the superposition of $|+->$ and $|-+>$ states is "projected" or "reduced" by a measurement into one of these states, e.g., $|+->$, and then further reduced - or "*disentangled*" - to the product of independent one-particle states $|+>|->$.

In the two-particle case (instead of just one particle making an appearance), when either particle is measured, we know instantly the now determinate properties of the other particle needed to satisfy the conservation laws, including its location equidistant from, but on the opposite side of, the source. But now we must also satisfy another conservation law, that of the total electron spin.

It is another case of "knowledge-at-a-distance," now about spin. If we measure electron 1 to have spin up, the conservation of electron spin requires that electron 2 have spin down, and instantly.

Just as we do not know their paths and positions of the electron before a measurement, we don't know their spins. But once we know one spin, we instantly know the other. And it is not that anything moved from one particle to "influence" the other.

Can Metaphysics Disentangle the EPR Paradox?

Yes, if the metaphysicist pays careful attention to the information available from moment to moment in space and time. When the EPR experiment starts, the prepared state of the two particles includes the fact that the total linear momentum and the total angular momentum (including electron spin) are zero. This must remain true after the experiment to satisfy conservation laws. These laws are the consequence of extremely deep properties of nature that arise from simple considerations of symmetry.

Physicists regard these laws as "cosmological principles." For the metaphysicist, these laws are metaphysical truths that arise from considerations of symmetry alone. Physical laws do not depend on the absolute place and time of experiments, nor their particular direction in space. Conservation of linear momentum depends on the translation invariance of physical systems, conservation of energy the independence of time, and conservation of angular momentum the invariance of experiments under rotations.

A metaphysicist can see that in his zeal to attack quantum mechanics, Einstein may have introduced an asymmetry into the EPR experiment that simply does not exist. Removing that asymmetry completely resolves any paradox and any conflict between quantum mechanics and special relativity.

To clearly see Einstein's false asymmetry, remember that a "collapse" of a wave function just changes probabilities everywhere into certainties. For a two-particle wave function, any measurement produces information about the particles' two new locations instantaneously. The possibilities of being anywhere that violate conservation principles vanish instantly.

At the moment one electron is located, the other is also located. At that moment, one electron appears in a spacelike separation from the other electron and a causal relation is no longer possible between them. Before the measurement, we know nothing about their positions. Either might have been "here" and the other "there." Immediately after the measurement, they are separated, we know where both are and no communication between them is possible.

Let's focus on Einstein's introduction of the asymmetry in his narrative that isn't there in the physics. It's a great example of going beyond the logic and the language to the underlying information we need to solve both philosophical and physical problems.

Just look at any introduction to the problem of entanglement and nonlocal behavior of two particles. It always starts with something like "We first measure the first particle and then..."

Here is Einstein in his 1949 autobiography...

"There is to be a system which at the time t of our observation consists of two partial systems S_1 and S_2, which at this time are spatially separated and (in the sense of the classical physics) are without significant reciprocity. [Such systems are not entangled!]

All quantum theoreticians now agree upon the following: If I make a complete measurement of S_1, I get from the results of the measurement and from ψ_{12} an entirely definite ψ-function ψ_2 of the system S_2... the real factual situation of the system S_2 is independent of what is done with the system S_1, which is spatially separated from the former." [5]

---

5   Einstein (1949) 'Autobiographical Notes,' *Albert Einstein: Philosopher-Scientist*, Ed. P. A. Schilpp, 1949, p.1, in German and English

But two *entangled* particles are not separable before the measurement. No matter how far apart they may appear *after* the measurement, they are inseparable as long as they are described by a single two-particle wave function ψ_{12} that cannot be the product of two single-particle wave functions. As Schrödinger made clear to Einstein in late 1935, they are only separable *after* they have become *disentangled*, by some interaction with the environment. If ψ_{12} has decohered, it can then be represented by the product of independent ψ-functions $\psi_1 * \psi_2$, and then what Einstein says about independent systems S_1 and S_2 would be entirely correct.

Schrödinger more than once told Einstein these facts about entanglement, but Einstein appears never to have absorbed them.

A proof that neither particle can be measured without instantly determining the other's position is seen by noting that a spaceship moving at high speed from the left sees particle 1 measured before particle 2. A spaceship moving in the opposite direction reverses the time order of the measurements. These two views expose the false asymmetries of assuming either measurement can be made prior to the other. In the *special frame* that is at rest with respect to the center of mass of the particles, the "two" measurements are simultaneous, because there is actually only one measurement "collapsing" the two-particle wave function.

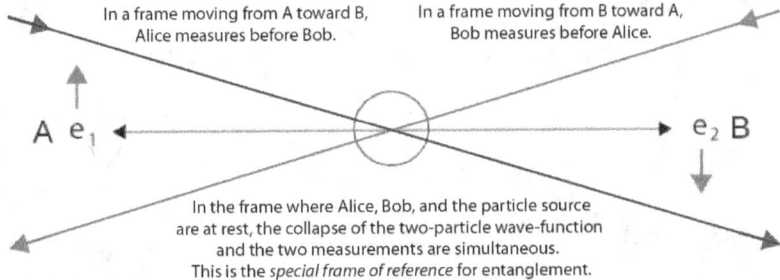

Figure 25-4. The special frame in which the two particles appear time symmetrically is the rest frame of the experiment.

Any measurement collapsing the entangled two-particle wave function affects the two particles instantly and symmetrically. We hope that philosophers and metaphysicians who pride themselves as critical thinkers will be able to explain these information and symmetry implications to physicists who have been tied in knots for so many decades by Einstein's introduction of an unreal asymmetry into the EPR paradox and entanglement.

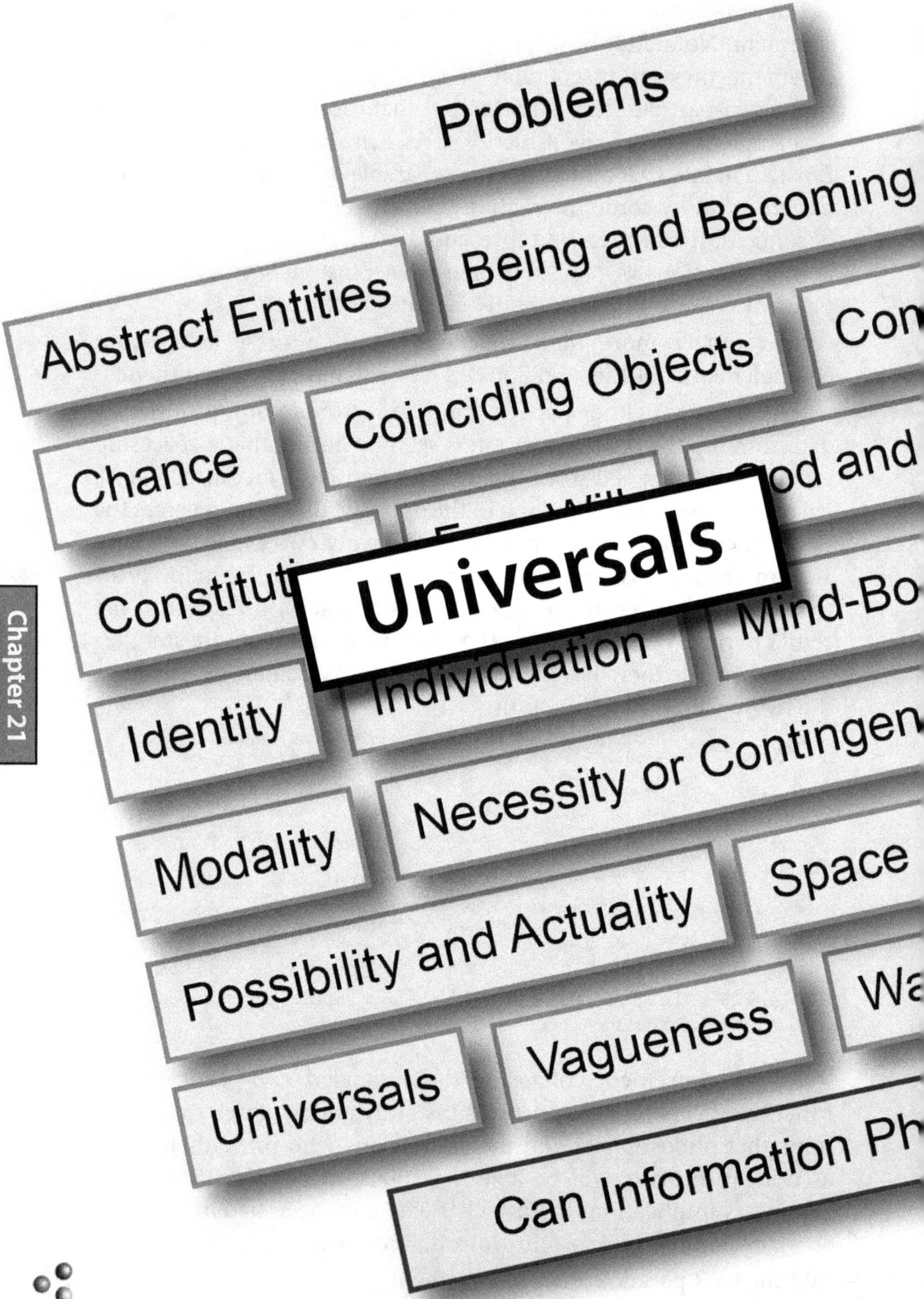

Chapter 21

Metaphysics

Problems

Abstract Entities

Being and Becoming

Coinciding Objects

Chance

Universals

Identity

Modality

Necessity or Contingency

Possibility and Actuality

Vagueness

Universals

Universals

Universals is another name for the Platonic Ideas or Forms. Plato thought these ideas pre-existed the things in the world to which they correspond. For example, a perfect circle is an idea to which any actual circle would only correspond approximately. Aristotle thought the universals were merely general versions of properties found in common in the particular things. Thus the general idea of a horse would be the bundle of common properties that are abstracted from and found in all *particular* horses.

The terminology is a bit confusing because Plato regarded these Ideas as "real" where today we regard the material things as real and the universals, which are purely abstract and immaterial, as ideal. The great problem of the universals has been "do they exist?"

Both Plato and Aristotle have anticipated the information philosophy view of universals. A universal is simply the information which is a limited subset of the common information found in all the particulars.

The great ontological and existential problem of the universals then becomes clear in information philosophy. The tangible existence of an idea depends on it being encoded somewhere, in a mind, in a physical or biological structure, etc. The information encoded might be a mathematical concept, for example a perfect circle as all the points equidistant from a reference point.

The mental abstraction of a universal away from any and all minds remains an issue with two resolutions. First, the universal idea has probably been encoded in human artifacts, books for example, now independent of any particular mind. This is our Sum of all information.

A "universal" in metaphysics is a property or attribute that is shared by many particular objects (or concepts). It has a subtle relationship to the problem of the one and the many.

Second, with Aristotle, we can imagine that many particulars pre-existed any minds and remain in the world in the absence of any mind. They "exist" for any future intelligence to discover.

This chapter on the web - metaphysicist.com/problems/universals

It is also the question of ontology. What exists in the world? Ontology is intimately connected with epistemology, how can we know what exists in the world?

Knowledge about objects consists in describing the objects with properties and attributes, including their relations to other objects. Rarely are individual properties unique to an individual object. Although a "bundle of properties" may uniquely characterize a particular individual, most properties are shared with many individuals.

The "problem of universals" is the existential status of a given shared property. Does the one universal property exist apart from the many instances in particular objects? PLATO thought it does. ARISTOTLE thought it does not.

Consider the property having the color red. Is there an abstract concept of redness or "being red?" Granted the idea of a concept of redness, in what way and where in particular does it exist? Nominalists (sometimes called anti-realists) say that it exists only in the particular instances, and that redness is the name of this property. Conceptualists say that the concept of redness exists only in the minds of those persons who have grasped the concept of redness. They might exclude color-blind persons who cannot perceive red.

Realism is the view that a "reality" of physical objects, and possibly of abstract concepts like redness, exists in an external world independently of our minds and perceptions.

Platonic Realism is the view that abstract things like numbers, perfect geometric figures, and other things that Plato called the Forms or the Ideas, have a real and independent existence, though they are not material objects.

But for his student, Aristotle, these "universals" exist only in the concrete objects which share some property. For him, the universal idea of a perfect circle is a shared property of the many actual circles in nature.

Naive realists think that we can access concrete physical objects directly and fully with our perceptual sense data. This is sometimes called the "copy theory." Our perceptions are fully apprehending the physical objects, so that the content of a perception is the same as the object of perception. In information philosophy terms, naive realism mistakenly assumes that the information in the perceived sense data (or the representation in the mind) is (quantitatively) equal to (a copy of) the information in the physical object. In the case of the abstract concept of redness, it may be that the copy-theory is most tenable. The perception of a red object may in a strong sense bring the concept of redness into existence (at least in the observer's mind).

Historically, realism is a metaphysical claim about this independently existing world where redness might be found. Since Aristotle's *Metaphysics*, two kinds of metaphysical questions (ontological and epistemological) are raised, what exists, and how can we know what exists.

The ontological status of abstract concepts is a completely different question from the ontology of concrete material objects, though these questions have often been confounded in the history of philosophy.

Information philosophy provides distinct answers to these two ontological questions. Material objects exist in the world of space and time. They are information structures embodied in matter and interacting with energy. Abstract concepts (like redness) are pure information, neither matter nor energy, although they need matter for their embodiment and energy for their communication.

The contrast between physical objects and abstract concepts can be illustrated by the difference between invention and discovery.

We discover physical objects through our perceptions of them. To be sure, we invent our ideas about these objects, their descriptions, their names, theories of how they are structured and how they interact energetically, with one another and with us. But we cannot arbitrarily invent the natural world. We must test our theories with experiment. The experimental results select those theories that best fit the data, the information coming to us from the world. This makes our knowledge of an independent external world scientific knowledge.

By contrast, we humans invent abstract concepts like redness. We know that these cultural constructs exist nowhere in nature as physical structures. We create them. Cultural knowledge is relative to and dependent on the society that creates it.

However, some of our invented abstract concepts seem to clearly have an existence that is independent of us, like the numbers and the force of gravity.

Critical realists, like scientists, start with observations and sense data, but they add hypotheses and experiments to develop theories about the physical objects and the abstract concepts in the external world. Nevertheless, the abstract representation in the mind is (quantitatively) much less information than the information in the physical object represented.

Universals generally contain miniscule amounts of information when compared to material objects which instantiate the property.

The idea of an independent reality claims that the reality known exists independently of the knowledge of it. And we can say that the *Sum* of human knowledge, the world of ideas, is a miniscule amount of information compared to that in the material world.

The British empiricists JOHN LOCKE and DAVID HUME argued that what we were "given" in our perceptions of sense data is limited to so-called "secondary qualities." These are properties that produce the sensations in the observer's senses - color, taste, smell, sound, and touch. Knowledge that comes from secondary qualities does not provide objective facts about things "in themselves."

IMMANUEL KANT described these secondary qualities as "phenomena" that could tell us nothing about the "noumena," which the empiricists called the "primary qualities." These are properties the objects have that are independent of any observer, such as solidity, extension, motion, number and figure. These qualities exist in the thing itself (Kant's *"Ding an sich"*). Kant thought that some of these qualities can be determined with certainty, as *"synthetic a priori"* truths. Some of these qualities are analytic truths, defined by the logical meanings of linguistic terms. For example, a round circle cannot be a square.

The One and the Many

Is there just one basic category that contains everything? Some philosophers are monists, arguing that the world must be a unity, one unchanging thing, and that all the multiplicity and change that we see is mere illusion.

Some are dualists, puzzled how the *immaterial* One (usually Mind or the Ideal) can possibly interact with the *material* Many (the Body or the World). There are other kinds of dualists, but the idealism/materialism divide has a long history in philosophy under dozens of different names through the ages.[1]

Monists, with their claim that "All is One," generally reduce the physical world to the ideal world, or vice versa. "Neutral monists" argue that the ideal and physical worlds are somehow both something else. But note the underlying dualism that remains in these monistic claims.

Some philosophers prefer triads, triplicities, or trinities as their fundamental structures, and in these we may find the most sensible way to divide the world as we know it into "worlds," realms, or orders.

Those who divide their philosophy into four usually arrange it two by two (Schopenhauer, Heidegger, Derrida - who did it in jest, and against Christian trinities). There are a few who think a pentad has explanatory power. Another handful look to the mystical seven (the number of planets and thus days of the week) for understanding.

Since the Pythagoreans drew their triangular diagram of the tetractus, ten has been a divine number for some. Aristotle found ten categories. The neo-Platonist Kabalists have ten sephiroth. In string theory, there are ten dimensions reflecting the components of Einstein's general relativity equations.

Kant, the most important philosopher since Aristotle, structured his architectonic into twelve categories, arranged four by three.

---

1   See chapter 9 of *Great Problems in Philosophy and Physics*.

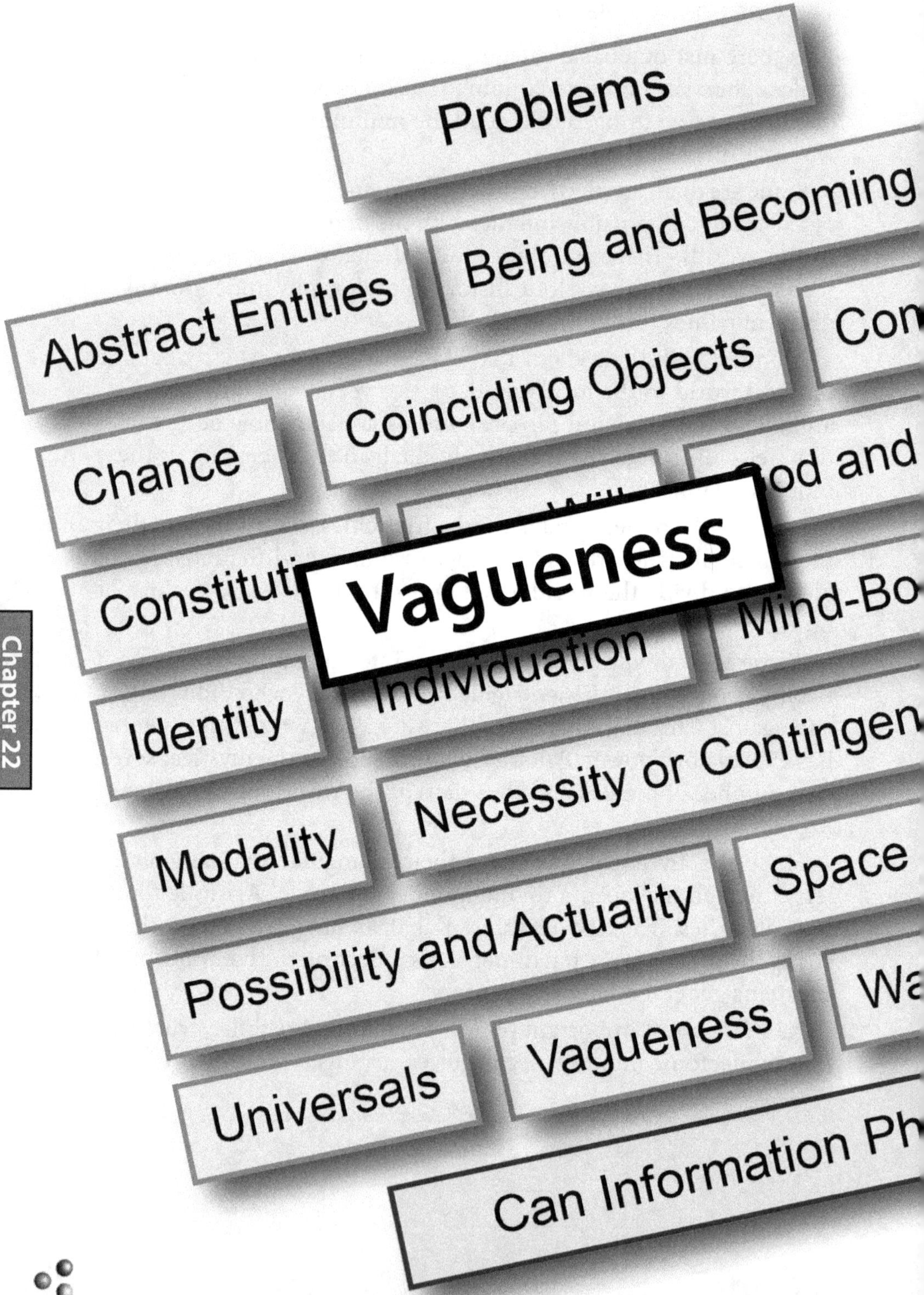
Problems
Being and Becoming
Abstract Entities
Coinciding Objects
Chance
Constituti
Vagueness
Mind-Bo
Individuation
Identity
Necessity or Contingen
Modality
Space
Possibility and Actuality
Universals
Vagueness
Can Information Ph

Vagueness

Vagueness of meaning was a concern in analytic language philosophy long before it referred to the fuzzy boundaries of material objects that led to PETER UNGER's "Problem of the Many."

Unger's vagueness comes from the lack of any precise boundary for a cloud in the sky,

> "as science seems clearly to say, our clouds are almost wholly composed of tiny water droplets, and the dispersion of these droplets, in the sky or the atmosphere, is always, in fact, a gradual matter. With pretty much any route out of even a comparatively clean cloud's center, there is no stark stopping place to be encountered. Rather, anywhere near anything presumed a boundary, there's only a gradual decrease in the density of droplets fit, more or less, to be constituents of a cloud that's there." [1]

The quantifiable information in any physical object far exceeds the amount that is picked out by human perceptions or conceptions of what the object is. A similar problem exists for an ideal or fictional object, especially as represented in human language, because of the fecundity of the human mind to imagine variations in meaning.

In our quest to understand the fundamental nature of reality, our understanding of quantum physics shows that the most microscopic objects have an irreducible vagueness in the form of Heisenberg's uncertainty principle. The wave function is a probabilistic estimate of the possible locations for finding a particle. The possible locations are virtually infinite compared to the particle size. We might say that quantum objects have the highest degree of metaphysical vagueness known.

In his 1975 article, "Vagueness, Truth, and Logic," KIT FINE gave specific examples of different types of vagueness in analytic language philosophy:

---

[1] Unger () 'Mental Problems of the Many.' *Oxford Studies in Metaphysics*, 23, Chapter 8. p.197.

"Suppose that the meaning of the natural number predicates, nice1, nice2, and nice3, is given by the following clauses:

(1) (a) n is nice1 if n > 15

(b) n is not nice1 if n < 13

(2) (a) n is nice2 if and only if n > 15

(b) n is nice2 if and only if n > 14

(3) n is nice3 if and only if n > 15

Clause (1) is reminiscent of Carnap's (1952) meaning postulates. Clauses (2) (a)-(b) are not intended to be equivalent to a single contradictory clause; somehow the separate clauses should be insulated from one an other. Then nice1 is vague, its meaning is under-determined; nice2 is ambiguous, its meaning is over-determined; and nice3 is highly general or un-specific. The sentence 'there are infinitely many nice3 twin primes' is possibly undecidable but certainly not vague or ambiguous." [2]

In the 1980 third edition of his *Reference and Generality*, PETER GEACH, asked how many hairs of a cat are essential to its identity.[3]

Perhaps the classic example of vagueness, in the sense of borderline cases which are transitions between relatively well-defined cases, is the Sorites paradox.[4]

The concept of vagueness as an intrinsic problem rooted in the ambiguity and contextuality of language alone was most clearly stated by Charles Sanders Peirce in 1902,

"A proposition is vague when there are possible states of things concerning which it is intrinsically uncertain whether, had they been contemplated by the speaker, he would have regarded them as excluded or allowed by the proposition. By *intrinsically uncertain* we mean not uncertain in consequence of any ignorance of the interpreter, but because the speaker's habits of language were indeterminate." [5]

---

[2] Fine (1975) 'Vagueness, truth and logic.' *Synthese* 30.3 (1975): 265-300.

[3] See Peter Geach in chapter 36.

[4] See chapter 32 for more details.

[5] Peirce (1902) *Dictionary of Philosophy and Psychology*, J.M. Baldwin (ed.), New York: MacMillan, p. 748.

Some "epistemicists" think that vagueness is caused by human ignorance. They often hold the related view that chance is not ontological, but only the result of human ignorance.

But as the Sorites paradox shows, there is no deductive or inductive logic that can establish the borderline case. It is not ignorance. It is, as Peirce says, intrinsic to the lack of a unique and determinate threshold case. While there is no connection with language, the indeterminate nature of physical boundaries or borderlines is related to the ontological nature of chance and possibilities.

Vagueness and the Two-Slit Experiment

We can define vagueness precisely as the volume of space around a particle trajectory where the square of the quantum wave function (we call this the "possibilities function") has a significant non-zero value. This is the volume where there is some probability of finding the particle.

When that vague probability spreads out so as to hit both slits, the famous interference pattern appears on the distant screen. If the non-zero probability, the vagueness, is narrowed or focussed to fall onto just one of the two slits, the interference pattern disappears. It is the information in the abstract probability that interferes with itself in the two-slit experiment.

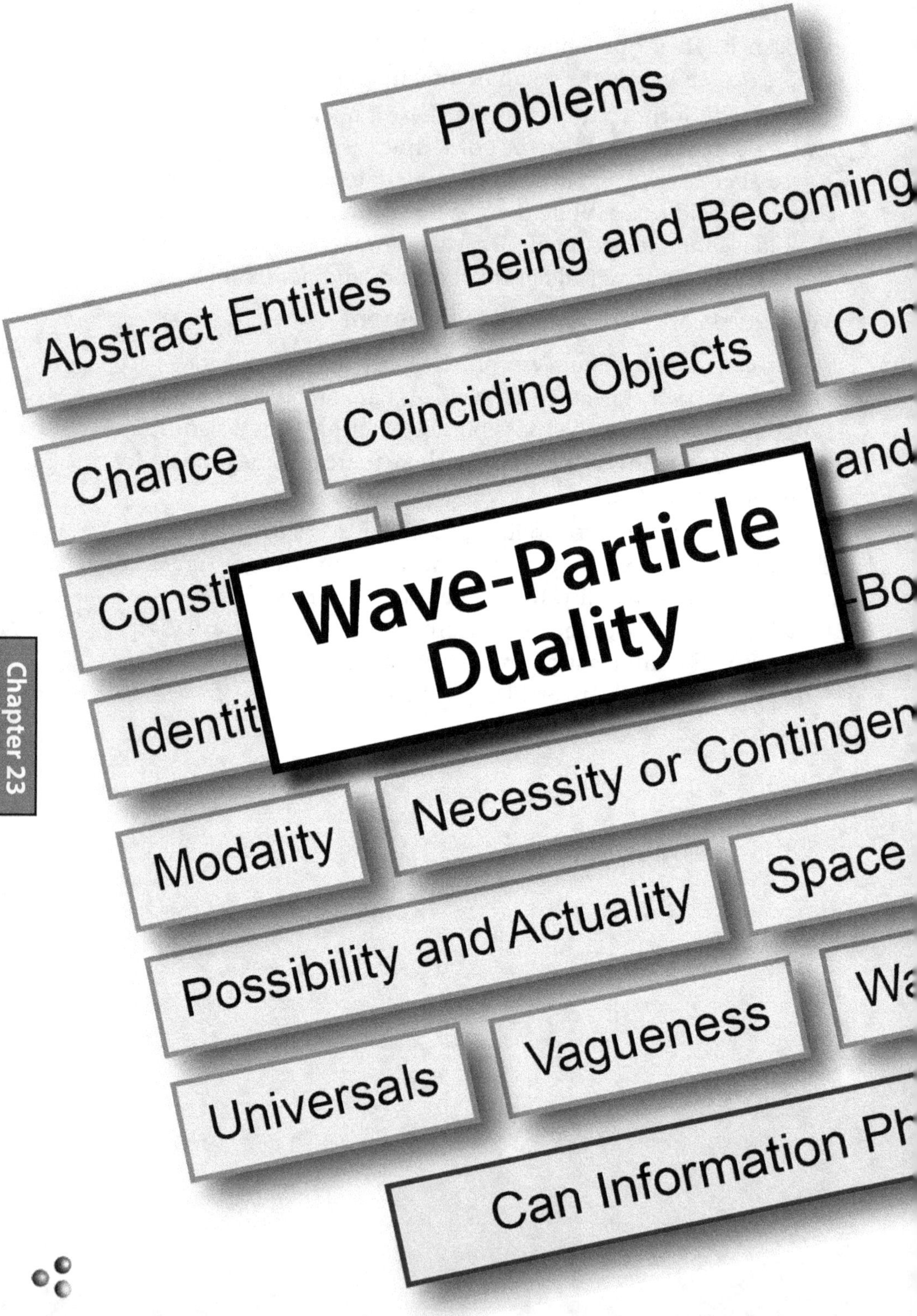
Problems
Being and Becoming
Abstract Entities
Coinciding Objects
Chance
Wave-Particle Duality
Modality
Possibility and Actuality
Vagueness
Universals

Chapter 23

Wave-Particle Duality

Of all the mysteries, puzzles, and paradoxes associated with modern physics, none is more profoundly metaphysical than the strange connection between waves and particles in quantum mechanics. And no philosophical method is better positioned to provide a metaphysical explanation than information philosophy, with an information analysis of the physics and the fundamental nature of physical reality, the so-called "quantum reality."

Most surprisingly, the solution to this most modern of scientific problems throws new light on perhaps the oldest philosophical problem, the ancient question about the existential status of ideas, and the relation between the ideal and the material.

Put most simply, the quantum wave function is an idea, pure information about the possible places that matter may be found. And perhaps most shocking, we can show that this abstract idea has causal power over the paths of the concrete particles, even as we can only learn about their paths statistically and not individually.

We present our solution with a historical view of the problem through the eyes of ALBERT EINSTEIN, who worried for decades about fundamental conflicts between quantum theory and his theories of special and general relativity. Using his thinking, we shall resolve the conflict with special relativity and show that in quantum mechanics the distribution of matter in space plays a role somewhat analogous to its role in general relativity, specifically, space having an influence on the motion of particles of matter.

No one understood wave-particle duality better than Einstein. Nevertheless, no one was more misunderstood than Einstein, by both his opponents and by his most avid supporters. No one thought about the problem longer. For over three decades from 1905 until 1935, Einstein had critical new insights into waves and particles that are today central parts of quantum mechanics. By comparison, the work of Einstein's opponents, the supposed "founders of quantum mechanics," was done in less than three years, from 1925 to 1927, and their theories have left scientists

This chapter on the web - metaphysicist.com/problems/wave-particle and philosophers with a tangled mess and dozens of conflicting "interpretations of quantum mechanics," all of them attempts to replace the original and muddled "Copenhagen interpretation."

The Heart of the Puzzle

Can something be, at one and the same time, both a discrete discontinuous particle (WERNER HEISENBERG) and a continuous wave field (ERWIN SCHRÖDINGER)?

The answer is similar to the solution we proposed for several ancient metaphysical paradoxes - something can be both a concrete substance and an *immaterial* form, both material and ideal.

In chapter 17 we contrasted necessity and contingency. We associated necessity with determinism and the logically *a priori*, contingency with chance and the *a posteriori*.

We can now say that the wave aspect of a quantum is perfectly deterministic and the particle aspect is fundamentally random.

For the quantum physicist doing calculations, it is always *either* a wave or a particle. The time evolution of a quantum system, an electron or a photon, for example, proceeds in two stages, similar in many ways to our two-stage model of free will. (Particles do not have a will, but, like humans, they are free, not pre-determined.)

The first wave stage is when the wave function explores all the *possibilities* available, given the configuration of surrounding particles, especially those nearby, which represent the boundary conditions used to solve the Schrödinger equation of motion for the wave function. Because the space where the possibilities are non-zero is large, we say that the wave function (or "possibilities function") is *nonlocal*. The time evolution of the possibilities function is completely deterministic.

The second stage is when a particle is found somewhere. An observer can not gain any empirical knowledge unless new information is irreversibly recorded, e.g., a particle has been localized in the experimental apparatus. This second stage is when the particle interacts with the apparatus' particles, leaving a record of its interaction. One of the nonlocal *possibilities* has then been "*actualized.*" The particle is now localized, but the new position is completely random, anywhere the possibilities function is non-zero..

Note that when particles are observed, they are totally localized. They are never found partly here, partly there.

When you hear or read that electrons are *both* waves and particles, you can operationally think "either-or" - first information in a wave of *possible* locations, then an *actual* particle location.

Think of the paradox or perhaps the irony in this temporal sequence. First, the possible positions evolve through space *deterministically*. The *average* position actually follows a classical path, just as the average behavior of large numbers of quantum particles approaches classical behavior. We call this "adequate determinism."

But then the actual position where an individual particle is found is *indeterministic*. The time that a radioactive particle decays is completely random. The time and direction a photon is emitted by an atom is the result of ontological chance, as Einstein first saw in 1916.

Many critics of quantum theory complain that these two aspects are logically contradictory. They may be antithetical, but they are not contradictory. Probabilities are determined, but the possibilities that are actualized are the result of ontological chance.

Let's now ask what it is that determines the evolution of the wave or "possibilities" function. Since we argue that the wave function is pure information, we must ask where does that information come from? What information in the physical world leads to the information about possible physical locations for particles?

The answer is quite simple. It depends only on the wavelength of the particle and the boundary conditions of the experiment. In the case of the two-slit experiment, boundary conditions are the wall with two slits and the detection screen.

But this has profound implications. Questions like which slit did the particle go through? or how does the particle going through slit A know that slit B is open?, can now be answered clearly.

The interference conditions that produce maxima and minima (even null points) in the number of particles found are present in the space where the particles will be allowed to travel.

Thinking temporally, the probability amplitudes and the possibilities function are present in the space before any particle arrives, determined by the particle wavelength and the spatial geometry.

We can note a loose parallel with Einstein's general relativity, which reimagines dynamical forces as the spatial curvature caused by the overall matter distribution. Particles are determined to follow shortest-distance paths (geodesics) that are present in space.

In our information analysis of quantum mechanics, particles follow paths determined by the probabilities function present in space, which is determined by material boundary conditions.

In both relativity and quantum mechanics, information present in space has a *causal* influence on the motion of material objects.

This is far from a reconciliation of quantum mechanics with general relativity. That requires giving up Einstein's field picture, with physical objects described by classical variables that depend only on local coordinates in his four-dimensional space-time continuum. Reconciliation means a replacement of continuous fields with a particles picture that has nonlocal and statistical behaviors.

Einstein knew that his dream of a unified field theory may not be possible. In 1949 he asked about the theoretical foundation of physics, "Will it be a field theory [or] will it be a statistical theory?"

But our information picture does reconcile quantum mechanics with special relativity, which was Einstein's earliest concern about nonlocality. The mistaken idea that the wave *is* in any sense the particle leads to the false belief that something (matter or energy, or at least a signal) must move when the wave function "collapses."

In our information analysis, all the information needed for quantum interference effects is already present in the space itself, e.g., the "knowledge" that slit B is open. With slit B closed, particles are distributed one way. With both slits open, positions on the screen that had particles with only A open, now have no particles.

The pure information about boundary conditions for waves in space is influencing the motion of material particles. But no part of the probability wave amplitude or the possibilities function has to move to the point where a particle is found, as was shown in Figure 20-2 of chapter 20. The interference pattern depends only on the particle wavelength and the boundary conditions, not on the moving particle. We can think of it as a standing wave.

Wave-Particle Duality

The History of Waves and Particles

That a light wave might actually be composed of quanta (later called *photons*) was first proposed by Einstein as his "light-quantum hypothesis." He wrote in 1905:

> In accordance with the assumption to be considered here, the energy of a light ray spreading out from a point source is not continuously distributed over an increasing space but consists of a finite number of energy quanta which are localized at points in space, which move without dividing, and which can only be produced and absorbed as whole units.[1]

On the modern quantum view, what spreads out to fill space is a "nonlocal" wave of probability amplitude, which gives the possibilities for absorption, followed by a whole photon actually being absorbed ("localized") somewhere.

In 1909, Einstein speculated about the connection between wave and particle views:

> When light was shown to exhibit interference and diffraction, it seemed almost certain that light should be considered a wave...A large body of facts shows undeniably that light has certain fundamental properties that are better explained by Newton's emission theory of light than by the oscillation theory. For this reason, I believe that the next phase in the development of theoretical physics will bring us a theory of light that can be considered a fusion of the oscillation and emission theories...
>
> Even without delving deeply into theory, one notices that our theory of light cannot explain certain fundamental properties of phenomena associated with light. Why does the color of light, and not its intensity, determine whether a certain photochemical reaction occurs? Why is light of short wavelength generally more effective chemically than light of longer wavelength? Why is the speed of photoelectrically produced cathode rays independent of the light's intensity? Why are higher temperatures (and, thus, higher molecular energies) required to add a short-wavelength component to the radiation emitted by an object?
>
> The fundamental property of the oscillation theory that engenders these difficulties seems to me the following. In the kinetic

---

1   Einstein (1905) "A Heuristic Viewpoint on the Production and Transformation of Light," *Annalen der Physik*, vol.17, p.133, English translation - *American Journal of Physics*, 33, 5, p.368

theory of molecules, for every process in which only a few elementary particles participate (e.g., molecular collisions), the inverse process also exists. But that is not the case for the elementary processes of radiation.

According to our prevailing theory, an oscillating ion generates a spherical wave that propagates outwards. The inverse process does not exist as an elementary process. A converging spherical wave is mathematically possible, to be sure; but to approach its realization requires a vast number of emitting entities. The elementary process of emission is not invertible. In this, I believe, our oscillation theory does not hit the mark. Newton's emission theory of light seems to contain more truth with respect to this point than the oscillation theory since, first of all, the energy given to a light particle is not scattered over infinite space, but remains available for an elementary process of absorption.[2]

Here Einstein sees the emission and absorption of radiation as *irreversible*. This microscopic irreversibility explains the macroscopic irreversibility of statistical mechanics and thermodynamics.[3]

Dueling Wave and Particle Theories

Not only do we have the problem of understanding wave-particle duality in a quantum system, we have a full-blown wave mechanics theory (de Broglie and Schrödinger) versus a particle mechanics theory (Heisenberg, Max Born, Pascual Jordan).

Before either of these theories was developed in the mid-1920's, Einstein in 1909 showed how both wave-like and particle-like behaviors are seen in light quanta, and in 1916 that the emission of light is done at random times and in random directions. This was the introduction of ontological chance (*Zufall*) into physics, over a decade before Heisenberg announced in his "uncertainty principle" paper of 1927 that quantum mechanics is *acausal*.

As late as 1917, Einstein felt very much alone in believing the reality (his emphasis) of light quanta:

"I do not doubt anymore the *reality* of radiation quanta, although I still stand quite alone in this conviction." [4]

---

2   Einstein (1909) 'On the Development of Our Views Concerning the Nature and Constitution of Radiation,' Phys. Zeit 10: 817.
3   See chapter 25 of *Great Problems of Philosophy and Physics*.
4   Einstein (1917a) quoted by Abraham Pais," "Subtle is the Lord...", p.411

Einstein in 1916 had just derived his A and B coefficients describing the absorption, spontaneous emission, and (his newly predicted) stimulated emission of radiation. In two papers, "Emission and Absorption of Radiation in Quantum Theory," and "On the Quantum Theory of Radiation," he derived the Planck law (for Planck it was mostly a guess at the formula to fit observations), he derived Planck's postulate E = hv, and he derived Bohr's second postulate

$E_m - E_n = hv$.

Einstein did this by exploiting the obvious relationship between the Maxwell-Boltzmann distribution of gas particle velocities and the distribution of radiation in Planck's law. He wrote in 1917:

> The formal similarity between the chromatic distribution curve for thermal radiation and the Maxwell velocity-distribution law is too striking to have remained hidden for long. In fact, it was this similarity which led W. Wien, some time ago, to an extension of the radiation formula in his important theoretical paper, in which he derived his displacement law...Not long ago I discovered a derivation of Planck's formula which was closely related to Wien's original argument and which was based on the fundamental assumption of quantum theory. This derivation displays the relationship between Maxwell's curve and the chromatic distribution curve and deserves attention not only because of its simplicity, but especially because it seems to throw some light on the mechanism of emission and absorption of radiation by matter, a process which is still obscure to us.[5]

But the introduction of Maxwell-Boltzmann statistical mechanical thinking to electromagnetic theory has produced what Einstein called a "weakness in the theory." It introduces the reality of an irreducibly objective and ontological chance!

Einstein saw that if light quanta are particles with energy $E = hv$ traveling at the velocity of light c, then they should have a momentum $p = E/c = hv/c$. When light is *absorbed* by a material particle, this momentum will clearly be transferred to the particle. But when light is *emitted* by an atom or molecule, a problem appears.

---

5   Einstein (1917) 'On the Quantum Theory of Radiation,' *Sources of Quantum Mechanics*, B. L. van der Waerden, Dover, 1967, p.63; *Physikalische Zeitschrift*, 18, pp.121–128, 1917

Conservation of momentum requires that the momentum of the emitted particle will cause an atom to recoil with momentum $h\nu/c$ in the opposite direction. However, the standard theory of spontaneous emission of radiation is that it produces a spherical wave going out in all directions. A spherically symmetric wave has no preferred direction. It can not cause a recoil.

> In which direction does the atom recoil?, Einstein asked:
> "Does the molecule receive an impulse when it absorbs or emits the energy ε? For example, let us look at emission from the point of view of classical electrodynamics. When a body emits the radiation ε it suffers a recoil (momentum) ε/c if the entire amount of radiation energy is emitted in the same direction. If, however, the emission is a spatially symmetric process, e.g., a spherical wave, no recoil at all occurs. This alternative also plays a role in the quantum theory of radiation. When a molecule absorbs or emits the energy ε in the form of radiation during the transition between quantum theoretically possible states, then this elementary process can be viewed either as a completely or partially directed one in space, or also as a symmetrical (nondirected) one. It turns out that we arrive at a theory that is free of contradictions, only if we interpret those elementary processes as completely directed processes." [6]

An outgoing light particle must impart momentum $h\nu/c$ to the atom or molecule, but the direction of the momentum can not be predicted! Neither can the theory predict the time when the light quantum will be emitted.

Such a random time was not unknown to physics. When ERNEST RUTHERFORD derived the law for radioactive decay of unstable atomic nuclei in 1902, he could only give the probability of decay times. Einstein saw the connection with radiation emission:

> "It speaks in favor of the theory that the statistical law assumed for [spontaneous] emission is nothing but the Rutherford law of radioactive decay." [7]

But the inability to predict both the time and the direction of light particle emissions, said Einstein in 1917, is "a weakness in the theory..., that it leaves time and direction of elementary processes to chance (*Zufall*)." It is only a weakness for Einstein, of course, because his God does not play dice.

---

6   Einstein (1917) 'On the Quantum Theory of Radiation,' p.65
7   Pais (1982) *Subtle is the Lord...* p.411

Einstein clearly saw in 1917 as none of his contemporaries did for many years, that since spontaneous emission is a statistical process, it cannot possibly be described with classical physics.

> "The properties of elementary processes required...make it seem almost inevitable to formulate a truly quantized theory." [8]

In his paper on the A and B coefficients (transition probabilities) for the emission and absorption of radiation, Einstein carried through his attempt to understand the Planck law. He confirmed that light behaves like waves (notably when a great number of particles are present and for low energies), at other times like the particles of a gas (for few particles and high energies).

Dirac on Wave-Particle Duality

> "Quantum mechanics is able to effect a reconciliation of the wave and corpuscular properties of light. The essential point is the association of each of the translational states of a photon with one of the wave functions of ordinary wave optics. The nature of this association cannot be pictured on a basis of classical mechanics, but is something entirely new. It would be quite wrong to picture the photon and its associated wave as interacting in the way in which particles and waves can interact in classical mechanics. The association can be interpreted only statistically, the wave function giving us information about the probability of our finding the photon in any particular place when we make an observation of where it is." [9]

Note that the information about the possibility of a photon at a given point does not have to be "knowledge" for some conscious observer. It is statistical information about the photon, even if it is never observed or recorded. Many years before the "founding" of quantum mechanics, Einstein realized that the connexion between light waves and photons has a statistical character. The wave function gives information about the probability of one photon being in a particular place. and not just the probable number of photons in that place. Einstein described this as "incomplete," when compared to classical mechanics, which it of course is.

Schrödinger agreed that the light wave at some point is the probable number of photons there. MAX BORN's "statistical interpretation" (the "Born Rule") simply extended Einstein's idea to electrons.

---

8   Pais, *ibid*.
9   Dirac (1930) *Principles of Quantum Mechanics*, 4th ed., Chapter 1, p.9

Chapter 24

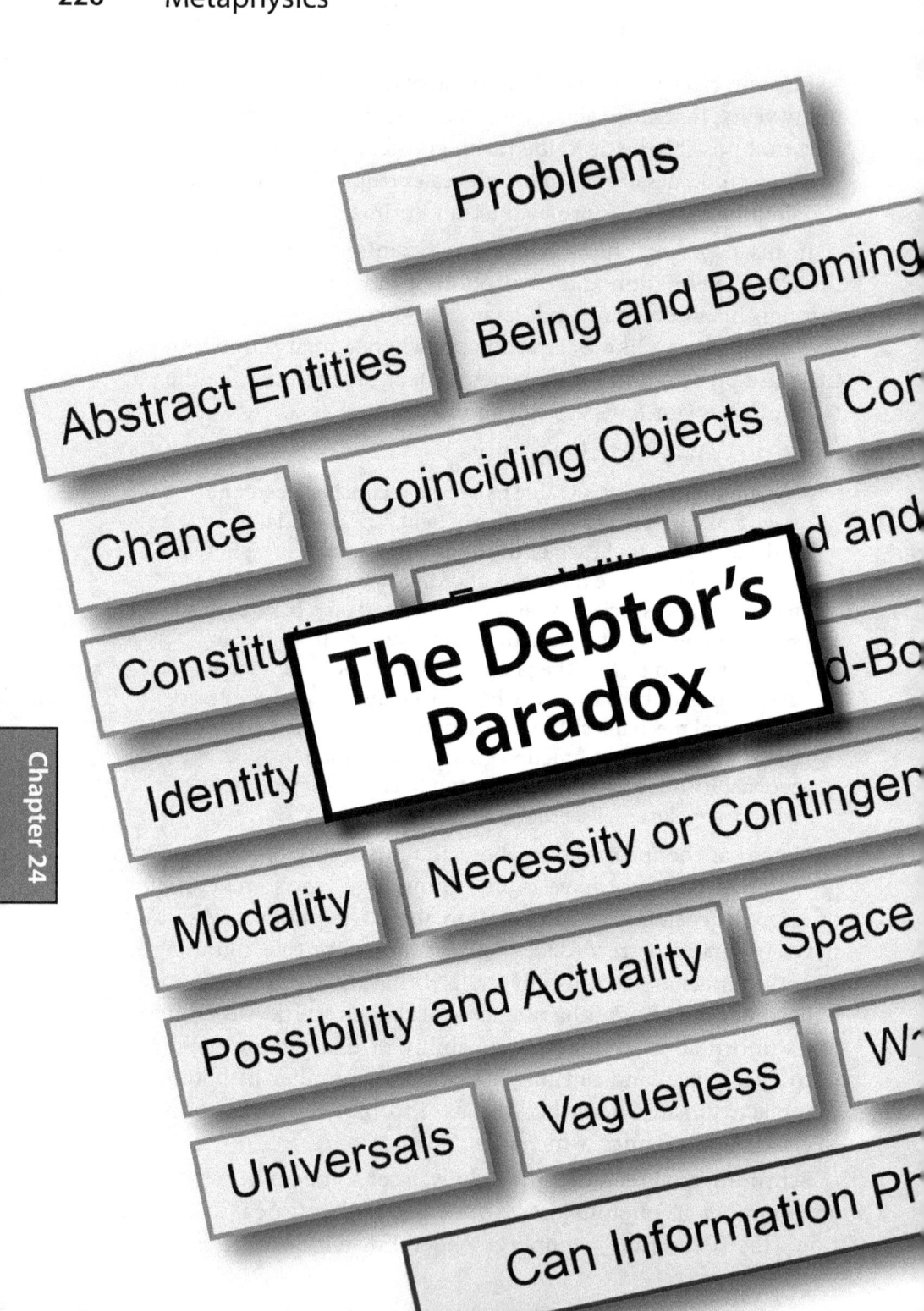

The Debtor's Paradox

EPICHARMUS of Syracuse (*fl*, 500-460 BCE) was one of the authors of early Greek comedies. He may have studied briefly with PYTHAGORAS. In one of his plays he used the ideas of HERACLITUS, that everything is in flux, all is change. If you can't step into the same river twice, he proposed that perhaps you are not the same person today that you were yesterday?

One of Epicharmus' comedies introduced a man who wants to break his contract with a lender on the grounds that he is not the same man that made the contract. The lender beats the debtor, who sues the lender for assault. When called before the courts, the lender uses the same argument, that he is now not the same as the person who committed the assault.

Modern metaphysicians also question the intrinsic connection between our "temporal parts." Are our bodies newly created at every instant? Can there be a principle of individuation that preserves our identity over time?[1]

Plutarch says that some Sophists used the Heraclitean doctrine of change to prove that a man who borrowed money in the past does not owe it in the present. In his Theaetetus (152D-E, 160D), Plato cites Epicharmus as saying "nothing is, but everything becomes" and that he and Homer are the founders of the Heraclitean tradition.

The Stoics opposed the ancient "Growing Argument" (*auxanomenos logos*), still being debated by the Academic Skeptics, that matter is the sole principle of individuation, so that any change of matter constitutes a change of identity.

The Stoics therefore anticipate the modern view of some (but not all) metaphysicians that material constitution is not identity.

The classicist DAVID SEDLEY reconstructed the debtor's paradox as follows, and why it had to wait for the Stoic era and Chrysippus for full resolution of the Growing Argument:

---

[1] See chapters 13 and 14 on identity and individuation.

"The story starts with a scene from an early Greek comedy. Its author is the Syracusan comic playwright Epicharmus, and it probably dates from the opening decades of the fifth century B.C. The following reconstruction is based on one verbatim quotation of twelve lines, plus two indirect references to it in later authors.

Character A is approached by Character B for payment of his subscription to the running expenses of a forthcoming banquet. Finding himself out of funds, he resorts to asking B the following riddle: 'Say you took an odd number of pebbles, or if you like an even number, and chose to add or subtract a pebble: do you think it would still be the same number?'

'No,' says B.

'Or again, say you took a measure of one cubit and chose to add, or cut off, some other length: that measure would no longer exist, would it?'

'No.'

'Well now,' continues A, 'think of men in the same way. One man is growing, another is diminishing, and all are constantly in the process of change. But what by its nature changes and never stays put must already be different from what it has changed from. You and I are different today from who we were yesterday, and by the same argument we will be different again and never the same in the future.'

B agrees. A then concludes that he is not the same man who contracted the debt yesterday, nor indeed the man who will be attending the banquet. In that case he can hardly be held responsible for the debt. B, exasperated, strikes A a blow. A protests at this treatment. But this time it is B who neatly sidesteps the protest, by pointing out that by now he is somebody quite different from the man who struck the blow a minute ago.

To subsequent generations, the argument used in this scene read like a remarkable anticipation of a philosophical doctrine associated with the names of Heraclitus and Plato, that of the radical instability of the physical world; and Plato himself was pleased to acknowledge such evidence of the doctrine's antiquity. But although the puzzle is a serious challenge to ordinary assumptions about identity, never in the fourth century

B.C., the era of Plato and Aristotle, does it meet with a proper philosophical analysis and repudiation. That is not to say that materials for answering it cannot be found in Aristotle's metaphysical writings.

My point is that it was not until the generation after Aristotle, with the emergence of the Stoic school, that the solution of such puzzles became an absolutely central route to philosophical discovery. This fact is becoming a familiar one with regard to Stoic logic, but very much less so when it comes to their metaphysics. In fact, the story which I shall be piecing together in this paper has as far as I know featured in none of the modem reconstructions of Stoic philosophy.

An especially important historical fact here is that when the Stoic school emerged in Athens at the opening of the third century B.C. there sprang up alongside it a dialectical gadfly, a new generation of radical sceptics, under the leadership of Arcesilaus, who had seized the reins of power in Plato's old school, the Academy. For the next two centuries every philosophical move by the Stoics was liable to be covered and challenged by these Academics, and Stoic theories were constantly designed and redesigned to circumvent the attacks. Many of the Academic countermoves exploited philosophical puzzles, some of which have remained classics." [2]

There is very little sign that modern metaphysicians have understood Stoic thinking well enough to see that they contain the solutions of these ancient puzzles if one interprets their "peculiarly qualified individuals" as *immaterial* information, as mental properties, rather than matter.

Information Philosophy Resolves the Debtor's Paradox

Most of our metaphysical puzzles start with a single object, then separate it into its matter and its form, giving each of them names and declaring them to be two coinciding objects. Next we postulate a change in either the matter or the form, or both. It is of course impossible to make a change in one without the other changing, since we in fact have only one object.

---

[2] Sedley (1982) 'The Stoic Criterion of Identity.' *Phronesis* 27: p.255

But our puzzle maker asks us to focus on one change and insist that the change has affected the status of only that one, usually claiming that the change has caused that one to cease to exist. This follows an ancient view that any change in material constitutes a change in . Has the debtor's identity really changed with a change in his material?

The modern metaphysicist knows that all objects are always changing and that a change in identity may always preserve some information of an entity. The puzzle claims that an aspect of the object persists if the relative identity, or identity "in some respect" has not changed.

To create a paradox, we use two of our three axioms about identity,[3]

Id1. Everything is identical to everything else in some respects.

Id2. Everything is different from everything else in some other respects.

We (in our minds) "pick out" one respect whose identity persists over time because of *Id1* and a second respect which changes in time because of *Id2*.

We now have one object that both persists and does not persist (in different respects, of course), the very essence of a paradox. We call them different objects to create the puzzle.

In the debtor's paradox, Epicharmus emphasizes the change in the debtor's matter. But *material constitution is not identity*, as we saw in chapter 9. Material parts of the debtor do not make contracts.

As the Stoics would have said, it is both material substance and immaterial qualities (the Skeptics suggested these are two things in one place?) taken together that constitute a person.

Just as Dion can survive the loss of a foot, just as human beings survive the almost complete replacement of their atoms and molecules - several times in a lifetime, so persons can survive the destruction and regeneration of their material parts.

---

3   See page 76 in chapter 9.

In the Academic Skeptic version of the Growing Argument, any change of material produces a numerically distinct individual. But the Stoics say this is just destruction and generation, not true growing. Real growth and decline happens to the entity whose identity we can trace through time by its bundle of peculiar qualities. This includes the debtor's memory of making the contract, when he falsely claims "I am not the same person who made that contract."

As Aristotle would have argued, it is the mindful thinking persons, of the debtor and the lender, who agreed on the contract. Their material bodies, and perhaps external materials such as paper and ink, merely embodied that contract.

The contract itself is *immaterial information*, a mere idea.

Chapter 25

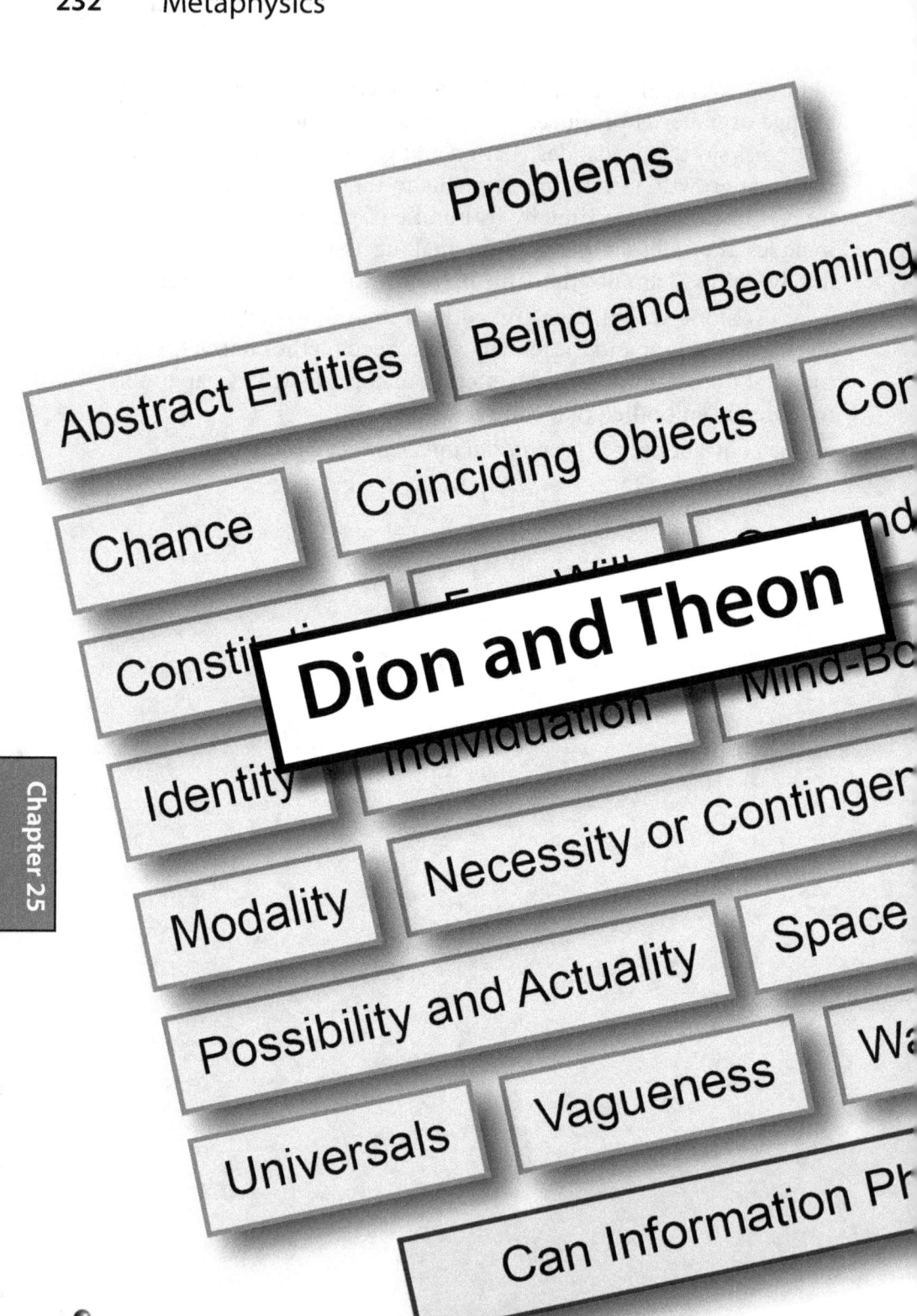

Dion and Theon

The puzzle of Dion and Theon was invented by the Stoic philosopher CHRYSIPPUS (c. 280 - 206 BCE). Some philosophers say that we have no clear idea of Chrysippus' purpose, but we can guess from Stoic views on existence and subsistence that Chrysippus was probably contrasting his Stoic view with the Academic Skeptic view of what constitutes "growing."

The Skeptics said entities cannot survive material change. Stoics say that the immaterial, peculiarly qualified individual (ἴδιος ποιὸν) does survive material change of the individual's body or substrate (ὑποκείμενον).

The only description of Chrysippus' Dion and Theon comes from an opponent, a later Academic Skeptic, Philo of Alexandria (c. 30 BCE.- 45 CE), who is here criticizing the Stoics as claiming two things can be in the same place at the same time.

"(1) Chrysippus, the most distinguished member of their school, in his work On the Growing [Argument], creates a freak of the following kind.

(2) Having first established that it is impossible for two peculiarly qualified individuals to occupy the same substance jointly,

(3) he says: 'For the sake of argument, let one individual be thought of as whole-limbed, the other as minus one foot. Let the whole-limbed one be called Dion, the defective one Theon. Then let one of Dion's feet be amputated.

(4) The question arises which one of them has perished, and his [Chrysippus'] claim is that Theon is the stronger candidate.

(5) These are the words of a paradox-monger rather than a speaker of truth. For how can it be that Theon, who has had no part chopped off, has been snatched away, while Dion, whose foot has been amputated, has not perished?

(6) 'Necessarily', says Chrysippus. 'For Dion, the one whose foot has been cut off, has collapsed into the defective substance of Theon. And two peculiarly qualified individuals cannot occupy the same substrate. Therefore it is necessary that Dion remains while Theon has perished'" [1]

---

1   Philo, 'On the indestructibility of the world,' in Stoic Ontology, *The Hellenistic Philosophers*, A. Long and D. Sedley, p.171-2

What Chrysippus May Have Been Doing

In his article "Chrysippus' Puzzle About Identity," John Bowin (2003) agrees with David Sedley (1982) that Chrysippus' argument was a *reductio ad absurdum* of the Skeptical version of the Growing Argument. We can agree and present the *reductio* in seven simple steps:

Two individuals cannot share the same space (Philo's point 2 about coincident beings)

Theon is another individual sharing a subset of Dion's space (contradicting point 2)

Dion's foot is amputated

Note that Dion survives the material loss, by the Stoic version of the Growing Argument

But now Dion and Theon share exactly the same space

This is absurd by the first premise about coincident beings (Philo's point 6)

Dion survives the material loss, which was Chrysippus' main point to the Skeptics. Theon has to go. In any case, Theon was only an *arbitrary undetached part* of Dion, with no natural justification. Theon was not a "proper part." Theon was always just a hypothetical "picking out" of a subset of Dion for dialectical purposes. Theon never did exist as a real object and separate individual.

Sometime in the early 1960's, PETER GEACH reframed Dion and Theon as *Tibbles, the Cat* and another cat, Tib, without a tail. Geach did not publish this version of Tibbles, but DAVID WIGGINS did in 1968. Wiggins begins with an assertion S*

> "S*: No two things of the same kind (that is, no two things which satisfy the same sortal or substance concept) can occupy exactly the same volume at exactly the same time.
>
> This, I think, is a sort of necessary truth...
>
> A final test for the soundness of S* or, if you wish, for Leibniz' Law, is provided by a puzzle contrived by Geach out of a discussion in William of Sherwood.
>
> A cat called Tibbles loses his tail at time t_2. But before t_2 somebody had picked out, identified, and distinguished from Tibbles a different and rather peculiar animate entity - namely, Tibbles minus Tibbles' tail. Let us suppose that he decided to

call this entity "Tib." Suppose Tibbles was on the mat at time t_1. Then both Tib and Tibbles were on the mat at t_1. This does not violate S*.

But consider the position from t_3 onward when, something the worse for wear, the cat is sitting on the mat without a tail. Is there one cat or are there two cats there? Tib is certainly sitting there. In a way nothing happened to him at all. But so is Tibbles. For Tibbles lost his tail, survived this experience, and then at t_3 was sitting on the mat. And we agreed that Tib ≠ Tibbles. We can uphold the transitivity of identity, it seems, only if we stick by that decision at t_3 and allow that at t_3 there are two cats on the mat in exactly the same place at exactly the same time. But my adherence to S* obliges me to reject this. So I am obliged to find something independently wrong with the way in which the puzzle was set up.

It was set up in such a way that before t_2 Tibbles had a tail as a part and Tib allegedly did not have a tail as a part. If one dislikes this feature (as I do), then one has to ask, "Can one identify and name a part of a cat, insist one is naming just that, and insist that what one is naming is a cat"? This is my argument against the supposition that one can: Does Tib have a tail or not? I mean the question in the ordinary sense of "have," not in any peculiar sense "have as a part." For in a way it is precisely the propriety of some other concept of having as a part which is in question.

Surely Tib adjoins and is connected to a tail in the standard way in which cats who have tails are connected with their tails. There is no peculiarity in this case. Otherwise Tibbles himself might not have a tail. Surely any animal which has a tail loses a member or part of itself if its tail is cut off. But then there was no such cat as the cat who at t_1 has no tail as a part of himself. Certainly there was a cat-part which anybody could call "Tib" if they wished. But one cannot define into existence a cat called Tib who had no tail as part of himself at t, if there was no such cat at t_1. If someone thought he could, then one might ask him (before the cutting at t_2), "Is this Tib of yours the same cat as Tibbles or is he a different cat?" " [2]

---

2   "Wiggins (1968) 'Being in the same place at the same time,"1968, *The Philosophical Review*, p.94

Wiggins sees that "one cannot define into existence a cat" or a cat-part at the same place and time as part of another cat. But the Tibbles version has left out what Chrysippus wanted to achieve with his explanation of growing, that an individual can survive material loss. This was his whole point in cutting off a foot, generally not appreciated by modern accounts.

In their great 1987 compilation of Hellenistic thought, A. A. Long and D. N. Sedley described Tibbles as an example of "two peculiarly qualified individuals coming to occupy one substance," something the Stoics explicitly denied. Long and Sedley clearly are following Wiggins' Tibbles, but they suggest that Chrysippus has given us an example of Dion surviving a diminution in his material without losing his identity, as opposed to what the Academic Skeptics claimed.

The key is to recognize this as the ancestor of a puzzle which has featured in recent discussions of place and identity. Take a cat, Tibbles, and assign the name Tib to that portion of her which excludes her tail. Tibbles is a cat with a tail, Tib is a cat without a tail. Then amputate Tibbles' tail. Tibbles, now tailless, occupies precisely the same space as Tib. Yet they are two distinct cats, because their histories are different. The conclusion is unacceptable, and the philosophical interest lies in pin-pointing the false step.

That Chrysippus' puzzle works along similar lines is made clear by Philo's later comments, in which he takes Theon to be related to Dion as part to whole. Dion corresponds to Tibbles, Theon to Tib, and Dion's foot to Tibbies' tail. The differences are twofold. First, the problem is about occupying the same substance, not the same place. Second, Chrysippus assumes both the validity of the opening steps of the argument and the truth of the principle that two peculiarly qualified individuals cannot occupy the same substance at the same time. He therefore concludes that one of the two must have perished, and his problem is to see why it should be one rather than the other. Philo's elliptical summary leaves unclear his reason for selecting Theon for this honour. Probably it is that if we are asked whose foot has been amputated we can only answer, 'Dion's'. Theon cannot have lost a foot which he never had.

"The title of Chrysippus' work shows that this puzzle was developed in connexion with the Growing Argument. But to what purpose? The following is a guess. According to the Growing Argument, matter is the sole principle of individuation, so that a change of matter constitutes a change of identity. Hence Socrates is a different person from the same individual with one extra particle of matter added. Now these two individuals are related as part to whole — just as Theon and Dion in the amputation paradox are related. Thus the paradox's presupposition that Dion and Theon start out as distinct individuals is not one that Chrysippus need endorse; it is a premise attributed for dialectical purposes to the Academic opponents, who cannot deny it without giving up the Growing Argument. But once they have accepted it, the Growing Argument is doomed anyhow. For whereas the Growing Argument holds that any material diminution constitutes a loss of identity. Chrysippus has presented them with a case, based on their own premises, where material diminution is the necessary condition of enduring identity: it is the diminished Dion who survives, the undiminished Theon who perishes." [3]

An Information Philosophy Analysis

The problems of Dion and Theon and Tibbles, the Cat both begin with denying that two objects can coincide and then immediately assuming that two objects are in the same place at the same time.

This is not a puzzle or a paradox. It is a *contradiction* that Chrysippus set up for dialectical purposes. What were his purposes?

1. First, the Stoic view was that a person is a combination of a material substance and what they called the "peculiarly qualified individual," which is approximately the bundle of qualities that individuates a person. This was essentially the Aristotelian view that a person combines a material body and an *immaterial* mind or soul. It is this soul that persists over time, growing, but not because of the body's material changes.

2. The Academic Skeptics exaggerated the Stoic position as claiming two things are occupying the same place at the same time.

"... since the duality which they say belongs to each body is differentiated in a way unrecognizable by sense-perception. For

---

3   Long and Sedley (1989) Stoic Ontology, *The Hellenistic Philosophers*, p.175

if a peculiarly qualified thing like Plato is a body, and Plato's substance is a body, and there is no apparent difference between these in shape, colour, size and appearance, but both have equal weight and the same outline, by what definition and mark shall we distinguish them and say that now we are apprehending Plato himself, now the substance of Plato? For if there is some difference, let it be stated and demonstrated." [4]

3. What the Stoics did claim, following Aristotle, is that the body is substance (something), which exists, plus the mind, which includes some not-things (ideas, information), which merely subsist. As Seneca described it,

"The Stoics want to place above this [existent] yet another, more primary genus... Some Stoics consider 'something' the first genus, and I shall add the reason why they do. In nature, they say, some things exist, some do not exist. But nature includes even those which do not exist — things which enter the mind, such as Centaurs, giants, and whatever else falsely formed by thought takes on some image despite lacking substance." [5]

4. The Skeptics claim that an increase or decrease in material substance means that an entity must cease to exist, based on the analogy with "numerically distinct" numbers. If we add or subtract 1 from the number 6, it becomes a different number, 7 or 5. It ceases to be 6.

5. For example, when we add some more clay to a lump of clay, Stoics believed that the original lump ceases to exist, replaced by a numerically distinct new lump. This is counterintuitive. But modern metaphysicians describe such changes as existential, when they mistakenly assume that material constitution is identity.

6. Note the similar claim of so-called "four-dimensionalists," who claim that material objects (and even personal identity) do not persist in time, but rather "perdure" as a sequence of distinct "temporal parts," each a separate object that comes into and goes out of existence in an instant.

7. The Stoics argued that this sort of material change should be called generation (γενέσεις) and destruction (φθοράς), since they transform the thing from what it is into something else. This is the

---

[4] Anonymous Academic treatise, Oxyrhynchus Papyrus 3008 in Stoic Ontology, *The Hellenistic Philosophers*, p.167

[5] Seneca, Letters 58.13-15 in Existence and Subsistence, Stoic Ontology, *The Hellenistic Philosophers*, p.162

Heraclitean philosophy of Becoming, that all is in flux, you can't step into the same river twice. If everything is always changing its material, what is to constitute its Parmenidean Being, especially a human being?

8. The Skeptic version of the Growing Argument is that matter is the sole principle of individuation, so that a change of matter constitutes a change of identity.

9. But according to the Stoics, material change is not growing. Something that grows and diminishes must subsist. It must retain its identity over time. Otherwise we cannot say that "it" is growing.

10. For the Stoics, what comes into existence, grows (αὐξήσεις), then diminishes (φθίσεις) and dies, is the peculiarly qualified individual (ἴδιος ποιὸν) that is coincident with a different amount of matter from time to time and that persists over time.

11. Thus material constitution is not identity, individuals are not their material substrate (ὑποκείμενον), but their qualities, which we can see as Aristotle's immaterial form.

12. The Stoics have therefore rejected matter as the principle of individuation.[6]

Information is a better principle of individuation.[7] It supports the relative identity of the persisting individual through time, even as the total information in an individual grows and diminishes.

Abstract information is neither matter nor energy, yet it needs matter for its concrete embodiment and energy for its communication. Information is *immaterial*.

It is the modern spirit, the ghost in the machine.

Immaterial information is perhaps as close as a physical or biological scientist can get to the idea of a soul or spirit that expires at death. When a living being dies, it is the maintenance of biological information that ceases. The matter remains.

---

6   See chapter 13.
7   See chapter 14.

Chapter 26

Frege's Puzzle

Frege's Puzzle

In his 1879 *Begriffsschrift* (or "Concept-Writing"), GOTTLOB FREGE developed a propositional calculus to determine the truth values of propositions from their general form, not from any particular predicates (using specific words, names, properties, attributes, relations, etc.) The propositional calculus, a truth-functional analysis of statements as a whole, is widely considered to be the greatest advance in logic since ARISTOTLE, whose logic of syllogisms was a predicate logic, where truths depend on the meaning of individual terms in the predicate (or the subject).

In Frege's 1892 *Über Sinn und Bedeutung* ("Sense and Reference"), he distinguished the reference (name, denotation, extension, signifier) from the sense (meaning, connotation, intension, significance). He called the reference "direct" and the sense "indirect." Frege was very clear about how the *Bedeutung*, literally the pointing out or indication of an object or concept, generates different ideas in the minds of different persons.

He says that all persons probably get a basic "sense" of a reference, from the common knowledge of things passed down through the generations, but that the particular ideas, or representations (*Vorstellung*) in each mind will be different, because everyone has had a different set of experiences, different memories. This agrees perfectly with our idea of an *experience recorder and reproducer* (ERR). Particular "meanings" are dependent on what a given mind plays back when stimulated by a new experience. Frege said ideas could only be compared if they were both present to the same consciousness, which is of course impossible.

What is sometimes called Frege's Puzzle is how two names for the same object can be distinct words (his example was the Morning Star and Evening Star) and yet in some respect be identical? His word was *Gleichheit* ("sameness"), mistranslated into English as identity by Peter Geach.

Here begins a vast problematic in philosophy that persists for the next one hundred and thirty-five years. Frege speculated that

This chapter on the web - metaphysicist.com/puzzles/frege

two references to the same object could therefore be considered "identical" *in that respect* even if the "names" are distinct.

Frege was following Gottfried Leibniz, who said, "To suppose two things indiscernible is to suppose the same thing under two names." Here is how Frege described it...

> "Sameness gives rise to challenging questions which are not altogether easy to answer. Is it a relation ? A relation between objects, or between names or signs of objects? In my Begriffsschrift I assumed the latter. The reasons which seem to favor this are the following: a = a and a = b are obviously statements of differing cognitive value; a = a holds a priori and, according to Kant, is to be labeled analytic, while statements of the form a = b often contain very valuable extensions of our knowledge and cannot always be established a priori...
>
> Now if we were to regard sameness as a relation between that which the names "a" and "b" refer to, it would seem that a = b could not differ from a = a (i.e., provided a = b is true).[1]
>
> A relation would thereby be expressed of a thing to itself, and indeed one in which each thing stands to itself but to no other thing. What is intended to be said by a = b seems to be that the signs or names "a" and "b" refer to the same thing, so that those signs themselves would be under discussion; a relation between them would be asserted. But this relation would hold between the names or signs only insofar as they named or designated something. It would be mediated by the connection of each of the two signs with the same designated thing. But this is arbitrary. Nobody can be forbidden to use any arbitrarily producible event or object as a sign for something. In that case the sentence a = b would no longer refer to the subject matter, but only to its mode of designation; we would express no proper knowledge by its means. But in many cases this is just what we want to do. If the sign "a" is distinguished from the sign "b" only as object (here, by means of its shape), not as sign (i.e., not by the manner in which it designates something), the cognitive value of a = a becomes essentially equal to that of a = b, provided a = b is true. A difference can arise only if the difference between the signs corresponds to a difference in the

---

[1] This works in mathematics, as Fitch and Quine saw, but not in ordinary language. See p.158.

mode of presentation of that which is designated...
If we found "a = a" and "a = b" to have different cognitive values, the explanation is that for the purpose of knowledge, the sense of the sentence, viz., the thought expressed by it, is no less relevant than its referent, i.e., its truth value. If now a = b, then indeed the referent of "b" is the same as that of "a," and hence the truth value of "a = b" is the same as that of "a = a." In spite of this, the sense of "b" may differ from that of "a," and thereby the sense expressed in "a = b" differs from that of "a = a." In that case the two sentences do not have the same cognitive value." [2]

Names and Reference

Frege's puzzle[3] is clear, the names "a" and "b" refer to the same thing, but the names are only identical *qua* references to the object. They may have different senses, or meanings.

Since Frege, generations of philosophers have puzzled over different names and/or descriptions referring to the same thing that may lead to logical contradictions when one term is *substituted* for the other in a logical statement. Frege's original example was the Morning Star and Evening Star (often called Hesperus and Phosphorus) as names that refer to the planet Venus. Do these names have differing cognitive value? Yes. Can they be defined *qua* references to uniquely pick out Venus. Yes.

The names are relations, words that are references to the objects. But words put us back into the ambiguous realm of language.

Over a hundred years of confusion in logic and language consisted of finding two expressions that can be claimed in some sense to be identical, but upon substitution in another statement, they do not preserve the truth value of the statement. Besides Frege, and a few examples from BERTRAND RUSSELL ("Scott" and "the author of Waverly." "bachelor" and "unmarried man"), WILLARD VAN ORMAN QUINE was the most prolific generator of paradoxes ("9" and "the number of planets," "Giorgione" and "Barbarelli," "Cicero" and "Tully," and others).

---

2   Frege (1892) in Geach and Black (1952) Sense and Reference, *Translations from the Philosophical Writings of Gottlob Frege*, pp.209, 230
3   Salmon (1986) . *Frege's Puzzle*.

Just as information philosophy shows how to pick out information in an object or concept that constitutes the "peculiar qualifications" that individuate it, so we can pick out the information in two designating references that provide what Quine called "purely designative references." Where Quine picks out information that leads to contradictions and paradoxes (he calls this "*referential opacity*"), we can "qualify" the information needed to make the terms referentially transparent.

Quine's Paradoxes

Quine generated a number of apparently paradoxical cases where truth value is not preserved when "quantifying into a modal context." But these can all be understood as a failure of substitutivity of putatively identical entities. Information philosophy shows that two distinct expressions that are claimed to be identical are never identical in all respects. So a substitution of one expression for the other may not be identical in the relevant respect. Such a substitution can change the meaning, the intension of the expression.

Perhaps Quine's most famous paradox is his argument about the number of planets:

(1) 9 is necessarily greater than 7

for example, is equivalent to

'9 > 7' is analytic

and is therefore true (if we recognize the reducibility of mathematics to logic)...[4]

Given, say that

(2) the number of planets is 9,

we can substitute 'the number of planets' from the non-modal statement (2) for '9' in the modal statement (1), which gives us the false modal statement

(3) The number of planets is necessarily greater than 7

But this is false, says Quine, since the statement,

(2) The number of planets is 9,

is true only because of circumstances outside of logic.

---

4   Quine (1943) 'Notes on Existence and Necessity,' p.121

Ruth Barcan Marcus analyzed this problem in 1961, which she calls the "familiar example" :

"(27) 9 eq the number of planets

is said to be a true identity for which substitution fails in

(28) □ (9 > 7)

for it leads to the falsehood

(29) □ (the number of planets > 7).

Since the argument holds (27) to be contingent (~ □ (9 eq the number of planets)), 'eq' of (27) is the appropriate analogue of material equivalence and consequently the step from (28) to (29) is not valid for the reason that the substitution would have to be made in the scope of the square." [5]

This *failure of substitutivity* can be understood by unpacking the use of "the number of planets." It is not a *purely designative* reference, as Quine calls it.

In (27), "the number of planets" is the empirical answer to the question "how many planets are there in the solar system?" It is not what Saul Kripke would call a "rigid designator" of the number 9. The intension of this expression, its reference, is the "extra-linguistic" fact about the quantity of planets (which Quine appreciated).

The expression '9' is an unambiguous mathematical (logical) reference to the number 9. It refers to the number 9, which is its meaning (intension). Kripke mistakenly claims that '9' is a rigid designator of the number 9 "in all possible worlds." This is false. Only the mathematical concept of the number 9 is true in all possible worlds, not its name.

We can conclude that (27) is not a true identity, unless before "the number of planets" is *quantified*, it is *qualified* as "the number of planets qua its numerosity, as a pure number." Otherwise, the reference is "opaque," as Quine describes it. But this is a problem of his own making.

As Marcus says, when we recognize (27) as contingent, ~□ (9 eq the number of planets), it is not necessary that 9 is equal to the number of planets, its reference to the number 9 becomes opaque. Indeed, today there are only eight planets, proving (27) was contingent.

---

5   Marcus (1961) "Modalities and Intensional Languages," p. 313

The substitution of a possible or contingent empirical fact that is not "true in all possible worlds" for a logical-mathematical concept that is necessarily true is what causes the substitution failure.

When all three statements are "in the scope of the square" (□), when all have the same modality, we can "quantify into modal contexts," as Quine puts it. Both expressions, '9' and 'the number of planets, *qua* its numerosity,' will be references to the same thing,

They will be identical in one respect, *qua* number. They will be "referentially transparent."

The New Theory of Reference[6]

Frege's Puzzle motivated several philosophers to develop a new theory of how words refer to objects, especially in modal contexts. It gave rise to Saul Kripke's theories about "possible world semantics."

When in the 1940's, RUTH C. BARCAN and RUDOLF CARNAP added modal operators to quantification theory, Quine strongly objected, developing his demonstrations that "quantifying into modal contexts" leads to "referential opacity" and logical nonsense like "the number of planets is necessarily greater than 7."

This was nothing but the fact first seen by Frege that different descriptions, different names that are "disguised descriptions," have different cognitive value, different "senses," that cannot be substituted for one another in any logical context, not just modal contexts, as Quine thought.

What we call a "concept" about a material object is some subset of the information in the object, accurate to the extent that the concept is isomorphic to that subset. By "picking out" different subsets, we can sort objects. We can compare objects, finding them similar *qua* one concept and different *qua* another concept. We can say that "a = b" *qua* color but not *qua* size.

Frege said that "the Morning Star = the Morning Star" is an identity and therefore tautological and tells us nothing. But "the Morning Star = the Evening Star" has additional cognitive value. In 1961, Ruth Barcan Marcus said it tells us something empirical about Venus in the morning and evening skies. She suggested less ambiguous,

---

6   See Humphreys and Fetzer (1999) *The New Theory of Reference*.

purely designative names would have no cognitive value beyond their reference to named objects.

Her work gave rise to the sophisticated but problematic modern idea of the "necessity of identity."[7]

In modern times, Frege's insight has been defended with elaborate modal logical arguments, beginning with Barcan (later Marcus) in 1947, using Leibniz's Law about identity and indiscernibility, that seem to suggest that for any a and b, if a = b (even contingently), then necessarily a = b.

$$\forall x \, \forall y \, (x = y) \supset [\Box(x = x) \supset \Box(x = y)]$$

This "indiscernibility of identicals" claims that if x = y, then x and y must share all properties, otherwise there would be a discernible difference. SAUL KRIPKE, following Marcus but not mentioning her, argues that one of the properties of x is that x = x, so if y shares the property of '= x,' we can say that y = x. Then, necessarily, x = y.

However, two distinct things, x and y, cannot be identical, because there is some difference in information between them. Instead of claiming that y has x's property of being identical to x, information philosophy can say only that y has x's property of being self-identical, thus y = y.

Then x and y remain distinct in at least this intrinsic property as well as in extrinsic properties like their distinct positions in space.

DAVID WIGGINS' eventually gave credit to Barcan Marcus,
"Miss Barcan's proof was long received with incredulity by those committed to the mutual assimilation (much criticized in more recent times by Kripke and others) of the categories of necessity and *a priority*, and rejected on the grounds that the identity of evening and morning star was an *a posteriori* discovery. But even if statement ascertainable *a priori* to be true and necessary true statement coincided perfectly in their extensions, Miss Barcan's theorem could still stand in our version. For the conclusion is not put forward here as a necessarily true statement. (On this we remain mute.)" [8]

---

7   See chapter 13 on Identity
8   Wiggins (1980) *Sameness and Substance*, pp. 110-111

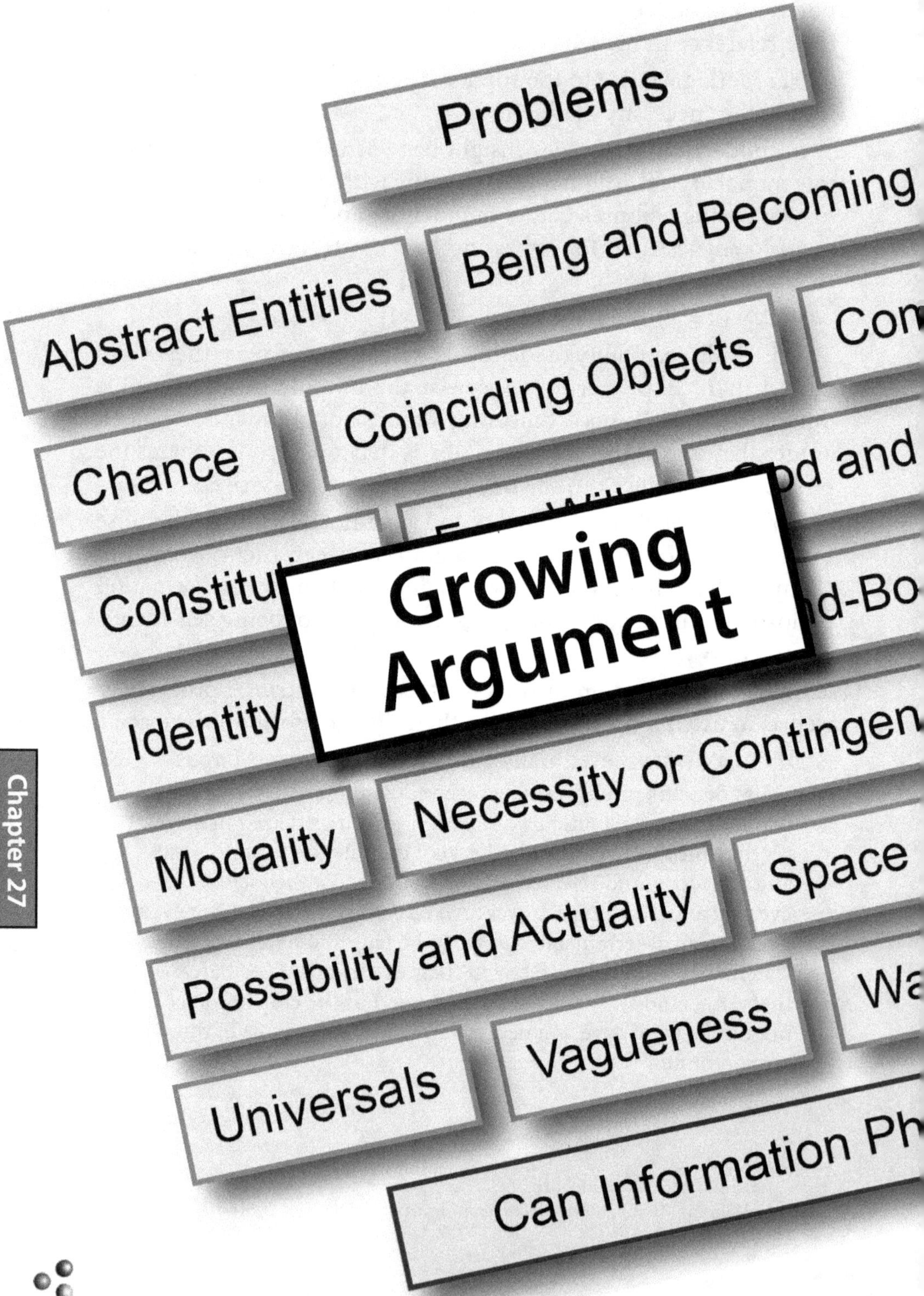
Problems
Being and Becoming
Abstract Entities
Coinciding Objects
Chance
Growing Argument
Identity
Modality
Space
Possibility and Actuality
Vagueness
Universals

The Growing Argument

The essential problem in Chrysippus' "Growing Argument" is whether an individual can survive (with its identity intact), when it suffers a partial loss (or a gain) of its material substance.

The Academic Skeptics argued that an individual cannot survive such material change. When any material is subtracted or added, the entity ceases to exist and a new numerically distinct individual comes into existence.

The Stoics, however, saw the identity of an individual as its *immaterial* bundle of properties or qualities that they called the "peculiarly qualified individual" or ἴδιος ποιὸν.

Following Aristotle, the Stoics called the material substance or substrate ὑποκείμενον (or "the underlying"). This material substrate is transformed when matter is lost or gained, but they said it is wrong to call such material changes "growth (αὐξήσεις) and decay (φθίσεις)." The Stoics suggested they should be called "generation (γενέσεις) and destruction (φθοράς)." These terms were already present in Aristotle, who said that the form, as essence, is not generated. He said that generation and destruction are material changes that do not persist (as does the Stoic peculiarly qualified individual).

> It is therefore obvious that the form (or whatever we should call the shape in the sensible thing) is not generated—generation does not apply to it—nor is the essence generated; for this is that which is induced in something else either by art or by nature or by potency. But we do cause a bronze sphere to be, for we produce it from bronze and a sphere; we induce the form into this particular matter, and the result is a bronze sphere...
>
> For if we consider the matter carefully, we should not even say without qualification that a statue is generated from wood, or a house from bricks; because that from which a thing is generated should not persist, but be changed. This, then, is why we speak in this way.[1]

It is important to see that the Aristotelian view is very similar to the Stoic - that individuals are combinations of matter and form.

---

1   Aristotle, *Metaphysics*, Book VII, § vii & viii

At times Aristotle made the matter the principle of individuation, at other times he stressed the immaterial qualities or "affections," as did the Stoics, with their peculiarly qualified individual.

"The term "substance" (οὐσία) is used, if not in more, at least in four principal cases; for both the essence (εἶναι), and the universal (καθόλου) and the genus (γένος) are held to be the substance of the particular (ἑκάστου), and fourthly the substrate (ὑποκείμενον). The substrate is that of which the rest are predicated, while it is not itself predicated of anything else. Hence we must first determine its nature, for the primary substrate (ὑποκείμενον) is considered to be in the truest sense substance.

Both matter and form and their combination are said to be substance (οὐσία). Now in one sense we call the matter (ὕλη) the substrate; in another, the shape (μορφή); and in a third, the combination of the two. By matter I mean, for instance, bronze; by shape, the arrangement of the form (τὸ σχῆμα τῆς ἰδέας); and by the combination of the two, the concrete thing: the statue (ἀνδριάς). Thus if the form is prior to the matter and more truly existent, by the same argument it will also be prior to the combination." [2]

The Skeptics attacked the Stoics, saying Stoics were making single things into dual beings, two objects in the same place at the same time, but indistinguishable.

"since the duality which they say belongs to each body is differentiated in a way unrecognizable by sense-perception. For if a peculiarly qualified thing like Plato is a body, and Plato's substance is a body, and there is no apparent difference between these in shape, colour, size and appearance, but both have equal weight and the same outline, by what definition and mark shall we distinguish them and say that now we are apprehending Plato himself, now the substance of Plato? For if there is some difference, let it be stated and demonstrated." [3]

The Skeptic Plutarch described the Growing Argument,
"(1) The argument about growth is an old one, for, as Chrysippus says, it is propounded by Epicharmus.[4]

---

2   Aristotle, *Metaphysics*, Book VII, § iii
3   Anonymous Academic treatise, Oxyrhynchus Papyrus 3008 in Stoic Ontology, *The Hellenistic Philosophers*, p.167
4   See the Debtor's Paradox in chapter 24

(2) For the argument is a simple one and these people grant its premises:

  a all particular substances are in flux and motion, releasing some things from themselves and receiving others which reach them from elsewhere;

  b the numbers or quantities which these are added to or subtracted from do not remain the same but become different as the aforementioned arrivals and departures cause the substance to be transformed;

  c the prevailing convention is wrong to call these processes or of growth and decay: rather they should be called generation and destruction, since they transform the thing from what it is into something else, whereas growing and diminishing are affections of a body which serves as substrate.

(3) When it is stated and proposed in some such way, what is the judgement of these champions of the evident, these yardsticks of our conceptions? That each of us is a pair of twins, two-natured and double ...two bodies sharing the same colour, the same shape, the same weight, and the same place, no man previously has seen them.[5]

4) But these men alone have seen this combination, this duplicity, this ambiguity, that each of us is two substrates, the one substance, the other <a peculiarly qualified individual>; ...nowhere providing sense-perception with a grasp of the difference.

(5) ... Yet this difference and distinction in us no one has marked off or discriminated, nor have we perceived that we are born double, always in flux with one part of ourselves, while remaining the same people from birth to death with the other.

(6) I am simplifying their account, since it is four substrates that they attribute to each of us; or rather, they make each of us four. But even the two are sufficient to expose the absurdity.

(7) If when we hear Pentheus in the tragedy say that he sees two suns and a double Thebes we say he is not seeing but misseeing, going crazy in his arithmetic...

(8) Here, actually, they can perhaps be excused for inventing different kinds of substrates, for there seems no other device available to people determined to save and protect the processes of growth." [6]

---

5 See chapter 7 on Coinciding Objects.

6 Plutarch, On common conceptions 1083A— 1084A in Stoic Ontology, *The Hellenistic Philosophers*, p.167

Chapter 28

The Infinite Regress

While strictly a problem in epistemology and not metaphysics, an infinite regress of justifications was one of the arguments that the Academic Skeptics leveled against the Stoics.

Since metaphysicians claim to get to the fundamental structure of reality, skeptics can always question metaphysical claims as to what underlies fundamental reality. If the metaphysicists say that it is X, skeptics can initiate an infinite regress by asking what underlies X, but nothing underlies information.

Plato in the *Theaetetus* (200D-201C) defined knowledge as justified true belief. Justification was providing some reasons (λόγος or συλλογισμῶ), a rational explanation for the belief. True opinion accompanied by reason is knowledge. (δόξαν ἀληθῆ μετὰ λόγου ἐπιστήμην εἶναι) (202C)

Although "justified true belief" is the traditional philosophical definition of knowledge, still in use in modern positions on epistemology, the ancients were already skeptical of this Platonic idea. Socratic dialogues normally did not reach any positive conclusions; they were "negative dialectics."

Indeed, the *Theaetetus* ends with Socrates' utter rejection of perception, true belief, or true belief combined with reasons or explanations as justification. Socrates says:

> "And it is utterly silly, when we are looking for a definition of knowledge, to say that it is right opinion with knowledge, whether of difference or of anything else whatsoever. So neither perception, Theaetetus, nor true opinion, nor reason or explanation combined with true opinion could be knowledge (epistéme)." [1]

An infinite regress arises when we ask what are the justifications for the reasons themselves.

If the reasons count as knowledge, they must themselves be justified with reasons for the reasons, and so on, *ad infinitum*.

---

1   Plato, *Theaetetus*, (210A-B)

This chapter on the web - metaphysicist.com/puzzles/regress

The problem of the infinite regress was a critical argument of the Skeptics in ancient philosophy.

SEXTUS EMPIRICUS tells us there are two basic Pyrrhonian modes or tropes that lead the skeptic to suspension of judgment (ἐποχῇ):

> "They [skeptics] hand down also two other modes leading to suspension of judgement. Since every object of apprehension seems to be apprehended either through itself or through another object, by showing that nothing is apprehended either through itself or through another thing, they introduce doubt, as they suppose, about everything. That nothing is apprehended through itself is plain, they say, from the controversy which exists amongst the physicists regarding, I imagine, all things, both sensibles and intelligibles; which controversy admits of no settlement because we can neither employ a sensible nor an intelligible criterion, since every criterion we may adopt is controverted and therefore discredited.
>
> And the reason why they do not allow that anything is apprehended through something else is this: If that through which an object is apprehended must always itself be apprehended through some other thing, one is involved in a process of circular reasoning or in regress ad infinitum. And if, on the other hand, one should choose to assume that the thing through which another object is apprehended is itself apprehended through itself, this is refuted by the fact that, for the reasons already stated, nothing is apprehended through itself. But as to how what conflicts with itself can possibly be apprehended either through itself or through some other thing we remain in doubt, so long as the criterion of truth or of apprehension is not apparent, and signs, even apart from demonstration, are rejected." [2]

The skeptic can always ask a philosopher for justifying reasons. When those reasons are given, he can demand their justification, and this in turn leads to an infinite regress of justifications.

The endless controversy and disagreement of all philosophers cautions us against accepting any of their arguments as knowledge.

---

2   Sextus Empiricus. *Outlines of Pyrrhonism*, Loeb Library, R.G.Bury tr., 1.178-79

Infinite Regress

Second only to Kant's "scandal" that philosophers cannot logically prove the existence of the external world, it is scandalous that professional philosophers to this day are in such profound disagreement about what it means to know something.

Epistemologists may not all be wrong, but with their conflicting theories of knowledge, how many of them are likely to be right?

This is especially dismaying for those epistemologists who still see a normative role for philosophy that could provide an *a priori* foundation for scientific or empirical *a posteriori* knowledge. Kant called this the synthetic *a priori*.

In recent years, professional epistemologists have been reduced to quibbling over "Gettier problems" - clever sophistical examples and counterexamples that defeat the reasoned justifications for true beliefs.

Following some unpublished work of Gregory O'Hair, DAVID ARMSTRONG identified possible ways to escape the Skeptic's infinite regress, including:[3]

Skepticism - knowledge is impossible

The regress is infinite but virtuous

Regress is finite, but no end (Coherence view)

The regress ends in self-evident truths, the axioms of geometry, for example (Foundationalist view)

Non-inferential credibility, such as direct sense perceptions

Externalist theories (O'Hair is the source of the term "externalist")

Causal view (Ramsey)

Reliability view (Ramsey)

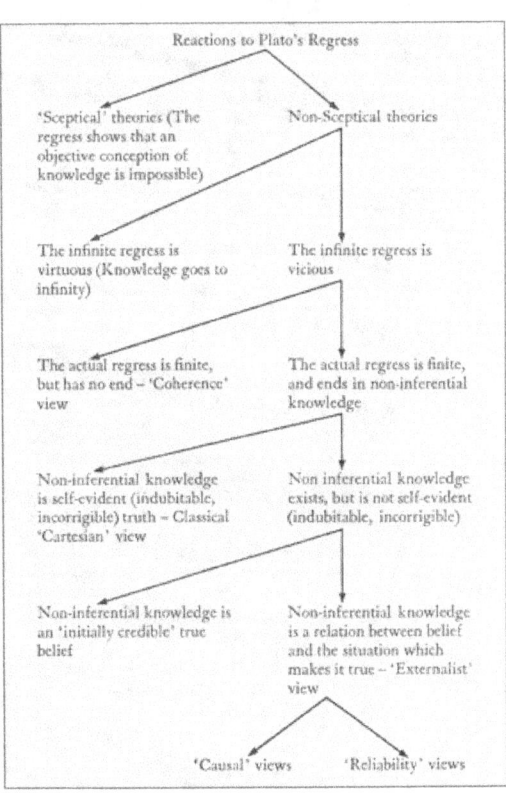

---

3   Armstrong (1973) *Belief, Truth, and Knowledge*. p.152

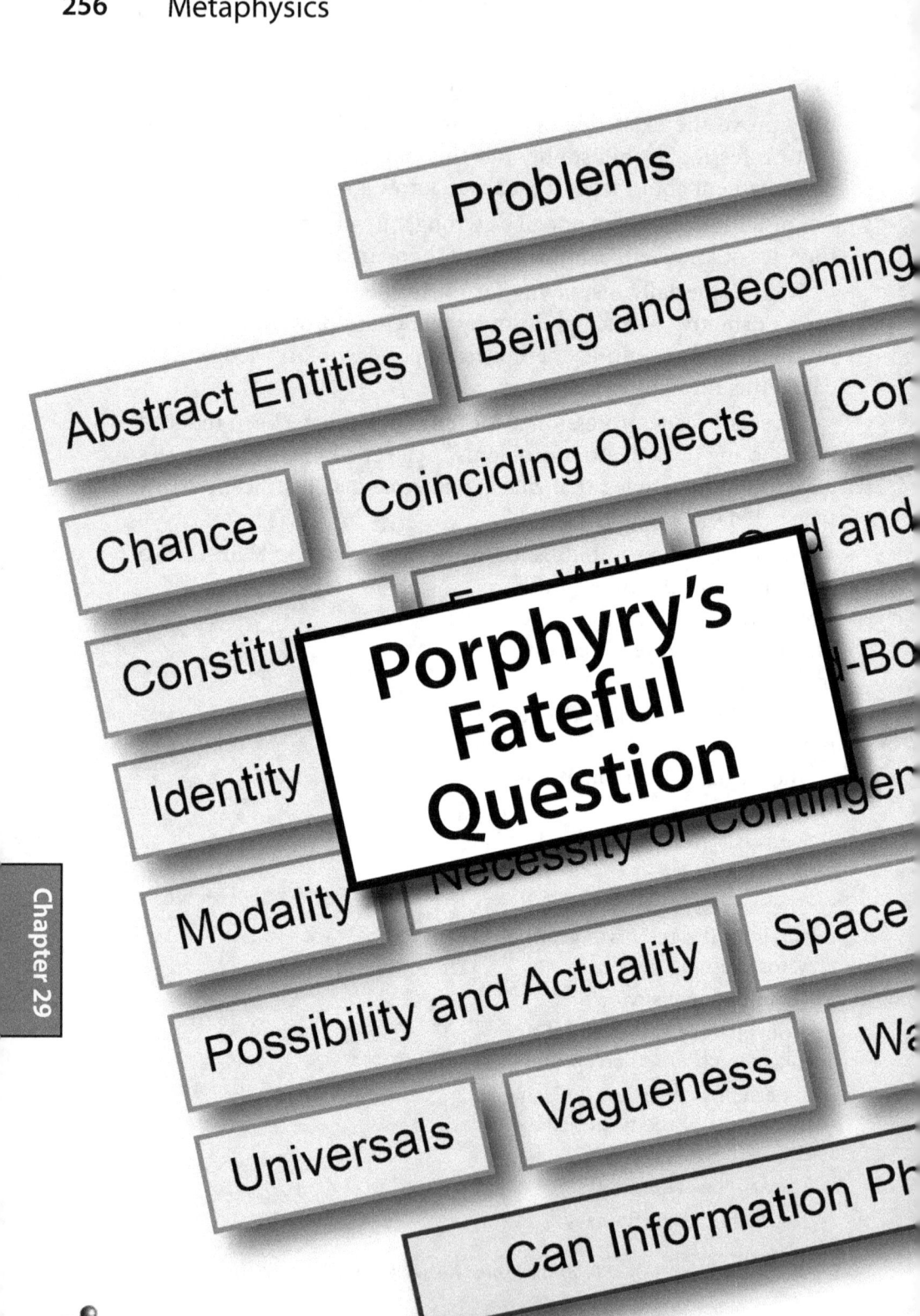

Porphyry's Fateful Question

Porphyry (c. 234 – c. 305) was a neoplatonist, a student of the leading neoplatonist Plotinus. Porphyry's criticism of the Aristotelian categories raised the profound question of their existential status. The categories are the most general "predicables," the things (the "concepts?") that can be said or predicated of "objects." In some sense, this is the beginning of analytic language philosophy. Later thinkers divided over whether the categories are real things (the "Realists") or just words or names (the "Nominalists").

Like Plato and all the neoplatonists, Porphyry disliked the idea of material things (including the body), regarding them as subordinate to the Platonic ideas" (ιδεα), and merely poor copies (*mimesis*) of those ideas. For Porphyry, the Platonic realm of ideas is the source of eternal "Being," whereas the material world is ephemeral and mere "Becoming." And the ultimate "Being" for Porphyry is the idea of "The One," which included the Platonic ideals of the True, the Good, and the Beautiful.

Where these ideas are perfectly singular, all lesser ideas contain internal differences, describable (or predicable) as properties or attributes of their substance. Thus Socrates (a substance) is a Man (a property). Aristotle's five categories[1] are definition (horos), genus (*genos*), difference (*diaphora*), property (*idion*), and accident (*symbebekos*). Porphyry substituted Plato's idea (*eidos*) for Aristotle's *horos*. Later writers use *species*.

In his Introduction to the Aristotelian Categories (the *Isagoge*), Porphyry raised what became known as his "fateful question." Can these categories be said to exist (in the same sense of material existence)? As a neoplatonist, Porphyry might have been quite satisfied to have the categories simply exist in the "metaphysical" realm of the ideas? He clearly sees that they are concepts. Information philosophy identifies Platonic Ideas as *immaterial information*. Yet they are physical things, some with *causal power*.

---

1 Aristotle *Topics*, a iv. 101 b 17-25

This chapter on the web - metaphysicist.com/puzzles/porphyry

Chapter 30

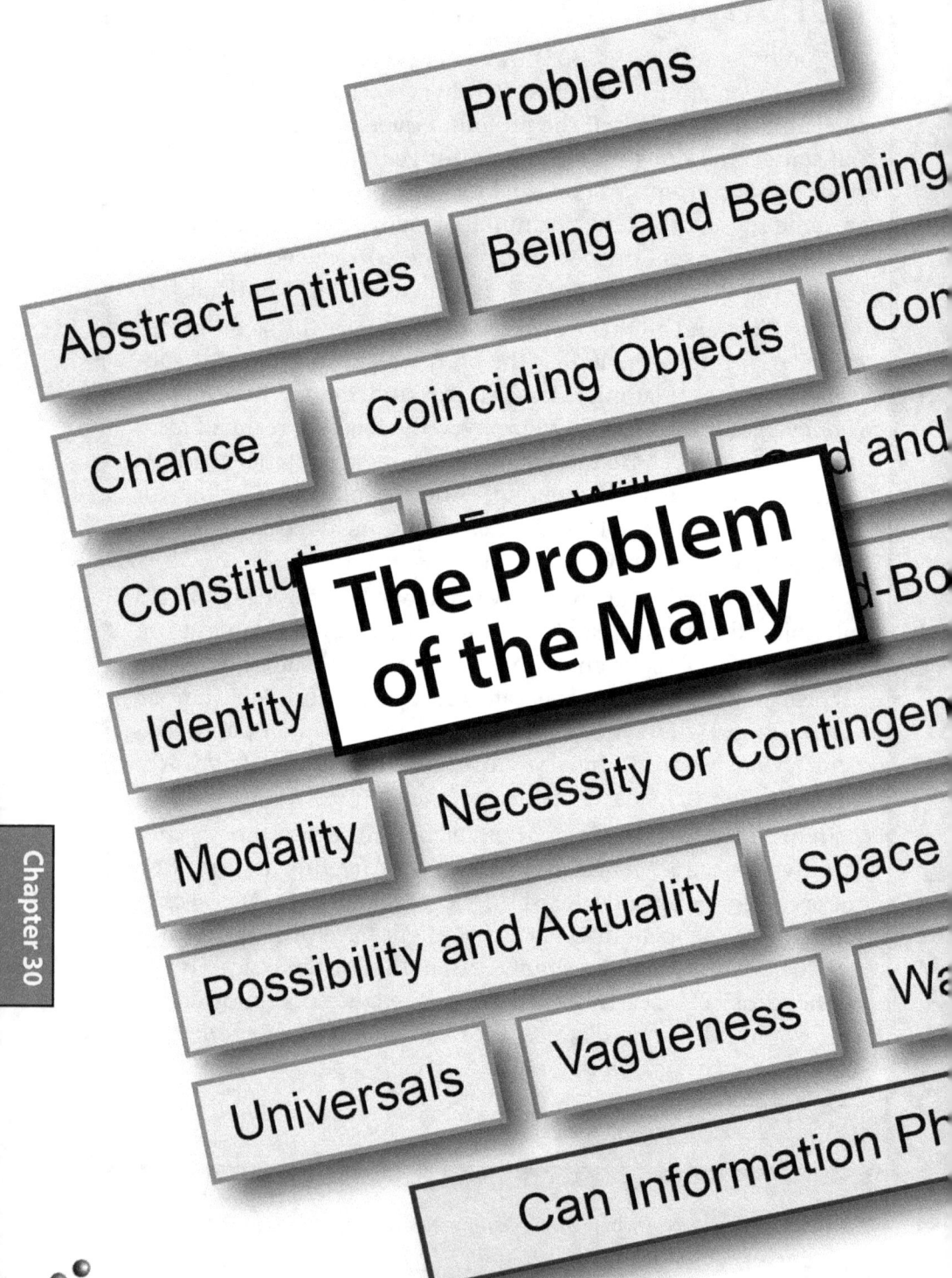

The Problem of the Many

Modern metaphysicians make the problem of *vagueness* the central issue in the Problem of the Many. Vagueness may also be involved in the Sorites paradox.

The *Problem of the Many* may also be a consequence of the significant use of set theory in analytic philosophy along with the view that inanimate "composite objects" are nothing but "simples arranged object-wise," as PETER VAN INWAGEN has maintained.

Van Inwagen criticized the tendency of metaphysicians to pick out selected "parts" or even just some properties of an object and claim to see another individual, as the Stoic CHRYSIPPUS did in his so-called "Growing Argument."

Recall that the Skeptics accused the Stoics of putting two entities at the same place and the same time, making us all double. Now this was only because the Stoics distinguished the substance (οὐσίας) or substrate (ὑποκείμενον) from the "peculiarly qualified individual" (ἴδιος ποιὸν), much as Aristotle saw a man as a combination of matter and form, body and mind.

Plutarch says if the Stoics add two individual qualifications to one and the same substance, there could also be three or four or more...

> "(1) One can hear them [the Stoics], and find them in many works, disagreeing with the Academics and crying that they confuse everything by their 'indiscernibilities' and force a single qualified individual to occupy two substances. (2) And yet there is nobody who does not think this and consider that on the contrary it is extraordinary and paradoxical if one dove has not, in the whole of time, been indiscernible from another dove, and bee from bee, wheat-grain from wheat-grain, or fig from proverbial fig. Adding a second individual to the same substance may refer to the puzzle of Dion and Theon?
> (3) What really is contrary to our conception is these people's assertions and pretences to the effect that two peculiarly qualified individuals occupy one substance, and that the same substance which houses one peculiarly qualified individual, on

This chapter on the web - metaphysicist.com/puzzles/many

the arrival of a second, receives and keeps both alike.

For, if two, there will be three, four, five, and untold numbers, belonging to a single substance; and I do not mean in different parts, but all the infinite number of them belonging alike to the whole." [1]

The *Problem of the Many* is mostly associated with the modern metaphysician PETER UNGER, who named it in 1980, and PETER GEACH, who the same year showed how his metaphysical cat Tibbles could be reimagined as 1,001 numerically distinct cats by plucking each of 1,000 cat hairs.

Losing hairs reminds us of a variation of the Sorites puzzle of the heap of grains of wheat. It asks for the exact moment that a man becomes bald as his last few hairs fall out.

DAVID WIGGINS tells us that Geach's first version of Tibbles was as a cat that loses just one part, his tail, in an update of the "body-minus" problem of Dion and Theon.

If we remove something inessential (say one water molecule from a cloud, one hair from the second Tibbles, a foot from Dion, a tail from the first Tibbles, a leg from Descartes, or replace one plank in the Ship of Theseus), do we have a new entity, as the Academic Skeptics first argued?

Is there a criterion of parthood that makes some "temporal part" mereologically essential to the identity of the whole?

If we could, that would stop dialectical claims about different sets of the simplest components of a material object that are picked out by a metaphysician to start an argument. Van Inwagen attacks this as the "*Doctrine of Arbitrary Undetached Parts*."[2]

Unger and van Inwagen independently came up with the extreme opposite position from the Problem of the Many, which became known as "mereological universalism," the belief in the existence of arbitrary "mereological sums." Give a set with a large number N of simple members, the Problem of the Many suggests that the N! different combinations of those members composes a new object.

---

1 Plutarch, Moralia, Against the Stoics on Common Conceptions 1077c—E, in *The Hellenistic Philosophers*, p.171

2 Van Inwagen (1981) 'Doctrine of Arbitrary Undetached Parts,' *Pacific Philosophical Quarterly* 62, 123-137

Peter Unger

In 1980 Peter Unger formulated what he called "The Problem of the Many." It led Unger to propose that *nothing exists* and that even he did not exist, a position known as *mereological nihilism*.

Today this is the metaphysical problem of material *composition* and of *vagueness*.

In 1999 Unger redescribed the problem in the *Oxford Studies in Metaphysics*

> "let us start by considering certain cases of ordinary clouds, clouds like those we sometimes seem to see in the sky.
>
> As often viewed by us from here on the ground, sometimes puffy "picture-postcard" clouds give the appearance of having a nice enough boundary, each white entity sharply surrounded by blue sky. (In marked contrast, there are other times when it's a wonder that we don't simply speak singularly of "the cloud in the sky", where each visible cloudy region runs so messily together with many other cloudy "parts of the sky".) But upon closer scrutiny, as may happen sometimes when you're in an airplane, even the puffiest, cleanest clouds don't seem to be so nicely bounded. And this closer look seems a more revealing one. For, as science seems clearly to say, our clouds are almost wholly composed of tiny water droplets, and the dispersion of these droplets, in the sky or the atmosphere, is always, in fact, a gradual matter. With pretty much any route out of even a comparatively clean cloud's center, there is no stark stopping place to be encountered. Rather, anywhere near anything presumed a boundary, there's only a gradual decrease in the density of droplets fit, more or less, to be constituents of a cloud that's there.
>
> With that being so, we might see that there are enormously many complexes of droplets, each as fit as any other for being a constituted cloud. Each of the many will be a cloud, we must suppose, if there are even as many as just one constituted cloud where, at first, it surely seemed there was exactly one. For example, consider the two candidates I'll now describe. Except for two "widely opposing" droplets, one on one side of two overlapping cloudy complexes, way over on the left, say, and

another way over on the right, two candidate clouds may wholly overlap each other, so far as droplets goes. The cited droplet that's on the left is a constituent of just one of the two candidates, not a component of the other; and the one on the right is a component of the other candidate, not the one first mentioned. So each of these two candidate clouds has exactly the same number of constituent droplets. And each might have exactly the same mass, and volume, as the other." [3]

In his 1990 book *Material Beings*, Peter van Inwagen said Unger's original insight that there are many ways to compose a cloud from innumerable water droplets should be called "*mereological universalism.*" Van Inwagen denies there is any way for simples to compose anything other than themselves, which van Inwagen calls "mereological nihilism.

Peter Geach

Geach worked on problems of identity and some time in the early 1960's reformulated Chrysippus's ancient problem of Dion and Theon as "Tibbles, the Cat."

In 1968, David Wiggins described Geach's first version of Tibbles. Where Theon is identical to Dion except he is missing a foot, we now have a cat named Tibbles and a second cat named Tib who lacks a tail.

In 1980, Geach repurposed his metaphysical cat Tibbles. Geach's second version of Tibbles is widely cited as a discussion of the problem of vagueness or what Peter Unger in the same year called the Problem of the Many.

If a few of Tibbles' hairs are pulled out, do we still have Tibbles, the Cat? Obviously we do. Have we created other cats, now multiple things in the same place at the same time? Obviously not.

Geach argues that removing one of a thousand hairs from Tibbles shows that there are actually 1,001 cats on the mat. He writes:

> The fat cat sat on the mat. There was just one cat on the mat. The cat's name was "Tibbles": "Tibbles" is moreover a name for a cat.—This simple story leads us into difficulties if we assume that Tibbles is a normal cat. For a normal cat has at least 1,000 hairs. Like many empirical concepts, the concept (single) hair is fuzzy

---

3   Unger (1999) 'Mental Problems of the Many.' *Oxford Studies in Metaphysics*, 23, Chapter 8. p.197

at the edges; but it is reasonable to assume that we can identify in Tibbles at least 1,000 of his parts each of which definitely is a single hair. I shall refer to these hairs as $h_1, h_2, h_3, \ldots$ up to $h_{1,000}$.[4]

Geach now proposes to pull one of these hairs and thus produce 1,000 cats identified by the missing hair on each one. This is parallel to the case of Dion and Theon, who has lost a leg and Geach's early version of Tibbles and Tib, who has lost a tail. Now Tibbles is losing just a single hair. Geach might have subtracted just a single atom and claim to have produced another unique cat.

Thus each one of the names "$c_1 ; c_2, \ldots c_{1,000}$ or again the name "c", is a name of a cat; but none of these 1,001 names is a name for a cat, as "Tibbles" is. By virtue of its sense "Tibbles" is a name, not for one and the same thing (in fact, to say that would really be to say nothing at all), but for one and the same cat. This name for a cat has reference, and it names the one and only cat on the mat; but just on that account "Tibbles" names, as a shared name, both c itself and any of the smaller masses of feline tissue like c_{12} and c_{279}; for all of these are one and the same cat, though not one and the same mass of feline tissue. "Tibbles" is not a name for a mass of feline tissue.

So we recover the truth of the simple story we began with. The price to pay is that we must regard "is the same cat as" as expressing only a certain equivalence relation, not an absolute identity restricted to cats; but this price, I have elsewhere argued, must be paid anyhow, for there is no such absolute identity as logicians have assumed.[5]

As David Wiggins has argued, we only have *relative identity* between two distinct objects. And as we have shown, the only absolute identity is the relation a thing has with itself at each instant of time. So the slightest modification, whether a leg, a tail, a hair, or even a single atom, represents the kind of change that occurs in all material entities over time. Their persistence or endurance is always only a partial or relative identity.

---

4   Geach (1962) *Reference and Generality*, 3rd edition, p.215.
5   *ibid*, p.216.

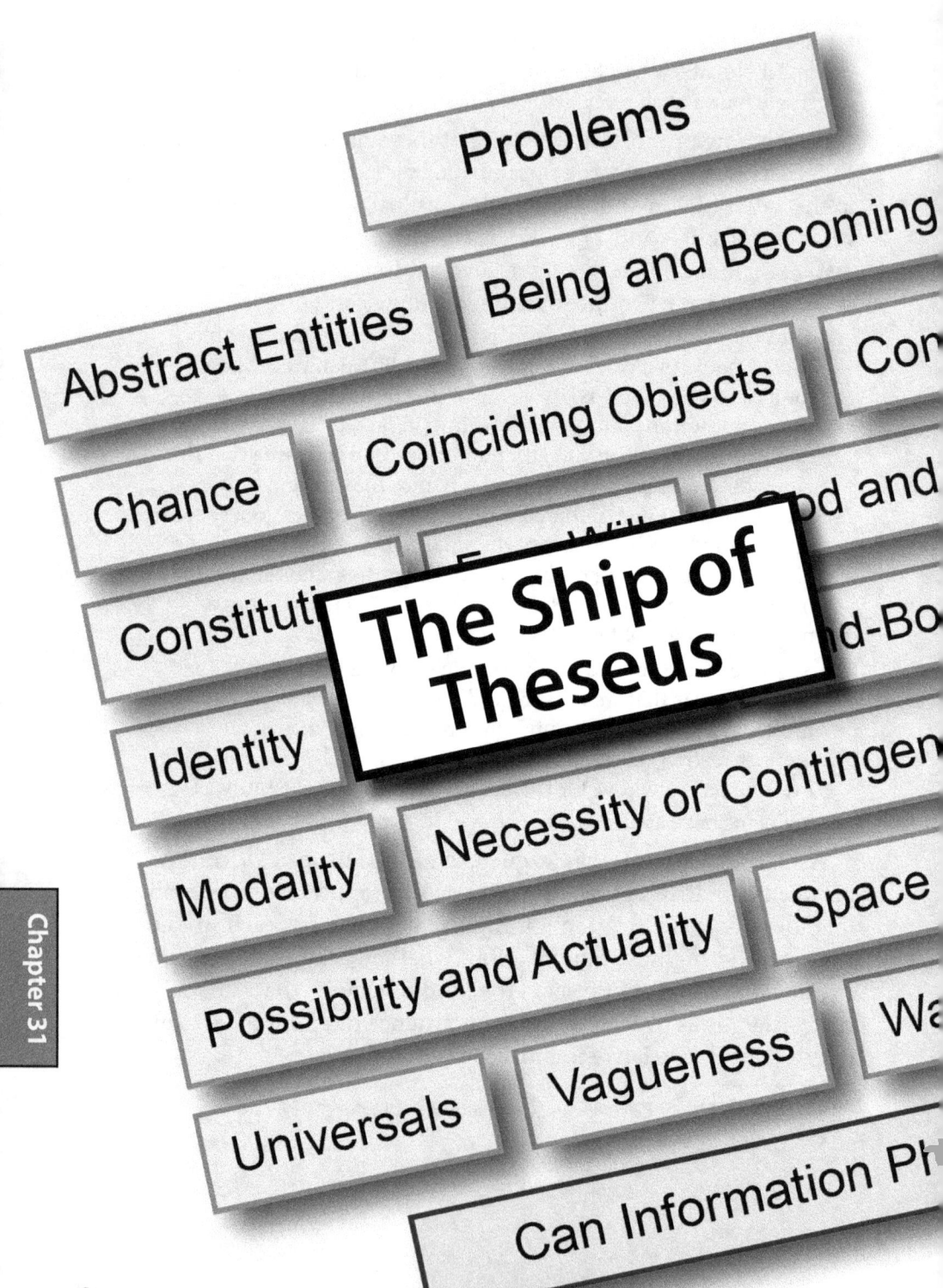

The Ship of Theseus

The Ship of Theseus was a famous vessel in early Greece. "The ship wherein Theseus and the youth of Athens returned had thirty oars, and was preserved by the Athenians down even to the time of Demetrus Phalereus, for they took away the old planks as they decayed, putting in new and stronger timber in their place, insomuch that this ship became a standing example among the philosophers, for the logical question as to things that grow; one side holding that the ship remained the same, and the other contending it was not the same." [1]

In his *De Corpore*, THOMAS HOBBES followed up an ancient suggestion that the ship's original planks might have been hoarded by a collector on land and reassembled, once every part had been replaced. Hobbes offered the reassembled ship as the true original. But he may have had his tongue in his cheek about the ambiguous use of language in truth claims. It is the true original, *qua* material, but not *qua* a functioning ship.

How Information Philosophy Resolves the Paradox

From an information philosophy perspective, the Ship of Theseus is just a quibble about naming. But the full facts of the matter provide the information needed to name the ship uniquely.

We have perfect information about the constituting planks, especially if they are carefully distinguished and stored for reassembly of the original planks as a museum copy (presumably the ship reassembled from old planks will not be seaworthy).

We have perfectly understandable and meaningful names for all the parts in this problem. We have the original ship. We have for example original plank 224, replacement plank 175, etc. We have the repaired ship with specific replacement planks in position. We can keep a diagram showing where all the planks fit. Finally we have the reassembled ship. We can see two numerically distinct ships (or at least collections of ship parts) at all times.

---

1   Plutarch 1880, 7-8

This chapter on the web - metaphysicist.com/puzzles/ship_theseus

The comparable problem of identifying parts of an organism, - specific cells, even atoms, is extremely difficult if not impossible. The exact boundaries of organs and limbs are vague, etc.

So apart from denials that composite inanimate objects exist at all, where is the deep metaphysical problem?

If it is the problem of identity through time, the information philosophy solution is straightforward.

Material constitution is not identity. So the specific planks, mere substrate, are not what the Stoics would have seen as a "peculiarly qualified individual."

It is the arrangement of functioning material parts that makes a functioning ship. As the Stoics would have said, it is both material substance and immaterial qualities (the Skeptics suspect two things in one place?) taken together that constitute the ship.

Just as Dion can survive the loss of a foot, just as human beings survive the almost complete replacement of their atoms and molecules - many times in a lifetime, so the working ship can survive any number of working replacement planks.

In the Academic Skeptic version of the Growing Argument, any change of material produces a numerically distinct ship. But the Stoics say this is just destruction and generation, not true growing. Real growth and decline happens to the entity whose identity we can trace through time by its bundle of peculiar qualities.

And there is one implicit quality that is ignored in the paradox, an important piece of information that identifies a unique ship. Only one of these ships carries Theseus and the youth of Athens, traveling back and forth across the Aegean.

Whatever the specific planks in use, the one that is uniquely The Ship of Theseus is the one sailing the Aegean down even to the time of Demetrus Phalereus.

How to Make Two Ships Out of One.

Most of our metaphysical puzzles start with a single object, then separate it into its matter and its form, giving each of them names and declaring them to be two coinciding objects. Next we postulate a change in either the matter or the form, or both. It is of course impossible to make a change in one without the other changing, since we in fact have only one object.

Although both form and matter must change together, our paradox monger insists that the change has affected the status of only one, usually claiming that the change has caused that one to cease to exist. This follows an ancient view that any change in material constitutes a change in identity. But the modern metaphysicist knows that all objects are always changing and that a change in identity may always preserve some information of an entity. The puzzle claims that an aspect of the object persists if the relative identity, or identity "in some respect" has not changed.

To create a paradox, we use two of our axioms about identity,

Id1. Everything is identical to everything else in some respects.

Id2. Everything is different from everything else in some other respects.

We (in our minds) "pick out" one respect whose identity persists over time because of Id1 and a second respect which changes in time because of Id2.

In cases of coinciding objects, we start with one object that both persists and does not persist (in different respects, of course), the very essence of a paradox. We call them different (coinciding) objects to create the puzzle.

In our case of the Ship of Theseus, we actually create two ships over time. We can look at this as creating two sets of coinciding objects, the matter and its form of function. In each case, we focus on the persistent aspect and ignore the changes.

One persists as a functioning ship, ignoring the changes in matter (the planks). The other persists over time with respect to its matter. They both can claim to have preserved their identity over time with the original ship, but in different respects, the first *qua* functioning ship, the second *qua* material.

In the first case, we ignore the changes in matter. In the second case and the more sophisticated Hobbes formulation, we ignore the loss of function and we ignore the loss of form until the rebuilding of a non-functional ship with the form of the original.

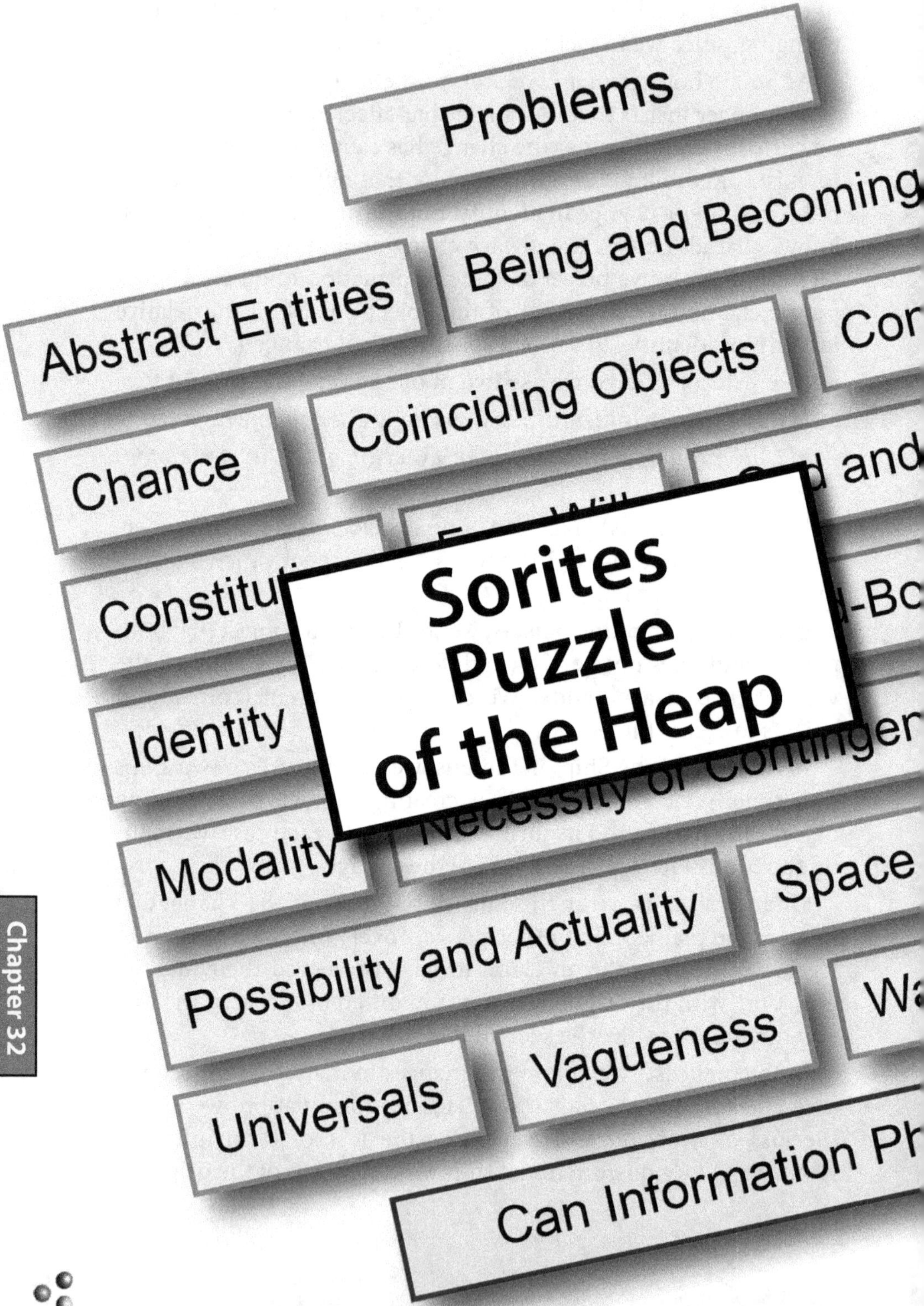

Chapter 32

Sorites Puzzle of the Heap

Sorites Puzzle

The Sorites problem was one of a number of paradoxes created by the 4th century BCE Megarian philosopher Eubulides, who was a pupil of Euclid.

The Greek word soros means 'heap' and gave its name to this "Heap Puzzle," which goes like this:
- Is a single grain of wheat a heap? Not at all.
- Would you describe two grains of wheat as a heap? No.
- How about three grains of wheat ? No.
- How about four, five, six? No.
- Surely several? Maybe…

Another variation is to start with a genuinely large heap, claim that the following two premises are true, then remove grains of sand.
- A million grains of sand is a heap of sand
- A heap of sand minus one grain is still a heap.

After removing enough grains, we get to the *borderline* cases of the paradox. The second premise shows that one grain is absolutely not a heap, because removing one grain leaves nothing, let alone a heap.

Sorites problems are also called "little by little" because small changes may be indiscernible in large objects but they become obvious when applied long enough and the object becomes small.

A characteristic of all Sorites puzzles is the breakdown of truth conditions at some point along the soritical chain of steps from one end to the other. This is often considered a logical paradox, but it seems to be created by our ambiguous language..

Sorites paradoxes appear to resemble proofs by mathematical induction. If $F_n \Rightarrow F_n+1$, and given any n where F_n is true, then it is true for all n.

The Stoics are said to have backed away from the strong conditional A implies B to a weaker material implication where A → B is true just in the case that either A is false or B is true, or not ($\neg A \lor B$) . But this did not help them.

Viewed from the point of the infinite series of mathematical induction, the problem can be found in the fact that for some n, F_n is false (in most Sorites examples - grains of sand, hairs on a bald head, poor or rich, small or large, few or many, - n is small), while for other values of n, F_n is true.

$$\forall n(F_n \to F_n+1)$$

But there is no particular point n along the chain where the failure is obvious, since each step seems too small to make the difference. Put another way, there is no transitivity of truth back and forth somewhere along the chain of steps in the argument. But exactly where the truth condition fails is vague.

Some philosophers regard this failure at some point midway between n = 1 and n very large as a full-blown paradox that might be soluble by a new metatheory, perhaps with non-bivalent logic or with declared gaps in truth values to cover the vague segments where the soritical chain has broken links. From the standpoint of information philosophy, one might say the sorites paradoxes are all consequences of the ambiguous nature of language. Or maybe it just be an overambitious attempt to "precisify" vague concepts with bivalent logic.

One semi-formal way out might be say that either/or soritical terms need a third option or even a "dialectical" acceptance of "both." This is similar but not identical to the failure of bivalence in statements about the future that are neither true nor false. We are often somewhere in the middle between extremes, neither rich nor poor, but middle class, neither hot nor cold, but the "just right" of Goldilocks' porridge. Accepting "both" might include statements like, "He's bald but he's not that bald."

Another workaround for sorites paradoxes might be to notice that neither/nor can be said of the truth value for situations in the *vagueness* gap. For example, somewhere between small and large, we might say it's neither small nor large. Then if we say that small = "not large," we can say that in the gap we have neither small nor not small is true. Since it is always true that everything is either small or not small, without knowing which, some metatheorists imagine a "supervaluation" condition $(P \vee \neg P)$ is needed to describe the vague middle terms, but this seems like logic and language games, since "He's bald but he's not that bald" might also describe the dialectical *both* $(P \wedge \neg P)$.

The fact that large objects appear not to change when small, indiscernible changes are made is also called a *vagueness*.[1] A classic example is PETER UNGER's observation that a few water molecules at the edge of a cloud may be removed with no obvious change in the cloud.

See also DAVID WIGGINS's version of Tibbles the Cat as really 1,001 cats by selectively excluding one of Tibbles' 1,000 hairs.[2] Unger's conclusion was that the water molecules may compose many clouds by selectively excluding or including just a few molecules. This is known as the *Problem of the Many*,[3] but Unger's first response was to say that the ambiguity meant that there are no clouds at all, a position known as *mereological nihilism* that was also endorsed by PETER VAN INWAGEN.

Liar Paradox

Eubulides also created a variation on Sorites with the number of hairs on a bald man's head as well as the much more famous Liar's Paradox

A man says that he is lying. Is what he says true or false?

A modern self-referential variation is Russell's Paradox

This statement is false.

---

1 See chapter 22.
2 Chapter 34.
3 Chapter 30.

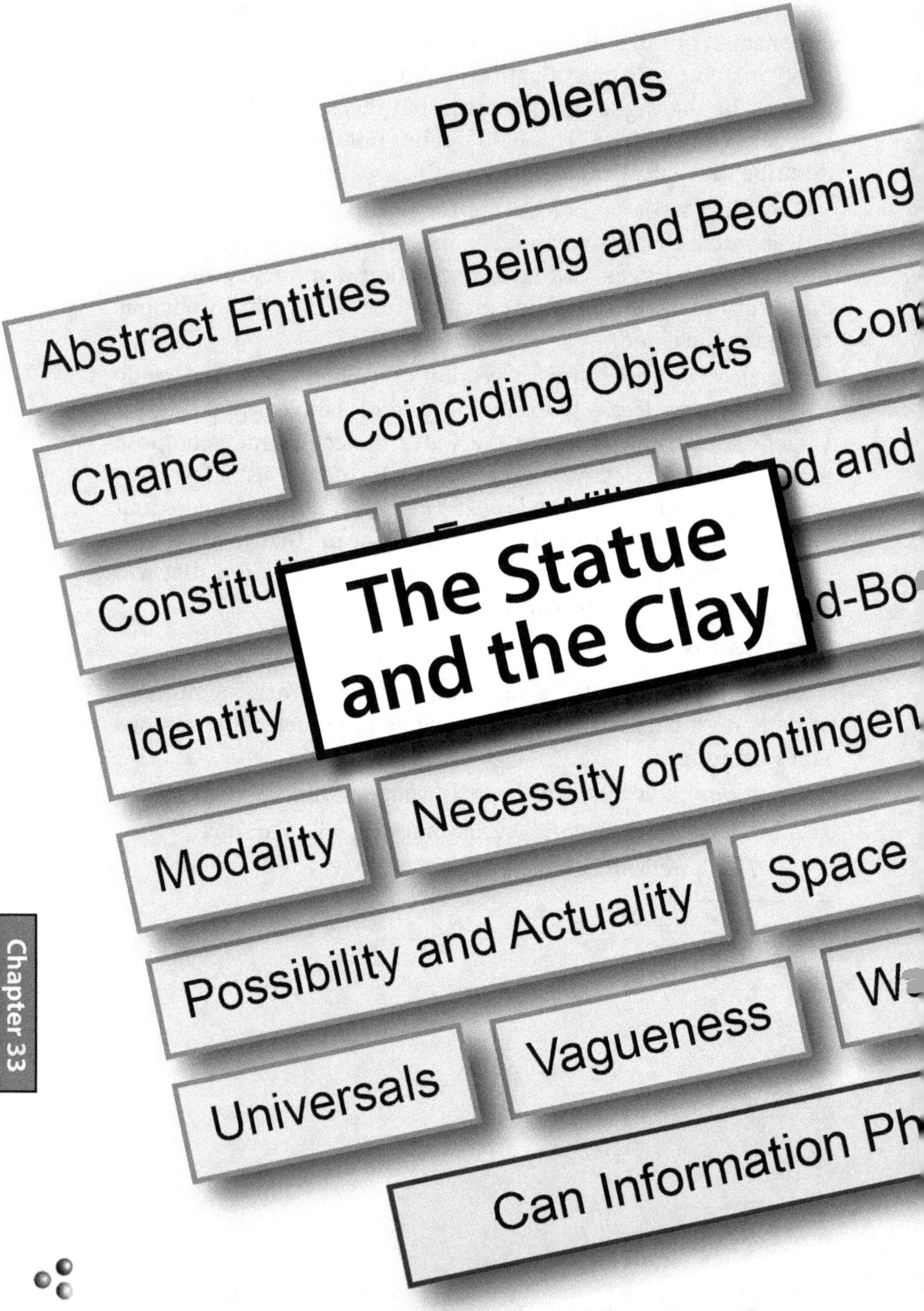

Chapter 33
The Statue and the Clay

The Statue and the Clay

Aristotle's *Metaphysics* has perhaps the earliest mention of the Statue and the Clay (actually bronze in his example), but his hylomorphic theory sees no problem with the coincidence of material (ὕλη) and the form (μορφή) of the statue. Is Aristotle here the source of the four Stoic genera or categories?

"The term "substance" (οὐσία) is used, if not in more, at least in four principal cases; for both the essence (εἶναι), and the universal (καθόλου) and the genus (γένος) are held to be the substance of the particular (ἑκάστου), and fourthly the substrate (ὑποκείμενον). The substrate is that of which the rest are predicated, while it is not itself predicated of anything else. Hence we must first determine its nature, for the primary substrate (ὑποκείμενον) is considered to be in the truest sense substance." [1]

Aristotle clearly sees a statue as both its form/shape and its matter/clay.

"Both matter and form and their combination are said to be substance (οὐσία). Now in one sense we call the matter (ὕλη) the substrate; in another, the shape (μορφή); and in a third, the combination of the two. By matter I mean, for instance, bronze; by shape, the arrangement of the form (τὸ σχῆμα τῆς ἰδέας); and by the combination of the two, the concrete thing: the statue (ἀνδριάς). Thus if the form is prior to the matter and more truly existent, by the same argument it will also be prior to the combination." [2]

Aristotle also sees no problem with the body and soul of a person being combined in one substance (οὐσία), but a hundred or so years after Aristotle, the Academic Skeptics attacked the Stoics, saying Stoics were making single things into dual beings, two objects in the same place at the same time, but indistinguishable.

---

1   Aristiotle *Metaphysics*, Book VII, § iii
2   *Ibid*.

This chapter on the web - metaphysicist.com/puzzles/clay_statue

The two objects are just Plato's body and his peculiarly qualified individual (ἴδιος ποιὸν),

> Aristotle would say they are his matter and his form. . .
> "since the duality which they say belongs to each body is differentiated in a way unrecognizable by sense-perception. For if a peculiarly qualified thing like Plato is a body, and Plato's substance is a body, and there is no apparent difference between these in shape, colour, size and appearance, but both have equal weight and the same outline, by what definition and mark shall we distinguish them and say that now we are apprehending Plato himself, now the substance of Plato? For if there is some difference, let it be stated and demonstrated." [3]

Perhaps the earliest statement of the classic puzzle of the Statue and the Clay was described by Mnesarchus of Athens, a Stoic philosopher who lived c. 160 - c. 85 BCE, as reported by the 5th century CE compiler of extracts from Greek authors, Joannes Stobaeus. Mnesarchus' puzzle is the origin of the observation that the clay and the statue have different persistence conditions.

> "That what concerns the peculiarly qualified is not the same as what concerns the substance, Mnesarchus says is clear. In this case, what goes in and out of existence is only what Aristotle called form (μορφή) or shape, the arrangement of the form (τὸ σχῆμα τῆς ἰδέας) For things which are the same should have the same properties. For if, for the sake of argument, someone were to mould a horse, squash it, then make a dog, it would be reasonable for us on seeing this to say that this previously did not exist but now does exist. So what is said when it comes to the qualified thing is different." [4]

This is no longer Aristotle's ancient problem of the coexistence of body versus mind (or soul), or the Stoic problem of the material substrate (ὑποκείμενον) of a person versus the "peculiarly qualified individual" (ἴδιος ποιὸν), because modern metaphysics has become materialist, or naturalist, denying the dualism of a separate mental substance.

---

3   Anonymous Academic treatise, Oxyrhynchus Papyrus 3008 in Stoic Ontology, *The Hellenistic Philosophers*, A. Long and D. Sedley, v.1, p.167

4   Stobaeus (I,177,21 - 179,17, in *The Hellenistic Philosophers*, v.1, p.168

It is now common for many identity theorists to say that the whole of one object and the whole of another can occupy just the same place at just the same time. This is the problem of coinciding objects.[5] Common sense says that two material objects cannot coincide.

In modern times, at least two puzzles are used to pose the problem of coinciding objects. One is the Statue and the Clay. The other is the ancient problem of Dion and Theon,[6] in recent years described as Tibbles the Cat [7] and a similar cat missing his tail.

How to Make Two Out of One

Most of our metaphysical puzzles start with a single object, then separate it into its matter and its form, giving each of them names and declaring them to be two coinciding objects. Next we postulate a change in either the matter or the form, or both. It is of course impossible to make a change in one without the other changing, since we in fact have only one object.

But our puzzle maker asks us to focus on one and insist that the change has affected the status of only that one, usually claiming that the change has caused that one to cease to exist. This follows an ancient view that any change in material constitutes a change in identity. But the modern metaphysicist knows that all objects are always changing and that a change in identity may always preserve some information of an entity. The puzzle claims that an aspect of the object persists if the relative identity, or identity "in some respect" has not changed.

To create a paradox, we use two of our axioms about identity,

Id1. Everything is identical to everything else in some respects.

Id2. Everything is different from everything else in some other respects.

---

5   See chapter 7.
6   Chapter 25.
7   Chapter 34.

We (in our minds) "pick out" one respect whose identity persists over time because of Id1 and a second respect which changes in time because of Id2. We have created a paradox.

We now have one object that both persists and does not persist (in different respects, of course), the very essence of a paradox. We call them different objects to create the puzzle.

In our case of the statue and the clay, Mnesarchus's original version assumes someone moulds a horse, then squashes it. We are asked to pick out the horse's shape or form. The act of squashing changes that shape into another relatively amorphous shape. The object changes its identity with respect to its shape. Mnesarchus said it would be reasonable to see this sequence of events as something coming into existence and then ceasing to exist. The most obvious thing changing is the horse shape that we name "statue."

By design, there is no change in the amount of clay, so the matter is identical over time with respect to the amount of clay. The clay persists.

We now claim to have seen a difference in persistence conditions. The object *qua* clay persists. The object *qua* statue goes in and out of existence.

But this is just a way of talking about what has happened because a human observer has "picked out" two different aspects of the one object. As the statue is being smashed beyond recognition, every part of the clay must move to a new position that accommodates the change in shape of the statue. There are changes in the clay with identical information to the change in the shape of the statue. These we ignore to set up the puzzle.

Notice that what we ignore is the identity of the statue and the clay. It is in fact the only true identity, the self-identity of any object with itself that is our third identity axiom.

Id3. Everything is identical to itself in all respects at each instant of time, but different in some respects from itself at any other time.

In more modern versions of the statue and clay puzzle, we can make a change in the matter, for example by breaking off an arm and replacing it with a new arm made of different material but restoring the shape. We now ignore the change in form, although it was obviously a drastic change until the restoration. For the paradox, we focus on the clay, making the absurd claim that the original clay has ceased to exist and new clay has come into existence. This is just sophistical talk. That part of the clay still in the statue still exists. So does the broken piece. It is just no longer a part of the statue.

There is a discontinuity when the arm is broken off and replaced, but after the replacement the newly repaired statue is still identical with itself at each instant, but following Id3 it is now a new self, different from its earlier, original self, with respect to the matter in the new arm.

All the paradoxes of coinciding objects are language games that ignore the fundamental identity of anything with itself.

In this puzzle, we are asked to make a change in only the form.

In other puzzles, we are asked to make a change in only the matter (The Ship of Theseus or The Debtor's Paradox), or in both matter and form (The Growing Argument, The Problem of the Many, or Dion and Theon). A careful focus on the information involved always finds identical changes in both the matter and the form.

The paradox maker asks us to focus on one and ignore the other.

Tibbles, the Cat

PETER GEACH was a younger colleague of LUDWIG WITTGENSTEIN. Geach worked on problems of identity and some time in the early 1960's reformulated CHRYSIPPUS's ancient problem of Dion and Theon as "Tibbles, the Cat."

In his 1968 article "On Being in the Same Place at the Same Time," DAVID WIGGINS described Geach's first version of Tibbles. Although Geach himself never published this version, Wiggins cites Geach as his source of a variation on the ancient problem of Dion and Theon, where Theon is identical to Dion except he is missing a foot. Wiggins describes a metaphysical cat named Tibbles and a second cat named Tib who lacks a tail.

Where Theon is defined as identical to Dion except he is missing a foot, we now have a cat named Tibbles and a second cat named Tib who lacks a tail.

Wiggins begins his argument with an assertion S*

"S*: No two things of the same kind (that is, no two things which satisfy the same sortal or substance concept) can occupy exactly the same volume at exactly the same time.

This, I think, is a sort of necessary truth...

A final test for the soundness of S* or, if you wish, for Leibniz' Law, is provided by a puzzle contrived by Geach out of a discussion in William of Sherwood. A cat called Tibbles loses his tail at time t_2. But before t_2 somebody had picked out, identified, and distinguished from Tibbles a different and rather peculiar animate entity-namely, Tibbles minus Tibbles' tail. Let us suppose that he decided to call this entity "Tib." Suppose Tibbles was on the mat at time t_1. Then both Tib and Tibbles were on the mat at t_1. This does not violate S*.

But consider the position from t_3 onward when, something the worse for wear, the cat is sitting on the mat without a tail. Is there one cat or are there two cats there? Tib is certainly sitting there. In a way nothing happened to him at all. But so is Tibbles. For Tibbles lost his tail, survived this experience, and then at t_3 was sitting on the mat. And we agreed that Tib

This chapter on the web - metaphysicist.com/puzzles/tibbles

≠ Tibbles. We can uphold the transitivity of identity, it seems, only if we stick by that decision at t_3 and allow that at t_3 there are two cats on the mat in exactly the same place at exactly the same time. But my adherence to S* obliges me to reject this. So I am obliged to find something independently wrong with the way in which the puzzle was set up."

This is a clear case of Peter van Inwagen's *Doctrine of Arbitrary Undetached Parts*[1]

"It was set up in such a way that before t_2 Tibbles had a tail as a part and Tib allegedly did not have a tail as a part. If one dislikes this feature (as I do), then one has to ask, "Can one identify and name a part of a cat, insist one is naming just that, and insist that what one is naming is a cat"? This is my argument against the supposition that one can: Does Tib have a tail or not? I mean the question in the ordinary sense of "have," not in any peculiar sense "have as a part." For in a way it is precisely the propriety of some other concept of having as a part which is in question."

As an arbitrary undetached part, Tib has been picked out and defined as coinciding with Tibbles, except for the tail Tibbles is about to lose. This violates S*

"Surely Tib adjoins and is connected to a tail in the standard way in which cats who have tails are connected with their tails. There is no peculiarity in this case. Otherwise Tibbles himself might not have a tail. Surely any animal which has a tail loses a member or part of itself if its tail is cut off. But then there was no such cat as the cat who at t_1 has no tail as a part of himself. Certainly there was a cat-part which anybody could call "Tib" if they wished. But one cannot define into existence a cat called Tib who had no tail as part of himself at t, if there was no such cat at t_1. If someone thought he could, then one might ask him (before the cutting at t_2), "Is this Tib of yours the same cat as Tibbles or is he a different cat?" [2]

---

1 Van Inwagen (1997). in Rea, *Material Constitution*, 191-208.
2 "Being in the same place at the same time," *The Philosophical Review*, p.94

In Geach's second account of Tibbles as an exemplar of a metaphysical problem, published some years later (1980), Tibbles is a cat with 1,000 hairs that can be interpreted as 1,001 cats, by "picking out" and then pulling out one of those cat hairs at a time and each time identifying a new cat..

Geach's second version of Tibbles is widely cited as a discussion of the problem of *vagueness* or what PETER UNGER called the *Problem of the Many*, also published in 1980. It is not the "body-minus" problem of the original Tibbles, but it is relevant to the problem of coinciding objects and the relation of parts to wholes.

If a few of Tibbles' hairs are pulled out, do we still have Tibbles, the Cat? Obviously we do. Have we created other cats, now multiple things in the same place at the same time? Obviously not.

Nevertheless, Geach attempts to show that removing one of a thousand hairs from Tibbles may mean that there are actually 1,001 cats on the mat.

> "The fat cat sat on the mat. There was just one cat on the mat. The cat's name was "Tibbles": "Tibbles" is moreover a name for a cat.—This simple story leads us into difficulties if we assume that Tibbles is a normal cat. For a normal cat has at least 1,000 hairs. Like many empirical concepts, the concept (single) hair is fuzzy at the edges; but it is reasonable to assume that we can identify in Tibbles at least 1,000 of his parts each of which definitely is a single hair. I shall refer to these hairs as h_1, h_2, h_3, ... up to $h_{1,000}$.
> Now let c be the largest continuous mass of feline tissue on the mat. Then for any of our 1,000 cat-hairs, say h_n, there is a proper part c_n of c which contains precisely all of c except the hair h_n; and every such part c_n differs in a describable way both from any other such part, say c_m, and from c as a whole. Moreover, fuzzy as the concept cat may be, it is clear that not only is c a cat, but also any part c_n is a cat: c_n would clearly be a cat were the hair h_n plucked out, and we cannot reasonably suppose that plucking out a hair generates a cat, so c_n must already have been a cat. So, contrary to our story, there was not just one cat called 'Tibbles' sitting on the mat; there were at least 1,001 sitting there!

All the same, this result is absurd. We simply do not speak of cats, or use names of cats, in this way; nor is our ordinary practice open to logical censure. I am indeed far from thinking that ordinary practice never is open to logical censure; but I do not believe our ordinary use of proper names and count nouns is so radically at fault as this conclusion would imply.

Everything falls into place if we realize that the number of cats on the mat is the number of different cats on the mat; and c_{13}, c_{279}, and c are not three different cats, they are one and the same cat. Though none of these 1,001 lumps of feline tissue is the same lump of feline tissue as another, each is the same cat as any other: each of them, then, is a cat, but there is only one cat on the mat, and our original story stands.

Thus each one of the names "c_1 ; c_2, ... $c_{1,000}$ or again the name "c", is a name of a cat; but none of these 1,001 names is a name for a cat, as "Tibbles" is. By virtue of its sense "Tibbles" is a name, not for one and the same thing (in fact, to say that would really be to say nothing at all), but for one and the same cat. This name for a cat has reference, and it names the one and only cat on the mat; but just on that account "Tibbles" names, as a shared name, both c itself and any of the smaller masses of feline tissue like c_{12} and c_{279}; for all of these are one and the same cat, though not one and the same mass of feline tissue. "Tibbles" is not a name for a mass of feline tissue.

So we recover the truth of the simple story we began with. The price to pay is that we must regard "is the same cat as" as expressing only a certain equivalence relation, not an absolute identity restricted to cats; but this price, I have elsewhere argued, must be paid anyhow, for there is no such absolute identity as logicians have assumed." [3]

As Geach has argued, we only have *relative identity* between any two objects.

And as Geach also recognizes so clearly, his selecting out arbitrary parts and giving them a separate identity from the whole is just an exercise in verbal quibbling. He has multiplied his original problem of Tibbles, which was just a restatement of the Academic Sceptic's Dion and Theon.

---

3   Geach (1980) *Reference and Generality*, 3rd edition, p.215

Geach might as well have removed a single atom of material from the cat and declared it was another cat, in which case he would have produced of the order of 10^{26} cats.

The puzzle of Tibbles, the Cat is closely related to these classic metaphysical problems:

- Constitution. For those metaphysicians who think that material constitution is identity, there is a doubt that Tibbles can survive the loss of his tail or Dion the loss of a foot. Chrysippus's so-called "growing argument" was designed to show that Dion survives, despite Skeptic claims.
- Composition. If we remove something inessential (say one atom, or one hair from Tibbles), do we have the same thing? Or are some "proper parts" mereologically essential to the identity of the whole?
- Identity. Different aspects of an single object may have different persistence conditions. Some of Tibbles' hairs fall out naturally. Does that create a new identity for Tibbles? Perdurantisists deny the possibility of identity through time. Endurantists emphasizes the subsets of total information that are unchanging over time as constituting the essential Tibbles.
- Coinciding Objects. The metaphysical notion of two things occupying the same space and time has always been a verbal quibble, a "picking out" of a part and seeing it as coincident with a part of the whole has been an absurd language game.
- Individuation. Given two equal amounts of matter, they are distinguished by their shape or form. Given two things with identical form, they are individuated by being embodied in different material. A living thing is a composite object that has a telos in the form of all its genetic information.

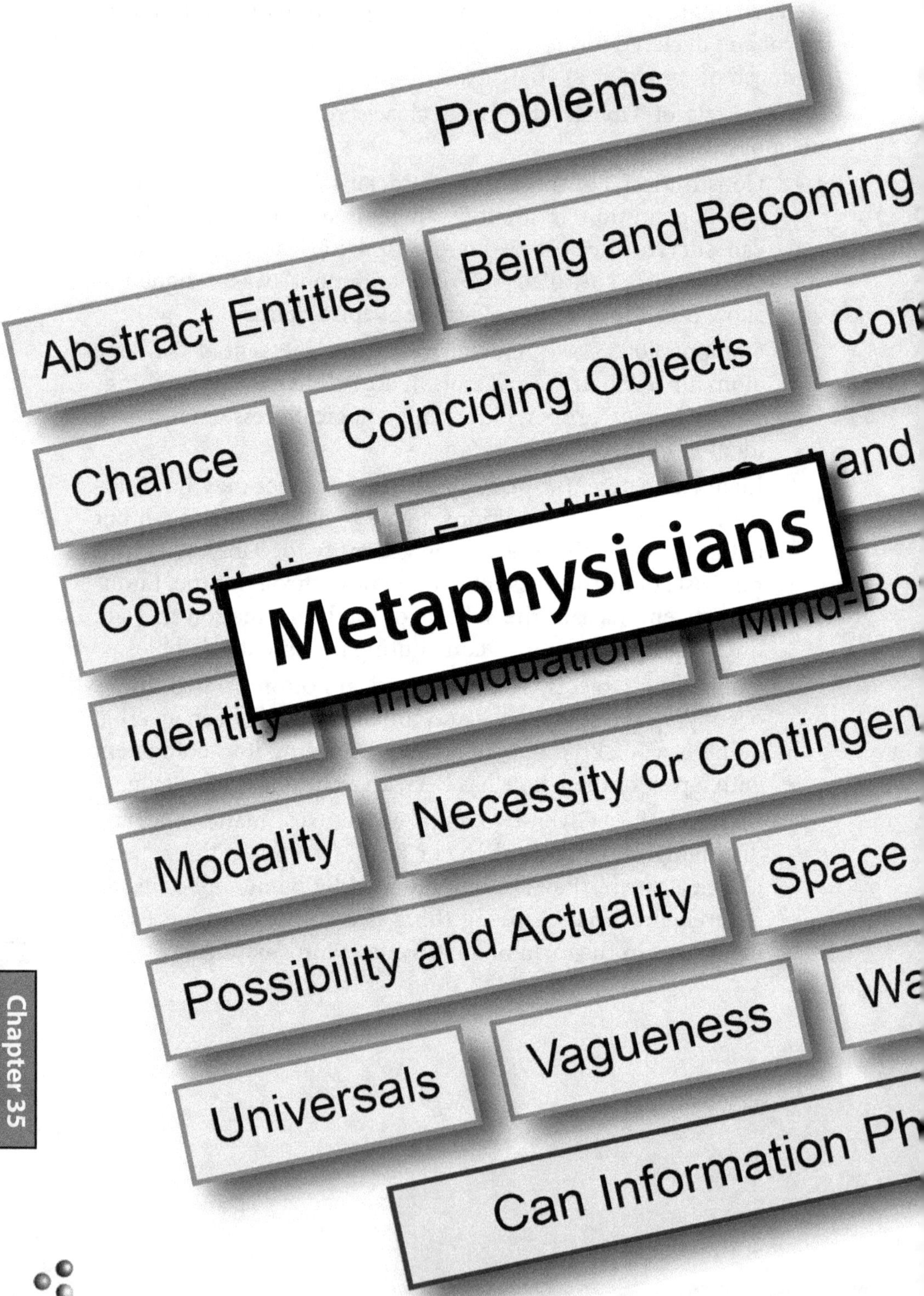

Chapter 35

Metaphysicians

Problems

- Abstract Entities
- Being and Becoming
- Chance
- Coinciding Objects
- Constitution
- Free Will
- Identity and Individuation
- Mind-Body
- Modality
- Necessity or Contingency
- Possibility and Actuality
- Space
- Universals
- Vagueness
- Can Information Physics...

Metaphysicians

David M. Armstrong

DAVID MALET ARMSTRONG's book *Belief, Truth and Knowledge* contains an important analysis of the infinite regress of inferences - "reasons behind the reasons" - first noticed by Plato in the *Theaetetus*.[1]

Knowledge traditionally entails true belief, but true belief does not entail knowledge.

Knowledge is true belief plus some justification in the form of reasons or evidence. But that evidence must itself be knowledge, which in turn must be justified, leading to a regress.

Following some unpublished work of Gregory O'Hair, Armstrong identified and diagramed several possible ways to escape Plato's regress, including:[2]

- Skepticism - knowledge is impossible
- The regress is infinite but virtuous
- The regress is finite, but has no end (Coherence view)
- The regress ends in self-evident truths (Foundationalist view)
- Non-inferential credibility, such as direct sense perceptions
- Externalist theories (O'Hair is the source of the term "externalist")
- Causal view (Ramsey)
- Reliability view (Ramsey)

Armstrong is cited by HILARY KORNBLITH and other recent epistemologists as restoring interest in "externalist" justifications of knowledge. Since Descartes, and perhaps Kant, epistemology had been focused on "internalist" justifications. Knowledge in information philosophy is a *correspondence* between information in the mind (the experience recorder and reproducer - ERR) and the external world that provides the experience.

---

1 Plato, *Theaetetus*, 200D-201C
2 Armstrong (1973) *Belief, Truth, and Knowledge*. p.152

Armstrong does not subscribe to traditional views of justifying true beliefs, but he cited "causal" and "reliabilist" theories as direct non-inferential validation of knowledge. Direct validation or justification avoids the problem of the infinite regress of inferences.

Causality and reliabilism also were not original with Armstrong. He referred to the 1929 work of FRANK RAMSEY. Today these ideas are primarily associated with the name of ALVIN GOLDMAN, who put forward both "causal" (in 1967) and "reliabilist" (in 1969) theories of justification for true beliefs. Goldman was apparently not familiar with the earlier Ramsey work, since it is not mentioned in the early Goldman papers?

Here is how Armstrong described "causal" and "reliabilist" views:

> According to "Externalist" accounts of non-inferential knowledge, what makes a true non-inferential belief a case of knowledge is some natural relation which holds between the belief-state, Bap ['a believes p'], and the situation which makes the belief true. It is a matter of a certain relation holding between the believer and the world. It is important to notice that, unlike "Cartesian" and "Initial Credibility" theories, Externalist theories are regularly developed as theories of the nature of knowledge generally and not simply as theories of non-inferential knowledge. But they still have a peculiar importance in the case of non-inferential knowledge because they serve to solve the problem of the infinite regress.
>
> Externalist theories may be further sub-divided into 'Causal' and 'Reliability' theories.

The source for both causal and reliabilist theories is Frank Ramsey (1929). Armstrong gets this right.

> Ramsey's brief note on 'Knowledge', to be found among his 'Last Papers' in The Foundations of Mathematics, puts forward a causal view. A sophisticated recent version of a causal theory is to be found in 'A Causal Theory of Knowing' by Alvin I. Goldman (Goldman 1967).
>
> Ramsey is the source for reliabilist views as well. Once again, Ramsey is the pioneer. The paper 'Knowledge', already mentioned, combines elements of the Causal and the Reliability view. There followed John Watling's 'Inference from the

Known to the Unknown' (Watling 1954), which first converted me to a Reliability view. Since then there has been Brian Skyrms' very difficult paper 'The Explication of "X knows that p"' (Skyrms 1967), and Peter Unger's 'An Analysis of Factual Knowledge' (Unger 1968), both of which appear to defend versions of the Reliability view. There is also my own first version in Chapter Nine of A Materialist Theory of the Mind. A still more recent paper, which I think can be said to put forward a Reliability view, and which in any case anticipates a number of the results I arrive at in this Part, is Fred Dretske's 'Conclusive Reasons' (Dretske 1971).

Here is Hilary Kornblith on Armstrong

> The terms "internalism" and "externalism" are used in philosophy in a variety of different senses, but their use in epistemology for anything like the positions which are the focus of this book dates to 1973. More precisely, the word "externalism" was introduced in print by David Armstrong in his book "*Belief, Truth and Knowledge*' (sic).

Michael Burke

MICHAEL BURKE is Professor Emeritus of Philosophy at Indiana University. He worked on problems of material constitution and critically examined the idea of coinciding objects (colocation), both Chrysippus's ancient problem of Dion and Theon and its modern version as Tibbles, the Cat. He wrote in 1994:

> The Stoic philosopher Chrysippus is said to have posed the following puzzle. Yesterday, there was a whole-bodied man called 'Dion' who had a proper part called 'Theon'. Theon was that part of Dion which consisted of all of Dion except his left foot. Today, Dion's left foot was successfully amputated. The Academic Skeptics said no individual can survive a material loss. Chrysippus argued that Dion could. Theon was just a name for a part of Dion, not a distinct individual, hypothesized for dialectical purposes So, if Dion and Theon both still exist, they are numerically different objects now occupying just the same place and wholly composed of just the same matter. Presuming this to be impossible, the question is which of the two, Dion or Theon, has ceased to exist.

At first thought, of course, it seems that neither has ceased to exist. It would seem absurd to deny that Dion is still with us. Surely, a man can retain his identity despite the loss of a foot. But it also seems undeniable that Theon still exists. Theon, it seems, has emerged from the surgery intact.

Might it be that Dion and Theon, who initially were two, have both survived, but now are one? Assuming the indiscernibility of identicals, a principle invoked even in Hellenistic philosophy, the answer is "no." For even now there is something true of Dion which is not true of Theon: that he once had two feet.

As will be obvious to those familiar with contemporary identity theory, the puzzle of Dion and Theon is of more than antiquarian interest. The same type of puzzle commands much attention today. (The example discussed most often is that of Tibbles the cat.) Interestingly, none of today's theorists would agree with Chrysippus that Theon has perished." [3]

Tibbles the Cat

The original suggestion of Tibbles by Peter Geach in the early 1960's may not have been what is called today a "body-minus" problem. It was a problem of the many. But in 1968, David Wiggins repurposed Geach's idea, imagined Tibbles as a cat without a tail, renaming of the problem of Dion and Theon that has eclipsed Chrysippus' account.

About the same time, Peter van Inwagen (1981) imagined a Descartes who had lost a leg.[4] Van Inwagen denied the legitimacy of a second individual occupying the same space and time as even a part of Dion. This is right, of course, it was just the deliberate setting up of the ancient paradox.

Wiggins described his Tibbles, beginning with an assertion that he calls a *necessary* truth.

> "S*: No two things of the same kind (that is, no two things which satisfy the same sortal or substance concept) can occupy exactly the same volume at exactly the same time.

---

[3] Burke (1994b) 'Dion and Theon: An essentialist solution to an ancient puzzle,' p.129

[4] Van Inwagen (1981) 'Doctrine of Arbitrary Undetached Parts,'

This, I think, is a sort of necessary truth...

A final test for the soundness of S* or, if you wish, for Leibniz' Law, is provided by a puzzle contrived by Geach out of a discussion in William of Sherwood." [5]

In their great 1987 compilation of Hellenic thought, A. A. Long and D. N. Sedley described Tibbles as an example of "two peculiarly qualified individuals coming to occupy one substance," something the Stoics explicitly denied is possible. Long and Sedley clearly are following Wiggins' 1968 version of Tibbles. They suggest that Chrysippus has given us an example of Dion surviving a diminution in his material without losing his identity, as the Academic Skeptics claimed.

> "The key is to recognize this as the ancestor of a puzzle which has featured in recent discussions of place and identity. Take a cat, Tibbies, and assign the name Tib to that portion of her which excludes her tail. Tibbies is a cat with a tail, Tib is a cat without a tail. Then amputate the tail. The result is that Tibbies, now tailless, occupies precisely the same space as Tib. Yet they are two distinct cats, because their histories are different. The conclusion is unacceptable, and the philosophical interest lies in pin-pointing the false step."[6]

In his 1996 article "Tibbles the cat: A Modern 'Sophisma,'" Burke claimed Tibbles was "scholastic in origin," which is puzzling as he knows the story of the Greek Dion and Theon very well (Burke 1994b). He describes Tibbles, clearly following Wiggins or Long and Sedley and not Geach.

> "Before us stands a 10-pound cat named 'Tibbles'. Before us also is that 9-pound part of Tibbles which consists of all of Tibbles except his tail. Following philosophical custom, call that bodily part, for which English has no common name, a 'puss'; and give Tibbies' puss the proper name 'Tib'. Further, assume that cats are wholly physical. (Or else let 'Tibbles' name the body of the cat, or even a toy cat.) Suppose now that Tibbles loses his tail. We are left with a tailless cat - and a puzzle. If Tib and Tibbles both still exist, they are numerically different physical objects, one a former 10-pounder, one not, which now consist of just the

---

5   Wiggins (1969) 'Being in the same place at the same time,', p.94
6   Stoic Ontology, *The Hellenistic Philosophers*, A. A. Long and D. N. Sedley, p.175

same matter and occupy just the same place. That, presumably, is impossible. Either Tib or Tibbles, therefore, has ceased to exist. But which one? The identity of a cat surely is not tied to its tail. So Tibbles still exists. But surely Tib has not ceased to exist: Tib lost none of its parts. Something has to give. But what?

Tibbles-type puzzles are a mainstay of revisionist metaphysics." [7]

Burke proposes a "novel and conservative solution" to the body-minus problem, based on the idea of "essentialism," the idea that properties of an object are essential to the object. Burke's argument agrees with Chrysippus' view that it is Dion who survives. Tib ceases to exist because she was a puss and, if she still existed, would now be a cat. Though Burke doubts this was Chrysippus' argument.

> "Here is what I propose to say about Tib and Tibbies: Initially we had a 10-pound cat, Tibbies, which contained a 9-pound puss, Tib. Before us now, following the loss of the tail, is a single 9-pound object, one which is both a cat and a puss. That object is Tibbies, which earlier had a tail but now is tailless. Tib has ceased to exist.
>
> What is novel in this account, and what will surely seem counterintuitive, is the claim that Tib has ceased to exist. After all, I allow that there was such a thing as the puss Tib. And I allow that there is a puss before us now. The latter is spatiotemporally continuous with Tib. And it is both qualitatively and compositionally identical to Tib. So how could it fail to be Tib? My answer, very simply, is that Tib was merely a puss, whereas the puss now before us is also a cat..." [8]

For more on Burke's thoughts on mereological essentialism, see his page on metaphysicist.com and chapter 10 on essentialism. Burke thought he could demystify problems of coinciding objects.

An information-based metaphysics shows that two "coinciding objects" are often just the matter and form of a single object, for example the statue and the lump of clay. But the *immaterial* form (abstract information) and the concrete material are not "parts" in the same sense. Does Burke make a "category mistake?"

> "We have before us a copper statue. In the same place, presumably, there is a piece of copper. Let's call the statue 'Statue' and

---

7   Burke (1996) 'Tibbles the cat: A Modern "Sophisma". *p.* 63
8   *ibid.*, pp.64-65

the piece of copper 'Piece'. Now what is the relationship between Statue and Piece? Among philosophers who reject the view that objects have temporal parts, by far the most popular account of such cases is one on which Statue and Piece are numerically different objects even though they consist of just the same matter and are wholly present in just the same place. What shows them to be different objects, according to this account, is that they have different persistence conditions: Piece could survive a drastic change in shape; Statue could not. Let's call this 'the standard account.'" [9]

Information philosophy denies these two are numerically distinct and yet "just the same matter." The Piece is wholly matter. The Statue is merely form. They have been picked out as "two" and named for their dialectical value as having different persistence conditions

In a 1994 article. Burke begins by arguing that the "standard account" for many metaphysical identity theorists is this:

"It is common for the whole of one object and the whole of another object to occupy just the same place at the same time. So say many identity theorists." [10]

The "identity theorists" he included are David Wiggins (1967), Saul Kripke (1971), Roderick Chisholm (1973), and E. Jonathan Lowe (1983).

Exceptions include Peter van Inwagen (1981), who Burke says calls it a "desperate expedient," David Lewis (1986), who wrote, "This multiplication of entities is absurd on its face," and Harold Noonan (1988), who says it "manifests a bad case of double vision." These are words the Ancient Skeptics used about the Stoic categories of material substrate or body and the 'peculiarly qualified individual' or person in their discussions of the Growing Argument)."

In his extensive article, Burke cites several examples of coinciding objects, the statue and clay, a tree and its molecules, cats and pusses, and persons and bodies.

Information philosophy, and an information-based metaphysics, analyzes all these problems as distinctions between the *immaterial*

---

9 Burke (1992) 'Copper Statues and Pieces of Copper: A Challenge to the Standard Account.' *Analysis* 52: 12-17

10 Burke (1994a) 'Preserving the Principle of One Object to a Place,' *Philosophy and Phenomenological Research*, 54(3), p.591

form (the information) and the material substance. As such, information philosophy is a *dualist* theory. Burke recognizes the importance of this distinction, potentially solving problems that are intractable for a modern materialist or naturalist philosopher, who denies anything *immaterial*, notably the *mind*.

> "Perhaps the most frequently cited example of coincidence is that of persons and their bodies. Let's briefly consider the example from both dualist and materialist points of view.
>
> On dualist theories of the human person, there is no threat of genuine coincidence. Dualist theories divide into those on which the body is a proper part of the person and those on which the body is something like a possession. On theories of the first type, it is true that a person occupies the place occupied by his body. But it's not the whole of the person that occupies that place; it's merely a part of him that does so. This is no more a case of coincidence than is the case of a pipe and its bowl... On theories of the second type, on which a person is a mind or soul that "possesses" a body, it is only in some non-literal sense that a person may be said to "occupy" the place occupied by her body. The sense is similar to that in which a general may be said to occupy the area occupied by his army, even if he commands the army from outside that area." [11]

In a 2004 article, "Dion, Theon, and the Many Thinkers Problem," Burke summarizes of his work, defending it against numerous criticisms. See his page on metaphysicist.com for details.

Rudolf Carnap

Carnap and his colleagues in the Vienna Circle added very little of lasting value to either science or philosophy with their strong ideas in the philosophy of science. They mistakenly believed that both subjects were reducible to language and logic.

Ludwig Wittgenstein had set the project for the Vienna Circle in the *Tractatus Logico-Philosophicus*.

> "4.11   The totality of true propositions is the whole of natural science (or the whole corpus of the natural sciences)" [12]

---

[11] Burke (1994a) "Preserving the principle of one object to a place," in Rea (1997) *Material Constitution*. p.261

[12] Wittgenstein (1922) *Tractatus Logico-Philosophicus* 4.11

In his 1928 book *Der Logische Aufbau der Welt*, and especially his 1934 work *Logische Syntax der Sprache* (published in 1937 as *The Logical Syntax of Language*), Carnap thought that he completed the Wittgenstein project, but with significant differences from some of Wittgenstein's views in the Tractatus.

The logical syntax of a language is a set of formal rules. They have nothing to do with the "meaning of the symbols (for example, the words) or the sequence of expressions (the sentences), but simply and solely to the kinds and order of the symbols from which the expressions are constructed."

As logical empiricists or positivists, they were committed to minimal "interpretations" of "reality" itself. Their goal was a "unified science" built up from pointer readings, from physical "observables." They were inspired by the early work on relativity by Albert Einstein, who had been inspired by Ernst Mach's positivism and opposition to metaphysics.

Limiting physics to observables, instead of a preconception about how reality must be, was behind Werner Heisenberg's uncertainty principle. Thus we can observe the spectral lines emitted by electrons when they jump from one orbit to another, but we cannot observe the orbiting electrons themselves.

For Carnap, a causal law was simply the fact that events are predictable. Quantum uncertainty put limits on that predictability, and some physicists spoke loosely of "the failure of the principle of causality only because it has become impossible to make predictions with any desired degree of accuracy."

David Chalmers

Chalmers is a philosopher of mind whose characterization of consciousness as "the hard problem" has set a very high bar for understanding the mind. He says that "the problem of quantum mechanics is almost as hard as the problem of consciousness."

Chalmers describes his position as a naturalistic dualism. He doubts that consciousness can be explained by physical theories, because consciousness is itself not physical. We agree, because all experiences are recorded and reproduced as immaterial information

- in both conscious and unconscious playback. But information, while not material, is embodied in the physical. It is a property of the material world.

Chalmers says that the failure of supervenience implies that materialism - as a monistic theory of the complete contents of the world, that there is "nothing but" matter, and that the world is "causally closed," for example - is "false." We agree with this and believe that the reductionist arguments of Jaegwon Kim can be shown wrong.

"In our world, there are conscious experiences.

There is a logically possible world physically identical to ours, in which the positive facts about consciousness in our world do not hold.

Therefore, facts about consciousness are further facts about our world, over and above the physical facts.

So materialism is false." [13]

Chalmers suggests that the dualistic (non-physical) element might be information. Indeed it might. With this idea too, information philosophy completely agrees. But information is physical. It is just *immaterial*. Mind/body is a property dualism.

Chalmers says that a "fundamental theory of consciousness" might be based on information. He says that "physical realization is the most common way to think about information embedded in the world, but it is not the only way information can be found. We can also find information realized in our phenomenology." (*ibid*, p.284)

He is quite correct. Information is neither matter nor energy. It needs matter to be embedded temporarily in the brain. And it needs energy to be communicated. Phenomenal experiences transmitted to us as visual perceptions, for example, consist of information that is pure radiant energy. The pure (mental) information content in one brain can be transmitted to other brains, by converting it to energy for communication; other brains can then embody the same information (perhaps with significant differences in the details) for use by other minds (the "multiply realizable" software in different brains' hardware).

---

13   Chalmers (1996) *The Conscious Mind*, p.123

Chalmers comes very close to our view of the mind as information. He describes his fundamental theory as a "double-aspect principle."

> "The treatment of information brings out a crucial link between the physical and the phenomenal: whenever we find an information space realized phenomenally, we find the same information space realized physically...It is natural to suppose that this double life of information spaces corresponds to a duality at a deep level. We might even suggest that this double realization is the key to the fundamental connection between physical processes and conscious experience. We need some sort of construct to make the link, and information seems as good a construct as any. It may be that principles concerning the double realization of information could be fleshed out into a system of basic laws connecting the physical and phenomenal domains.
>
> We might put this by suggesting as a basic principle that information (in the actual world) has two aspects, a physical and a phenomenal aspect. Wherever there is a phenomenal state, it realizes an information state, an information state that is also realized in the cognitive system of the brain. Conversely, for at least some physically realized information spaces, whenever an information state in that space is realized physically, it is also realized phenomenally...
>
> Information seems to be a simple and straightforward construct that is well suited for this sort of connection, and which may hold the promise of yielding a set of laws that are simple and comprehensive. If such a set of laws could be achieved, then we might truly have a fundamental theory of consciousness.
>
> It may just be...that there is a way of seeing information itself as fundamental."[14]

In his conclusions, Chalmers declares himself to be a mind-body dualist, even a *panpsychist*.

> "I resisted mind-body dualism for a long time, but I have now come to the point where I accept it, not just as the only tenable view but as a satisfying view in its own right. It is always possible that I am confused, or that there is a new and radical possibility that I have overlooked; but I can comfortably say that I think dualism is very likely true. I have also raised the possibility of a

---

14   *Ibid.*, pp.284-7

kind of panpsychism. Like mind-body dualism, this is initially counterintuitive, but the counterintuitiveness disappears with time. I am unsure whether the view is true or false, but it is at least intellectually appealing, and on reflection it is not too crazy to be acceptable." [15]

In recent years, Chalmers has explored panpsychism, the thesis that some fundamental entities have mental states. THOMAS NAGEL and GALEN STRAWSON have also examined panpsychism. Since information is a universal property of matter, it "goes all the way down," so the basis of mentality - information - is present in the simplest physical structures, but there is no mind in the worlds of physics and chemistry, which have minimal histories and no use of information to manage the *arrangement* of matter.

Roderick Chisholm

Chisholm studied at Harvard but was strongly opposed to behaviorist analytic philosophers like Quine. His major work was titled *Person and Object* to draw the contrast with analytic language philosophy implicit in Quine's famous *Word and Object*.

Chisholm was a libertarian who distinguished "agent causation" from "event-causation" (see his book *Freedom and Action*), which is a major distinction made by current incompatibilist philosophers, though later in life he recanted this distinction.

> "In earlier writings on this topic, I had contrasted agent causation with event causation and had suggested that "causation by agents" could not be reduced to "causation by events." I now believe that that suggestion was a mistake. What I had called agent causation is a subspecies of event causation. My concern in the present study is to note the specific differences by reference to which agent causation can be distinguished from other types of event causation." [16]

In his 1964 Lindley Lecture, Chisholm saw free will as a metaphysical problem. He asserts that a man who performs an act is completely free and uncaused, a *causa sui*.

---

15   Ibid., p.357
16   Chiholm (1995) Agents, Causes, and Events: The Problem of Free Will,' in *Agents, Causes, and Events*, ed. T. O'Connor,

"The metaphysical problem of human freedom might be summarized in the following way: "Human beings are responsible agents; but this fact appears to conflict with a deterministic view of human action (the view that every event that is involved in an act is caused by some other event); and it also appears to conflict with an indeterministic view of human action (the view that the act, or some event that is essential to the act, is not caused at all)." To solve the problem, I believe, we must make somewhat far-reaching assumptions about the self of the agent — about the man who performs the act.

Perhaps it is needless to remark that, in all likelihood, it is impossible to say anything significant about this ancient problem that has not been said before.

Let us consider some deed, or misdeed, that may be attributed to a responsible agent: one man, say, shot another. If the man was responsible for what he did, then, I would urge, what was to happen at the time of the shooting was something that was entirely up to the man himself. There was a moment at which it was true, both that he could have fired the shot and also that he could have refrained from firing it. And if this is so, then, even though he did fire it, he could have done something else instead. (He didn't find himself firing the shot "against his will," as we say.) I think we can say, more generally, then, that if a man is responsible for a certain event or a certain state of affairs (in our example, the shooting of another man), then that event or state of affairs was brought about by some act of his, and the act was something that was in his power either to perform or not to perform.

Chisholm reprises the standard argument against free will.

The ascription of responsibility conflicts with a deterministic view of action. Perhaps there is less need to argue that the ascription of responsibility also conflicts with an indeterministic view of action — with the view that the act, or some event that is essential to the act, is not caused at a

If the act — the firing of the shot — was not caused at all, if it was fortuitous or capricious, happening so to speak "out of the blue," then, presumably, no one — and nothing — was responsible for the act. Our conception of action, therefore, should be neither deterministic nor indeterministic. Is there any other possibility?

We must not say that every event involved in the act is caused by some other event, and we must not say that the act is something that is not caused at all. The possibility that remains, therefore, is this: We should say that at least one of the events that are involved in the act is caused, not by any other events, but by something else instead. And this something else can only be the agent — the man.

If there is an event that is caused, not by other events, but by the man, then there are some events involved in the act that are not caused by other events. But if the event in question is caused by the man, then it is caused and we are not committed to saying that there is something involved in the act that is not caused at all." [17]

René Descartes

In his 1644 *Principles of Philosophy*, Descartes identified freedom with actions that are not pre-determined, even by the existence of divine foreknowledge.

Descartes was of course the origin of the central problem in metaphysics that divided the world into *mind* (the ideal realm of thoughts) and *body* (the material world). For him, the physical world was a *deterministic* machine, but our ideas and thoughts can be free (*indeterminate*) and could change things in the material world (through the pineal gland in the brain, he thought). Here are the relevant sections in Descartes' Principles.

39. The freedom of the will is self-evident.

There is freedom in our will, and that we have power in many cases or withhold our assent at will, is so evident that it must be counted among the first and most common notions that are innate in us. This was obvious earlier on when, in our attempt to doubt everything, we went so far as to make the supposition of some supremely powerful author of our being who was attempting to deceive us in every possible way. For in spite of that supposition, the freedom which we experienced within us was nonetheless so great as to enable us to abstain from believing

---

17   Chisholm (1964) '*Human Freedom and the Self,*' The Lindley Lecture

whatever was not quite certain or fully examined. And what we saw to be beyond doubt even during the period of that supposition is as self-evident and as transparently clear as anything can be.

40. It is also certain that everything was preordained by God.

But now that we have come to know God, we perceive in him a power so immeasurable that we regard it as impious to suppose that we could ever do anything which was not already preordained by him. And we can easily get ourselves into great difficulties if we attempt to reconcile this divine preordination with the freedom of our will, or attempt to grasp both these things at once.

41. How to reconcile the freedom of our will with divine preordination.

But we shall get out of these difficulties if we remember that our mind is finite, while the power of God is infinite — the power by which he not only knew from eternity whatever is or can be, but also willed it and preordained it. We may attain sufficient knowledge of this power to perceive clearly and distinctly that God possesses it; but we cannot get sufficient grasp of it to see how it leaves the free actions of men undetermined. Nonetheless, we have such close awareness of the freedom and indifference which is in us, that there is nothing we can grasp evidently or more perfectly. And it would be absurd, simply because we do not grasp one thing, which we know must by its very nature be beyond our comprehension, to doubt something else of which we have intimate grasp and which we experience within ourselves.[18]

    1. Haldane and Ross translate *indifferentiae*, perhaps influenced by the liberty of indifference, and by *indeterminata* in the prior line, as indeterminacy.

    "We are so conscious of the freedom and indeterminacy which exist in us, that there is nothing we comprehend more clearly and perfectly"

---

18   Descartes. *Principles of Philosophy*, Part One, Section 41, trans. Haldane and Ross, 1911, p.235

Peter Geach

Peter Geach was a young colleague of Ludwig Wittgenstein. Geach tried to synthesize analytic philosophy and Thomism.

He worked on problems of identity, and some time in the early 1960's created "Tibbles, the Cat," as a character in two important problems in metaphysics, Chrysippus's ancient problem of Dion and Theon and the problem of the many.

In 1968, David Wiggins wrote an article, "On Being in the Same Place at the Same Time," in which he described Geach's Tibbles. Where Theon is identical to Dion except he is missing a foot, we now have a cat named Tibbles and a second cat named Tib who lacks a tail.

In Geach's second account of Tibbles as an exemplar of a metaphysical problem, published some years later (1980), Tibbles is a cat with 1,000 hairs that can be interpreted as 1,001 cats, by "picking out" and then pulling out one of those cat hairs at a time and each time identifying a new cat..

Geach's second version of Tibbles is widely cited as a discussion of the problem of vagueness or what Peter Unger called the Problem of the Many, also published in 1980. It is not the "body-minus" problem of Geach's original Tibbles.

If a few of Tibbles' hairs are pulled out, do we still have Tibbles, the Cat? Obviously we do. Have we created other cats, now multiple things in the same place at the same time? Obviously not.

Geach argues that removing one of a thousand hairs from Tibbles shows that there are actually 1,001 cats on the mat.

> "The fat cat sat on the mat. There was just one cat on the mat. The cat's name was "Tibbles": "Tibbles" is moreover a name for a cat.—This simple story leads us into difficulties if we assume that Tibbles is a normal cat. For a normal cat has at least 1,000 hairs. Like many empirical concepts, the concept (single) hair is fuzzy at the edges; but it is reasonable to assume that we can identify in Tibbles at least 1,000 of his parts each of which definitely is a single hair. I shall refer to these hairs as $h_1, h_2, h_3, \ldots$ up to $h_{1,000}$. Now let c be the largest continuous mass of feline tissue on the mat. Then for any of our 1,000 cat-hairs, say h_n, there is a proper

part cn of c which contains precisely all of c except the hair hn; and every such part c_n differs in a describable way both from any other such part, say c_m, and from c as a whole. Moreover, fuzzy as the concept cat may be, it is clear that not only is c a cat, but also any part c_n is a cat: cn would clearly be a cat were the hair h_n plucked out, and we cannot reasonably suppose that plucking out a hair generates a cat, so c_n must already have been a cat. So, contrary to our story, there was not just one cat called 'Tibbles' sitting on the mat; there were at least 1,001 sitting there!

All the same, this result is absurd...

Everything falls into place if we realize that the number of cats on the mat is the number of different cats on the mat; and c_{13}, c_{279}, and c are not three different cats, they are one and the same cat. Though none of these 1,001 lumps of feline tissue is the same lump of feline tissue as another, each is the same cat as any other: each of them, then, is a cat, but there is only one cat on the mat, and our original story stands.

So we recover the truth of the simple story we began with. The price to pay is that we must regard "is the same cat as" as expressing only a certain equivalence relation, not an absolute identity restricted to cats; but this price, I have elsewhere argued, must be paid anyhow, for there is no such absolute identity as logicians have assumed." [19]

Geach worked on problems of identity and debated for years with DAVID WIGGINS about relative identity.

For Geach and Wiggins, relative identity means "x is the same F as y," but "x may not be the same G as y." Wiggins argued against this idea of relative identity, but accepted what he called a sortal-dependent identity, "x is the *same what* as y." Geach called this a "criterion of identity."

> "I had here best interject a note on how I mean this term "criterion of identity". I maintain that it makes no sense to judge whether x and y are 'the same', or whether x remains 'the same', unless we add or understand some general term—"the same F". That in accordance with which we thus judge as to the identity, I call a criterion of identity." [20]

---

19   Geach (1980) *Reference and Generality*, 3rd edition, p.215
20   Geach (1980) *Reference and Generality*, p.63 (1962, p.39;)

In his 1967 article "Identity," in the *Review of Metaphysics*, Geach had written

> "I am arguing for the thesis that identity is relative. When one says "x is identical with y", this, I hold, is an incomplete expression; it is short for "x is the same A as y", where "A" represents some count noun understood from the context of utterance." [21]

David Hume

Hume thought and wrote a great seal about necessity and liberty. Has the necessitism of modal logic as metaphysics settled any of the problems raised by Hume?

Hume redefined the term "necessity" to describe the inference of the human mind that discovers *causality* in the regular succession of events, that postulates "uniformity of nature" to assume that the laws of nature will continue tomorrow to be the same as today, and even to describe the assumption that we can predict future behaviors of an agent based on our observations of the agent's habitual behaviors.

Modern uses of Hume's word "necessity" lead many philosophers to misunderstand Hume. Today we should say that the empirical observations of all these regularities only justify our assigning high probabilities to such predictions, and never the "certainty" that is associated with a physical causal determinism or a logical necessity. Hume's usage may be closer to the eighteenth-century use of the terms "moral necessity" or "moral certainty."

Indeed, now that quantum mechanics has shown that the laws of nature are fundamentally probabilistic, there is evidence that Hume's "necessity" was in fact only such a high probability.

> "It seems evident that, if all the scenes of nature were continually shifted in such a manner that no two events bore any resemblance to each other, but every object was entirely new, without any similitude to whatever had been seen before, we should never, in that case, have attained the least idea of necessity, or

---

21 See chapter 13 on identity for more details.

of a connexion among these objects...Inference and reasoning
concerning the operations of nature would, from that moment,
be at an end; and the memory and senses remain the only canals,
by which the knowledge of any real existence could possibly
have access to the mind. Our idea, therefore, of necessity and
causation arises entirely from the uniformity observable in the
operations of nature, where similar objects are constantly con-
joined together, and the mind is determined by custom to infer
the one from the appearance of the other...it must follow, that all
mankind have ever agreed in the doctrine of necessity, and that
they have hitherto disputed, merely for not understanding each
other." [22]

"We must not, however, expect that this uniformity of human
actions should be carried to such a length as that all men, in
the same circumstances, will always act precisely in the same
manner, without making any allowance for the diversity of
characters, prejudices, and opinions. Such a uniformity in every
particular, is found in no part of nature. On the contrary, from
observing the variety of conduct in different men, we are enabled
to form a greater variety of maxims, which still suppose a degree
of uniformity and regularity." [23]

Hume here is cautious and circumspect. He knows that perfect uniformity has never been seen. Agents may act differently even in the same circumstances.

Our careful reading shows that Hume backs away from strict necessity and says the inferences are only probabilistic, with certainty only "more or less."

"Above one half of human reasonings contain inferences of a
similar nature, attended with more or less degrees of certainty
proportioned to our experience of the usual conduct of mankind
in such particular situations." [24]

---

22   Hume (1748) Enquiry Concerning Human Understanding, Section VIII, "Of Liberty and Necessity," pp.81-82
23   ibid., p.85
24   ibid., p.91

Whatever Hume thought about reduced certainty, for him there was no such thing as chance. It is human ignorance that leads to all our ideas of probability. This was the view of all the great mathematicians who developed the calculus of probabilities - ABRAHAM DE MOIVRE before Hume and PIERRE-SIMON LAPLACE after him. And, following de Moivre, Hume called chance a mere word.

> "Though there be no such thing as Chance in the world; our ignorance of the real cause of any event has the same influence on the understanding, and begets a like species of belief or opinion." [25]

Most compatibilists and determinists since Hobbes and Hume never mention the fact that a causal chain of events going back before our birth would not provide the kind of liberty they are looking for. But Hume frankly admits that such a causal chain would be a serious objection to his theory.

> "I pretend not to have obviated or removed all objections to this theory, with regard to necessity and liberty. I can foresee other objections, derived from topics which have not here been treated of. It may be said, for instance, that, if voluntary actions be subjected to the same laws of necessity with the operations of matter, there is a continued chain of necessary causes, pre-ordained and pre-determined, reaching from the original cause of all to every single volition, of every human creature. No contingency anywhere in the universe; no indifference; no liberty. While we act, we are, at the same time, acted upon." [26]

Is it the case that modern metaphysicians, with their tendencies to eliminative materialism, tacitly accept this lack of contingency?

Immanuel Kant

Kant reacted to the Enlightenment, to the Age of Reason, and to Newtonian mechanics (which he probably understood better than any other philosopher), by accepting determinism as a fact in the physical world, which he calls the *phenomenal* world. Kant's goal was to rescue the physical sciences from the devastating and unanswerable skepticism of David Hume, especially Hume's assertion

---

25 *Enquiry*, Book VI, Of Probability, p. 56
26 *Enquiry*, Book VIII, Of Liberty and Necessity, p. 99

that no number of "constant conjunctions" of cause and effect could logically prove causality. Today we know that nothing is logically true of the world, but Kant called Hume's assertion the "*crux metaphysicorum*." If Hume is right, he said, metaphysics is impossible. Kant's goal for his *Critique of Pure Reason* was to prove that Hume was wrong.

Neither Hume's Idea of "natural belief" nor Kant's "concepts of the understanding" are the apodeictic and necessary truths sought by metaphysicians. They are *abstract theories* about the world, whose information content is validated by experiments. Hume criticized the Theory of Ideas of his fellow British empiricists JOHN LOCKE and GEORGE BERKELEY. If, as they claim, knowledge is limited to perceptions of sense data, we cannot "know" anything about external objects, even our own bodies. But Hume said that we do have a *natural belief* in the external world and in causal laws.

Hume's idea of the mind having a "feeling" (not a reason) that leads to natural beliefs became Kant's "second Copernican revolution" that the mind projects "concepts of the understanding" and "forms of perception" on the external world.

Kant's main change in the second edition of the Critique of Pure Reason was an attempted refutation of this British idealism (B 274). He thought he had a proof of the existence of the external world. Kant thought it a scandal in philosophy that we must accept the existence of material things outside ourselves merely as a belief, with no proof.

> "The only thing which might be called an addition, though in the method of proof only, is the new refutation of psychological idealism, and the strict (and as I believe the only possible) proof of the objective reality of outer intuition. However innocent idealism may be considered with respect to the essential purposes of metaphysics (without being so in reality), it remains a scandal to philosophy, and to human reason in general, that we should have to accept the existence of things outside us (from which after all we derive the whole material for our knowledge, even for that of our inner sense) merely on trust, and have no satisfactory proof with which to counter any opponent who chooses to doubt it." [27]

---

27   Preface to Second Edition, *Critique of Pure Reason*, B XL

Saul Kripke

Saul Kripke is a philosopher and logician and emeritus professor at Princeton. He attacked the theory that proper names are descriptions, for examples bundles of properties, as espoused by GOTTLOB FREGE and especially BERTRAND RUSSELL.

The Frege-Russell *theory of descriptions* was also a theory of meaning. The meaning of a proper name was said to consist in all the properties attached to the named person. The Frege-Russell theory was also a theory of reference, of denotation, of terms that "pick out" or identify an individual, whether a human being, an inanimate object, or a natural kind.

Frege and Russell said that some of these properties can be substituted in statements for the name and preserve the truth value of the statement. For example, George Washington can be replaced by "the first president of the United States." But descriptive properties can be problematic.

Kripke's modal analysis of alternative possibilities shows that the first president of the United States might not have been Washington. Things might have been otherwise. Washington might have died in the Revolutionary War.

But his proper name, given as a child by his parents, told to family and friends and then to people widely through a chain of communications that grew worldwide, could only be a reference to this unique individual, a reference that identifies him more strongly than any accidental property.

Kripke says that proper names are "rigid designators" that only refer to the objects they designate. They contain none of the likely accidental properties that accrue to persons during their lifetimes, such as "first president." Rigidity of proper names refers to their unchanging, even *necessary* character, says Kripke, colorfully described as "true in all possible worlds," as today's modal philosophers like to say, even "*necessary a posteriori*," which is only "true" within a logical system, not a fact in the irreducibly *contingent* material world.

Kripke says that once an object is "baptized" with the first use (the origin) of its name, it more reliably denotes that individual than any of the properties the individual might acquire during a lifetime that might evolve in multiple possible ways.

But note that the rigidity of a proper name is only relative to its early date. Any property that was established in the past is now unchangeable – "necessary ex post facto?" – even if it could have been otherwise, so it too might serve as a rigid designator.

Reference and Identity

Using the ancient example of "Hesperus is Phosphorus," the two ancient names for the planet Venus that appears as both the Evening star and the Morning star, Kripke claims that since the two names refer to the same thing, they are identical. But this seems extreme.

Granted that someone who knows that Venus can appear on either side of the sun, Hesperus and Phosphorus refer to the same thing. But there is no way the names themselves (as words) are identical to one another. We must select a subset of the information contained in the two words and in factual, even scientific and empirical knowledge available, to pick out the fact that these words refer to the same object.

There are not two things (names) here that are identical to one another. Identical terms should be substitutable for one another in propositions and preserve the truth value. Hesperus and Phosphorus are two different words. They contain significantly different information. They are examples of Quine's failure of substitutivity.

One name describes a morning phenomenon. So, there is no truth to the statement "Phosphorus is the Evening Star." Phosphorus never appears in the evening. Circumlocutions are needed like "What we call Phosphorus is a planet that sometimes appears as Hesperus."

Part of the information content here is that we have two words referring to one thing. But each word provides different knowledge about the planet Venus, one telling that Venus sometimes appears to the East of the Sun, the other that it sometimes appears to the West. It is false that "The Morning Star *Is* The Evening Star," except in a limited sense.

Most all statements of identity between two things should be paraphrased as "these two things are identical in some respect." They are only the same if we ignore their differences. For example, Hesperus and Phosphorus are identical *qua* referents to the planet Venus

GOTTFRIED LEIBNIZ's famous law about the "identity of indiscernibles" can not be an absolute statement. The only absolute identity is self-identity. All things are identical only to themselves. Two indiscernibles are only indiscernible *qua* – in some respects. They are easily discerned to be two objects, in different places for example.

But any two things are similar if we ignore all their differences, just as they are different if we ignore their similarities. Exceptions are the identical and "indistinguishable" elementary particles of quantum physics, a deep problem for quantum mechanics and for metaphysics.

Hesperus and Phosphorus are identical only *qua* referents to a planet, and there is nothing necessary about this fact except that it began in the past and is now a convention and tradition, and as such Hesperus and Phosphorus are Kripke rigid designators.

But we cannot forget the obvious fact from linguistic theory, whether Peirce semiotics or Saussure semiology, that the names Hesperus and Phosphorus are *arbitrary* symbols, with no information in common with the planet Venus. In ancient languages, the planet was *Ishtar*, *Ashtoreth* in the Bible, in Greek *Astarte*, for centuries before the Latin name for the love goddess.

Given the fact that all human language terms are *contingent* and historically accidental, we must struggle to understand Kripke's claim for the names' necessity.

Necessary A Posteriori?

Kripke has defined a different kind of necessity from that usually identified with the *analytic* and the *a priori*. He thus alters the traditional distinction between the necessary and the contingent.

Kripke calls his idea *metaphysical necessity* to distinguish it from epistemic necessity. Kripke further distinguishes analyticity and a prioricity from necessity. For him, *analyticity* is a *semantic* notion, *a priori* is *epistemic*, and his *necessity* is a *metaphysical* notion.

Analyticity covers everything known to be true or false by definition of the terms involved. This includes logical and mathematical truths, such as "A is A," and "7 + 5 = 12." He says, "an analytic statement is, in some sense, true by virtue of its meaning and true in all possible worlds by virtue of its meaning. Then something which is analytically true will be both necessary and a priori. (That's sort of stipulative.)"[28]

Metaphysical necessity concerns facts that are known to be the case by the nature of a physical object. This is based on the physical presumption that the way the world is, for example the laws of nature, could not have been otherwise. It may also be based on the fact that any event in the past is now fixed and so can be called metaphysically necessary? In any case, Kripke believes that we discover the essential properties, the essence of physical objects empirically.[29]

Anything that has been empirically determined to be the case thus can be called metaphysically necessary or "necessary a posteriori," says Kripke.

Consider the modal claim 'Necessarily, water is H_2O.' It is said to follow from the empirical and a posteriori claim 'Water is H_2O' together with an *a priori* claim, such as 'If water is H_2O, then necessarily, water is H_2O'.[30] But this seems dangerously like the redundancy in 'If water is H_2O, then it is true that water is H_2O'?

Kripke's other examples include: it is necessary that gold is necessarily a metal, that it is yellow, and has atomic number 79; lightning is necessarily an electrical discharge; "This table (pointing at a table in the room) is necessarily made of wood," if it was made of wood. Indeed, he says that the table was by metaphysical necessity made of the exact wood that it was made of.

We can take Kripke's "metaphysical necessity" with a metaphorical grain of salt (necessarily NaCl). This is because the physical world contains the possibility that the carpenter could have chosen a different piece of wood, or the table could have been made of ice.[31]

---

28 Kripke (1981) *Naming and Necessity*, p.39
29 *Ibid.*, p.110
30 *Ibid.*, p.128
31 Kripke's cryptic alternative, *ibid.*, p.114

Possible Worlds

Kripke and DAVID LEWIS are both famous for using the concept of possible worlds, but there are some extreme and very important differences between them. Kripke thinks that Lewis's idea has "encouraged philosophical pseudo-problems and misleading pictures." One major difference is that Lewis thinks of his super-infinity of possible worlds as actually existing in an infinite space-time continuum, where Kripke thinks his possible worlds are merely ways of talking about the alternative possibilities in our actual world. He says that "possible worlds' are total 'ways the world might have been', or states or histories of the entire world, or 'counterfactual situations' might even be better.

> "I will say something briefly about 'possible worlds'. (I hope to elaborate elsewhere.) In the present monograph I argued against those misuses of the concept that regard possible worlds as something like distant planets, like our own surroundings but somehow existing in a different dimension, or that lead to spurious problems of 'transworld identification'. Further, if one wishes to avoid the Weltangst and philosophical confusions that many philosophers have associated with the 'worlds' terminology, I recommended that 'possible state (or history) of the world', or 'counterfactual situation' might be better. One should even remind oneself that the 'worlds' terminology can often be replaced by modal talk—'It is possible that . . .'
>
> 'Possible worlds' are little more than the miniworlds of school probability blown large. It is true that there are problems in the general notion not involved in the miniature version. The miniature worlds are tightly controlled, both as to the objects involved (two dice), the relevant properties (number on face shown), and (thus) the relevant idea of possibility. 'Possible worlds' are total 'ways the world might have been', or states or histories of the entire world. To think of the totality of all of them involves much more idealization, and more mind-boggling questions, than the less ambitious elementary school analogue. Certainly the philosopher of 'possible worlds' must take care that his technical apparatus not push him to ask questions whose meaningfulness is not supported by our original intuitions of possibility that gave

the apparatus its point. Further, in practice we cannot describe a complete counterfactual course of events and have no need to do so." [32]

When thinking about different possibilities in the actual world, e.g., what if Nixon had lost the 1968 presidential election and Humphrey won it, Nixon in Kripke's alternative possible world is the same individual, differing only in the property of losing the election. All of Kripke's possible worlds are different ways our actual world might have been.

By contrast, David Lewis describes a Nixon in an alternate world as not the same individual, but a "counterpart" of Nixon who has the same bundle of properties as the actual Nixon, with the exception of the election loss. This raises the troubling problem of a "trans-world individual." Clearly no matter how similar, individuals in two different worlds are not identical.

> "I wish at this point to introduce something which I need in the methodology of discussing the theory of names that I'm talking about. We need the notion of 'identity across possible worlds' as it's usually and, as I think, somewhat misleadingly called.
>
> (Misleadingly, because the phrase suggests that there is a special problem of 'transworld identification', that we cannot trivially stipulate whom or what we are talking about when we imagine another possible world. The term 'possible world' may also mislead; perhaps it suggests the 'foreign country' picture. I have sometimes used 'counterfactual situation' in the text; Michael Slote has suggested that 'possible state (or history) of the world' might be less misleading than 'possible world'. It is better still, to avoid confusion, not to say, 'In some possible world, Humphrey would have won' but rather, simply, 'Humphrey might have won'. The apparatus of possible words has (I hope) been very useful as far as the set-theoretic model-theory of quantified modal logic is concerned, but has encouraged philosophical pseudo-problems and misleading pictures.)
>
> One of the intuitive theses I will maintain in these talks is that names are rigid designators. Certainly they seem to satisfy the intuitive test mentioned above: although someone other than the U.S. President in 1970 might have been the U.S. President

---

32   Kripke (1981) *Naming and Necessity*, pp.15-20

in 1970 (e.g., Humphrey might have), no one other than Nixon might have been Nixon. In the same way, a designator rigidly designates a certain object if it designates that object wherever the object exists; if, in addition, the object is a necessary existent, the designator can be called strongly rigid. For example, 'the President of the U.S. in 1970' designates a certain man, Nixon; but someone else (e.g., Humphrey) might have been the President in 1970, and Nixon might not have; so this designator is not rigid.

In these lectures, I will argue, intuitively, that proper names are rigid designators, for although the man (Nixon) might not have been the President, it is not the case that he might not have been Nixon (though he might not have been called 'Nixon'). Those who have argued that to make sense of the notion of rigid designator, we must antecedently make sense of 'criteria of transworld identity' have precisely reversed the cart and the horse; it is because we can refer (rigidly) to Nixon, and stipulate that we are speaking of what might have happened to him (under certain circumstances), that 'transworld identifications' are unproblematic in such cases.

(Of course I don't imply that language contains a name for every object Demonstratives can be used as rigid designators, and free variables can be used as rigid designators of unspecified objects. Of course when we specify a counterfactual situation, we do not describe the whole possible world, but only the portion which interests us.)" [33]

It is critical to note that metaphysicians proposing possible worlds are for the most part materialists and determinists who do not believe in the existence of ontological possibilities in our world.

First, they "index" our world as the "actual world." They are actualists who say that the only possibilities have always been whatever actually happened. This is DANIEL DENNETT's position, for example, not that far from the original actualist, DIODORUS CRONUS.

Moreover, all of their infinite number of possible worlds are governed by deterministic laws of nature. This means that there are no actual possibilities in any of their possible worlds, only actualities there as well. Every possible world is deterministic!

---

33   Kripke (1981) *Naming and Necessity*, pp.47-49

Now this is quite ironic, since the invention of possible worlds was initially proposed as a superior way of talking about counterfactual possibilities in our world.

Since information philosophy defends the existence of alternative possibilities leading to different futures, we can adopt a form of modal discourse to describe these possibilities as possible future worlds for our to-be-actualized world.

It turns out there is an infinity of such possible future worlds. The infinity is not as large as the absurdly extravagant number in David Lewis's possible worlds, which have counterparts for each and every living person with every imaginable difference in each of our counterparts, each counterpart in its own unique world.

Thus there are Lewisian worlds in which your counterpart is a butcher, baker, candlestick maker, and every other known occupation. There are possible worlds in which your counterpart eats every possible breakfast food, drives every possible car, and lives in every block on every street in every city or town in the entire word.

This extravagance is of course part of Lewis's appeal. It makes HUGH EVERETT III's "many worlds" of quantum mechanics (which split the universe in two when a physicist makes a quantum measurement) minuscule, indeed quite parsimonious, by comparison.

Specifically, when an Everett universe splits into two, it doubles the matter and energy in the new universe(s) – an extreme violation of the principle of the conservation of matter/energy – and it also doubles the information. Apart from that absurdity, the two universes differ by only one bit of information, for example, whether the electron spin measured up or down in the quantum measurement.

Similarly, for every Lewisian universe, the change of one bit of information implies one other possible universe in which all the infinite number of other bits stay exactly the same. But Lewis imagines that every single bit in the universe may be changed at any time, an order of physical infinities that rivals the greatest number that Georg Cantor ever imagined. Is David Lewis ontologically committed to such a number?

Although Kripke does not seem to have said anything about the problem of free will, his view of "possible worlds" may be sympathetic to human freedom, since he describes the worlds as "ways the world might have been."

In our two-stage model of free will, we can describe the alternative possibilities for action generated by an agent in the first stage as "possible worlds." They are "counterfactual situations" in Kripke's sense, involving a single individual. Suppose the agent is considering five different courses of action. During the second stage of evaluation and deliberation only one of the five options (each a "possible world") will become actualized.

The agent is the same individual of interest in these five possible worlds. There are no Lewisian "counterparts." There is no problem of "transworld identification."

Note that these five possible worlds are extremely close to one another, "nearby" in the sense of their total information content. We can focus on the "miniworld" of the five options and hold the rest of the universe constant. As Kripke described it, "the 'counterfactual situation' could be thought of as a miniworld or a ministate, restricted to features of the world relevant to the problem at hand."

Quantification over the information in each world shows that the difference between them is very small number of bits, especially when compared to the typical examples given in possible worlds cases. In the case of Humphrey winning the election, millions of persons would have to have done something different. Such worlds are hardly "nearby" one another.

For typical cases of a free decision, the possible worlds require only small differences in the mind of a single person. Kripke argued against the identity of mind and body (or brain), and in this example it would only be the thoughts of the agent that pick out the possible world that will be actualized.

Our thoughts are free. Our actions are willed by an adequately determined evaluation and decision process, not one that was predetermined by the mechanical laws of nature acting on our material bodies.

David Lewis

The analytic language philosopher David Lewis was a possibilist. He developed the philosophical methodology known as modal realism based on the idea of possible worlds. He claims that

- Possible worlds exist and are just as real as our world.
- Possible worlds are the same sort of things as our world – they differ in content, not in kind.
- Possible worlds cannot be reduced to something more basic – they are irreducible entities in their own right.
- Actuality is indexical. When we distinguish our world from other possible worlds by claiming that it alone is actual, we mean only that it is our world.
- Possible worlds are unified by the spatiotemporal interrelations of their parts; every world is spatiotemporally isolated from every other world.
- Possible worlds are causally isolated from each other.

Modal realism implies the existence of infinitely many parallel universes, an idea similar to the many-worlds interpretation of quantum mechanics. In the information interpretation of quantum mechanics, quantum systems evolve in two ways: the first is the wave function deterministically exploring all the possibilities for interaction; the second is the particle randomly choosing one of those possibilities to become actual.

Possible worlds and modal reasoning made "counterfactual" arguments extremely popular in current philosophy. Possible worlds, especially the idea of "nearby worlds" that differ only slightly from the actual world, are used to examine the validity of modal notions such as necessity and contingency, possibility and impossibility, truth and falsity.

Lewis appears to have believed that the truth of his counterfactuals was a result of believing that for every non-contradictory statement there is a possible world in which that statement is true.

True propositions are those that are true in the actual world.

False propositions are those that are false in the actual world.

Necessarily true propositions are those that are true in all possible worlds.

Contingent propositions are those that are true in some possible worlds and false in others.

Possible propositions are those that are true in at least one possible world.

Impossible propositions are those that are true in no possible world.

E. Jonathan Lowe

E. J. Lowe was an Oxford-trained philosopher who worked on the philosophy of action and philosophy of mind since the late 1970's. He developed a version of psychophysical dualism that he called non-Cartesian substance dualism. It is an interactionist substance dualism. (Cf. JOHN ECCLES and early KARL POPPER.) The non-Cartesian "substance" proposed by Lowe is the acting Self, whose (free) will has an irreducible causal power.

Lowe argued, however, that events (both mental and physical) should properly not be thought of as causes, because only actors (human or animal agents - or inanimate physical agents) can cause things. Events are more properly simply happenings, some caused, some uncaused. (If quantum indeterminism is correct, some are only statistically caused - perhaps then uncaused and neither determined nor pre-determined).

For Lowe, reasons, motives, beliefs, desires, etc., should also not be described as causes of human actions. To do so neglects the will of the agent. He says, "Behavior that is caused by an agent's beliefs and desires is, on that very account, not rational, free action." Describing behavior as caused by reasons, etc. is just a *façon de parler*. Events are causally impotent

> In my view, only entities in the category of substance -— that
> is, persisting, concrete objects — possess causal powers. Strictly

speaking, an event cannot do anything and so cannot cause anything. For causings are a species of doings — that is, in a very broad sense, actions — and doings are themselves happenings. Thus, talk of an event doing something either involves a gross category mistake — because, understood literally, it implies that one happening is done by another — or else, taken less seriously, it may be dismissed as being no more than a misleading manner of speaking.[34]

Lowe defends mental events (and mental causation) as distinct from physical events (and physical causes) but equally real. Information philosophy sees them as physical, but *immaterial.*

Lowe is opposed to the notion of *causal closure*, the idea that everything that happens in the world is caused by physical objects in the world. Causal closure is a requirement for current "materialist/physicalist" views in the philosophy of mind, which regard mental events as identical to physical (brain) events, or perhaps merely epiphenomena. That mental states (or processes) are unable to cause anything to happen in the world is the modern version of the Cartesian mind-body problem. Lowe opposes this view with his idea of a non-Cartesian "self" (or mind) which has causal power.

Philosophers DONALD DAVIDSON and Jaegwon Kim have discussed the possibility of a non-reductive physicalism, in which mental events might not be reducible to physical events.

Davidson hoped to describe mental events as emergent from lower physical levels in the hierarchy. Kim denies the possibility of emergence or of a "non-reductive physicalism." Both describe mental events as supervenient on events in lower hierarchical levels.

Lowe asks three questions important for his interactionist non-Cartesian substance dualism:

"(1) Are all causes events, or are at least some causes agents?

(2) Are free actions uncaused, at least by antecedent events? and

(3) Are an agent's reasons for action causes of that agent's actions?" [35]

---

34   Lowe (2010) *Personal Agency*, p.4
35   *Ibid.* p.2

And Lowe proposes three answers, plus a new claim:

"(1) In the most fundamental sense of 'cause', only agents are causes — although 'agents' understood in a very broad sense, to include inanimate objects as well as human beings.

(2) Free actions are completely uncaused — but they need not on that account be deemed to be merely random or chance occurrences. [Chance is not the direct cause of actions.]

(3) A rational agent's reasons for action are never causes of his or her actions.

In addition, I shall make the following claim:

(4) All free actions either consist in, or are initiated by, an act of will — in other words, a volition — on the part of the agent." [36]

Ruth Barcan Marcus

In 1947, Ruth C. Barcan (later Marcus) wrote an article on "The Identity of Individuals, " the first assertion of the "necessity of identity." Her work was written in the dense expressions of symbolic logic, with little verbal explanation or commentary.

2.33*. $\vdash (\beta_1 I(\beta_2) \equiv (\beta_1 I_m(\beta_2)).$

$((\beta_1 1_m(\beta_2)) (\beta_1 I(\beta_1))$ hook $(\beta_1 1(\beta_2))$ 2.21, 2.3, subst, *14.26*

$(\beta_1 I_m(\beta_2))$ hook $(\beta_1 I(\beta_2))$ 2.6, 2.32*, subst, adj, *18.61*, mod pon

$(\beta_1 I(\beta_2) \equiv (\beta_1 I_m(\beta_2))$ *18.42*, 2.23, subst, adj, def

Five years later, Marcus's thesis adviser, Frederick B. Fitch, published his book, *Symbolic Logic*, which contained the simplest proof ever of the necessity of identity, by the simple mathematical substitution of b for a in the necessity of self-identity statement.

23.4

(1) a = b,

(2) □ [a = a],

then (3) □ [a = b], by identity elimination. [37]

Clearly this is mathematically and logically sound. Fitch substitutes b from (1), for a in the modal context of (2). This would be fine if these are just mathematical equations. But as Barcan Marcus knew very well from Lewis's work on strict implication, substitutivity in statements also requires that the substitution is intensionally mean-

---

36 Lowe (2010) *Personal* Agency, p.2-3
37 Fitch (1952) *Symbolic Logic*, p.164

ingful. In the sense that b is actually just a, substituting b is equivalent to keeping a there, as a tautology, something with no new information. To be informative and prove the necessary truth of the new statement, we must know more about b, for example, that its *intrinsic* information in b is identical to that of a.

Marcus reprised the proof of her claim about the necessity of identity. She explicitly added Leibniz's Law relating identicals to indiscernibles to her argument.[38]

(x)(y) (x = y) ⊂ □ (x = y),

which reads "for all x and for all y, if "x = y," then necessarily "x = y."

In a formalized language, those symbols which name things will be those for which it is meaningful to assert that *I* holds between them, where ' *I* ' names the identity relation... If 'x' and 'y' are individual names then

(1) x *I* y

Where identity is defined rather than taken as primitive, it is customary to define it in terms of indiscernibility, one form of which is

(2) x *Ind* y $=_{df}$ (φ)(φx eq φy)

(3) x eq y = x *I* y

Statement (2) is Leibniz's Law, the indiscernibility of x from y, by definition means that for every property φ, both x and y have that same property, φx eq φy.

In her third article back in 1947, Barcan Marcus had first proved the necessity of identity. This result became a foundational principle in the modern incarnation of Leibniz's "possible worlds" by Kripke and David Lewis.

Fourteen years after her original identity article, Marcus presented her work at a 1961 colloquium at Boston University attended by Quine and Kripke.

A few years after Marcus' 1961 presentation, David Wiggins developed a five-step proof of the necessity of identity, using Leibniz' Law, as had Marcus. Wiggins did not mention her.

---

38   Marvus (1961) *Modalities and Intensional Languages*, pp. 5-7

Moreover, the great work on necessity and identity cited by most modal logicians is usually credited to Kripke's 1965 article "Identity and Necessity." This has stirred a great deal of controversy about giving proper credit to women working in academic fields formerly occupied primarily by men.[39]

Trenton Merricks

Trenton Merricks is a relatively young professor of philosophy and metaphysics at the University of Virginia. He is one of the staunch defenders of *mereological nihilism*, the idea that there are no composite objects, only "simples" arranged to look like objects. There are "no tables, only simples arranged tablewise," said Peter van Inwagen in his 1990 book *Material Beings*.

Van Inwagen made an exception for living things, an abstruse argument based on Descartes' idea that humans are thinking beings and "I think, therefore I am (existing?)."

Merricks follows van Inwagen in accepting human organisms as existing objects. But he goes beyond van Inwagen by denying reductionist arguments that the physical world is "causally closed" from the "bottom up."

Merricks adapts the reductionist claims of JAEGWON KIM that say properties in a complex system can be "reduced" to the lower-level properties of the system's components. For example, the laws and properties of chemistry can be reduced to the laws of physics.

More specifically, the properties of molecules can be reduced to those of atoms, the properties of biological cells can be reduced to those of molecules, plants and animals can be reduced to those of cells, and mind can be reduced to neurons in the brain. So far, Merricks agrees, any composite object is reducible to its simples - atoms or whatever the latest physics tells us are the most fundamental material objects.

Kim argues that mental events are redundant because for every event in a "mind," there must be a corresponding physical event in the brain that is doing the real causal work. Kim calls for "excluding" the mental events, describing them as "overdetermining" actions.

---

[39] Humphreys, P., & Fetzer, J. H. (Eds.). (1999). *The New Theory of Reference: Kripke, Marcus, and its Origins*

Merricks develops a powerful analogy between Kim's mental events and van Inwagen's non-existing composite objects. His prime example is a baseball breaking a window, which he calls his 'Overdetermination Argument'.

> "Consider the following argument about an alleged baseball causing atoms arranged windowwise to scatter, or, for ease of exposition, causing 'the shattering of a window'.
> (1) The baseball—if it exists—is causally irrelevant to whether its constituent atoms, acting in concert, cause the shattering of the window.
> (2) The shattering of the window is caused by those atoms, acting in concert.
> (3) The shattering of the window is not overdetermined. Therefore,
> (4) If the baseball exists, it does not cause the shattering of the window." [40]

For Merricks, the idea of the composite "baseball" can be excluded as overdetermining the shattering of the window. The analogy is powerful because the baseball is just an idea, just some information about the structure of the object, just its "form," like the form of a statue in the famous metaphysical puzzle of The Statue and the Clay.

The statue cannot survive the squashing of a lump of clay, but the lump can survive. Metaphysicians claim that the lump of clay and the statue have different persistence conditions.

Eliminative materialists deny the causal power of such abstract ideas or "forms." For them, only matter enters into causal relations. Form is separated from matter in many metaphysical puzzles and paradoxes. Form was imagined to be a numerically distinct object by the ancient Skeptics, but such pure ideas in minds are thought unable to move material.

Why Humans Exist

Merricks' argument for the existence of humans goes well beyond that of van Inwagen. It brings up more subtle metaphysical problems and leads to some surprising conclusions, including the fact that humans have free will.

---

40   Merricks (2003) *Objects and Persons*. p.56

He begins by arguing that Kim's Exclusion Argument does not succeed in denying mental causation in humans! And his own Overdetermination Argument, based originally on Kim's Exclusion, also does not apply, because humans have causal mental properties that cause things that are not caused by our constituent atoms.

> "Sometimes my deciding to do such and such is what causes the atoms of my arm to move as they do. Presumably my so deciding won't ever be the only cause of their moving. There will also be a cause in terms of microphysics or microbiology, in terms of nerve impulses and the like. But at some point in tracing back the causal origin of my arm's moving (if it is intended), we will reach a cause that is not microphysical, that just is the agent's deciding to do something." [41]

Composite objects that cause things that their parts do not redundantly cause can resist the eliminative sweep of the Overdetermination Argument. We humans—in virtue of causing things by having conscious mental properties—are causally non-redundant. So the Overdetermination Argument fails to show that we do not exist. So I conclude that we do. For we should assume that we exist unless we are shown otherwise. Any conscious composita presumably survive the Overdetermination Argument just as we do. So I conclude that dogs and dolphins, among other animals, exist.[42]

> "Human organisms do not dodge the Overdetermination Argument on a mere technicality of which baseballs, for example, cannot avail themselves for some intuitively irrelevant reason. Rather, human organisms have non-redundant causal powers and so can exercise downward causation. Baseballs, on the other hand, would not—even if they existed—have nonredundant causal powers or exercise downward causal control over their parts. This deep, fundamental difference between the powers of human organisms and the powers of alleged baseballs (and statues and rocks and stars and so on) makes all the difference with respect to the Overdetermination Argument." [43]

Merricks' defense of free will is straightforward. He denies the thesis that "humans have no choice about what their constituent atoms do or are like." He says that

---

41 *Ibid.*, p.110
42 *Ibid.*, p.114
43 *Ibid.*, p.116

"human persons have downward causal control over their constituent atoms. And surely downward causal control of this sort is sufficient for having a choice about what one's atoms do or are like...

On the assumption that we are human organisms, I have argued that we exercise downward causation...

I say that the downward causal control we exercise over our atoms makes room for our having free will. And, as we saw in the previous section, that same downward causal control undermines the Micro Exclusion Argument for mental epiphenomenalism. I think free will requires mental causation. So I think it bodes well for my metaphysics that its defence of free will turns on the same fact about humans as does its defence of mental causation." [44]

Merricks is correct that we have some downward mental control over some of our atoms.[45]

Huw Price

Huw Price was born in Oxford, England and was a professor of logic and metaphysics at Edinburgh. But he developed his original philosophical ideas in Australia as professor of philosophy at the University of Sydney. He is now Bertrand Russell Professor of Philosophy and a Fellow of Trinity College at the University of Cambridge. There he directs the Centre for Time and propose that physicists and philosophers look at the world from the perspective of an "Archimedean point" outside space and time that provides a symmetric view of the past and the future.

Price's ideas are inspired by the "block universe" of Einstein-Minkowski special relativity. A generation before Price was in Sydney, Australian philosopher J. J. C. SMART developed a "tenseless" theory of space and time and maintained that there is but one possible future.

Smart was one of the original architects of the standard argument against free will and Price developed an argument based on the work of JOHN BELL that giving up free will (what NIELS BOHR and

---

44 *Ibid.*, p.159-160
45 See Doyle (2016) Mental Causation, Great *Problems in Philosophy and Physics*, chapter 16.

Werner Heisenberg called the "free choice" of the experimenter) could remove a conflict between special relativity and the measurements of entangled systems in which something appears to be traveling faster than the speed of light.

The free choice of the experimenter was explored by John Conway and Simon Kochen. They claim that if free choice exists, it shows that atoms themselves must have free will, something they call the *Free Will Theorem*.

In his 1996 book, *Time's Arrow and Archimedes' Point*, Price proposes an Archimedean point "outside space and time" as a solution to the problem of nonlocality in the Bell experiments in the form of an "advanced action."

John Bell, and more recently, following Bell, Nicholas Gisin and Antoine Suarez claim that something might be coming from "outside space and time" to correlate the results in the spacelike-separated experimental tests of Bell's Theorem.

Rather than a "superdeterministic" common cause coming from "outside space and time" (as proposed by Bell, Gisin, Suarez, and others), Price argues that there might be a cause coming *backwards in time* from some interaction in the future. Roger Penrose and Stuart Hameroff have also promoted this idea of "backward causation," sending information backward in time in the Libet experiments and in the EPR experiments.

John Cramer's *Transactional Interpretation* of quantum mechanics and other Time-Symmetric Interpretations like that of Yakir Aharonov and K. B Wharton also search for Archimedean points "outside space and time."

But there is another way to get a time-symmetric point of view that resolves the EPR paradox of "influence" traveling faster than the speed of light. In his chapter on John Bell in *Time's Arrow...*, Price cites a BBC interview in which Bell suggested that a preferred frame of reference might help to explain nonlocality and entanglement.

The standard explanation of entangled particles usually begins with an observer A, often called Alice, and a distant observer B, known as Bob. Between them is a source of two entangled particles.

The two-particle wave function describing the indistinguishable particles cannot be separated into a product of two single-particle wave functions.

The problem of faster-than-light signaling arises when Alice is said to measure particle A and then puzzle over how Bob's (later) measurements of particle B can be perfectly correlated, when there is not enough time for any "influence" to travel from A to B.

Price describes the problem:

"the results of measurement on one particle enable us to predict the results of corresponding measurements on the other particle. For example, we might predict the position of particle 1 by measuring the position of particle 2, or predict the momentum of particle 2 by measuring the momentum of particle 1.[46]

Information physics has explained entanglement as the instantaneous collapse of the two-particle wave function everywhere when it is measured anywhere.[47]

Willard Van Orman Quine

In the early 1950's, Quine challenged the ancient analytic-synthetic distinction, arguing that in the end the "truth" of analytic statements, the proofs of mathematical theorems, and the use of logic, also depend on empirical verification.

The key idea of Quine's empiricism (and of DAVID HUME's) is to deny the existence of any *a priori* knowledge of the world, whether analytic or synthetic.

As CHARLES SANDERS PEIRCE had said, nothing is logically and necessarily true of the physical world. Logical truths like the *Principles of Non-Contradiction* and *Bivalence (Excluded Middle)* might be true in all possible worlds, but they tell us nothing about our physical world, unless they are applicable and empirically verified.

Epistemology Naturalized

Nearly twenty years later, Quine argued that epistemology, the justification of knowledge claims, should be "naturalized." All

---

46   Price (1997) *Time's Arrow and Archimedes' Point*, p.202
47   See chapter 20 above and chapter 21 of Doyle (2016) *Great Problems in Philosophy and Physics*.

knowledge claims should be reduced to verification by the methods of natural science. "For suppose we hold," he says, "with the old empiricist Peirce, that the very meaning of a statement consists in the difference its truth would make to possible experience."

> Every term and every sentence is a label attached to an idea, simple or complex, which is stored in the mind. When on the other hand we take a verification theory of meaning seriously, the indeterminacy would appear to be inescapable. The Vienna Circle espoused a verification theory of meaning but did not take it seriously enough. If we recognize with Peirce that the meaning of a sentence turns purely on what would count as evidence for its truth, and if we recognize with Duhem that theoretical sentences have their evidence not as single sentences but only as larger blocks of theory, then the indeterminacy of translation of theoretical sentences is the natural conclusion. And most sentences, apart from observation sentences, are theoretical. This conclusion, conversely, once it is embraced, seals the fate of any general notion of propositional meaning or, for that matter, state of affairs.[48]

Ontology

Quine began his famous essay "On What There Is" claiming it has a trivial answer,

> A curious thing about the ontological problem is its simplicity. It can be put in three Anglo-Saxon monosyllables: 'What is there?' It can be answered, moreover, in a word—'Everything' —and everyone will accept this answer as true. However, this is merely to say that there is what there is. There remains room for disagreement over cases; and so the issue has stayed alive down the centuries.[49]

Alexius Meinong disagreed, and in a way most disagreeable to Quine, insisting that "objects exist which do not exist," by which he meant things that do not have an ordinary material existence, such as *abstract entities* like numbers and Platonic Ideas. Meinong also meant impossible objects, like the "round square," which have meaning but do not have denotation, any reference to an example or an instance of such an object.

---

48 Quine (1969) 'Epistemology Naturalized,' *Ontological Relativity and Other Essays*. pp.80-3
49 Quine (1961) 'On What There Is,' *From a Logical Point of View*, p.1

Quantified Modal Logic and Identity

Quine was perhaps best-known in the philosophy of logic for his views on quantification, which was an essential part of ARISTOTLE's *Prior Analytics* and was formalized by GOTTLOB FREGE in 1879 in his *Begriffsschrift* or "Concept Writing."

Frege replaced the familiar sentences (or statements or propositions) of the "first-order" predicate logic of Aristotle's syllogisms - "All men are mortal' - with the notion of quantification operators working on propositional functions, formulas that include variables, some of which are "free" and others "bound" by the quantification operator.

The idea of "for all x" becomes $\forall x$ and is called the universal quantification operator. The notion of "for some x" is called the existential operator $\exists x$. This is often read "there exists an x such that..."

In his 1940 book Mathematical Logic, Quine commented on identity, explaining it in terms of class membership.

"WE TURN now to the problem of so defining 'x = y', in terms of '∈' and our other primitives, that it will carry the intended sense 'x and y are the same object'. In the trivial case where y is not a class, indeed, x ∈ y if and only if x = y in this sense (cf. § 22); but our problem remains, since 'x ∈ y' diverges in meaning from ' x = y' in case y is a class. We must find a formula, composed of 'x' and ' y ' by means of '∈' and our other primitives, which will be true just in case x and y are the same object — whether a class or a non-class. The requirement is met by:

(1) (z)(z ∈ x . = . z ∈ y)

when x and y are classes, since classes are the same when their members are the same (cf. § 22). Moreover, (1) continues to meet the requirement when x and y are not classes. For, in this case 'z ∈ x' and 'z ∈ y ' identify z with x and with y; and (1) as a whole then says that whatever is the same as x is the same as y, thus identifying x and y. Both where x and y are classes and where they are not, therefore, (1) meets our requirements; (1) is true if and only if x and y are the same. We are thus led to introduce 'x = y' as an abbreviation of (1)...

Variables and abstracts will be spoken of collectively as terms. Now let us supplement our Greek-letter conventions to this extent: just as we use 'φ', 'ψ', and 'χ', to refer to any formulae, and 'α', 'β', 'γ', and 'δ' to refer to any variables, so let us use 'ζ', 'η', and 'θ' (along with their accented and subscripted variants) to refer in general to any terms. With help of this convention we can express the general definition of identity as follows, for application to variables and abstracts indifferently:

D10. ⌜$(\zeta = \eta)$⌝ for ⌜$(\alpha)(\alpha \in \zeta . = . \alpha \in \eta)$⌝." [50]

In 1943, a few years before RUTH BARCAN MARCUS introduced her two new modal operators, ◊ for possibility, and □ for necessity (the square was suggested by her thesis adviser, F. B. Fitch), Quine published an important paper on existence and necessity.

Here is the converse of Leibniz's Law, first given its converse name by Quine:

> "One of the fundamental principles governing identity is that of substitutivity - or, as it might well be called, that of indiscernibility of identicals. It provides that, given a true statement of identity, one of its two terms may be substituted for the other in any true statement and the result will be true. It is easy to find cases contrary to this principle. For example, the statements:
>
> (1) Giorgione = Barbarelli,
>
> 2) Giorgione was so-called because of his size
>
> are true; however, replacement of the name 'Giorgione' by the name 'Barbarelli' turns (2) into the falsehood:
>
> Barbarelli was so-called because of his size." [51]

Frege had warned about the confusion possible between the bare denotation or name and the sense intended by the speaker and interpreted by the listener. C. I. LEWIS said we need to consult the intension, the meaning, to draw the right logical conclusions. Lewis felt Quine's extensionality, based on set membership, is not enough.

The proper resolution of this word quibble and quasi-paradox is to take the intension of "Barbarelli" as a second name for the same thing named by "Giorgione" - "big George." Barbarelli, *qua* Giorgione, was so-called because of his size.

---

50   Quine (1940) *Mathematical Logic*, p.134 in the 1951 edition.

51   Quine (1943) 'Notes on Existence and Necessity,' *Journal of Philosophy* 40(5) p.113

In his brief discussion of necessity, Quine, following Rudolf Carnap, said
> Among the various possible senses of the vague adverb 'necessarily', we can single out one - the sense of *analytic* necessity - according to the following criterion: the result of applying 'necessarily' to a statement is true if, and only if, the original statement is analytic.
>
> (16) Necessarily no spinster is married,
>
> for example, is equivalent to:
>
> (17) 'No spinster is married' is analytic,
>
> and is therefore true.

Quine concludes that the notion of necessity may simply not be susceptible to quantification, and suggest extensionality is the best approach, because there is no need for intensionality in mathematics!
> The effect of these considerations is rather to raise questions than to answer them. The one important result is the recognition that any intensional mode of statement composition, whether based on some notion of "necessity" or, for example, on a notion of "probability" (as in Reichenbach's system), must be carefully examined in relation to its susceptibility to quantification. Perhaps the only useful modes of statement composition susceptible to quantification are the extensional ones, reducible to '-' and '.'. Up to now there is no clear example to the contrary. It is known, in particular, that no intensional mode of statement composition is needed in mathematics.[52]

In 1947, Ruth C. Barcan (later Marcus) wrote an article on "The Identity of Individuals, " the first assertion of the "necessity of identity." Five years later, Marcus's thesis adviser, Frederic B. Fitch, published his book, *Symbolic Logic*, which contained the simplest proof ever of the necessity of identity, by the simple mathematical substitution of b for a in the necessity of self-identity statement.

23.4

(1) $a = b$,

(2) $\Box [a = a]$,

then (3) $\Box [a = b]$, by identity elimination. [53]

---

52   Quine (1943) 'Notes on Existence and Necessity,' p.124-5
53   Fitch (1952) *Symbolic Logic*, p.164

Fitch substitutes b from (1) for a in the modal context of (2). This is mathematically and logically sound. This would be fine if these are just mathematical or logical equations (as Quine hoped). But as Barcan Marcus knew very well from C.I.Lewis's work on strict implication, substitutivity in statements also requires that the substitution is *intensionally meaningful*. In the sense that b is actually just a, substituting b is equivalent to keeping a there, a tautology, something with no new information. To be informative and prove the necessary truth of the new statement, we must know more about b, for example, that *intrinsic* information in b is identical to that of a.

Fourteen years after her original identity article, Marcus presented her work at a 1961 colloquium at Boston University attended by Quine and Saul Kripke.

Marcus reprised the proof of her claim about the necessity of identity. She explicitly added Leibniz's Law relating identicals to indiscernibles to her argument.

$(x)(y) (x = y) \subset \square (x = y)$

Many years after Quine's attempts to refute Marcus' arguments quantifying into modal logic, her work is widely accepted by present-day metaphysicians.

Michael Rea

Rea is a professor of philosophy at Notre Dame and director of the Center for Philosophy and Religion. He is also a professorial fellow at the University of St. Andrews, specializing in analytic and exegetical theology.

Rea's 1997 book, *Material Constitution: A Reader*, is an anthology of 17 articles on the problems of coincident entities, contingent identity, mereological nihilism, and problems of identity.

In a landmark 1995 article in the *Philosophical Review*, Rea arranged some classic puzzles and paradoxes in material constitution (The Statue and the Clay, The Ship of Theseus, Dion and Theon, Tibbles, the Cat, and The Growing Problem, as criticized by Chryssipus).

Metaphysicians

Rea saw all these problems could be grouped together under a single problem of material constitution.[54]

> "What I intend to show is that there is one problem underlying these four familiar puzzles (and their many variants). This problem I will call "the problem of material constitution." I say it underlies the four puzzles for the following reason: every solution to the problem of material constitution is equally a solution to each of these four puzzles, though not vice versa." [55]

Rea saw five assumptions at the core of each of the puzzles.

> "Informally, they are: (i) there is an F and there are ps that compose it, (ii) if the ps compose an F, then they compose an object that is essentially such that it bears a certain relation R to its parts, (iii) if the ps compose an F, then they compose an object that can exist and not bear R to its parts, (iv) if the ps compose both a and b, then a is identical with b, and (v) if a is identical with b then a is necessarily identical with b. Let us call these assumptions, respectively the Existence Assumption, the Essentialist Assumption, (with apologies to Frankfurt) the Principle of Alternative Compositional Possibilities (or PACP for short), the Identity Assumption, and the Necessity Assumption." [56]

Information philosophy maintains that there is no necessity in the material world. Necessity is an essential concept in the logical world of ideas. Rea showed that any possible solutions to these puzzles can be grouped in a taxonomy of assumptions. He divided the possible solutions into those that deny the Identity Assumption, those that deny the Necessity Assumption, and those that deny one or more of the remaining three. The Identity Assumption is roughly the idea that "constitution is identity." At least one assumption must be incompatible with the others, he says.

The most flawed assumption, from an information philosophy point of view, is the identity assumption, especially the idea that material constitution is identity. This assumption, which dates from the pre-Socratics, was challenged by the Stoics, especially by Chrysippus' puzzling description of Dion and Theon.

---

54 See chapter 9.
55 Rea (1995) 'The Problem of Material Constitution.' *Philosophical Review*, 104(4), 525
56 *Ibid.*, p.527.

Dion/Theon is best interpreted as an attack on the Growing Argument, which the Academic Skeptics used to challenge the Stoic claim that their "peculiarly qualified individuals" can survive material change. The Stoics accepted the ancient claim that a change of material causes an object to cease to exist and a new "numerically distinct" object comes into existence.

But the Stoics argued that this sort of material change should be called generation and destruction, since they transform the thing from what it is into something else. This is the Heraclitean philosophy of Becoming, that all is in flux, you can't step into the same river twice. If everything is always changing its material, what is to constitute its Parmenidean Being, especially a human being?

The Academic Skeptic version of the Growing Argument was that matter is the sole principle of individuation, so that a change of matter constitutes a change of identity.

But according to the Stoics, material change is not growing. Something that grows and diminishes must subsist. It must retain its identity over time. Otherwise we cannot say that "it" is growing.

For the Stoics, what comes into existence, grows, then diminishes and dies, is the peculiarly qualified individual (ἴδιος ποιὸν) that is coincident with a different amount of matter from time to time.

But material constitution is not identity, individuals are not their material substrate (ὑποκείμενον), but their unique qualities, which we can take to be Aristotle's *immaterial* form and our *information*.

The Stoics have therefore rejected matter as the principle of individuation.

Alan Sidelle

Sidelle is a professor of philosophy at the University of Wisconsin who argues that many "truths" in philosophy are merely conventional. This should include all the analytical language statements that are true by definition, because these are clearly conventional.

Information philosophy assumes that the concept of truth should be limited to logic. Truths are logical *a priori* statements. Facts are empirical *a posteriori* statements.

Despite IMMANUEL KANT's failure to prove the existence of *synthetic a priori* truths, some metaphysicians talk about some that are *necessary a posteriori*. This is the idea that once something is a fact, it is now a *necessarily true* fact.

Information philosophy considers claims such as "If P, then P is true" to be redundant, adding no information to the (true) assertion of the statement or proposition "P." Further redundancies are equally vacuous, such as "If P is true, then P is necessarily true" and "If P is true, then P is necessarily true in all possible worlds."

In fact, that is to say in the empirical world, any fact F is only probably true, with the probability approaching certainty in cases that are adequately determined. And, in any case, any past F could have been otherwise. That is to say, ontologically real possibilities exist as ideas, pure abstract information, alongside material objects.

In metaphysics, Sidelle's "No Coincidence Thesis" denies the existence of *coinciding objects*.

> "One central such view I call 'The No Coincidence Thesis' (NC): There cannot be two material objects wholly located in the same place at the same time (some prefer: No two objects can wholly consist, at a time, of just the same parts). This principle conflicts with our everyday judgments that there are both ordinary objects-sweaters, trees and cows-and 'constituting' objects-pieces of yarn and wood, maybe aggregates of cells or quarks combined with our views about how these things move through time, which, more theoretically, underlie our views about the persistence conditions for these sorts of things. Since the 'macro' objects can go from existence while the constituting objects persist, and more generally, since the histories traced by each can differ, an object and its 'constituting' object cannot, in general, be identified, so we are committed to coinciding objects (Wiggins (1968)). NC also plays a role in Van Inwagen's (1981) modern version of the ancient Dion/Theon puzzle; he shows that this principle is inconsistent with our belief in arbitrary undetached parts, combined with the view that objects can lose parts (plus an intuitive judgment that undetached parts persist if all their parts persist arranged in just the same way)." [57]

---

57 Sidelle (2002) 'Is There a True Metaphysics of Material Objects?,' *Noûs*, Vol. 36, Supplement: Philosophical Issues, 12, Realism and Relativism (2002), p.118

Sidelle also questions the use of arbitrary distinctions, such as those involved in Peter van Inwagen's Doctrine of Arbitrary Undetached Parts. This is the problem that Plato called "carving nature at the joints"

> "Another theoretical idea often invoked in criticism of ordinary (and other) views is a proscription against arbitrary distinctions. Arbitrariness, or its appearance, can show up in judgments about which portions of the world do, and which do not, contain objects, and in judgments about how things persist through change - what changes are 'substantial', and how things move through time. For instance, we commonly think cells arranged in certain ways constitute cows, but that no object is constituted by this paper and my eye. But one may wonder whether there is any difference here which can, in an appropriate way, substantiate such a distinction, especially when science reveals how much space there is between small particles making up cows. What of our judgment that something ceases to exist when a cow dies, but not when a hoof is clipped, or it catches cold? In each case, it seems that something persists, but some properties change. Or why does a car become larger when bumpers are attached, but not when a trailer is?" [58]

Arbitrariness is invoked in the problem of composite objects. Mereological nihilists deny there are any composite objects, with Peter van Inwagen and others making an ill-justified exception for living things.

For mereological universalists, David Lewis for example, arbitrary mereological sums are considered to be composite objects. Considering the Statue of Liberty and Eiffel Tower a composite object is an example of arbitrary unrestricted composition. Considering Theon (Dion missing his left leg) or Tibbles minus one hair are arbitrary disjunctions. Such arbitrariness hardly carves nature at the joints.

Between these two absurd extremes of mereological nihilism and universalism, information philosophy provides strong reasons for why things are composite objects. They also include "proper parts" that are composite objects. We can call these "integral" parts as they have a function in the integrated object.

These same reasons show that artifacts are composite objects.

---

58   Ibid., p.119

Artifacts and living things have a purpose which Aristotle called final cause or "telos." They are "teleonomic." For example, "simples arranged tablewise" have been arranged by a carpenter, whose "telos" was to make a table. This telos carves the artifact at the joints (legs, top). The arrangement or organization is pure abstract information.

Living things were described by Aristotle as "entelechy, "having their telos within themselves." They are more than just matter and static form like an artifact. They have internal messaging between their integral parts that helps to achieve the teleonomic end of maintaining themselves against degradation by the second law of thermodynamics. Many such integral parts are themselves wholes, from vital organs down to the individual cells. The boundaries of integral parts "carve nature at the joints."

Living things also contain many "biological machines" that include "biological computers" or information processors that respond to those messages. The messages are written in meaningful biological codes that are analogous to and the precursor of human languages.

Ted Sider

Sider is a leading metaphysician who defends four-dimensionalism, the idea that objects persist over time as distinct "temporal parts." Here is his definition

> "According to 'four-dimensionalism', temporally extended things are composed of temporal parts. Most four-dimensionalists identify ordinary continuants—the persisting objects ordinary language quantifies over and names—with aggregates of temporal parts ('space-time worms'), but an attractive alternate version of four-dimensionalism identifies ordinary continuants with instantaneous temporal slices and accounts for temporal predication using temporal counterpart theory." [59]

Four-dimensionalism is a variation of the Academic Skeptic argument about growth, that even the smallest material change destroys an entity and another entity appears. In this case, a change in the instant of time also destroys every material object, followed instantaneously by the creation of an "identical" object.

---

59   Sider (2001) *Four-Dimensionalism*: An Ontology of Persistence and Time (abstract)

WILLARD VAN ORMAN QUINE proposed a similar idea that he called object "stages." The great Anglo-American philosopher ALFRED NORTH WHITEHEAD attributed the continued existence of objects from moment to moment to the intervention of God. Without a kind of continuous creation of every entity, things would fall apart. This notion can also be traced back to the American theologian JONATHAN EDWARDS, for whom God intervenes in all human actions, creating the world anew at every instant. DAVID LEWIS's theory of temporal parts argues that at every instant of time, every individual disappears, ceases to exist, to be replaced by a very similar new entity, with its own properties that he calls "temporary intrinsics."

Lewis proposed temporal parts as a solution to the problem of *persistence*. He calls his solution "perdurance," which he distinguishes from "endurance," in which the whole entity exists at all times.

In his thinking about persistence, Sider has been inspired (as have many metaphysicians) by Einstein's theory of special relativity. The idea of a four-dimensional manifold of space and time supports the idea that the "temporal parts" of an object are as distinct from one another as its spatial parts. This raises questions about the continued identity of an object as it moves in space and time.

There is no physical basis for the wild assumptions of past metaphysicians and theologians that the contents of the universe cease to exist and then reappear *de novo* at the next instant. This notion violates one of the most fundamental of physical laws, the conservation of matter and energy.

More metaphysically significant, neither temporal nor spatial "slices" carve nature at the joints. They are arbitrary mental constructions imposed on the world by philosophers that have little to do with "natural" objects and their "integral" component parts.

Ironically, Sider claims that the fundamental nature of reality is to be found in his latest claim that "structure" is the most fundamental "underlying" notion that includes concepts, notions, primitive expressions, in short an ideology that carves nature at the joints.

"In order to perfectly describe the world, it is not enough to speak truly. One must also use the right concepts - including the right logical concepts. One must use concepts that "carve at the joints", that give the world's *structure*. There is an objectively correct way to "write the book of the world". Metaphysics, as traditionally conceived, is about the fundamental nature of reality; in the present terms, metaphysics is about the world's structure. Metametaphysics - inquiry into the status of metaphysical questions - turns on structure. The question of whether ontological, causal, or modal questions are "substantive" is in large part a question of whether the world has ontological, causal, and modal structure - whether quantifiers, causal relations, and modal operators carve at the joints.

Although philosophical doubts can be raised about structure, it is sensible to follow David Armstrong and David Lewis in taking the idea at face value. As will be seen in the rest of the book, the idea illuminates metametaphysics. Some critics think that certain questions of metaphysics are "insubstantial" (or merely verbal), in something like the way in which the question of whether the pope is a bachelor is insubstantial. Whether they are right depends on whether the key notions in the questions carve at the joints." [60]

Information philosophy offers a model close to Sider's notion of "structure" as fundamental reality, we maintain that the world consists of information structures, bits of matter arranged with an abstract form that can be quantified over. Some of these information structures have internal integrity that depends on the way they were formed. For example, astronomical and geological objects were formed respectively by gravitation and chemical forces that gave them their forms.

Artifacts, by contrast, are created for a *purpose*. Some of their "proper parts" may be essential (though not logically necessary) to that purpose, in which case they are parts that are essential to the whole and can be called "integral parts," since they perform a function and contribute to the holistic integrity of the entity.

Sider says that he is a mereological nihilist, like PETER VAN INWAGEN, whereas DAVID LEWIS, Sider's source of naturalness (carving nature at the joints), favors mereological sums or unrestricted composition.

---

60   Sider (2011) *Writing the Book of the World*. Oxford University Press.

Now the "time slices" that are the "temporal parts" of Sider's four-dimensionalism do not "carve nature at the joints," any more than his putatively analogous slices in any spatial dimension. Indeed, any two-dimensional spatial slice perpendicular to the third spatial dimension would normally destroy a physical object and kill any living thing.

An actual temporal slice, cutting the continuity between an object and its future existence, would also destroy the object, which was the ancient view of the Greek philosophers and the commonsense view today.

Perhaps Sider thinks of his arbitrary slicing as not "real" but merely as an analytic tool, like the CAT scan of the human brain that gives us the information in the slice without harming the patient? But David Lewis insisted that his extravagant proliferation of infinite possible worlds was real and he probably meant his temporal parts with their "temporary intrinsic" properties to be numerically distinct real objects?

Peter Unger

In 1980, Unger formulated what he called "The Problem of the Many." It led Unger to propose that nothing exists and that even he did not exist, a position known as *nihilism*.

Today this includes the metaphysical problems of *material composition* and of *vagueness*.

> "let us start by considering certain cases of ordinary clouds, clouds like those we sometimes seem to see in the sky.
>
> As often viewed by us from here on the ground, sometimes puffy "picture-postcard" clouds give the appearance of having a nice enough boundary, each white entity sharply surrounded by blue sky...But upon closer scrutiny, as may happen sometimes when you're in an airplane, even the puffiest, cleanest clouds don't seem to be so nicely bounded. And this closer look seems a more revealing one. For, as science seems clearly to say, our clouds are almost wholly composed of tiny water droplets, and the dispersion of these droplets, in the sky or the atmosphere, is always, in fact, a gradual matter. With pretty much any route out of even

a comparatively clean cloud's center, there is no stark stopping place to be encountered. Rather, anywhere near anything presumed a boundary, there's only a gradual decrease in the density of droplets fit, more or less, to be constituents of a cloud that's there.

With that being so, we might see that there are enormously many complexes of droplets, each as fit as any other for being a constituted cloud. Each of the many will be a cloud, ..where, at first, it surely seemed there was exactly one." [61]

In his 1990 book *Material Beings*, PETER VAN INWAGEN said Unger's original insight that there are many ways to compose a cloud from innumerable water droplets should be called *"mereological universalism."* Van Inwagen denies there is any way for simples to compose anything other than themselves, which van Inwagen calls *"mereological nihilism."*

Free Will

Unger developed a unique theory combining science and philosophy hat he called "Scientiphicalism." He wrote about free will:

"In the terms of our dominant Scientiphical Metaphysic, it's hard to think of myself as an entity that engages in activity he himself chooses from available alternatives for his action.

Rather than discussing a form of Incompatibilism discussed for centuries, I'm now trying to introduce for discussion new forms of Incompatibilism.

Let's return to consider our Scientiphical Jane. Composed of very many Particles, and nothing else metaphysically basic, all Jane's powers must derive, in such a straightforwardly physical fashion, from the basic propensities of her quite simple physical constituents...

More philosophers now take an urgent interest in another issue concerning full choice that, at least nowadays, may be the real heart of "the problem of free will." This more urgent issue may be presented by way of an argument strikingly forceful for reasoning so sketchy and bare:

---

61   Unger (1999) 'Mental Problems of the Many.' *Oxford Studies in Metaphysics*, 23, Chapter 8. p.197.

First Premise: If Determinism holds, then, as everything we do is inevitable from long before we existed, nothing we do is anything we choose from available alternatives for our activity.

Second Premise: If Determinism doesn't hold, then, [while some things we do may be inevitable from long before our existence and, as such, it's never within our power to choose for ourselves] it may be that some aren't inevitable - but, as regards any of these others, it will be a matter of chance whether we do them or not, and, as nothing of that sort is something we choose to do - nothing we do is anything we choose from available alternatives for our activity.

Third Premise: Either Determinism holds or it doesn't.

Therefore,

Conclusion: Nothing we do is anything we choose from available alternatives for our activity.

This argument is quite disturbing. Indeed, nowadays, able thinkers often take it to suggest that our concept of full choice is an incoherent idea, never true of any reality at all." [62]

Peter van Inwagen

Van Inwagen made a significant reputation for himself by bucking the trend among philosophers in most of the twentieth century to accept compatibilism, the idea that free will is compatible with a strict causal determinism. This fits in with the majority of thinkers who embraced some form of eliminative materialism and behaviorism.

Van Inwagen's major contribution was to change the language and the framing in the free will debates. Opposing compatibilism, he proposed the idea of *incompatibilism* that has been very popular in the last few decades. He asserted that the old problem of whether we have free will or whether determinism is true was no longer being debated. In the first chapter of his landmark 1983 book, *An Essay on Free Will*, van Inwagen says:

"1.2 It is difficult to formulate "the problem of free will and determinism" in a way that will satisfy everyone. Once one might

---

62 Unger (2002) 'Free Will and Scientiphicalism.' *Philosophy and Phenomenological Research*, vol. 65(1), 1-24.

have said that the problem of free will and determinism — in those days one would have said 'liberty and necessity' — was the problem of discovering whether the human will is free or whether its productions are governed by strict causal necessity. But no one today would be allowed to formulate "the problem of free will and determinism" like that, for this formulation presupposes the truth of a certain thesis about the conceptual relation of free will to determinism that many, perhaps most, present-day philosophers would reject: that free will and determinism are incompatible. Indeed many philosophers hold not only that free will is compatible with determinism but that free will entails determinism. I think it would be fair to say that almost all the philosophical writing on the problem of free will and determinism since the time of Hobbes that is any good, that is of any enduring philosophical interest, has been about this presupposition of the earlier debates about liberty and necessity. It is for this reason that nowadays one must accept as a fait accompli that the problem of finding out whether free will and determinism are compatible is a large part, perhaps the major part, of "the problem of free will and determinism"." [63]

Incompatibilism

Just as PETER. F. STRAWSON in 1962 changed the subject from the existence of free will, from the question of whether determinism or indeterminism is true, and just as HARRY FRANKFURT changed the debate to the question of the existence of *alternative possibilities*, so Van Inwagen made a major change, at least in the terminology, to the question of whether free will and determinism are compatible, indeed whether free will entails determinism, as he says above.

Van Inwagen replaces the traditional problem of "liberty and necessity," finding out whether determinism is true or false, and thus whether or not we have free will, with a new problem that he calls the compatibility problem.

"I shall attempt to formulate the problem in a way that takes account of this fait accompli by dividing the problem into two problems, which I will call the Compatibility Problem and the Traditional Problem. The Traditional Problem is, of course, the problem of finding out whether we have free will or whether

---

63 Van Inwagen (1983) *An Essay on Free Will*, p.1

determinism is true. But the very existence of the Traditional Problem depends upon the correct solution to the Compatibility Problem: if free will and determinism are compatible, and, a fortiori, if free will entails determinism, then there is no Traditional Problem, any more than there is a problem about how my sentences can be composed of both English words and Roman letters." [64]

Despite the obvious over-reaching claim that the Traditional Problem would disappear, which was nonsense, van Inwagen's new framing proved immensely popular over the next few decades. And the new framing introduced a new jargon term that is in major use today, the position of "Incompatibilism." Earlier writers, CARL GINET and WILFRED SELLARS, for example, had said that free will is "incompatible" with determinism. But that was simply the original position of all libertarians, in opposition to both the determinists and the compatibilists (WILLIAM JAMES' "soft" determinists), who were following what Sellars called the traditional Hume-Mill solution, which "reconciled" free will with determinism, liberty with necessity.

Before van Inwagen then, incompatibilists were libertarians, opposing the idea that free will is compatible with determinism.

But after van Inwagen, the new emphasis on "incompatibilism" drew attention to the idea that James' "hard" determinists were also incompatibilist in the sense of denying compatibilism.

Unfortunately for the clarity of the dialectic, this new category of incompatibilism is very confusing, because it now contains two opposing concepts, libertarian free will and hard determinism!

And like determinism versus indeterminism, compatibilism versus incompatibilism is a false and unhelpful dichotomy. J. J. C. Smart once claimed he had an exhaustive description of the possibilities, determinism or indeterminism, and that neither one neither allowed for free will. (Since Smart, dozens of others have repeated this standard logical argument against free will.)

---

64   Ibid., p.2

The Consequence Argument and Mind Argument

Van Inwagen developed his own terminology for the two-part standard argument against free will, dividing it into what he now called the Consequence Argument and the Mind Argument.

Van Inwagen defines determinism very simply. "Determinism is quite simply the thesis that the past determines a unique future."[65]

He concludes that such a determinism is not true, because we could not then be responsible for our actions, which would all be simply the consequences of events in the distant past that were not "up to us."

Van Inwagen's Consequence Argument is just a renaming of the perennial determinism objection in the standard argument against free will.[66] The Consequence Argument has proved very popular in philosophy courses taught by professors with little knowledge of the history of the free will problem.

In recent decades, centuries-old debates about free will have been largely replaced by debates about moral responsibility. Since Peter Strawson, many philosophers have claimed to be agnostic on the traditional problem of free will and determinism and focus on whether the concept of moral responsibility itself exists. Some say that, like free will itself, moral responsibility is *an illusion*. Van Inwagen is not one of those. He hopes to establish moral responsibility based on a libertarian free will, in opposition to prevailing compatibilist views.

Van Inwagen also notes that quantum mechanics shows indeterminism to be "true." He is correct. But we still have a very powerful and "adequate" determinism. It is this adequate determinism that R. E. HOBART and others have recognized when he wrote that "Free Will Involves Determination and is Inconceivable Without It." Our will and actions are *adequately determined*, by our reasons, motives, feelings, etc., not in any way *pre-determined* from before we begin thinking, evaluating, and selecting one of the *alternative possibilities* in our thoughts. It is our thoughts and the open future that are undetermined.

---

65   Ibid., p.2
66   See Doyle (2011) *Free Will: The Scandal in Philosophy*, chapter 4

Sadly, many philosophers mistake indeterminism to imply that nothing is causal and therefore that everything is completely random. This is the Randomness Objection in the standard two-part argument against free will.

Van Inwagen states his Consequence Argument as follows:
"If determinism is true, then our acts are the consequences of the laws of nature and events in the remote past. But it is not up to us what went on before we were born, and neither is it up to us what the laws of nature are. Therefore, the consequences of these things (including our present acts) are not up to us." [67]

Exactly how this differs from the arguments of centuries of Libertarians is not clear, but van Inwagen is given a great deal of credit in the contemporary literature for this obvious argument. See for example, Carl Ginet's article "Might We Have No Choice?"[68]

We note that apparently Ginet also thought his argument was original. What has happened to philosophers today that they so ignore the history of philosophy?

Mereological Universalism

Van Inwagen has been an outspoken opponent of mereological universalism, the idea that an arbitrary collection of objects or parts of objects can be considered a conceptual whole – a "mereological sum" – for some purpose or other (mostly to provoke an empty debate with other metaphysicians).

Modern metaphysics examines the relations of parts to whole, whole to parts, and parts to parts within a whole using the abstract axioms of set theory, a vital part of analytic language philosophy today. Because a set can be made up of any list of things, whether they have any physical integrity or even any conceivable connections, other than their membership in the arbitrary set. Remember the "whole" made up of the Eiffel Tower and the Statue of Liberty!

Mereology is a venerable subject. The Greeks worried about part/whole questions, usually in the context of the persistence of an object when a part is removed and the question of an object's identity. Is

---

[67] *Ibid.*, p.16

[68] Ginet (1966) 'Might We Have No Choice', *Freedom and Determinism*, Ed. K. Lehrer, 1966

the Ship of Theseus the same ship when some of the planks have been replaced? Does Dion survive the removal of his foot?

The idea that an arbitrary collection of things, a "mereological sum," can be considered a whole, does violence to our common sense notion of a whole object. It is an extreme example of the arbitrary connection between words and objects that is the bane of analytic language philosophy.

Mereological universalism also leads to the idea that there are many ways to compose a complex material whole out of a vague collection of simple objects. This is what Peter Unger called the Problem of the Many.

It led Peter van Inwagen to his equally extreme position of *mereological nihilism*, that there are no composite wholes of any kind. Van Inwagen says there are no tables, only "simples arranged table-wise." The "arrangement" is the *information structure* in the table. When we can identify the origin of that information, we have the deep metaphysical reason for it essence. Aristotle called the arrangement "the scheme of the ideas."

> By matter I mean, for instance, bronze; by shape, the arrangement of the form (τὸ σχῆμα τῆς ἰδέας); and by the combination of the two, the concrete thing: the statue (ἀνδριάς).[69]

Van Inwagen makes an exception of living things, and Unger has abandoned his own form of nihilism in recent years. Both Unger and van Inwagen now accept the idea that the two of them exist as composite objects.

Van Inwagen's says that his argument for living beings as composite objects is based on the Cartesian "cogito," *I think, therefore I am.* He proposes,

> (∃y the xs compose y) if and only if the activity of the xs constitutes a life.

> If this answer is correct, then there are living organisms: They are the objects whose lives are constituted by the activities of simples, and, perhaps, by the activities of subordinate organisms such as cells; they are the objects that have proper parts...My argument for the existence of organisms, it will be remembered, involved in an essential way the proposition that I exist.[70]

---

69   Aristotle, *Metaphysics*, Book VII, § vii
70   Van Inwagen (1990b) *Material Beings*, p.213

Living things involve many, many "proper parts," above the cellular level and below, all of them full of teleonomic purpose. And van Inwagen's tables also have a purpose, albeit external, namely the carpenter who gave it its form, the holistic shape that makes it a table.

David Wiggins

Wiggins speculated on the *necessity of identity* in 1965.

"The connexion of what I am going to say with modal calculi can be indicated in the following way. It would seem to be a necessary truth that if a = b then whatever is truly ascribable to a is truly ascribable to b and vice versa (Leibniz's Law). This amounts to the principle

(1) $(x)(y)((x = y) \supset (\varphi)(\varphi x \supset \varphi y))$

Suppose that identity-statements are ascriptions or predications.! Then the predicate variable in (1) will apparently range over properties like that expressed by '(= a) ' and we shall get as consequence of (1)

(2) $(x)(y)((x = y) \supset (x = x \, . \supset . \, y = x))$

There is nothing puzzling about this. But if (as many modal logicians believe), there exist de re modalities of the form

□ (φa) (i.e., necessarily (φa)),

then something less innocent follows. If '(= a) ' expresses property, then '□ (a=a)', if this too is about the object a, also ascribes something to a, namely the property □ (= a). For on a naive and pre-theoretical view of properties, you will reach an expression for a property whenever you subtract a noun-expression with material occurrence (something like ' a ' in this case) from a simple declarative sentence. The property

□ (= a) then falls within the range of the predicate variable in Leibniz's Law (understood in this intuitive way) and we get

(3) $(x)(y)(x = y \supset (\Box (x = x) \, . \supset . \, \Box (y = x)))$

Hence, reversing the antecedents,

(4) $(x)(y)(\Box (x = x) \, . \supset . \, (x = y) \supset \Box (x = y))$

But (x) (□ (x=x)) ' is a necessary truth, so we can drop this antecedent and reach

(5) $(x)(y)((x = y) \, . \supset . \, \Box (x = y))$" [71]

---

[71] Wiggins (1965) 'Identity Statements', in *Analytical Philosophy*, Second Series, 1965, Oxford: Blackwell. pp.40-41

Peter Geach worked on problems of identity and debated for years with David Wiggins about *relative identity*.

For Geach and Wiggins, relative identity means "x is the same F as y," but "x may not be the same G as y."

Wiggins argued against this idea of relative identity, but accepted what he called a sortal-dependent identity, "x is the same F as y." Geach called this a "criterion of identity."

Free Will

Inspired by the libertarian philosophers RODERICK CHISHOLM and RICHARD TAYLOR, Wiggins provided a vigorous defense of libertarianism (or an attack on compatibilism) in a 1965 paper read to the Oxford Philosophical Society. Part of that paper was rewritten as "Towards a reasonable libertarianism" in Ted Honderich's 1973 *Essays on Freedom of Action*.

This paper caught the eye of DANIEL DENNETT, who expanded on Wiggins' theme of figuring out what libertarians say they want, and trying to give it to them. Wiggins described his goals:

"One of the many reasons, I believe, why philosophy falls short of a satisfying solution to the problem of freedom is that we still cannot refer to an unflawed statement of libertarianism…Compatibilist resolutions to the problem of freedom must wear an appearance of superficiality, however serious or deep the reflections from which they originate, until what they offer by way of freedom can be compared with something else, whether actual or possible or only seemingly imaginable, which is known to be the best that any indeterminist or libertarian could describe.

A sympathetic and serviceable statement of libertarianism cannot be contrived overnight, nor can it be put into two or three sentences, which is all that some utilitarian and compatibilist writers have been willing to spare for the position. If they were more anxious to destroy or supersede libertarianism than to understand and improve it, this was natural enough; but time or human obstinacy have shown that the issue is too complex for such summary treatment. What follows is offered as a small step in the direction of a more reasonable exposition… I still hope to have shown that the libertarian perceived something which was missed by all extant compatibilist resolutions of the problem of freedom; and that the point the libertarian was making must bear upon any future reconstruction of our notions and practices." [72]

Wiggins proposed a specific form of (quantum mechanical) indeterminism as a variation on an idea of ARTHUR STANLEY EDDINGTON and BERTRAND RUSSELL. Here is Russell's suggestion

"for those who are anxious to assert the power of mind over matter it is possible to find a loophole. It may be maintained that one characteristic of living matter is a condition of unstable equilibrium,...so delicate that the difference between two possible occurrences in one atom suffices to produce macroscopic differences in the movements of muscles. And since, according to quantum physics, there are no physical laws to determine which of several possible transitions a given atom will undergo, we may imagine that, in a brain, the choice between possible transitions is determined by a psychological cause called "volition." All this is possible, but no more than possible; there is not the faintest positive reason for supposing that anything of the sort actually takes place." [73]

Dennett called this "Russell's Hunch" in his 1978 book *Brainstorms*. Note that Wiggins' variation does not get away from the error of making chance a direct cause of action, since he simply amplifies microscopic indeterminacy to macroscopic indeterminacy, as Eddington and Russell had done.

Dennett cleverly avoided that error in his two-stage decision model (which was based on Wiggin's work, Paul Valery's comments, and perhaps ARTHUR HOLLY COMPTON's ideas as interpreted by KARL POPPER). Dennett limits the indeterminism to the early stages of deliberation (where in a two-stage model they can generate *alternative possibilities*). But Dennett refused to endorse his own excellent model, because as a determinist he denied any role for quantum uncertainty. And with his computational model of mind he thought pseudo-random number generation was all a mind needed.

72　Wiggins (1973) *Towards a reasonable libertar*ianism, p.33
73　Russell (1948) 'The Physiology of Sensation and Volition,' Part One, Chapter V, *Human Knowledge: Its Scope and Limits*, 1948, p.52

Wiggins had amplified the quantum indeterminacy directly. "For indeterminism maybe all we really need to imagine or conceive is a world in which (a) there is some macroscopic indeterminacy founded in microscopic indeterminacy, and (b) an appreciable number of the free actions or policies or deliberations of individual agents, although they are not even in principle hypothetico-deductively derivable from antecedent conditions, can be such as to persuade us to fit them into meaningful sequences. We need not trace free actions back to volitions construed as little pushes aimed from outside the physical world. What we must find instead are patterns which are coherent and intelligible in the low level terms of practical deliberation, even though they are not amenable to the kind of generalisation or necessity which is the stuff of rigorous theory. On this conception the agent is conceived as an essentially and straightforwardly enmattered or embodied thing. His possible peculiarity as a natural thing among things in nature is that his biography unfolds not only non-deterministically but also intelligibly; non-deterministically in that personality and character are never something complete, and need not be the deterministic origin of action; intelligibly in that each new action or episode constitutes a comprehensible phase in the unfolding of the character, a further specification of what the man has by now become." [74]

This indeterminism at each new step of character formation is essentially the basis for ROBERT KANE's theory of "Self-Forming Actions."

"I was not a fully formed person before I chose (and still am not, for that matter). Like the author of the novel, I am in the process of writing an unfinished story and forming an unfinished character who, in my case, is myself." [75]

Timothy Williamson

Timothy Williamson is a principal architect of *necessitism*, the claim that everything that exists necessarily exists. Ontology is necessary. Things could not have been otherwise. The universe could not have evolved differently.

---

74 Wiggins (1973). *Towards a reasonable libertarianism*, p.52
75 Kane (2009) 'Libertarianism.' in Fischer et al. *Four Views on Free Will*, p.42.

Necessitism is opposed to the idea of contingency, which denies that necessarily everything that is something is necessarily something. Ontology is contingent. Things could have been otherwise. There is ontological chance in the universe.

Necessitism grows out of the introduction of modal logic into quantification theory by Ruth Barcan Marcus in 1947, in which she proved the necessity of identity.

Before Marcus, most philosophers limited the necessity of identity to self-identity. Since her work, David Wiggins in 1965 and Saul Kripke in 1971 suggested there is no *contingent* identity.

Williamson reads Barcan Marcus as proving that everything is necessarily what it is, everything that exists necessarily exists. Williamson writes her argument as

> "The logical arguments for the necessity and permanence of identity are straightforward, and widely accepted in at least some form. Suppose that x is identical with y. Therefore, by the indiscernibility of identicals, x is whatever y is. But y is necessarily identical with y. Therefore x is necessarily identical with y. By analogous reasoning, x is always identical with y. More strongly: necessarily always, if x is identical with y then necessarily always x is identical with y. Of course, we understand 'x' and 'y' here as variables whose values are simply things, not as standing for definite descriptions such as 'the winning number' that denote different things with respect to different circumstances." [76]

There is a serious flaw in the reasoning that "x is whatever y is. But y is necessarily identical with y. Therefore x is necessarily identical with y." Wiggins and Kripke also made this error. The proper reasoning is "x has the same properties as y. But y is necessarily self-identical with y. Therefore x is necessarily self-identical, i.e., with x."

Numerically distinct objects cannot have identical extrinsic external information, the same relations to other objects in their

---

76   Williamson (2013) *Modal Logic as Metaphysics*, pp.25-26

neighborhood, the same positions in space and time, unless they are one and the same object.

Barcan Marcus' work is correct as it applies to a universe of discourse described by first-order logic. As Rudolf Carnap proposed, the first-order object language can be analyzed for truth values of propositional functions in a second-order meta-language.

But these are literally just "ways of talking." And information philosophy is an attempt to go "beyond logic and language."

Propositions that are perfectly *substitutable* in quantified modal logic contexts are necessarily identical. But there are no numerically distinct physical objects that are perfectly identical. Information philosophy shows that numerically distinct objects can have a *relative identity* if their intrinsic internal information is identical.

Information philosophy has established the existence of metaphysical possibility in two ways. The first is quantum mechanical indeterminacy. The second is the increasing information in the cosmological and biological universe. There can be no new information without possibilities, which depend on ontological chance.

Since information philosophy has shown that the increase in information in our universe is a product of chance events, without possibilities there can be no new information created. In our metaphysics, ontology is irreducibly contingent. *Nothing is necessary.*

Since information philosophy has shown that the increase in information in our universe is a product of chance events – without possibilities there can be no new information created – in our metaphysics, the ontology of is irreducibly contingent.

In a deterministic universe (one without contingency or possibility), the total information is a constant, there is but one possible future, the evolution of the universe is entirely present at all times.

This might fit well with Williamson's parallel interest in permanentism, which is a form of pre-determinism or pre-destination that fits with some theological views.

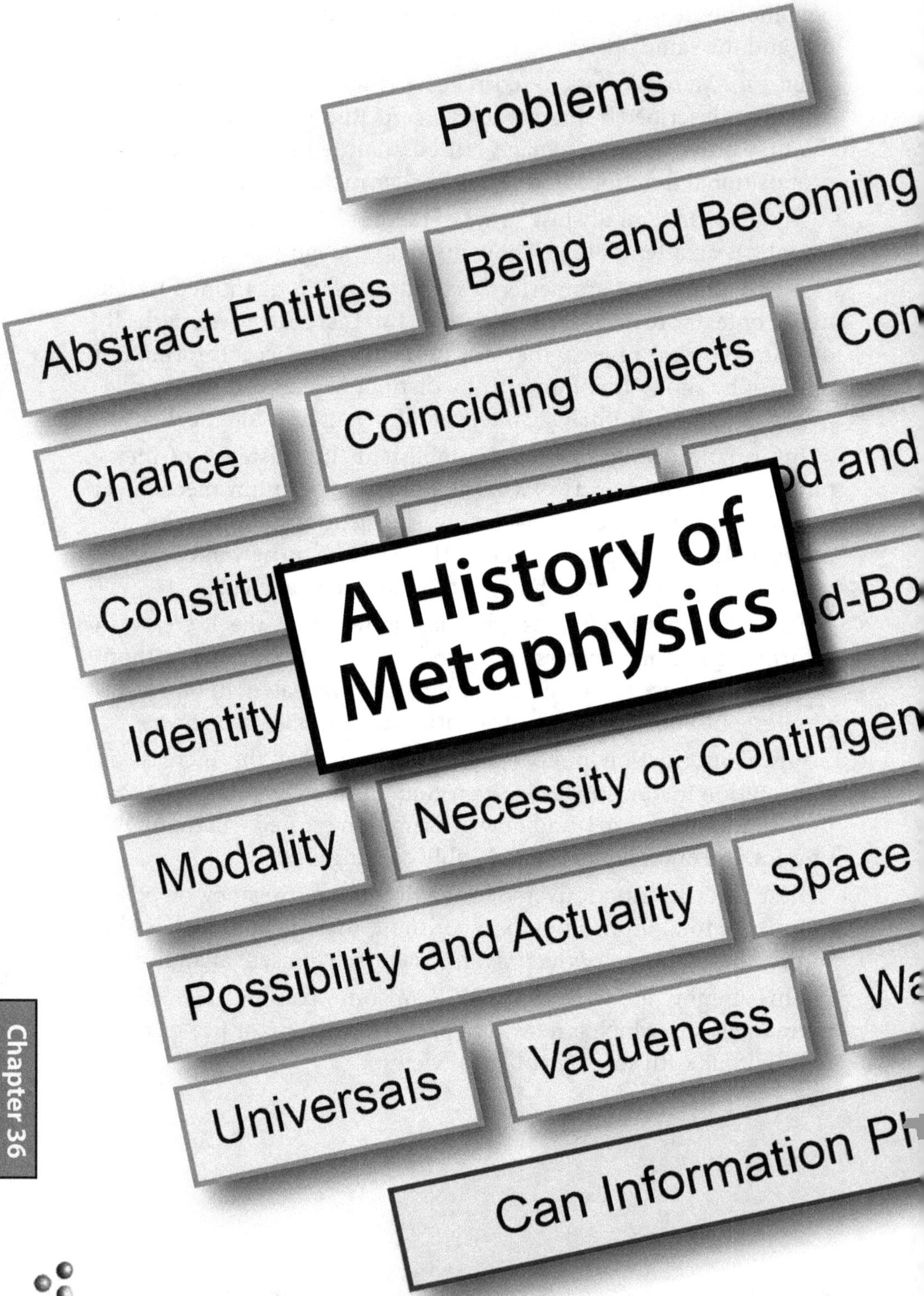

Chapter 36

A History of Metaphysics

Problems · Being and Becoming · Abstract Entities · Coinciding Objects · Chance · Constitution · Identity · Modality · Necessity or Contingency · Possibility and Actuality · Space · Vagueness · Universals · Can Information Ph...

A History of Metaphysics

The Presocratics

Although metaphysics properly begins with ARISTOTLE's search for the underlying principles of reality, he looked to the claims of the pre-Socratics as possible answers to deep questions such as "what is there?" and what are the causes behind everything.

Most of their pre-Socratic claims were speculations about the physical nature of the cosmos and its origins. In some ways, the pre-Socratics might be viewed as the earliest natural scientists, with their strong interest in physics, chemistry, astronomy, geology, meteorology, and even psychology. By contrast, SOCRATES would change the subject to ethical issues. It took Aristotle to return to cosmological, theological, and metaphysical issues first raised by the pre-Socratic philosophers and great authors like Homer and Hesiod.

The two great antagonist views were from PARMENIDES and HERACLITUS. For Parmenides, "All is One," there is no such thing as nothing (the void of the atomists), and change is an illusion (all of Zeno's paradoxes of motion supported his master's claims).

For Heraclitus, by contrast, "All is Flux." There is nothing but change. "You can't step in the same river twice." The one great positive insight of Heraclitus was that behind all changes there are laws – the "Logos." He clearly anticipates the modern notion of the laws of nature that control all change.

Aristotle gives great credit to several pre-Socratic philosophers, starting with Thales of Miletus, for attempting "natural" explanations for phenomena where earlier thinkers had given only poetic, mythological, or theological stories. Although the explanations were very simple, they were as basic as could be. Thales said "All is Water." This means everything material now is somehow made from water. This is the sort of basic principle and discovery of basic elements of nature that Aristotle was after.

This chapter on the web - metaphysicist.com/history

For Anaximander of Miletus, the first principle is a sort of indefinite and unbounded moving element. For Anaximenes, another Milesian, the primal element from which all is made is air. For his primal element, Heraclitus chose Fire, because unlike Thales's Water and Anaximenes' Air (and of course Earth), Fire is always rapidly changing.

PYTHAGORAS gave PLATO the idea that mathematics could supply the most fundamental explanations of reality, namely the Forms, the organization and arrangement of things in the universe. Most other pre-Socratics were focused on material explanations, especially the atomists, DEMOCRITUS and LEUCIPPUS, who were physical determinists, and EPICURUS, who agreed about the atoms and void, but made the atoms swerve to add an element of *indeterminism* to events.

Socrates and Plato

Considered as a metaphysicist, Plato's greatest contribution was to promote the Forms or "Ideas." Plato coined the Greek word for idea (ιδέα) from the past tense of the verb "to see." For Plato, ideas are something we have seen when souls made their great circuit of the heavens before coming to Earth.

Plato was inspired by Pythagoras. Other than Pythagoras, whose fundamental understanding of reality was based on mathematics, the other pre-Socratics were all materialists.

Socrates had no interest in the materialists and their physical theories. He wanted to understand the human being and ethical values. He famously insisted that "virtue is knowledge." Anyone doing an evil thing must be doing it out of ignorance of the Good.

Ironically, Socrates spent his life showing that very few, if any, people understand what it is to know anything.

Aristotle

Metaphysics has signified many things in the history of philosophy, but it has not strayed far from a literal reading of "beyond the physical." The term was invented by the 1st-century BCE head of Aristotle's Peripatetic school, Andronicus of Rhodes. Andronicus edited and arranged Aristotle's works, giving the name Metaphysics (τα μετα τα φυσικα βιβλια), literally "the books beyond the physics," perhaps the books to be read after reading Aristotle's books on nature, which he called the Physics. The Greek for nature is *physis*, so metaphysical is also "beyond the natural." Proponents of modern naturalism deny the existence of anything metaphysical, which some regard as "supernatural.".

Aristotle never used the term metaphysics. For Plato, Aristotle's master, the realm of abstract ideas was more "real" than that of physical. i.e., material or concrete, objects, because ideas can be more permanent (the Being of Parmenides), whereas material objects are constantly changing (the Becoming of Heraclitus). Where Plato made his realm of ideas the "real world," Aristotle made the material world the source of ideas as mere abstractions from common properties found in many concrete objects. Neoplatonists like PORPHYRY worried about the existential status of the Platonic ideas. Does Being exist? What does it mean to say "Being Is"?

In recent centuries then, metaphysical has become "beyond the material." Metaphysics has become the study of *immaterial* things, like the mind, which is said to "supervene" on the material brain. Metaphysics is a kind of idealism, in stark contrast to "eliminative" materialism. And metaphysics has failed in proportion to the phenomenal success of naturalism, the idea that the laws of nature alone can completely explain the contents of the universe.

The books of Aristotle that Andronicus considered "beyond nature" included Aristotle's "First Philosophy" — ontology (the science of being), cosmology (the fundamental processes and original causes of physical things), and theology (is a god required as "first cause?").

Aristotle's Physics describes the four "causes" or "explanations" (*aitia*) of change and movement of objects already existing in the universe (the ideal formal and final causes, vs. the efficient and material causes). Aristotle's metaphysics can then be seen as explanations for existence itself. What exists? What is it to be? What processes can bring things into (or out of) existence? Is there a cause or explanation for the universe as a whole?

In critical philosophical discourse, metaphysics has perhaps been tarnished by its Latinate translation as "supernatural," with its strong theological implications. But from the beginning, Aristotle's books on "First Philosophy" considered God among the possible causes of the fundamental things in the universe. Tracing the regress of causes back in time as an infinite chain, Aristotle postulated a first cause or "uncaused cause." Where every motion needs a prior mover to explain it, he postulated an "unmoved first mover." These postulates became a major element of theology down to modern times.

Modern metaphysics is described as the study of the fundamental structure of reality, and as such foundational not only for philosophy but for logic, mathematics, and all the sciences. Some see a need for a foundation for metaphysics itself, called metametaphysics, but this invites an infinite regress of "meta all the way down (or up)."

Aristotle's First Philosophy included theology, since first causes, new beginnings or genesis, might depend on the existence of God. And there remain strong connections between many modern metaphysicians and theologians.

The Stoics

The Stoics divided their philosophy into three parts, logic, ethics, and physics.

Stoic logic included rhetoric, dialectic, grammar, epistemology and a philosophy of language. They developed theories of concepts, propositions, perception, and thought. Their logic was propositional, rather than the Aristotelian logic of syllogisms and predicates. They defined five fundamental logical tools:

if p then q; p; therefore q (*modus ponens*);

if p then q; not q; therefore not-p (*modus tollens*);

either p or q; p; therefore not-q;

either p or q; not p; therefore q;

not both p and q; p; therefore not-q;

They had a strict interpretation of the principle of bivalence (Aristotle's non-contradiction) and the law of the excluded middle. Every statement is either true or false, even statements about the future, as DIODORUS CRONUS maintained. But Aristotle denied the present truth or falsity of future statements with his analysis of future contingency (e.g., the Sea Battle).

The Stoic philosophy of language had a theory of signs long before CHARLES SANDERS PEIRCE's semiotics or FERDINAND DE SAUSURRE's semiology. A signifier is an utterance of a name, a proper noun (*onoma*). The name-bearer is the object or concept that gets signified. The signification consists of the immaterial qualities that they called *lekta*, or 'sayables,' predicates that are true or false of the signified. The sayables are that which subsists (grows and decays), the "peculiar qualifications" of an individual.

Stoic physics included a wide range of topics including ontology, cosmology, theology, psychology, and metaphysics. The basic principles of the universe (Aristotle's *archai*) are two - matter and *pneuma*, a breath or *psyche*. Pneuma combined two of the four fundamental elements, fire and air, representing hot and cold, as the active principle. A passive principle combined earth and water as the basis for material objects. The Stoics regarded matter as "unqualified" and inert. Changes in the material in an object they described as generation and destruction (following Aristotle).

Pneuma is the cause (*aition*) of change in the peculiar qualities of an individual that constitute growth and decay, corresponding to the Platonic and Aristotelian forms and ideas that shape a material object. Pneuma endows the bodies with different qualities as a result. The pneuma of inanimate object is called a 'tenor' (*hexis*, "having"). What it "has" are qualities. Pneuma in plants has a (*phusis*, 'nature'). Pneuma in animals the Stoics called soul (*psychê*) and in rational animals pneuma includes the commanding faculty (*hêgemonikon*)

The Stoics saw the identity of an individual as its immaterial bundle of properties or qualities that they called the "peculiarly qualified individual" or ἴδιος ποιὸν.

Zeno of Cytium had formulated a psychological theory of how we acquire beliefs that are justified empirically and not by reasoning. To form a belief is to give one's assent to an "impression" (a phenomenal appearance: *phantasia*) about the material substrate of an object. Some perceptions are 'cognitive' or self-warranting. Assenting to them is a cognition or grasp (*katalêpsis*) of their objects. Assent should be restricted to these cognitive or kataleptic impressions. Cognitive impressions give us infallible knowledge or wisdom. Our beliefs will then be constituted entirely by self-warranting perceptual cognitions. Zeno argued that a cognitive impression "stamps" the form of the object (its peculiar qualities) on our mind or soul (pneuma), just as we now see *immaterial* information embodied in the material brain, experiences recorded in our ERR.

Following Aristotle, the Stoics called the material substance or substrate ὑποκείμενον (or "the underlying"). This material substrate is transformed when matter is lost or gained, but they said it is wrong to call such material changes "growth (αὐξήσεις) and decay (φθίσεις)." The Stoics suggested they should be called "generation (γενέσεις) and destruction (φθοράς)." These terms were already present in Aristotle, who said that the form, the essence, is not generated. He said that generation and destruction are material changes that do not persist (as does the Stoic peculiarly qualified individual).

> "It is therefore obvious that the form (or whatever we should call the shape in the sensible thing) is not generated—generation does not apply to it—nor is the essence generated; for this is that which is induced in something else either by art or by nature or by potency. But we do cause a bronze sphere to be, for we produce it from bronze and a sphere; we induce the form into this particular matter, and the result is a bronze sphere... For if we consider the matter carefully, we should not even say without qualification that a statue is generated from wood, or a house from bricks; because that from which a thing is generated should not persist, but be changed. This, then, is why we speak in this way." [1]

It is important to see that the Aristotelian view is very similar to the Stoic - that individuals are combinations of matter and form. At times Aristotle made the matter the principle of individuation, at other times he stressed the immaterial qualities or "affections," as did the Stoics, with their peculiarly qualified individual (ἴδιος ποιὸν).

---

1   Aristotle, *Metaphysics*, Book VII, § vii & viii

Is Aristotle here the source of the four Stoic genera or categories? The term "substance" (οὐσία) is used, if not in more, at least in four principal cases; for both the essence and the universal and the genus are held to be the substance of the particular (ἑκάστου), and fourthly the substrate (ὑποκείμενον). The substrate is that of which the rest are predicated, while it is not itself predicated of anything else. Hence we must first determine its nature, for the primary substrate (ὑποκείμενον) is considered to be in the truest sense substance.

Aristotle clearly sees a statue as an integral combination of its form/shape and its matter/clay, not two distinct things, as Skeptics would claim. Now in one sense we call the matter (ὕλη) the substrate; in another, the shape (μορφή); and in a third, the combination. Both matter and form and their combination are said to be substrate. of the two. By matter I mean, for instance, bronze; by shape, the arrangement of the form (τὸ σχῆμα τῆς ἰδέας); and by the combination of the two, the concrete thing: the statue (ἀνδριάς). Thus if the form is prior to the matter and more truly existent, by the same argument it will also be prior to the combination.[2]

The Academic Skeptics attacked the Stoics, saying Stoics were making single things into dual beings, two objects in the same place at the same time, but indistinguishable.

> "... since the duality which they say belongs to each body is differentiated in a way unrecognizable by sense-perception. For if a peculiarly qualified thing like Plato is a body, and Plato's substance is a body, and there is no apparent difference between these in shape, colour, size and appearance, but both have equal weight and the same outline, by what definition and mark shall we distinguish them and say that now we are apprehending Plato himself, now the substance of Plato? For if there is some difference, let it be stated and demonstrated." [3]

Many of the classic metaphysical puzzles are arguments over this dual nature of something as matter and form, especially Dion and Theon, Tibbles, the Cat, The Growing Argument, The Ship of Theseus, and The Statue and the Clay.

---

2   Aristotle, *Metaphysics*, Book VII, § iii, 1-2

3   Anonymous Academic treatise, Oxyrhynchus Papyrus 3008 in Stoic Ontology, *The Hellenistic Philosophers*, A. Long and D. Sedley, p.167

Modern metaphysicians mistakenly think that matter alone constitutes an entity.

Academic Skeptics

Fundamentally, the Skeptics attempted to deny knowledge, including epistemology and metaphysics.

Arcesilaus, the sixth head or scholarch of the Platonic Academy. Under him, the Academy returned to the Socratic method and engaged in negative dialectics that denied the possibility of knowledge (*akatalêpsia*). Arcesilaus realized that he could not say that he knows nothing without making a knowledge claim. This mitigated absolute skepticism.

The Academic Skeptics refused to accept any philosophical arguments that claimed to justify knowledge. Whatever reasons are used to justify something must themselves be justified, leading to an infinite regress. The Skeptics recommended that their followers therefore suspend (*epochê*) all judgments.

Most of Arcesilaus's best known arguments were dialectical attacks on the Stoics. His major Stoic opponent was CHRYSIPPUS, whose philosophy of "assent" was more or less the opposite of Arcesilaus' epochê. Stoic epistemology was more empirical than the logical and rational approach of the Skeptics, which allowed them to generate several dialectical puzzles and paradoxes from the Stoic premises or first principles.

The Scholastics

For medieval philosophers, metaphysics was understood as the science of the supersensible. Albertus Magnus called it science beyond the physical. THOMAS AQUINAS narrowed it to the rational cognition of God. JOHN DUNS SCOTUS disagreed, arguing that only study of the world can yield knowledge of God. Aquinas and Scotus can be seen as the founders of the great division in philosophy between continental rationalism and British empiricism.

It began as a theological dispute over the freedom of God. Does God have freedom of the will or is God constrained by Reason? If God must be rational, then one can deduce everything about the world by reasoning in an ivory tower. If God was free to create anything, knowledge requires an empirical investigation of the world.

Scholastic philosophers mostly returned metaphysics to the study of being in itself, that is, ontology, which again today is the core area of metaphysical arguments. In renaissance Germany, Christian Wolff broadened metaphysics to include psychology, along with ontology, cosmology, and natural or rational theology. In renaissance England, Francis Bacon narrowed metaphysics to the Aristotelian study of formal and final causes, separating it from natural philosophy which he saw as the study of efficient and material causes.

Descartes

RENÉ DESCARTES made a turn from what exists to knowledge of what exists. He changed the emphasis from a study of being to a study of the conditions of knowledge or epistemology.

Descartes was the origin of the mind-body problem.[4] He famously divided the world into mind (the ideal realm of thoughts) and body (the material world). For him, the physical world was a deterministic machine, but our ideas and thoughts could be free (undetermined) and could change things in the material world (through the pineal gland in the brain, he thought).

Information philosophy restores an *immaterial* mind to the impoverished and deflated metaphysics that we have had since empiricism and naturalism rejected the dualist philosophy of René Descartes and its troublesome mind-body problem.

Leibniz

GOTTFRIED LEIBNIZ had a vision of a universal ambiguity-free language based on a new symbol set, a *characterica universalis*, and a machine-like *calculus ratiocinator* that would automatically prove all necessary truths, true in "all possible worlds." GOTTLOB FREGE called Leibniz's idea "a system of notation directly appropriate to objects." In the three hundred years since Leibniz had this vision, logical philosophers and linguistic analysts have sought those truths

---

4   See chapter 15.

in the form of "truth-functional" propositions and statements formulated in words, but they have failed to find any necessarily "true" connection between words and objects.

Information philosophy uses such system of notation, not in words, but in bits of digital information. And the interconnected computers of the Internet are not only Leibniz's *calculus ratiocinator*, but humanity's storehouse of shared experiences and accumulated knowledge. Like the individual *experience recorder and reproducer* (ERR) in each human mind, the World Wide Web is our shared Knowledge Recorder and Reproducer. Computer simulations of physical and biological processes are the best representations of human knowledge about the external world of objects.

Leibniz's *Principle of Sufficient Reason* says that every event has a reason or cause in the prior state of the world. This appears to commit him to a necessary determinism, but like the ancient compatibilist Chrysippus, Leibniz argued that some empirical things are contingent.

Leibniz formulated many logical principles that play a major role in current metaphysical debates.

One is his *Principle of Contradiction* (Aristotle's *Principle of Non-Contradiction*). A proposition cannot be true and false at the same time, and that therefore A is A and cannot be not A.

That A is A follows from what Leibniz called the *Identity of Indiscernibles*, the idea that no differences are perceivable between identical things. This came to be known as Leibniz's Law.

The Metaphysics of Identity

Leibniz calls identity of any object with itself as a primary truth. "Primary truths are those which either state a term of itself or deny an opposite of its opposite. For example, 'A is A', or 'A is not not-A'; If it is true that A is B, it is false that A is not B, or that A is not-B'; again, 'Each thing is what it is', 'Each thing is like itself, or is equal to itself, 'Nothing is greater or less than itself—and others of this sort which, though they may have their own grades of priority, can all be included under the one name of 'identities'.

All other truths are reduced to primary truths by the aid of definitions—i.e. by the analysis of notions; and this constitutes a priori proof, independent of experience. I will give an example. A proposition accepted as an axiom by mathematicians and all others alike is 'The whole is greater than its part', or 'A part is less than the whole'. But this is very easily demonstrated from the definition of 'less' or 'greater', together with the primitive axiom, that of identity. The ' less' is that which is equal to a part of another ('greater') thing. (This definition is very easily understood, and agrees with the practice of the human race when men compare things with one another, and find the excess by taking away something equal to the smaller from the larger.) So we get the following reasoning: a part is equal to a part of the whole (namely to itself: for everything, by the axiom of identity, is equal to itself). But that which is equal to a part of the whole is less than the whole (by the definition of 'less'); therefore a part is less than the whole.[5]

4. There are no two individuals indiscernible from one another... Two drops of water or milk looked at under the microscope will be found to be discernible. This is an argument against atoms, which, like the void, are opposed to the principles of a true metaphysic.

5. These great principles of a Sufficient Reason and of the Identity of Indiscernibles change the state of metaphysics, which by their means becomes real and demonstrative; whereas formerly it practically consisted of nothing but empty terms.

6. To suppose two things indiscernible is to suppose the same thing under two names." [6]

Information philosophy restores the metaphysical existence of a Cartesian realm that is "beyond the natural" in the sense since at least David Hume and Immanuel Kant that the "laws of Nature" completely determine everything that exists, everything that happens, everything that exists in the phenomenal and material world.

---

5 Leibniz.. 'Primary Truths,' in *Philosophical Writings*, ed. G. H. R. Parkinson, p.87
6 Leibniz. "'Correspondence with Clarke," in *Philosophical Writings*, p.216

While information philosophy is a form of Descartes' idealism/materialism dualism, it is not a substance dualism. Information is a physical, though *immaterial*, property of matter. Information philosophy is a property dualism.

Abstract information is neither matter nor energy, although it needs matter for its embodiment and energy for its communication.

Information is *immaterial*. It is the modern spirit, the ghost in the machine. It is the mind in the body. It is the soul. And when we die, our personal information and its communication perish. The matter remains.

The Empiricists

For empiricists in England like JOHN LOCKE and DAVID HUME, metaphysics included the "primary" things beyond psychology and the "secondary" sensory experiences. They denied that any knowledge was possible apart from experimental and mathematical reasoning. Hume thought the metaphysics of the Scholastics is sophistry and illusion.

> If we take in our hand any volume; of divinity or school metaphysics, for instance; let us ask, Does it contain any abstract reasoning concerning quantity or number? No. Does it contain any experimental reasoning concerning matter of fact and existence? No. Commit it then to the flames: for it can contain nothing but sophistry and illusion.[7]

Hume criticized the Theory of Ideas of his fellow British empiricists John Locke and George Berkeley. If, as they claim, knowledge is limited to perceptions of sense data, we cannot "know" anything about external objects, even our own bodies. But Hume said that we do have a "natural belief" in the external world and causal laws.

Hume's idea of the mind having a "feeling" (not a reason) that leads to natural beliefs became Kant's "second Copernican revolution" that the mind projects "concepts of the understanding" and "forms of perception" on the external world.

---

7   Hume (1748) *Enquiry Concerning Human Understanding*, section XII

Kant

In Germany, IMMANUEL KANT's *Critiques of Reason* claimed a transcendental, non-empirical realm he called *noumenal*, for pure, or *a priori*, reason beyond or behind the phenomena. Kant's phenomenal realm is deterministic, matter governed by Newton's laws of motion. Kant's *immaterial noumena* are in the metaphysical non-empirical realm of the "things themselves" along with freedom, God, and immortality. Kant identified ontology not with the things themselves but, influenced by Descartes, what we can think - and reason - about the things themselves. In either case, Kant thought metaphysical knowledge might be impossible for finite minds.

Kant reacted to the Enlightenment, to the Age of Reason, and to Newtonian mechanics (which he probably understood better than any other philosopher), by accepting determinism as a fact in the physical world, which he called the phenomenal world. Kant's goal was to rescue the physical sciences from the devastating and unanswerable skepticism of David Hume, especially Hume's assertion that no number of "constant conjunctions" of cause and effect could logically prove causality.

Kant called Hume's assertion the "*crux metaphysicorum*." If Hume is right, he said, metaphysics is impossible. Kant's *Critiques of Reason* were to prove that Hume was wrong.

Neither Hume's Idea of "natural belief" nor Kant's "concepts of the understanding" are the apodeictic and necessary truths sought by metaphysicians. They are abstract theories about the world, whose information content is validated by experiments. Hume's idea of the mind having a "feeling" (not a reason) that leads to natural beliefs became Kant's "second Copernican revolution" that the mind projects "concepts of the understanding" and "forms of perception" on the external world.

Kant's main change in the second edition of the *Critique of Pure Reason* was an attempted refutation of this British idealism (B 274). He thought he had a proof of the existence of the external world. Kant thought it a scandal in philosophy that we must accept the existence of material things outside ourselves merely as a belief, with no proof.

> "The only thing which might be called an addition, though in the method of proof only, is the new refutation of psychological idealism, and the strict (and as I believe the only possible) proof of the objective reality of outer intuition. However innocent idealism may be considered with respect to the essential purposes of metaphysics (without being so in reality), it remains a scandal to philosophy, and to human reason in general, that we should have to accept the existence of things outside us (from which after all we derive the whole material for our knowledge, even for that of our inner sense) merely on trust, and have no satisfactory proof with which to counter any opponent who chooses to doubt it." [8]

Kant's noumenal world outside of space and time is a variation on Plato's concept of Soul, Descartes' mental world, and the Scholastic idea of a world in which all times are present to the eye of God. His idea of free will is a most esoteric form of *compatibilism*. Kant's decisions are made in our souls outside of time and only appear determined to our senses, which are governed by our built-in *a priori* forms of sensible perception, like space and time, and built-in categories or concepts of intelligible understanding.

Positivisms

The motto of the information philosopher is "beyond logic and language." Specifically, we must show that logical positivism and logical empiricism, whose attack on metaphysics began as early as Auguste Compte in the early nineteenth century, have done nothing to solve any of the deep problems about the fundamental nature of reality.

Positivism is the claim that the only valid source of knowledge is sensory experience, reinforced by logic and mathematics. Together these provide the empirical evidence for science. Some see this as the "naturalizing" of epistemology.

ERNST MACH's positivism claimed that science consists entirely of "economic summaries" of the facts (the results of experiments). He rejected theories about unobservable things like LUDWIG

---

8   Kant (1787) Preface to Second Edition, *Critique of Pure Reason*, B XL

BOLTZMANN's atoms, just a few years before ALBERT EINSTEIN used Boltzmann's own work to prove that atoms exist.

This "linguistic turn" and naturalizing of epistemology can be traced back to Kant and perhaps even to Descartes. The logical positivism of BERTRAND RUSSELL and LUDWIG WITTGENSTEIN claimed that all valid knowledge must be scientific knowledge, though science is often criticized for "reducing" all phenomena to physical or chemical events. The logical positivists may have identified ontology not with the things themselves but what we can say - using concepts and language - about the things themselves.

The idea that all knowledge can be described by true statements began with Leibniz's vision of a universal ambiguity-free language based on a new symbol set, a *characterica universalis*, and a machine-like *calculus ratiocinator* that would automatically prove all necessary truths, true in "all possible worlds."

In the three hundred years since Leibniz had this vision, logical philosophers and linguistic analysts following Gottlob Frege have sought those truths in the form of "truth-functional" propositions and statements formulated in words, but they have failed to find any necessarily "true" connection between words and objects.

Frege had an enormous influence on Russell, who shared Frege's dream of reducing mathematics, or at least arithmetic, to logic. The great *Principia Mathematica* of Russell and ALFRED NORTH WHITEHEAD was the epitome of that attempt. It failed with the discovery of Russell's Paradox and later Gödel's incompleteness proof.

Russell hoped to work with the young Ludwig Wittgenstein to develop the "logical atoms," the simplest propositions, like "red, here, now," upon which more complex statements could be built. He saw the major problems of philosophy as problems of language and logic, that complete understanding of the natural world could be obtained through a complete set of logical propositions.

Wittgenstein's *Tractatus Logico-Philosophicus* was the height of logical positivism - the idea that all knowledge, including all science, can be represented in logically true statements or propositions. The Tractatus includes the first hint of its own failure, with its dark comments about how little can be said.

"The totality of true propositions is the total natural science (or the totality of the natural sciences)." [9]

"We feel that even if all possible scientific questions be answered, the problems of life have still not been touched at all." [10]

Logical positivists and the logical empiricists of the Vienna Circle not only asserted that all knowledge is scientific knowledge derived from experience, i.e., from verifiable observations, they also added the logical analysis of language as the principal tool for solving philosophical problems. They divided statements into those that are reducible to simpler statements about experience and those with no empirical basis. These latter they called "metaphysics" and "meaningless." While language is too slippery and ambiguous to serve as a reliable tool for philosophical analysis, quantitative information, which underlies all language use, is such a tool.

Logical positivists and empiricists mistakenly claim that physical theories can be logically deduced (or derived) from the results of experiments. A second flaw in all empiricist thinking since Locke et al. is the mistaken idea that all knowledge is derived from experience, written on the blank slate of our minds, etc. In science, this is the flawed idea that all knowledge is ultimately experimental. To paraphrase Kant and CHARLES SANDERS PEIRCE, theories without experiments may be empty, but experiments without theories are blind.

By contrast, the modern hypothetical-deductive method of science maintains that theories are not the logical (or inductive) consequences of experiments. As Einstein put it, after shaking off his early enthusiasm for Mach's positivistic ideas, theories are "free inventions of the human mind." Theories begin with hypotheses, mere guesses, "fictions" whose value is shown only when they can be confirmed by the results of experiments. Again and again, theories have predicted behaviors in as yet untested physical conditions that have surprised scientists, often suggesting new experiments that have extended the confirmation of theories, which again surprise us. As pure information, scientific knowledge is far beyond the results of experiments alone.

---

9 Wittgenstein (1922) *Tractatus Logico-Philosophicus*, 4.11
10 *Ibid*, 6.52

Linguistic Analysis

The central figure in the transition from logical empiricism to linguistic analysis was Ludwig Wittgenstein.

Modern anglo-american metaphysicians think problems in metaphysics can still be treated as problems in language, potentially solved by conceptual analysis. They are today still analytical language philosophers, despite a general failure of words to describe objects in any deeply meaningful way. Language is too flexible, too ambiguous and full of metaphor, to be a diagnostic tool for metaphysics. We must go beyond logical puzzles and language games to the underlying information contained in a concept, and in the material things that embody the concept. And it is now transparently obvious that the description of objects, aside from the scientific discovery of the natural laws governing their behavior, is best done with information, with computer simulations and dynamic animations of material objects, both inanimate and living.

Although many metaphysicians claim to be exploring the fundamental structure of reality, the overwhelming fraction of their writings is about problems in analytic linguistic philosophy, that is to say problems with words. Many questions appear to be verbal quibbles. Others lack meaning or have no obvious truth value, dissolving into paradoxes.

Based on current practice, we can sharpen the definition of a metaphysician to be an analytic language philosopher who discusses metaphysical problems.

By contrast, a metaphysicist is an information philosopher who is familiar with modern physics, chemistry, and biology, as well as the interpretation of quantum physics. The fundamental structure of reality today must be built on an understanding of quantum reality.

For example, the wave function of a quantum particle is pure information. Interpretations of quantum mechanics are fundamentally metaphysical, problems for a metaphysicist.

What are we to say about a field of human inquiry whose problems have hardly changed over two millennia? Metaphysicians today still analyze logic and language in the puzzles and paradoxes that have been used for millennia to wrestle with metaphysical problems. Debates between metaphysicians have changed relatively little in recent centuries, despite great advances in human knowledge.

Most of these problems are the result of assuming that the contents of the universe are pure material. They depend on the idea that material alone constitutes complete knowledge - the identity - of any physical thing.

Analytic language philosophers are largely materialist, even eliminative materialists, many denying the existence of mind, for example. They are also mostly determinist, denying the existence of alternative possibilities in our actual universe, while investing a great deal of their energy in the study of inaccessible possible worlds (in each of which there are also no possibilities, only actuality).

The new light thrown by information philosophy on many metaphysical problems, puzzles, and paradoxes comes from establishing an *immaterial*, yet physical, realm of ideas alongside the material realm. No physical object is completely known without understanding its form in terms of quantifiable information. Information philosophy goes beyond logical puzzles and language games.

Modal Logic

Although the modes of necessity, possibility, and impossibility had been part of Aristotelian logic (indeed, even future contingency was analyzed), Gottlob Frege's logic of propositional functions included only one mode - simple affirmation and denial of statements and the universal and existential quantifiers. Bertrand Russell's *Principia Mathematica* followed Frege and ignored other modalities.

Although the Scholastics considered some questions of modality, it was the Harvard logician C.I. LEWIS who advanced beyond Aristotle and developed the first modern version of modal logic. He wrote two textbooks, *A Survey of Symbolic Logic* in 1918 and *Symbolic Logic*, written with C. H. Langford, in 1927.

Lewis was critical of the *Principia* for its non-intuitive concept of "material implication," which allows irrelevant, even false premises p to imply any true consequences. Lewis proposed that implication must include "intensional" and meaningful, even causal, connections between antecedents and consequences, a revision he called "strict implication."

Lewis's inclusion of intension (meaning) was criticized by WILLARD VAN ORMAN QUINE, who thought symbolic logic should be limited to "extensional" arguments, based on the members of classes in a set theory basis for logic. In Quine's 1943 article, "Notes on Existence and Necessity," (revised to appear ten years later as part of the chapter "Reference and Modality" in his landmark book *From a Logical Point of View*, Quine saw no need for "intensional" statements in mathematics. Truth values are all that are needed, he says

> "These latter are intensional compounds, in the sense that the truth-value of the compound is not determined merely by the truth-value of the components...any intensional mode of statement composition...must be carefully examined in relation to its susceptibility to quantification...It is known, in particular, that no intensional mode of statement composition is needed in mathematics." [11]

Quine saw the need for serious restrictions on the significant use of modal operators.[12] Just three years later, RUTH BARCAN MARCUS, publishing under her maiden name Ruth C. Barcan, added a modal axiom for possibility to the logical systems S2 and S4 of C.I. Lewis. Lewis was pleasedwith her work, although by that time, he had given up his own work on logic.

Quine, however, reacted negatively to Marcus's suggestion in 1946 that modal operators (Lewis's diamond '$\lozenge$' for possibly, and a box '$\square$' for "necessarily" suggested by Barcan's thesis adviser, F. B. Fitch) could be transposed or interchanged with universal and existential quantification operators (an inverted A '$\forall$' for "for all" and a reversed E '$\exists$' for "for some"), while preserving the truth values of the statements or propositions.

Marcus asserted the commuting of quantification and modal operators in what A.N. Prior called the "Barcan formulas."

$\forall x \, \square Fx \supset \square \, \forall x \, Fx.$ $\forall x \, \lozenge Fx \supset \lozenge \, \forall x \, Fx.$
$\exists x \, \square Fx \supset \square \exists x \, Fx.$ $\exists x \, \lozenge Fx \supset \lozenge \exists x \, Fx.$

---

11   Quine (1943) 'Notes on Existence and Necessity,' in *Journal of Philosophy*, 40 p.123-125
12   Ibid., p,127

In his 1943 article, Quine had generated a number of apparently paradoxical cases where truth value is not preserved when "quantifying into a modal context." But these can all be understood as a failure of *substitutivity* for putatively identical entities.

Information philosophy has shown that two distinct expressions that are claimed to be identical are never identical in all respects. So a substitution of one expression for the other may not be identical in the relevant respect. Such a substitution can change the meaning, the intension of the expression. Quine called this "referential opacity." This is a problem that can be solved with unambiguous references.

Frege had insisted that we must look past the reference or designator (his "*Bedeutung*) to the sense ("*Sinn*") of the reference, which is just what Lewis was attempting to do with his attempted addition of intension and "strict" implication..

Perhaps Quine's most famous paradox of referential opacity is this argument about the number of planets:

"(1) 9 is necessarily greater than 7

for example, is equivalent to

'9 > 7' is analytic

and is therefore true (if we recognize the reducibility of mathematics to logic)..." [13]

Given, say that

(2) The number of planets is 9,

we can substitute 'the number of planets' from the non-modal statement (2) for '9' in the modal statement (1) which gives us the false modal statement

(3) The number of planets is necessarily greater than 7.

But this is false, says Quine, since the statement

(2) The number of planets is 9

is true only because of circumstances outside of logic.

Marcus analyzed this problem in 1961, which she called the "familiar example,"

---

[13] Quine (1943) 'Notes on Existence and Necessity,' p.121

"(27) 9 eq the number of planets

is said to be a true identity for which substitution fails in

(28) □ (9 > 7)

for it leads to the falsehood

(29) □ (the number of planets > 7).

Since the argument holds (27) to be contingent (~□(9 eq the number of planets)), 'eq' of (27) is the appropriate analogue of material equivalence and consequently the step from (28) to (29) is not valid for the reason that the substitution would have to be made in the scope of the square." [14]

The failure of substitutivity can be understood by unpacking the use of "the number of planets" as a purely designative reference, as Quine calls it.

In (27), "the number of planets" is the empirical answer to the question "how many planets are there in the solar system?" It is not what Ruth Barcan Marcus would call a "tag" of the number 9. The intension of this expression, its reference, is the "extra-linguistic" fact about the current quantity of planets.

The expression '9' is an unambiguous mathematical (logical) reference to the number 9. It refers to the number 9, which is its meaning (intension).

We can conclude that (27) is not a true identity, unless before "the number of planets" is quantified, it is qualified as "the number of planets *qua* its numerosity, as a pure number." Otherwise, the reference is "opaque," as Quine describes it. But this is a problem of his own making.

As Marcus says, when we recognize (27) as contingent, ~□(9 eq the number of planets), it is not necessary that 9 is equal to the number of planets, its reference to the number 9 becomes opaque.

The substitution of a possible or contingent empirical fact that is not "true in all possible worlds" for a logical-mathematical concept that is necessarily true is what causes the substitution failure.

When all three statements are "in the scope of the square" (□), when all have the same modality, we can "quantify into modal con-

---

14   Marcu (1961) Modalities and Intensional Languages," p. 313

texts," as Quine puts it. Both expressions, '9' and 'the number of planets, *qua* its numerosity,' will be references to the same thing,

They will be identical in one respect, *qua* number. They will be "referentially transparent."

The Necessity of Identity

In her third article back in 1947, "The Identity of Individuals," Barcan had first proved the necessity of identity. This result became a foundational principle in the modern incarnation of Leibniz's "possible worlds" by SAUL KRIPKE and DAVID LEWIS.

Her proof combined a simple substitution of equals for equals and Leibniz's Law.

Quine described this in his 1953 "Reference and Modality" (p.153) as in the form

(x)(y) (x = y) ⊃ □ (x = y),

reading "for all x and for all y, if "x = y," then necessarily "x = y."

Quine found this relationship in the 1952 textbook, *Symbolic Logic*, by F. B. Fitch, who was Ruth Barcan's thesis adviser. Although Fitch mentions her work in his foreword, he does not attribute this specific result to her where he presents it. His proof is based on the assumption of *substitutability*, which he calls "identity elimination."

23.4 (1) a = b, (2) □[a = a], then (3) □[a = b], by identity elimination.[15]

Then in 1961, Marcus published a very brief proof of her claim, using Leibniz's Law relating identicals to indiscernibles.

> "In a formalized language, those symbols which name things will be those for which it is meaningful to assert that I holds between them, where 'I ' names the identity relation... If 'x' and 'y' are individual names then
>
> (1) x I y
>
> Where identity is defined rather than taken as primitive, it is customary to define it in terms of indiscernibility, one form of which is
>
> (2) x Ind y =df (φ)(φx eq φy)" [16]

---

15   Fitch (1952) *Symbolic Logic*, p.164
16   Marcus (1961) Modalities and Intensional Languages,' p. 305

Statement (2) says that the indiscernibility of x from y, by definition means that for every property φ, both x and y have that same property, φx eq φy.

A few years after Marcus' 1961 presentation, David Wiggins developed a five-step proof of the necessity of identity, using Leibniz' Law, as had Marcus. He did not mention her.

David Wiggins on Identity

DAVID WIGGINS and PETER GEACH debated back and forth about the idea of "relative identity" for many years after Geach suggested it in 1962.

Ruth Barcan Marcus published her original proof of the necessity of identity in 1947 and repeated her argument at a 1961 Boston University colloquium.

Whether Wiggins knew of Marcus's 1961 presentation is not clear. He should have known of her 1947 paper, and his work is similar to her 1961 derivation (which uses Leibniz's Law). Wiggins gives no credit to Marcus, a pattern in the literature for the next few decades and still seen today ignoring the work of female philosophers.

SAUL KRIPKE clearly modeled much of his four-step derivation after Wiggins, especially his criticism of the derivation as "paradoxical". Kripke gives no credit to either Marcus or Wiggins for the steps in the argument, but his quote from Wiggins, that such a claim makes contingent identity statements impossible, when they clearly are possible, at least tells us he has read Wiggins. And we know Kripke heard Marcus's presentation at the 1961 B. U. colloquium.

Here is Wiggins in 1965,

> "I WANT to try to show (i) that there are insuperable difficulties any term + relation + term or subject + predicate analysis of statements of identity, (ii) that, however important and helpful the sense-reference distinction is,[1] this distinction does not make it possible to retain the relational or predicative analysis of identity statements, and (iii) that a realistic and radically new account is needed both of ' = ' and of the manner in which noun-phrases occur in identity-statements.
>
> Till we have such an account many questions about identity

and individuation will be partly unclear, and modal logics will continue without the single compelling interpretation one might wish.

The connexion of what I am going to say with modal calculi can be indicated in the following way. It would seem to be a necessary truth that if a = b then whatever is truly ascribable to a is truly ascribable to b and vice versa (Leibniz's Law). This amounts to the principle

(1) $(x)(y)((x = y) \supset (\varphi)(\varphi x \supset \varphi y))$

Suppose that identity-statements are ascriptions or predications.¹ Then the predicate variable in (1) will apparently range over properties like that expressed by '(= a)'² and we shall get as consequence of (1)

(2) $(x)(y)((x = y) \supset (x = x . \supset . y = x))$

There is nothing puzzling about this. But if (as many modal logicians believe), there exist de re modalities of the form

$\Box (\varphi a)$ (i.e., necessarily (φa)),

then something less innocent follows. If '(= a)' expresses property, then '$\Box$ (a=a)', if this too is about the object a, also ascribes something to a, namely the property $\Box$ (= a). For on a naive and pre-theoretical view of properties, you will reach an expression for a property whenever you subtract a noun-expression with material occurrence (something like ' a ' in this case) from a simple declarative sentence. The property

$\Box$ (= a) then falls within the range of the predicate variable in Leibniz's Law (understood in this intuitive way) and we get

(3) $(x)(y)(x = y \supset (\Box (x = x) . \supset . \Box (y = x)))$

Hence, reversing the antecedents,

(4) $(x)(y)(\Box (x = x) . \supset . (x = y) \supset \Box (x = y))$

But $(x)(\Box (x=x))$ ' is a necessary truth, so we can drop this antecedent and reach

(5) $(x)(y)((x = y) . \supset . \Box (x = y))$

Now there undoubtedly exist contingent identity-statements. Let 'a = b' be one of them. From its simple truth and (5) we can derive '$\Box (a = b)$'. But how then can there be any contingent identity-statements?...

1 G. Frege, 'On Sense and Reference', Translations from the Philosophic Writings of Gottlob Frege, ed. P. T . Geach and M. Black (Oxford, 1952), pp. 56-4]

2 Quotation marks are used under the convention that they serve to form a designation of whatever expression would result in a particular case from rewriting the expression within the quotation-marks with genuine constants in the place of free variables and dummy-expressions." [17]

Saul Kripke on Identity

Kripke does not cite Wiggins directly as the source of the argument, but just after his exposition above, Kripke quotes David Wiggins as saying in his 1965 "Identity-Statements"

> Now there undoubtedly exist contingent identity-statements. Let a = b be one of them. From its simple truth and (5) [= (4) above] we can derive '□(a = b)'. But how then can there be any contingent identity statements?[18]

Kripke goes on to describe the argument about b sharing the property " = a" of being identical to a, which we read as merely self-identity, and so may Kripke.

> "If x and y are the same things and we can talk about modal properties of an object at all, that is, in the usual parlance, we can speak of modality *de re* and an object necessarily having certain properties as such, then formula (1), I think, has to hold. Where x is any property at all, including a property involving modal operators, and if x and y are the same object and x had a certain property F, then y has to have the same property F. And this is so even if the property F is itself of the form of necessarily having some other property G, in particular that of necessarily being identical to a certain object. [viz., = x]
>
> Well, I will not discuss the formula (4) itself because by itself it does not assert, of any particular true statement of identity, that it is necessary. It does not say anything about statements at all. It says for every object x and object y, if x and y are the same object, then it is necessary that x and y are the same object. And this, I think, if we think about it (anyway, if someone does not think so, I will not argue for it here), really amounts to something very little different from the statement (2). Since

---

17   Wiggins (1965) Identity Statements,' in *Analytical Philosophy* pp.40-41
18   Kripke (1971) 'Identity and Necessity,' p. 136

x, by definition of identity, is the only object identical with x, "(y)(y = x ⊃ Fy)" seems to me to be little more than a garrulous way of saying 'Fx' and thus (x) (y)(y = x ⊃ Fx) says the same as (x)Fx no matter what 'F' is — in particular, even if 'F' stands for the property of necessary identity with x. So if x has this property (of necessary identity with x), trivially everything identical with x has it, as (4) asserts. But, from statement (4) one may apparently be able to deduce various particular statements of identity must be necessary and this is then supposed to be a very paradoxical consequence." [19]

The indiscernibility of identicals claims that if x = y, then x and y must share all their properties, otherwise there would be a discernible difference. Now Kripke argues that one of the properties of x is that x = x, so if y shares the property of '= x,' we can say that y = x. Then, necessarily, x = y.

However, two distinct things, x and y, cannot be identical, because there is some difference in extrinsic external information between them. Instead of claiming that y has x's property of being identical to x ("= x") , we can say only that y has x's property of being self-identical, thus y = y. Then x and y remain distinct in at least this intrinsic property as well as in extrinsic properties like their distinct positions in space.

David Lewis on Identity

David Lewis, the modern metaphysician who built on Leibniz' possible worlds to give us his theory of "modal realism," is just as clear as Leibniz on the problem of identity.

"[W]e should not suppose that we have here any problem about identity. We never have. Identity is utterly simple and unproblematic. Everything is identical to itself; nothing is ever identical to anything else except itself. There is never any problem about what makes something identical to itself, nothing can ever fail to be. And there is never any problem about what makes two things identical; two things never can be identical." [20]

Except, says an information philosopher, "in some respects."

---

19   Kripke (1971) 'Identity and Necessity,' p. 137-138
20   Lewis (1988) 'Counterparts or Double Lives,' *On the Plurality of Worlds*, p.192

Modal Logic and Possible Worlds

In the "semantics of possible worlds," necessity and possibility in modal logic are variations of the universal and existential quantifiers of non-modal logic. Necessary truth is defined as "truth in all possible worlds." Possible truth is defined as "truth in some possible worlds." These abstract notions about "worlds" – sets of propositions in universes of discourse – have nothing to do with physical possibility, which depends on the existence of real contingency.

Propositions in modal logic are required to be true or false. Contingent statements that are neither true or false are not allowed. So much for real possibilities, which cannot be based on truths in some possible worlds.

Historically, the opposition to metaphysical possibility has come from those who claim that the only possible things that can happen are the actual things that do happen. To say that things could have been otherwise is a mistake, say eliminative materialists and determinists. Those other possibilities simply never existed in the past. The only possible past is the past we have actually had.

Similarly, there is only one possible future. Whatever will happen, will happen. The idea that many different things can happen, the reality of modality and words like "may" or "might" are used in everyday conversation, but they have no place in metaphysical reality. The only "actual" events or things are what exists. For "presentists," even the past does not exist. Everything we remember about past events is just a set of "Ideas." And philosophers have always been troubled about the ontological status of Plato's abstract "Forms," entities like the numbers, geometric figures, mythical beasts, and other fictions.

Traditionally, those who deny possibilities in this way have been called "Actualists."

In the last half-century, one might think that metaphysical possibilities have been restored with the development of modal logic. So-called modal operators like "necessarily" and "possibly" have been added to the structurally similar quantification operators "for all" and "for some." The metaphysical literature is full of talk about "possible worlds."

The most popular theory of "possible worlds" is David Lewis's "modal realism," an infinite number of worlds, each of which is just as actual (eliminative materialist and determinist) for its inhabitants as our world.

It comes as a shock to learn that every "possible world" is just as actual, for its inhabitants, as our world is for us. There are no alternative possibilities, no contingency, that things might have been otherwise, in any of these possible worlds. Every world is as physically deterministic as our own.

Modal logicians now speak of a "rule of necessitation" at work in possible world semantics. The necessarily operator ' $\Box$ ' and the possibly operator ' $\Diamond$ ' are said to be "duals" - either one can be defined in terms of the other ($\Box = \sim\Diamond\sim$, and $\Diamond = \sim\Box\sim$), so either can be primitive. But most axiomatic systems of modal logic appear to privilege necessity and de-emphasize possibility. They rarely mention contingency, except to say that the necessity of identity appears to rule out contingent identity statements.

The rule of necessitation is that "if p, then necessarily p," or $p \supset \Box p$. It gives rise to the idea that if anything exists, it exists necessarily. This is called "necessitism." The idea that if two things are identical, they are necessarily identical, was "proved" by Ruth Barcan Marcus in 1947, by her thesis adviser F.B.Fitch in 1952, and by Willard Van Orman Quine in 1953. David Wiggins in 1965 and Saul Kripke in 1971 repeated the arguments, with little or no reference to the earlier work.

This emphasis on necessitation in possible-world semantics leads to a flawed definition of possibility that has no connection with the ordinary and technical meanings of possibility.

Modal logicians know little if anything about real possibilities and nothing at all about possible physical worlds. Their possible worlds are abstract universes of discourses, sets of propositions that are true or false. Contingent statements, that may be true or false, like statements about the future, are simply not allowed.

They define necessary propositions as those that are "true in all possible worlds." Possible propositions are those that are only "true in some possible worlds." This is the result of forcing the modal operators $\Box$ and $\Diamond$ to correspond to the universal and existential quantification operators for all $\forall$ and for some $\exists$. But the essential nature of possibility is the conjunction of contingency and necessity. Contingency is not impossible and not necessary ($\sim\sim\Diamond \land \sim\Box$).

We propose the existence of a metaphysical possibilism alongside the notion necessitism.

"Actual possibilities" exist in minds and in quantum-mechanical "possibility functions" It is what call "actual possibilism," the existence in our actual world of possibilities that may never become actualized, but that have a presence as abstract entities that have been embodied as ideas in minds. In addition, we include the many possibilities that occur at the microscopic level when the quantum-mechanical probability-amplitude wave function collapses, making one of its many possibilities actual.

Actual possibles can act as causes when an agent chooses one as a course of action.

Why Modal Logic Is Not Metaphysics

Modal logicians from Ruth Barcan Marcus to Saul Kripke, David Lewis, and the necessicist Timothy Williamson are right to claim metaphysical necessity as the case in the purely abstract informational world of logic and mathematics. But when information is embodied in concrete matter, which is subject to the laws of quantum physics and ontological chance, the fundamental nature of material reality is contingent and possibilist.

There are two reasons for the failure of modal logic to represent metaphysical reality. The first is that information is vastly superior to language as a representation of reality. The second is that truths and necessity cannot be the basis for metaphysical possibility.

Possible world semantics is a way of talking about universes of discourse - sets of true propositions - that considers them "worlds." It may be the last gasp of the attempt by logical positivism and analytic language philosophy to represent all knowledge of objects in terms of words.

Ludwig Wittgenstein's core idea from the Tractatus had the same goal as Gottfried Leibniz's ambiguity-free universal language,

> The totality of true propositions is the total natural science (or the totality of the natural sciences).[21]

Information philosophy has shown that the meaning of words depends on the experiences recalled in minds by the Experience Recorder and Reproducer. Since every human being has a different set of experiences, there will always be variations in meaning about words between different persons, as Gottlob Frege pointed out.

The goal of intersubjective agreement in an open community of inquirers hopes to eliminate those differences, but representation of knowledge in words will always remain a barrier and source of philosophical confusion. The physical sciences use analytic differential equations to describe the deterministic and continuous time evolution of simple material objects, which is a great advance over ambiguous words. But these equations fail at the quantum level and where discrete digital messages are being exchanged between biological interactors. Moreover, while mathematical methods are precise, their significance is not easily grasped.

The very best representation of knowledge is with a dynamic and interactive model of an information structure, what Wittgenstein imagined as a "picture of reality." Today that is a three-dimensional model implemented in a digital computer with a high-resolution display, even a virtual reality display. While computer models are only "simulations" of reality, they can incorporate the best "laws" of physics, chemistry, and biology. And since computer models are pure information, abstract ideas, they seem "beyond physical" and reaching the metaphysical.

Sadly, modal logicians have never proposed more than a handful of specific propositions for their possible worlds, and many of these generated controversies, even paradoxes, about substitutivity of presumed identicals in modal contexts. Word and object have degenerated to words and objections. By comparison, molecular models of the biological machines that have evolved to keep us alive and let us think can be "shown," not said, as Wittgenstein imagined.

---

21   Wittgenstein (1922) *Tractatus Logico-Philosophicus*, 4.11

His later work can be summed up as the failure of language to be a picture of reality. Information philosophy gives us that picture, not just a two-dimensional snapshot, but a lifelike animation and visualization of the fundamental nature of metaphysical reality.

Our information model incorporates the irreducible ontological chance and future contingency of quantum physics. The claimed "necessity of identity," and the "necessary a posteriori" of natural and artificial digital "kinds" with identical intrinsic information content are just more "ways of talking." There is no necessity in the physical world.

Truths and necessity are ideal concepts "true in all possible worlds," because they are independent of the physical world. They have great appeal as eternal ideas and "outside space and time."

Possible worlds semantics defines necessity as "propositions true in all possible worlds" and possibility as "propositions true in some possible worlds." There is no contingency here, as the only allowed propositions are either true or false. Modal logicians have little knowledge of our actual physical world and zero factual knowledge, by definition, of other possible worlds. The possible worlds of "modal realism" are all actual worlds, deterministic and eliminatively materialist. There are no possibilities in possible worlds, even in the "many worlds" of physics.

A necessicist metaphysics is only a half-truth. Without metaphysical possibility, we cannot account for the information in the universe today, nor can we explain the cosmic, biological, and human creation of new information in our free and open future.

Necessitism and possibilism are perhaps another congruence with the great duals of idealism and materialism.

The Return of Metaphysics and Its Paradoxes

In the last few decades, metaphysicians have celebrated the failures of logical positivists and logical empiricists, especially their loud claims that metaphysics is nonsense or meaningless.

The sad failure of analytic language philosophy to solve any meaningful problems in philosophy has also encouraged a number of philosophers to return to metaphysical questions.

But can they make any progress on the fundamental nature of reality if their tools are still only logic and language analysis? The information philosopher thinks not. We must go beyond logical puzzles and language games to underlying information structures.

Now academic philosophers have never failed to teach all the classic problems, paradoxes, and puzzles, mostly presenting them as insoluble, which gives them a form of job security, but this must be discouraging for would-be future philosophers.

The well-known lack of progress in philosophy compared to the advances in knowledge made in the sciences is more than an embarrassment, it is in some cases a scandal, as the information philosopher has tried to show.

Even in the sciences, the deference shown to philosophers by the special sciences, when it comes to the fundamental nature of reality, has held back those sciences.

Notably, the deep belief in natural laws that are deterministic has held back the essential role of chance in physics and biology. The claims of eliminative materialism have held back progress on the mind-body problem and the free will problem in psychology.

Indirectly caused by philosophical views, these are scandals in the special sciences themselves. The philosophical notion that many genuine problems about reality must be taught as mysteries, not only paradoxes and puzzles, is a disservice to generations of students, who come away not only confused, but ill-informed.

Consider these negative comments from a recent important study of *metametaphysics*, the foundations of metaphysics itself.

> "When one is first introduced to a dispute that falls within the purview of metaphysics — or perhaps even after years of thinking hard about it — one can experience two sorts of deflationary intuitions. First one may sense that nothing is really at issue between the disputants. The phenomenology here resembles that of countering merely 'verbal' or 'terminological' disputes in ordinary conversation...
>
> We come now to the second type of intuition that is elicited by metaphysical disputes. Even when we sense that something might really be at issue when it comes to a question of

metaphysics, we may still get the impression that the answer is more or less *trivial* —it can be known by drawing out consequences of truisms that we all accept or by reflecting on a conceptual framework that we all share.

These two deflationary intuitions threaten the robustly realist approach that is dominant today — at least among analytic philosophers who specialize in metaphysics, Most contemporary metaphysicians think of themselves as concerned, not primarily with the representations of language and thoughts, but with the reality that is represented." [22]

Information philosophy hopes to *reinflate* metaphysics by adding back the *immaterial* ideas that have been eliminated by naturalists and materialists, with their claims that the world is *causally closed*.

Information physics shows that the universe is open, continually expanding and generating creative new possibilities for the future.

Careful analysis of the information content (the abstract form that shapes a concrete object, arranging its parts) has given us plausible solutions for several classic paradoxes and puzzles in metaphysics.

Information is neither matter nor energy, although it needs matter for its embodiment and energy for its communication. It is *immaterial*. It is the modern spirit, the ghost in the machine.

Living things use information to control the flows of matter and energy through their bodies. Information is the mind in the body. It is the soul. And when we die, our personal information and its communications perish. The matter remains.

---

22   Chalmers, et al., (2009) *Metametaphysics*, pp.1-3 *passim*.

Metaphysics

Great Problems Solved?

A careful analysis of their information content suggests solutions to a number of problems in physics, cosmology, psychology, biology, philosophy, and of course in metaphysics in particular.

In physics...

Quantum Mechanics. We offer a new interpretation in which the wave function is just abstract information about the probability of finding particles somewhere. We show that this information depends only on the wavelength of a particle and the boundary conditions of the experiment, such as the two slits in a wall and the detection screen beyond. Information exists in the form of standing waves, whether or not a particle is entering the apparatus. It depends only on whether one or two slits are open.

Origin of Irreversibility. The great problem in statistical mechanics is how we can explain macroscopic irreversibility (entropy increase) when microscopic collisions are thought to be reversible, even in quantum mechanics. We have shown that whenever microscopic collisions or other processes involve radiation, they are not reversible.[1] Outgoing spherical waves of radiation are the norm, but time-reversed incoming spherical waves are *never seen in nature*. Interactions of photons and electrons involve *ontological chance*, because the photon direction is random, as ALBERT EINSTEIN found in 1916. Every collision involving radiation erases the path information about the history of the particles that would have been needed for the collision to be time reversible.

Entropy and the Second Law. Abstract immaterial information is mathematically, phenomenologically, and experimentally related to the physical quantity in thermodynamics and statistical mechanics called the entropy. The second law of thermodynamics says that a closed system, left to itself, approaches a state of maximum entropy, or disorder. This change is "irreversible" without input of low-entropy free energy from outside the system.

The macroscopic irreversibility of the entropy law depends on microscopic irreversibility, as LUDWIG BOLTZMANN suspected.

---

1   See chapter 25 of *Great Problems in Philosophy and Physics*.

Chance is Real. Without chance and the generation of possibilities, no new information can come into the world. Without chance, there can be no *creativity*. Without the creation of new information, new ideas, the information content of the universe would be a constant - "nothing new under the sun." In an eliminatively materialist and determinist world, there is but one possible future. Information philosophy shows that possibilities are real, if *metaphysical,* and chance is ontological.

The ultimate source of chance is the interaction of radiation and matter responsible for microscopic irreversibility.

Laws of Nature Are Statistical. With the exception of deep principles like conservation laws, symmetry considerations, and the constancy of light velocity, many laws of nature based on empirical evidence are in fact statistical laws. Microscopic atomic processes are governed by quantum physics, which is a *statistical* theory. These laws give us probabilities, not certainties. For material objects containing large numbers of atomic particles, the statistical uncertainty approaches zero and the laws are *adequately but only statistically deterministic.*

Quantum mechanical *probabilities* (the wave functions) evolve deterministically and continuously according to the Schrödinger equation, but the *actual* outcomes occur discontinuously and *statistically.* This may seem like a logical contradiction, but it's not.

The average value of *possible* particle positions moves according to classical mechanical laws, but the *actual* position where a particle is found is indeterminate (random), following quantum mechanical laws. "Determinism" is only an "adequate" *statistical determinism.*

Actualizing a Possibility. The existential status of possibilities is problematic, because they are not things, not physical material objects. They belong to the Platonic realm of ideas, an "ideal world" contrasted with the "material world." The status of possibilities is a problem in metaphysics. Many metaphysicians today defend *necessitism*, especially the *necessity of identity*. The information philosopher and metaphysicist defend *metaphysical possibilism*.

Note that the "possible worlds" of metaphysicians like DAVID LEWIS and the "many worlds" of physicists like HUGH EVERETT III are perfectly deterministic, each with only one possible future. Real possibilities mean there is more than one possible future.

Collapse of the Wave Function. The paradigmatic example in physics of infinite possibilities realized as a single actuality is the so-called "collapse of the wave function" or "reduction of the wave packet." Information philosophy provides a common-sense, intuitive picture of this process, so often taught as a deep mystery. RICHARD FEYNMAN called it "the only mystery in quantum mechanics." Information philosophy hopes to *demystify* it.

The wave function is a complex quantity known as a probability amplitude which can interfere with itself. When it is squared it gives us a positive number that represents the probability of finding a particle somewhere. This tells us the specific possibilities of finding a particle in different places. When we make a measurement, we find the particle in one actual place. The possibilities of finding it anywhere else vanish. Nothing material "collapses" in the sense of moving from place to place. This is a perfect example of ambiguous words confusing us about what is really going on.

The Two-Slit Experiment. Information philosophy simplifies this puzzling experiment by showing that the wave function is just *immaterial information* about where the particle may be found. Given the wavelength of the particle, the wave function is completely determined by the boundary conditions – the locations and size of the two slits and the distance to the screen. In the past, we have said that wave and particle are alternate descriptions, because we picture a wave between measurements and a particle when a measurement is made. But we were simply wrong to say "sometimes a wave, sometimes a particle." These are two distinct aspects or properties.

Nonlocality and Entanglement. When one particle decays into two particles that separate from a central point with equal and opposite velocities, ALBERT EINSTEIN saw that a measurement of one particle's position instantly tells us where the other particle is (assuming there has been no interaction with the environment).

We know because of the conservation laws for energy, momentum, angular momentum, and particle spin. This allows us to calculate the second particle's position. But this is not "action at a distance," as Einstein feared. We call it "knowledge at a distance." It is central to demystifying the puzzle of entanglement, where two particles are described with a single wave function.

For reasons that we can not yet comprehend, Einstein introduced a false *asymmetry* into a symmetric situation. This asymmetry has confused the interpreters of quantum mechanics for decades.[2]

Two entangled particles resulting from an irreversible single particle decay are described by a two-particle wave function that cannot be separated into a product of single-particle wave functions. When they are "measured" in the rest frame of the original particle decay, their positions are determined simultaneously. The original rest frame is a "special frame." Other moving frames may make one particle's measurement *appear* to be before the other, contributing to the "mystery" of entanglement.

Reconciling Quantum Mechanics and Special Relativity. As we saw on page 204 above, Einstein assumed that the entangled particles can be separated and measured independently. But they cannot separate without some interaction that *decoheres* the two-particle wave function into the product of two single-particle wave functions. The first measurement or interaction with anything external instantly locates the particles in a spacelike separation that satisfies the conservation laws, for example equidistant from the origin, with spins that add up to the original spin. Before that measurement, the particles could have been anywhere the two-particle wave function was non-zero (the essence of nonlocality), but wherever they were they must have been satisfying the conservation laws.

Nothing moves faster than light in the collapse of the two-particle wave function, reconciling quantum mechanics and relativity.

In cosmology...

The Expanding Universe. Expansion creates more phase space per particle, more possible ways to arrange material, more room for information structures. The increase in positive entropy (disorder) does not mean a decrease in negative entropy (potential informa-

---

2   See our forthcoming book *My God, He Plays Dice! How Albert Einstein Invented Most of Quantum Mechanics.*

tion). Both entropy and information, both disorder and order, have been increasing since the beginning of the universe. Today's information structures, the galaxies, stars, and planets, including our Sun and our Earth, emerged. Information about them did not exist at the origin of the universe, as many philosophers and theologians have thought.

The Cosmic Creation Process. Information philosophy explains the creation and *emergence* of new information in the universe as a two-step process beginning with an *irreversible* quantum event (in which possibilities become actualized) and ending with some positive entropy carried away from the resulting low-entropy information structure, to satisfy the second law of thermodynamics.

This process underlies the creation of every single bit of information, whether the formation of a hydrogen atom from a proton and electron, a complex physical measurement like discovering the Higgs boson, or the creation of a new idea in a human mind.

The Universe is Open. It began in a state of total disorder, with the maximum entropy possible for the initial conditions, some 13.75 billion years ago. How then can the universe today contain such rich information structures as galaxies, stars, and planets like Earth, with its rich biological information-processing systems? Why isn't the universe still in thermal equilibrium?

This is the fundamental question of information philosophy.

Our answer is that the maximum entropy of the early universe was tiny compared to the maximum possible entropy today, as a result of the expansion of the universe. And because the universe has not had time to reach its potential maximum of disorder, new information (negative entropy) has been and is now being created.

The Arrow of Time. The expansion of the universe is the fundamental *arrow of time*. It enables untold numbers of irreversible microscopic events, each of which has an arrow in the same time direction. The so-called radiation arrow is the fact of only outgoing spherical waves. Incoming spherical waves are never seen in nature.

Negative Entropy has Value. The source for all potential information can serve us as a basis for *objective value*. It is the *sine qua non* of anything interesting and useful in the universe.

In psychology ...

The Experience Recorder and Reproducer. The extraordinarily sophisticated connection between words and objects is made in human minds, mediated by the brain's *experience recorder and reproducer* (ERR). Words stimulate neurons to start firing and to play back relevant experiences that include the objects. The neuroscientist DONALD HEBB famously said that "neurons that fire together get wired together." Our ERR model says neurons that were wired together by old experiences will fire together again when a new experience resembles the old in any way, instantly providing guidance to deal with the new.

Mind-Body Problem. Since experiences are stored as immaterial information embodied in the neurons of the brain, information philosophy agrees that the *mind is software in the brain hardware*. But how can immaterial ideas move the material body? A specific example of the mind causing an action, while not itself being caused by antecedent events is the following. Faced with a decision of what to do next, the mind considers several possible alternatives, at least some of which are creatively invented based on random ideas that just "come to mind." Other possible alternatives might be familiar options, even habits, that have frequently been done in earlier similar situations.

All these mental alternatives show up as "neural correlates" - brain neurons firing. When the alternatives are evaluated and one is selected, the selected action results in still other neurons firing, some of which connect to the motor cortex that signals muscles to move the body. Apart from the occasional indeterministic generation of creative new alternative ideas, this whole causal process is adequately determined and it is downwardly causal. Mental events are causing physical body events.

The Two-stage Model of Free Will. Since every free act creates information, free will events are intimately related to events of cosmic creation, because they both begin with the generation of *alternative possibilities* for action, and they both end with one possibility being *actualized*. You can think of your thoughts as free, your actions as willed. You can think of both as cosmic events bringing new information into the universe.

Determinism is an illusion. Determinism has had a long and successful history in philosophy and physics, but it is an unwarranted assumption, not supported by the evidence. The material world is quantum mechanical, and ontological chance is the result of quantum indeterminacy. An *adequate* and *statistical* determinism does *appear* when macroscopic objects contain large numbers of microscopic particles so that quantum events can be averaged over. But every free event shows that the universe is not *pre-determined*.

In philosophy...

Knowledge is an isomorphism. Information *represents* a concept or an object better than an imprecise description in language. Information is the *form* in all concrete objects as well as the *content* in non-existent, merely possible, *abstract entities*. Knowledge is an *information structure* in a mind that is a partial *isomorphism* (a mapping) of an information structure in the external world. Information philosophy is the ultimate *correspondence* theory.

Beyond Logic and Language. But there is no isomorphism, no information in common, no necessary connection, between *words and objects*. Although language is an excellent tool for human communication, its arbitrary and ambiguous nature makes it ill-suited to represent the world directly. Language does not picture reality. It is not the best tool for solving philosophical problems.

The teachable elements of information philosophy are not words or concepts, but *dynamical models of information structures*. They go far beyond logic and language as a *representation* of the fundamental nature of reality. They "write" directly into our mental experience recorders. By contrast, words must be *interpreted* in terms of earlier experiences. Without words and related experiences previously recorded in your mental experience recorder, you could not comprehend spoken or written words. They would be mere noise, with no meaning. Compare these two representations of a cat.

CAT

Linguistic and picture/model representations compared.

Compared to a spoken or printed word, a photograph or a moving picture with sound can be seen and mostly understood by human beings, independent of their native tongue.

Computer animated dynamical models can incorporate all the laws of nature, from the differential equations of quantum physics to the myriad processes of biology. At their best, such simulations are not only our most accurate knowledge of the physical world, they may be the best teaching tools ever devised. We can transfer knowledge non-verbally to coming generations and most of the world's population via the Internet and ubiquitous smartphones.

A dynamic information model of an information structure in the world is presented immediately to the mind as a look-alike and act-alike simulation, which is experienced for itself, not mediated through arbitrary and ambiguous words.

Axioms of Identity. We propose three axioms of identity, with which many puzzles are solved about the persistence of objects.

Id1. Everything is identical to everything else in some respects.

Id2. Everything is different from everything else in some other respects.

Id3. Everything is identical to itself in all respects at each instant of time, but different in some respects from itself at any other time.

We can rewrite these axioms in terms of information.

I1. Any two things have some information in common.

I2. Any two things have some different information.

I3. The identity of anything over time is changing because the information in it (and about it) is changing with time.

In biology...

Origin of Life Because of microscopic irreversibility, the paths of material particles do not always tell us where they have been in the past, though some determinist physicists think so. Cosmological and geological objects have an evolutionary history. And so does biology. Matter and energy (with low entropy) flows through living things, maintaining their dynamical information structures and much of their history.

To discover the origin of life, it will be easier to work backwards in time through the history of biological evolution than to start from physics and chemistry, which know little of preserving information.

Information in Biology. Despite many controversies about the role of information in biology over the past several decades, we can now show that the creation and communication of information is not only necessary to understand biology, but that biology is a proper, if tiny, subset of information creation in the material universe, including the evolution of human minds and the abstract ideas created or discovered by our minds that constitutes our knowledge.

As biosemioticians have long claimed, biocommunications use arbitrary codes and symbols that are precursors to human language.

Evolution. Material information creation, in the form of planets, stars, and galaxies, went on for perhaps ten billion years before biological "agents" formed. At some time between three and four billion years ago, processes appeared that replicated macromolecules, multiplying their information. Perfect replication does not produce *new* information, only copies of pre-existing information. Copying *errors* and genetic mutations provided the random changes needed for evolution by variation and natural selection.

Some two billion years ago, multicellular biological agents began to communicate with their component parts and with one another, processing and sharing information.

With the appearance of living things, agency, purpose, meaning, and values entered the universe.

This is not a teleological purpose, a "telos" that pre-existed life. It is what COLIN PITTENDRIGH, JACQUES MONOD, and ERNST MAYR suggested we call teleonomy, a "built-in" purpose. Aristotle called it "entelechy," which means "having a purpose within."

The goal for information philosophy is to write a new story of biological evolution as the growth of information processing and communication, connecting it back into cosmological evolution as the creation of information structures, and illustrating the total dependence of biology on cosmological sources of negative entropy (potential information).

Bibliography

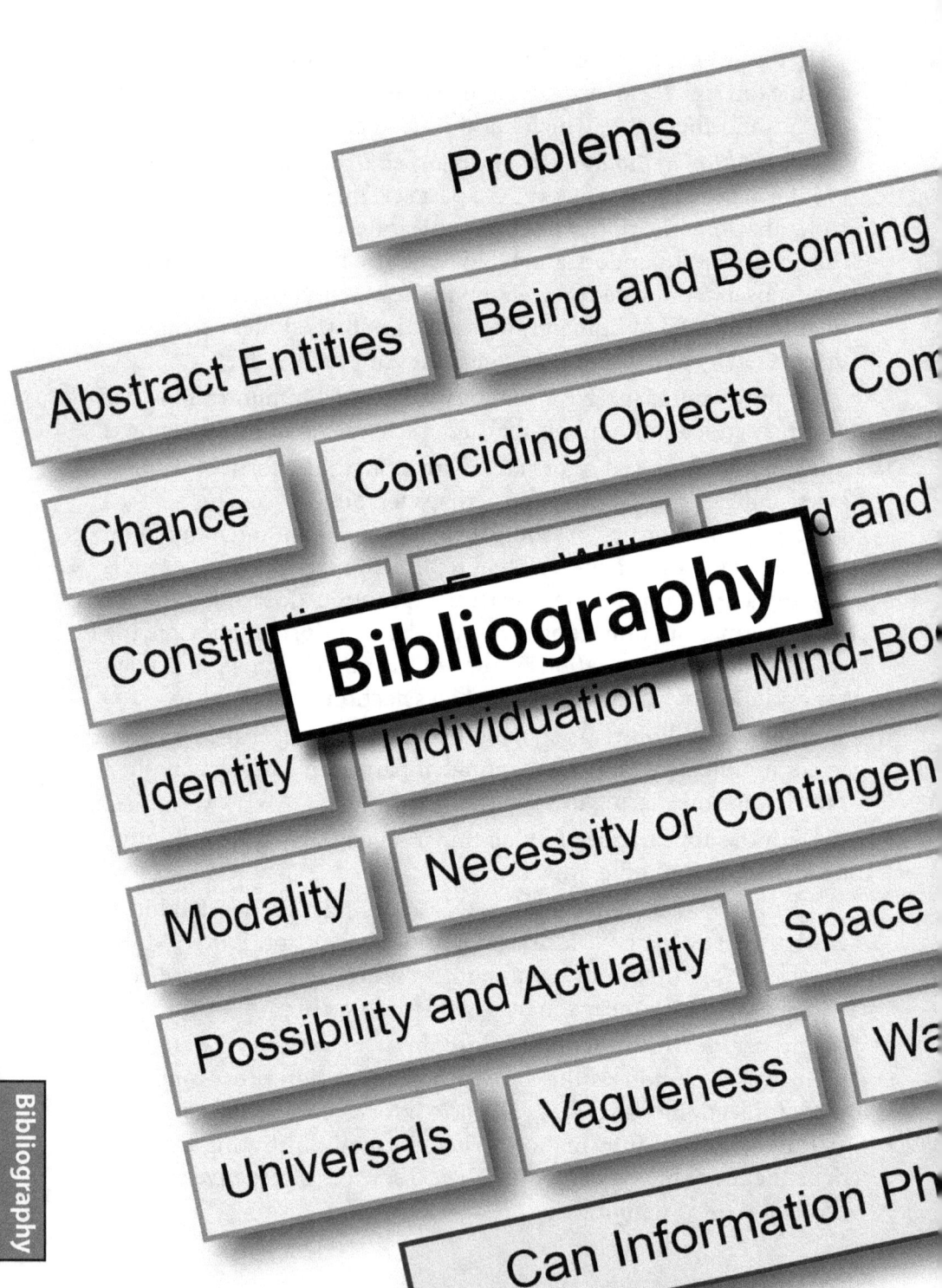

Bibliography

Aristotle, *Metaphysics*, *The Loeb Library*, Harvard University Press.

Armstrong, D. M. (1973). *Belief, Truth and Knowledge*. Cambridge University Press

Bacciagaluppi, G. and A. Valentini, (2009). *Quantum Theory at the Crossroads: Reconsidering the 1927 Solvay Conference*, Cambridge University Press

Baker, L. R. (1997). 'Why constitution is not identity.' *The Journal of Philosophy*, 94(12), 599-621.

Barcan, R. C. (1946a). 'A functional calculus of first order based on strict implication.' *The Journal of Symbolic Logic*, 11(01), 1-16.

Barcan, R. C. (1946b). 'The deduction theorem in a functional calculus of first order based on strict implication.' *The Journal of Symbolic Logic*, 11(04), 115-118.

Barcan, R. C. (1947). 'The identity of individuals in a strict functional calculus of second order.' *The Journal of Symbolic Logic*, 12(01), 12-15.

Black, Max. (1952). 'The Identity of Indiscernibles.' *Mind* 61: 153-64.

Bowin, J. (2003). 'Chrysippus' Puzzle About Identity.' Oxford Studies in Ancient Philosophy 24: 239-251

Burke, M. B. 1992. 'Copper Statues and Pieces of Copper: A Challenge to the Standard Account.' *Analysis* 52: 12-17.

Burke, M. B. (1994a). 'Preserving the principle of one object to a place: A novel account of the relations among objects, sorts, sortals, and persistence conditions.' *Philosophy and Phenomenological Research*, 54(3), 591-624.

Burke, M. B. (1994b). 'Dion and Theon: An essentialist solution to an ancient puzzle.' *The Journal of Philosophy*, 91(3), 129-139.

Burke, M. B. (1996). Tibbles the cat: A Modern "Sophisma". *Philosophical Studies*, 84(1), 63-74.

Burke, M. B. (1997). 'Coinciding objects: reply to Lowe and Denkel.' *Analysis*, 57(1), 11-18.

Burke, M. B. (2004). 'Dion, Theon, and the many-thinkers problem.' *Analysis*, 64(3), 242-250.

Bruno, G. (2011). *On the infinite universe and worlds*.

Carnap, R. (1946). *Meaning and necessity: a study in semantics and modal logic*. University of Chicago Press.

Carter, W. R. (1982). 'On Contingent Identity and Temporal Worms.' *Philosophical Studies* 41: 213-30.
Chalmers, D. J. (1996). *The conscious mind: In search of a fundamental theory*. Oxford University Press.
Chalmers, D., Manley, D., & Wasserman, R. (2009). *Metametaphysics: new essays on the foundations of ontology*. Oxford University Press.
Chisholm, R. M. (1973). 'Parts as essential to their wholes.' *The Review of Metaphysics*, 581-603.
Chisholm, Roderick M. (1989) *On Metaphysics*. Minneapolis: University of Minnesota Press, .
Cohen, S. M. (1984). 'Aristotle and Individuation.' *Canadian Journal of Philosophy*, 14(sup1), 41-65.
De Moivre, A. (1718) *The Doctrine of Chances: or, A Method of Calculating the Probability of Events in Play*.
Dirac, P. (1930) *The Principles of Quantum Mechanics*, Oxford University Press.
Doyle, B. (2011). *Free Will: The Scandal in Philosophy*. Cambridge: I-Phi Press
Doyle, B. (2016). *Great Problems in Philosophy and Physics, Solved?* Cambridge: I-Phi Press
Einstein, A. (1905) 'A Heuristic Viewpoint on the Production and Transformation of Light,' *American Journal of Physics*, 33, 5, 367
Einstein, A. (1933) 'On the Methods of Thoretical Physics." (Herbert Spencer Lecture) *Philosophy of Science*, Vol. 1, No. 2 (Apr., 1934)
Einstein, A. (1936), 'Physics and Reality,' *Journal of the Franklin Institute*, Vol.221, No.3.
Einstein (1949) *Albert Einstein: Philosopher-Scientist*, Ed. Paul Arthur Schilpp,
Einstein, A. (1954). *Ideas and Opinions*. New York: Crown.
Einstein, A. (1989). *The collected papers of Albert Einstein*. Princeton University Press.
Feynman, R. (1964) *The Feynman Lectures on Physics*, vol III, p.1-1
Field, Hartry (2008). *Saving Truth from Paradox*, Oxford University Press.
Fischer, J. M., Kane, R., Pereboom, D., & Vargas, M. (2009). *Four views on free will*. John Wiley & Sons.
Fitch, F. B. (1952) *Symbolic Logic*, New Haven,Yale University Press
Frege, G. (1952). *Translations from the Philosophical Writings of Gottlob Frege*. Edited by Peter Geach and Max Black. Basil Blackwell, Oxford.
Geach, P. T. (1967). 'Identity.' *Review of Metaphysics* 21: 3-12.

Geach, P. T. (1980). *Reference and Generality*. 3d ed. Ithaca, NY: Cornell University Press.
Gibbard, A. (1975). 'Contingent Identity.' *Journal of Philosophical Logic*, 4(2), 187-221.
Griffin, N. (1977) *Relative Identity*, Clarendon Press, Oxford.
Hale, B. (1987). *Abstract Objects*, Basil Blackwell, New York
Hale, B. (2013). *Necessary beings: An essay on ontology, modality, and the relations between them*. Oxford University Press.
Hale, B., & Hoffmann, A. (2010). *Modality: metaphysics, logic, and epistemology*. Oxford University Press.
Heisenberg, W. (1930). *The physical principles of quantum mechanics*. U. Chicago Press, Chicago,
Hirsch, E. (1992). *The Concept of Identity*. Oxford University Press.
Hughes, G. E. and M. J. Cresswell. (1996). *New Introduction to Modal Logic*. London: Routledge.
Hume, D. (1739) *Treatise on Human Nature*, Oxford University Press (1978).
Hume, D. (1748). *Enquiries Concerning the Human Understanding: And Concerning the Principles of Morals*. Oxford University Press (1975).
Humphreys, P., & Fetzer, J. H. (Eds.). (1999). *The New Theory of Reference: Kripke, Marcus, and its origins* (Vol. 270). Springer Science & Business Media.
Johnston, M. (1992). 'Constitution is not identity.' *Mind*, 101(401), 89-105.
Kant, Immanuel. (1787) *Prolegomena to Any Future Metaphysics*, Hackett (1977)
Kant (1784) *Idea for a Universal History*
Kim, J. (2007). *Physicalism, or something near enough*. Princeton University Press.
Kripke, Saul. (1971). 'Identity and Necessity.' In Munitz 1971, 135-164.
Kripke, Saul. (1981). *Naming and Necessity*. Blackwell Publishing.
James, W. (1899). *The Will to Believe and Other Essays in Popular Philosophy*. Dover (1956).
Johnston, M. (1992). 'Constitution is not identity.' *Mind*, 101(401), 89-105.
Layzer, D. (1991). *Cosmogenesis: the Growth of Order in the Universe*. Oxford University Press.
Leibniz, G. (1973) *Philosophical Writings*, ed. G. H. R. Parkinson, London: Dent and Sons.
Lehrer. K. (1966) *Freedom and Determinism*. Random House
Leonard, H. S., & Goodman, N. (1940). 'The calculus of individuals

and its uses.' *The Journal of Symbolic Logic*, 5(2), 45-55.
Lewis, D. K. (1973). *Counterfactuals*. Oxford: Blackwell.
Lewis, D. K. (1986). *On the plurality of worlds*. Oxford: Blackwell.
Lewis, D. (1993). 'Many, but almost one.' *Ontology, causality and mind*, 23-42. Chicago
Lloyd, A. C. (1970). 'Aristotle's' Principle of Individuation.' *Mind*, 79 (316), 519-529.
Locke, J. (1959). *An essay concerning human understanding*. Dover
Long, A. A., & Sedley, D. N. (1989). *The Hellenistic Philosophers: Greek and Latin Texts with Notes and Bibliography*. Cambridge University Press.
Lowe, E. J. (1982a). 'The paradox of the 1,001 cats.' *Analysis*, 42(1), 27-30. Chicago
Lowe, E. J. (1982b). 'On being a cat.' *Analysis*, 42(3), 174-177.
Lowe, E. J. (1987). 'Lewis on perdurance versus endurance.' *Analysis*, 47(3), 152-154.
Lowe, E. J. (1995a). 'Coinciding objects: in defence of the "standard account".' *Analysis*, 55(3), 171-178.
Lowe, E. J. (1995b). 'The Problem of the Many and the Vagueness of Constitution,' *Analysis*, 55(3), 179-182.
Lucretius. *De Rerum Natura, The Loeb Library,* Harvard University Press.
Lukasiewicz, J., E. Anscombe and K. Popper (1953) 'Symposium: The Principle of Individuation,' *Proceedings of the Aristotelian Society*, Supplementary Volumes, Vol. 27, (1953), pp. 69-120
Marcus, R. B. (1961). 'Modalities and intensional languages.' *Synthése*, 13(4), 303-322.
Marcus, R. B. (1993). *Modalities: Philosophical Essays*. Oxford University Press.
Merricks. T. (2003) *Objects and Persons*. Oxford University Press
McCulloch, G. (1989). *The game of the name: introducing logic, language, and mind*, Oxford University Press.
Mugnai, M. (2001). 'Leibniz on Individuation: From the Early Years to the "Discourse" and Beyond.' *Studia Leibnitiana*, (H. 1), 36-54.
Munitz, Milton, ed. (1971). *Identity and Individuation*. New York: New York University Press.
Noonan, Harold. (1985b). 'The Closest Continuer Theory of Identity,' *Inquiry* 28: 195-229.
Noonan, H. W. (1993). 'Constitution is identity.' *Mind*, 102(405), 133-146.
O'Connor, T. (1995). *Agents, causes, and events: Essays on indeterminism and free will*. Oxford University Press
Pais, A. (1982). *Subtle is the Lord: The Science and the Life of Albert*

Einstein. Oxford University Press, USA.
Pap, A (1958) 'The Linguistic Theory of Logical Necessity,' *Semantics and Necessary Truth*, Yale University Press.
Parsons, T. (1980). *Nonexistent Objects*. Yale University Press.
Peirce, C. S. (1933) *Collected Papers of Charles Sanders Peirce*. Harvard University Press
Peirce, C. S. (1902) *Dictionary of Philosophy and Psychology*, J.M. Baldwin (ed.), New York: MacMillan,
Plato, *The Loeb Library*, Harvard University Press.
Price, H. (1997). Time's arrow and Archimedes' point: new directions for the physics of time. Oxford University Press.
Poincaré, H (1914) *Science and Method*, Courier Corporation (2013)
Quine, W. (1940). *Mathematical Logic*. Harvard University Press.
Quine, W. V. (1943). 'Notes on Existence and Necessity,' *The Journal of Philosophy*, 40 (5) p.113
Quine, W. V. (1947). 'The Problem of Interpreting Modal Logic,' *The Journal of Symbolic Logic* 12 (2) p.43
Quine, W. V. (1980). *From a Logical Point of View*, 2d ed. Cambridge, MA: Harvard University Press.
Ramsey, F. P. (1960). *Foundations of mathematics and other logical essays*. Routledge Kegan Paul
Rea, M. C. (1997). *Material Constitution: A Reader*. Lanham, MD: Rowman & Littlefield.
Rea, M. C. (1995). 'The problem of material constitution.' *The Philosophical Review*, 104(4), 525-552.
Rea, M. C. ed. (2008) *Metaphysics*. 5 vols. New York: Routledge.
Rea, M. C. (2009). *Arguing about metaphysics*. New York, Routledge.
Regis, E. (1976). 'Aristotle's' Principle of Individuation.' *Phronesis*, 157-166.
Russell, B. & Whitehead, A. N. (1912). *Principia Mathematica* (Vol. 1). Cambridge University Press.
Russell, B. (1914). *Our knowledge of the external world as a field for scientific method in philosophy*. Open Court.
Salmon, Nathan. (1986). *Frege's Puzzle*. Bradford, Cambridge:.
Salmon, Nathan. (2005). *Reference and Essence*, Prometheus Books, Amherst, New York.
Schrödinger, Erwin. (1922) 'What Is a Law of Nature?,' *Science and the Human Temperament*. New York: Norton.
Sedley, David. (1982). 'The Stoic Criterion of Identity.' *Phronesis* 27: 255-75.
Shoemaker, S. and R. Swinburne, (1984), *Personal Identity*. Oxford:

Blackwell

Sidelle (2002) 'Is There a True Metaphysics of Material Objects?,' *Noûs*, Vol. 36, Supplement: Philosophical Issues, 12, Realism and Relativism (2002), p.118

Sider, Ted, (2001). *Four-Dimensionalism*, Oxford: Oxford University Press.

Sider, Ted, (2011). *Writing the Book of the World.* Oxford University Press

Sider, T., J. Hawthorne, and D. W. Zimmerman. (2008) *Contemporary Debates in Metaphysics*, Blackwell Publishing.

Sinnott-Armstrong, W., Raffman, D., & Asher, N. (1995). *Modality, Morality and Belief: Essays in Honor of Ruth Barcan Marcus.* Cambridge University Press.

Sperry (1969) 'A Modified Concept of Consciousness,' *Psychological Review*, 76, 6.

Stalnaker, R. (1999). *Context and Content*, Oxford University Press.

Stalnaker, R. (2003). *Ways a World Might Be*, Clarendon Press, Oxford.

Stalnaker, R. (2012). *Mere Possibilities*, Princeton University Press.

Taylor, R.. (1963) *Metaphysics*. Foundations of Philosophy Series. Englewood Cliffs, N.J: Prentice-Hall.

Taylor, Richard, (1955). 'Spatial and Temporal Analogues and the Concept of Identity,' *The Journal of Philosophy*, 52, 599–612.

Thomson, J. J. (1983). 'Parthood and identity across time.' *The Journal of Philosophy*, 80(4), 201-220.

Thomson, J. J. (1998). 'The statue and the clay.' Noûs, 32(2), 149-173.

Unger, Peter. (1979a). 'There Are No Ordinary Things.' *Synthése* 41: 117-54.

Unger, Peter. (1979b). 'Why There Are No People.' In *Midwest Studies in Philosophy*. Vol 4. pp. 177-222 Minneapolis: University of Minnesota Press.

Unger, Peter. (1980a) 'Skepticism and Nihilism.' *Noûs* 14: 517-45.

Unger, Peter. (1980b). 'The Problem of the Many.' In *Midwest Studies in Philosophy*. Vol. 5 Studies in Epistemology, ed. P. French, T. Uehling, and H. Wettstein Minneapolis: Univ. of Minnesota Press.

Unger, P. (1999). 'Mental Problems of the Many.' *Oxford Studies in Metaphysics*, 23, Chapter 8. p.195.

Van der Waerden, B. L. (1968). *Sources of Quantum Mechanics*. Dover

Van Heijenoort, J. (1967). *From Frege to Gödel: a source book in mathematical logic, 1879-1931*. Harvard University Press.

Van Inwagen, P. (1981). 'The Doctrine of Arbitrary Undetached Parts,' *Pacific Philosophical Quarterly*, 62, 123-137.

Van Inwagen, P. (1983). *An Essay on Free Will.* New York: Oxford,
Van Inwagen, P.. (1987). 'When Are Objects Parts?' In *Philosophical Perspectives.* Vol. 1
Van Inwagen, P., (1990a), 'Four-Dimensional Objects,' *Noûs,* 24: 245–55.
Van Inwagen, P., (1990b), *Material Beings,* Cornell
Van Inwagen, P. (2014) *Metaphysics.* Fourth Edition, Boulder: Westview Press.
Van Inwagen, P., and D. W. Zimmerman. (2008) *Metaphysics: The Big Questions,* 2nd Ed., Blackwell Publishing.
Varzi, Achille, *Mereology,* Stanford Encyclopedia of Philosophy
Whiting, J. E. (1986). 'Form and individuation in Aristotle.' *History of Philosophy Quarterly,* 3(4), 359-377.
Wiggins, D. (1965). 'Identity Statements,' In RJ Butler (ed.), *Analytic Philosophy,* 2nd edition. Basil Blackwell 40-71
Wiggins, D. (1967). *Identity and Spatio-Temporal Continuity.* Oxford: Blackwell.
Wiggins, D. (1968). 'On being in the same place at the same time.' *The Philosophical Review,* 90-95.
Wiggins, D. (2001). *Sameness and Substance Renewed.* Cambridge University Press.
Williams, B. A. O. (1964). 'Personal identity and individuation,' *Essays in Philosophical Psychology* (pp. 324-345). Palgrave Macmillan UK.
Williams, C. J. F. (1989). *What Is Identity?* Oxford University Press.
Williamson, T. (1990). *Identity and Discrimination,* Basil Blackwell, Cambridge, MA
Williamson, T. (1994). *Vagueness,* Routledge, London
Williamson, T. (2002). 'Necessary existents.' *Royal Institute of Philosophy Supplement,* 51, 233-251. Chicago.
Williamson (2010) 'Necessitism, Contingentism and Plural Quantification,' *Mind,* 119, pp.657-748
Williamson, T. (2013). *Modal Logic as Metaphysics,* Oxford University Press.
Whitehead, A. N., & Russell, B. (1912). *Principia mathematica* (Vol. 1). University Press. Cambridge.
Wittgenstein, L. (1922) *Tractatus Logico-Philosophicus.* tr. C. K. Ogden, Routledge Kegan Paul
Zalta, E. (2012). *Abstract objects: An introduction to axiomatic metaphysics.* Springer Science & Business Media.

Index

A

abstract entities
  and being 21, 76
  as information 47–48, 127
  identity and 104
  immaterial 13–19, 129, 131
  information explains 3, 5–7
  possibilities as 155
  universals as 209
Academic Skeptics
  and change 175
  and growing 227, 249, 332
  and identity 236, 260, 287
  and Stoics 56–58, 64, 105, 137, 273, 359–360
  on infinite regress 253
acausality 45
accident 26, 69, 80, 104, 131, 137
action-at-a-distance
  as immaterial information 393
  as knowledge at distance 393
  Einstein and 199–201
  gravitation as 31–32
actualism 184–185
  and Master Argument 169
  as necessitism 173
  as necessity 161–162
  as tenseless 178
adequate determinism
  and necessity 167, 171
  and physical laws 185
  and R.E.Hobart 343
  as result of averaging 219
  defined 43
  free will and 90–92, 315
agent causation
  and free will 89
  as self-determination 219
  Chisholm and 296
Aharonov, Yakir 325
Albertus Magnus 360
alternative possibilities
  and free creation 33, 148
  and free will 10, 83–87, 390
  and future contingency 155, 159
  and necessity 170
  and possible worlds 182

determinists deny 370
Frankfurt and 341
Kripke and 310
Lewis and 193, 380
analytic language philosophy
  and David Lewis 213, 315, 369
  and determinism 91, 370
  and Leibniz 163
  and quantification 102
  and true propositions 153, 167, 382–384
  and vagueness 213
  going beyond 48
  metaphysicians and 9–10
  on composition 68–70
  on constitution 75
analytic synthetic distinction 28
Anaximander of Miletus 354–356
Anaximenes 354–356
Andronicus of Rhodes 354–356
a priori
  Frege and 242
  Hume and 28–29
  Kant and 29–30, 210
  Kripke and 309
  necessity and 161–163
  Peirce and 41
  Russell and 6–7
  theories and 153
Aquinas, Thomas
  and Being 22–23
  and certainty 30
  as Scholastic 360
  on individuation 138
Aristotle
  and bivalence 155
  categories 257
  essentialism 81
  four causes of 26
  hylomorphic theory 48–50
  on arrangement 71, 273
  on coinciding objects 56, 65, 273
  on identity 104
  on individuation 135
  on universals 207
Armstrong, David M. 285–287
  and infinite regress 255
arrangement
  and change 47–49
  and composition 67–71, 71–73
  and constitution 75–76

Index 405

and necessity 169
and Ship of Theseus 266
and van Inwagen 64
Aristotle on 273
as form of matter 4, 26
as information 18
Averroes 137–139
Avicenna 137–139

B

Bacon, Francis 30
Bain, Alexander 41
becoming 21–23, 257
  as change 48
  as Heraclitean flux 239, 332
being
  and becoming 7, 21–23, 257
  as essence 64, 80
  Parmenidean 48, 76, 131, 239
bell curve 39
Berkeley, George 305, 364
Big Bang 52
biocommunication 64
biology
  and identity 132
  and individuation 135–140
  and mental causation 144
  as teleonomic 68
biomer
  definition 5
  essentialism 72
  in composition 64–65
biomereology 72
biosemiotics 8
bivalence. See excluded middle
  and free will 91
  and Peirce 326
  and Sorites 270
  Aristotle and 155
  Diodorus and 169
  excluded middle 151
body-minus 56, 77, 288, 300. See also Dion and Theon
Bohr, Niels
  and completeness 201
  and free choice 324
  second postulate 223
British empiricists 210
Broglie, Louis de

wave theory 222
Buckle, Thomas Henry 40–41
Burke, Michael 55, 287–292
Burke on 290

C

Carnap, Rudolf 151, 163, 173, 246, 292
carving nature at joints 334, 338
cash value 17, 173
category mistake 290, 317
causal chain 16, 27, 35, 86
  and Hume 304
  and mind 144
  new 156
  of determinism 90–91, 148, 170–171, 184
causality 25–33, 357
  and actualism 184
  and chance 35
  and Hume 129, 171, 302
  and Kant 305, 365
  and knowledge 286
  and necessity 171
  Hume and 129
causally closed 144, 184, 294, 321, 385
causa sui 25, 27, 35, 297
cause
  agent causation 89
  and mind 144
  Aristotle four causes 26
  causal chain 16, 27, 35, 86, 90
  information as 16
certainty 6, 30, 152, 161, 185
  Hume on 302
Chalmers, David 10, 293–295
change 47–53
  and Becoming 7, 21–23
  and colocation 59
  and constitution 75–77
  and debtor's paradox 227–231
  and individuation 140
  and information 200
  and persistence 175–179
  and Sorites 269
  biology and 5
  in material 233, 237–239, 249, 266–267
  of identity 130–132
  the future 184
Chisholm, Roderick 55, 291, 296–298
  mereological essentialism 63, 69–70

Chrysippus
  and free will 92
  and necessity 170
  on chance 35
  on Dion and Theon 233–239, 279, 287–291
  on growing 56, 176, 227, 249–250, 259
  on individuation 137
coinciding objects 55–61
collapse of the wave function 389
  and chance 45
  and many worlds 185, 193
  as information change 200
  Von Neumann on 187–188
colocation 55–61
communication
  and abstract entities 16
  and change 47
  and composition 64, 72
  and constitution 77
  and identity 102, 127–131
  and information 4–11
  Shannon and 186
compatibilism 340–343, 347, 366
composition 63–73, 261, 335, 338, 339
comprehensive compatibilism 63
Compte, August 366, 369
conceptual analysis 9, 369
consciousness 10, 133, 140, 147–149, 241
conservation
  laws 44, 66, 201–204, 224
  of matter and energy 49, 131, 177–178, 193
constitution 75–77
contingency 151–153, 161–173, 181–184
  and necessitism 350
  and possible worlds 379–382
  Hume on 304
  of future 357, 370
continuity 40, 140, 339
continuous 379
Copenhagen Interpretation 189, 218
Copernican revolution 27, 305, 364–365
copy theory 208
correspondence theory 390
cosmic creation process 5, 96–97, 387
cosmology 96, 355
counterfactual 183–185, 314–315, 355
Cramer, John 325
creativity 3, 53, 389
Crick, Francis 190
criterion of identity xiii, 101, 125, 301

Cronus, Diodorus 159, 169, 184, 313
crux metaphysicorum 28, 305
cybernetics 96, 190

D

de Broglie, Louis 222
debtor's paradox 176, 227–231
deduction 30–33
Democritus 38, 91, 170, 354
Dennett, Daniel 159, 184, 313, 347–349
Derrida, Jacques 211
Descartes, Rene 3, 7, 298–300
  on certainty 169
  on mind-body 73, 143–144
determination 39, 343
  self- 87–91
determinism
  adequate 219
  and actualism 184–185
  and Being 23
  and causality 25–29
  and chance 35–45
  and compatibilism 340–344
  and Einstein 32
  and free will 86–93
  and Hume 302
  and Kant 305, 365
  and Leibniz 362
  and mind-body 144–148
  and necessity 161, 167, 170–172
  as illusion 390
  in many worlds 193
Dion and Theon 57, 72, 233–239
Dirac, P.A.M.
  and certainty 152
  on wave-particle 225
Donald, Merlin 225
downward causation
  composites and 73
  mental causation as 145
Doyle, Bob xiv
dualism
  idealism-materialism 7, 14
  in neutral monism 211
  mind-body 7, 143–149
  of Chalmers 293–296
  of information philosophy 4, 364
  of Lowe 316–317
  property 7, 364

substance 7
dynamic information model 391

E

Eddington, Arthur Stanley 348
Eiffel, Alexandre-Gustave 69
Einstein, Albert
  and block universe 324
  and entanglement 196–205, 393
  and positivism 32, 293
  and relativity 178, 195, 211, 220–225, 336
  free creations of mind 9, 16, 32, 149, 368
  on atoms existence 367
  on chance 36–38, 43–45, 97, 219–225, 388
  on field theory 220
  on hypotheses 32–33
  on indistinguishability 141
  on irreversibility 222
  on light quantum 221, 222–225
  on nonlocality 196–205
  on wave-particle 217–225
Einstein-Podolsky-Rosen 200, 203
eliminative materialism 5–7, 304, 340, 355, 384
emergence 47
  composition as 73
  cosmic creation as 387
  possibility of 318
endurance
  Lewis on 193, 336
  of composites 66–67
  vs perdurance 177–179
entanglement
  and Einstein 196–205
  and Schrödinger 196
  as collapse 325
  a special frame 205, 325
  knowledge at a distance 393
entelechy 72, 79, 169, 335, 338
entropy 37, 47, 50–52, 97–98, 187–190, 387–388
  second law and 387–389
Epicurus 170, 354
epistemology xi, 6, 173, 208, 253, 285, 326, 366
Ergod 96–99
ERR. *See* experience recorder and reproducer
essentialism 3–11, 79, 290
  Aristotelian 64
  biomereological 5, 64, 72
  mereological 63, 69, 290
Everett III, Hugh 66, 156, 159, 185, 193, 313
evil 96
excluded middle 91, 151, 169, 326. *See also* bivalence
existential status
  of abstract entities 3
  of a property 208
  of aspects 60
  of categories 257
  of ideas 16, 143, 155, 217, 355
  of possibilities 389
Exner, Franz S. 37–40
experience 354
experience recorder and reproducer 18, 77, 85, 104, 127, 133, 140, 391
  consciousness and 149
  Donald Hebb and 392
  Frege and 241, 382
  mind as 146
externalism 287
extrinsic information. *See* intrinsic information

F

faster-than-light 196–199
Feynman, Richard 202
  only mystery 389
Fine, Kit 213
Fitch, Frederick B. 116, 119–120, 158, 182, 319
flows 47
  matter and energy 73, 385, 392
fluctuations
  in mind brain 92
  in statistical physics 145, 388
flux 48, 76, 130, 227, 239, 353
foreknowledge 95–97
Fouillée, Alfred 40
Fourier, Joseph 39
free will 10, 83–93
  and experimenter 324–325
  chance and 42
  Chisholm and 297
  contingency and 170
  Kant on 39, 366
  Kripke and 314
  Merricks and 322–324
  Peirce on 41
  two-stage model of 218, 314, 390–391
  Van Inwagen on 340–344

Metaphysics

Wiggins and 347–349
Frege, Gottlob 158
  and ERR 382
  and modal logic xiii
  Geach on 125–126
  Kripke and 306
  Leibniz and 361
  Morning Star 130, 158–159
  on ideas 103
  on identity 106
  puzzle 241
  Quine and 327
  sense and reference 108–112, 117, 119
  triad of 15
Frege's puzzle 241–247
fusion 241–244

G

galaxies, stars, and planets 53, 388
Gamow, George 190–193
Geach, Peter
  on relative identity 68, 121, 125–128, 157, 347
  on Tibbles, the cat 234, 260, 279, 288, 300
  on vagueness 214
  translating Frege 241
ghost field 197–200
ghost in the machine 8, 47, 136, 148, 239
God 95–99
  and chance 39
  and preordination 299–300
  Aristotle on 356
  as first cause 355
  intervention of 177, 336–339
  Kant on 365–366
  Scholastics on 360
God does not play dice 38–41, 44–45, 225
Gödel, Kurt
  incompleteness theorem 167, 367
  paradox 107
Goldman, Alvin 17, 286
good 286
Goodman, Nelson 63
growing argument 249–251, 291, 332
  and coinciding objects 56
  and debtor's paradox 227
  and Dion and Theon 234–239
  and persistence 176
  and Ship of Theseus 266
  and Tibbles, the cat 283

problem of many 259

H

half-life 43
Hebb, Donald 149, 392
Hegel, Georg W.F. 40
Heidegger, Martin 9, 21–22, 211
Heisenberg, Werner 218
  on Einstein nonlocality 200
  on free choice 324
  on uncertainty 36, 45, 213, 222, 293
Heraclitus 21, 227, 353
Hobbes, Thomas 265
Honderich, Ted 347
Hume, David 302–306
  constant conjunction 33, 305
  Hume's fork 28
  naturalism 9, 305–306
  on causality 25, 28–33, 129, 171
  on induction 29–33
  on metaphysics 28
  on secondary qualities 210
  sophistry and illusion 28

I

idealism 4–11
ideas
  and Being 21, 48, 76
  and free will 90
  as immaterial 16
  as information 17, 168
  causal power of 16, 17, 73
  come to mind 148
  eliminativists deny 13, 72
  ERR association of 147
  existential status of 16, 155, 257
  free creations 149, 170
  Frege and 103, 241
  mind-independent 14, 167
  Platonic 14, 79, 135, 143, 207–209
  possibilities as 155–156, 183
identity 101–133, 315
  absolute and relative 3, 157, 239, 263, 275
  and change 48, 249–251, 275–277
  and composition 63
  and essence 79
  and individuation 135
  and persistence 175
  as substitutivity 328

constitution as 75–76, 238–239, 239, 266–267
contingent identity 157, 166
necessity of 157–158, 165, 247, 318, 346
of coinciding objects 55, 59, 274, 291
of debtor 227, 230
over time 239, 266–267, 332
personal identity 238
self-identity 3, 165, 276–277, 308
transworld 85, 311–312
identity of indiscernibles 108, 165, 166, 247, 308
illusion
determinism as 390
immaterial 4–7
abstract entities as 13
arrangement as 68
experiences as 168
God as 95
hypotheses as 31
ideas as 21
information as 8, 47
knowledge as 169
logic as 151
mind as 10, 53, 76, 143
immortality 98
indeterminism. *See* determinism
indistinguishability 308
individuation 135–141
induction 29–33
infinite regress 253–255
information
abstract 4
as immaterial 8
communication of 8
creation of new 28
mind as 8
not matter or energy 8
philosophy 3–11
realism 8
information structures
dynamic models of 391
galaxies, stars, planets as 388
knowledge in minds as 390
material objects as 209
intention 68, 73
Husserl on 80, 103–133
Peirce on 111

internalism 287
intrinsic information 48, 68, 80
and identity 101–107, 112, 124, 131, 157, 247
and individuation 141
and relative identity 124
invention 3, 6, 9, 209–211
irreversibility 45, 197–205, 222–225, 387
isomorphism 10, 6–11
knowledge as 390

J

James, William 17, 41–45, 149, 342
justified true belief 17
knowledge as 253-255

K

Kane, Robert 86, 88–89, 349
Kant, Immanuel 305, 365–366
architectonic 211
Copernican revolution 27
dogmatic slumbers 29
laws determined 39
on Hume 29
on metaphysics 29
on noumena and phenomena 210
on skepticism 305–306
scandal 255
space and time 195
synthetic a priori 29, 33, 153, 162
Kim, Jaegwon 4, 76, 144, 294, 318, 321
knowledge 208, 390
as isomorphism 6
information in minds 6–10
knowledge at a distance 201, 203, 393
Kornblith, Hilary 285, 287
Kripke, Saul 306–315
and Marcus 158
and Wiggins 122–124
metaphysical necessity 167, 179, 182, 309
necessary a posteriori 157, 162, 167, 307, 309
on alternative possibilities 159, 306, 310
on free will 83, 314
on identical objects 107, 307
on identity 122–124, 157–158, 307
on identity of indiscernibles 158, 308
on naming and necessity 108, 167
on natural kinds 102, 157–159
on necessity of identity 106, 158–159
on possible worlds 159, 183, 307, 310

rigid designator 245, 307–308
ways world might be 192, 310

L

Land, Edwin 18
Langford, C. H. 164, 371
language games 6–10, 104, 271, 277, 283, 369
Laplace's demon 23, 25, 96
large numbers
  and induction 33
  average over 28, 43, 145, 219, 390
  law of 36, 40
  statistical determinism 392
law of errors 39
laws of nature 9, 13, 33, 53
  and free will 86
  and language 153
  deterministic 39, 42, 144, 159, 161
  Heraclitus on 353
  Hume on 302–304, 363
  in possible worlds 86, 159, 313
  Kant on 39
  Kripke on 309
  Poincaré on 42
  statistical 37, 392
  Van Inwagen on 344
Leibniz, Gottfried 6
  ambiguity-free language 151
  and Frege 109, 242
  and Lewis 126
  and Peirce 111
  and possible worlds 191
  identity of indiscernibles 106, 308
  lingua characterica 107
  necessary truths 106, 162–163
  on contingency 170
  on identity 107
  on substitutability 108
Leibniz's law 108–124, 158, 165, 247
Leonard, Henry 63
Leśniewski, Stanislaw 63
Leucippus 38, 91, 161, 354
Lewis, C.I. 117, 163, 329, 371
Lewis, David 315
  counterpart theory 159, 311, 314
  Kripke on 310
  modal realism 83, 182, 192

on composites 22
on identity 126
on temporl parts 66, 177
possible worlds xiii, 106, 156, 182, 310
liar paradox 271
libertarian 88–92, 170, 296, 342–348
Locke, John
  on colocation 55
  on essences 79
  on free will 89
  on secondary qualities 210, 305, 364
logic
  modal xiii, 3, 106–107
    and identity 247
    and possible worlds 181–183
    necessity in 151, 163–167, 172–173
    quantified 118–119, 327, 350
  predicate 163, 241, 327
  propositional xiii, 163, 241, 327
  symbolic 63, 106, 112, 118, 163, 172
logical positivism 32, 366–369, 382
logical puzzles 6–10
Long, Anthony A. 236, 289
Loschmidt, Josef 37
Lowe, E. Jonathan 10, 291, 316–318

M

Mach, Ernst 32, 293
many worlds 156, 159, 193, 313, 316, 383
Marcus, Ruth Barcan 107, 179, 182–184, 328–331, 380–381
  and Kripke 121–123
  and Wiggins 120–122
  necessity of identity 120, 158, 318, 350, 371
  substitutivity 120, 245–247
  substitutivity failure 245
master argument 169, 184
materialism 4–7
Maxwell, James Clerk 37, 40–41, 190, 223
Maxwell's Demon 190
Mayr, Ernst 64
McTaggart, John 22, 178
meaning. See substitutivity
  analyticity and 167
  as ERR responses 104, 127, 147–149
  as use 9
  Frege and 241–245
  intension and 80, 103, 117, 120, 371

Kripke and 306–310
picture theory of 127
Quine on 115, 118–119, 326–330
sense and 108, 110, 130
Meinong, Alexius 326
mental causation 144–145, 317–318, 322–323
mereology 67–73, 335
Burke on 290
mereological essentialism 63, 69, 80–81, 260
mereological nihilism 63, 68, 73, 261, 271
mereological sum 63–64, 69–70, 75, 102, 127
mereological universalism 63, 68, 70, 260, 344
Merricks on 320
Rea on 331
Sider on 338
Unger on 340
Van Inwagen on 344–345
Merricks, Trenton 320–323
metametaphysics 22, 337
Metaphysical Club 41
metaphysician xi, 3–11, 285–351
metaphysicist 9–11, 13–19, 59, 127, 370
and biology 139
and contingency 161
and information 253
on space and time 195–205
metaphysics
Aristotle's 209
possibilities in 389
possibility of 29, 305
universals and 207
microscopic irreversibility 45, 197, 222, 388
mind 3
as immaterial 3
software in hardware 13
mind-body
identity theory 315
Minkowski, Hermann 22, 178, 324
Mnesarchus 57, 276
modality 151–159
modal logic. *See* logic, modal
modal realism 126, 159, 182, 192, 315
model structure 84–85
Moivre, Abraham de 36, 39, 304
molecular disorder 37, 44
Monod, Jacques 64, 72, 139
moral responsibility 85, 88, 91–93

N

naturalism 7, 292–293, 355, 385
natural kinds 70, 79–80, 102, 157–159
Kripke on 306
necessary a posteriori 157, 162, 167, 307–310, 333
necessitism 157–159
rule of necessitation 182
necessity 6–11
necessity of 162
of identity 157–158, 165, 389
negative entropy 50–52, 97–98, 187, 387–388
as value 97
information as 388
neoplatonist 187
Newton, Isaac 29–32, 37–43, 221–222, 365
Nietzsche, Friedrich 9
nominalism 208
non-existent objects 3–5, 13–14, 47, 157, 172
nonlocality 195–197, 200–204, 218–221, 324–325, 393
nonseparability 202–205
normal distribution 36
nothing but 4–8, 294–298
noumenal 10, 210–211
nuclear decay 43–45, 224–225

O

O'Hair, Gregory 255
one possible future 42–45, 171, 181–185, 389
determinism and 26, 35, 351
in block universe 324
ontological chance 168
and contingency 7, 381–384
and free will 86, 92
and new ideas 3, 351
Einstein discovery of 43–45, 97, 219–225
in quantum physics 37, 152, 156, 186, 390
ontology 5–11, 208
other minds 13, 295
otherwise 154, 159, 161, 181–183
do otherwise 83, 87
outside space and time 4, 7, 163, 324–325, 383

P

Pap, Arthur 163
paradoxes
debtor's paradox 227–231
Diodorus' 169
Dion and Theon 233–239

EPR paradox 201, 325
how to create 59
liar's paradox 271
of analytic philosophy 130, 154
of increase 249
Quine's 244–246, 372
Russell's 167, 271
Ship of Theseus 265
Sorites 214, 269–270
wave-particle 217
Zeno's 48, 67, 353
Parmenides 7, 21–23, 353
parts
  proper 64–72, 77, 81, 234, 260
  temporal 66–67, 139, 177–179, 193
peculiar qualifications 57, 80, 101–111, 137, 357
Peirce, Charles Sanders 357
  and chance 41, 43–45
  and pragmatism 17
  and social physics 41
  on arbitrary symbols 308
  on identity 111
  Quine on 326
  triads 15, 31, 40–41
perdurance 177–179, 193
  Lewis on 66–68
persistence 56–61, 63–65, 75–77, 175–179, 336–338
  of identity 131–133
Philo of Alexandria 233–235
picking out 14, 59–61, 68
  essence 79–81
  identity 101–103, 234
  information 213, 244–246
  parts 259–261, 280–283, 291, 300
  qualities 110, 165
  resemblances 127
Pittendrigh, Colin 64, 72
Plato 7, 208
Platonic Academy 360
Platonic ideas 4, 208, 389
Plutarch 58, 176, 227, 250, 259
Poincaré, Henri 42
Popper, Karl 15, 147, 317, 348
Porphyry's question 257
Posidonius 257
positivism 348

possibilism 173, 183, 381–383, 389
possibilities
  abstract entities as 183, 381
possible worlds 6
  semantics of 183, 246
Presocratics 353–354
Price, Huw 324–325
Principia Mathematica 112
Prior, A.N. 372
probabilities 259
problem of the many 259–263
Providence 9
pseudo-problems 310
purpose 8
Putnam, Hilary 157
puzzle maker 59, 230
puzzles 227
Pythagoras 227, 354

Q

qua 101, 103, 126
quantification 68, 102–103, 246
  Frege and 109
  Marcus and 331, 350
  of information 315
  operators 181–182, 246
  Quine and 117, 244, 327–330
quantum mechanics
  and causality 25–26
  and chance 36–38, 45
  and free will 93
  and individuation 140–141
  and many worlds 159, 193
  and mental causation 144–146
  and possibilities 183–189
  Einstein and 196–205, 217–225
quantum reality xiii, 217, 370
quantum world 141, 145, 189
Quine, Willard Van Orman
  and Marcus 118–122
  knowledge as synthetic 130, 162–163
  naming and identity 108–112
  naturalizing epistemology xi
  on identity 115–119
  on quantification 68
  opposes quantified modal logic xiii, 118
  paradoxes 244

R

Ramsey, Frank 114, 255

Rea, Michael 331–333
reference
  and identity 307–308
  Frege on 108–110, 130, 158, 241–243
  Kripke on 306
  Marcus on 245
  Names and 110–111
  new theory of 246
  purely designative 245
  Quine on 110, 245, 371–375
  Wiggins on 376–377
referential opacity 245–246
relativity
  and quantum mechanics 195, 199–205, 217
  general 195–196, 198, 211, 220–222
  special 22, 32, 178, 184, 195
Renouvier, Charles 40–42
rigid designator 307
rule of necessitation 182
Russell, Bertrand
  all knowledge scientific 367
  and Wittgenstein 367
  Frege and 367
  on descriptions 306–308
  on deterministic causation 25, 42, 171
  on free will 348
  paradox 167, 271, 367
  Principia Mathematica 112
  Wittgenstein on 113–114
Rutherford, Ernest 43–45, 224

S

scandal 384
  Kant's 255, 305–306, 365
Scholastics 30, 136, 360–361, 364, 371
Schopenhauer, Arthur 211
Schrödinger equation 185–189, 202, 218
  determinism and 392
Schrödinger, Erwin
  laws deterministic 38, 145, 187
  laws statistical 38
  on entanglement 196, 205
  on visualization 201–202
Scotus, John Duns 30, 138, 360
second law 37–38, 51, 98, 335–338, 387
  and cosmic creation 387
  and measurement 187–188
Sedley, David N. 236, 289
semantics 83–85, 118, 181–183, 246–247, 379–383
sense (meaning) 103, 108–110, 117–120, 130, 241–247
  and non-sense xi, 107–109, 112, 124
  and reference. *See* reference
Sextus Empiricus 254
Shannon, Claude 190
  entropy 52
  principle 186
Ship of Theseus 70, 265–267, 345
Sidelle, Alan 333–335
Sider, Ted 336–339
Skeptics. *See* Academic Skeptics
Smart, J.J.C. 22, 324, 342
smartphone 95, 99, 391
Socrates 57–58, 109, 136, 253, 353–354
software in the hardware 7, 13–14, 53, 143, 295, 392
sorites puzzle 269–271
sortal 79, 125, 234, 279, 288
space and time 195–205
  outside of 4, 7, 324–325, 383
spirit 8, 47
standard argument 91, 297, 324, 343
statistical determinism. *See* determinism, adequate
  laws of nature and 392
statue and the clay 3, 59–60, 273–277, 290–291, 322
  Aristotle on 49
Stobaeus, Joannes 57–58, 136, 274
Stoics 26, 35
  and peculiar qualities 80, 105, 115, 137, 175
  and Skeptics 56–58, 64, 227, 233–239, 253
  on growing argument 249–251
Suárez, Francisco 138
substitutivity 126, 158, 245, 306–307, 307
  Leibniz on 108
substrate 175–176, 233, 239, 249–251, 259
supernatural 9
synthetic a priori 29, 210, 333

T

teleonomy 8–9, 64–72, 75–76, 335, 338–339
telos 8–9, 26, 64, 68, 72
thermodynamics
  entropy and 387
time
  A- and B-series 22–23, 178–179

space and 195–205
transworld identity 85, 314
triads 15–16
truth xi, 6–11, 28
  Hume's fork 28
Turing, Alan 190–191

U

uncertainty principle 45, 133, 153, 195, 213
Unger, Peter
  mereological nihilism 63, 68, 340, 345
  problem of many 71, 213, 260–263, 281, 339
universals 207–211
up to us 27, 343
use, meaning as 9–11

V

vagueness 213–215
value 388
Van Inwagen, Peter 259–262, 291, 344, 340–346
  consequence argument 343–344
  mereological nihilist 338
  simples arranged 63, 68, 71–72, 259, 320–322
  undetached parts 280, 334–335
Vienna Circle 292, 326, 368

W

Watson, James 190–193
wave function
  and interference 97, 197
  and many worlds 66, 185, 193
  as abstract information 10, 217–220
  collapse of 45, 145, 183, 185–190, 197–205
wave-particle duality 197, 217–225
Whitehead, Alfred North 177–178, 336–337, 367
wholes 3, 5, 55, 63–73, 75
Wiggins, David 10
  on Barcan Marcus 247, 320
  on coinciding objects 55, 291, 300
  on free will 347–349
  on identity 72, 107, 121–125, 301, 375–377
  on necessity of identity 157–158, 346, 350
  on TIbbles, the cat 234, 260–263, 271, 279, 288
Williamson, Timothy 173, 179, 349–351, 381
Wittgenstein, Ludwig 154
  and language games 369
  meaning as use 9

on identity 107, 113–114
on tautologies 163
picture theory 127–128, 382
science as logical truths 292–293, 367, 382
shown, not said 383
words and objects xi, 296, 383, 391
  and analytic philosophy 70, 118, 167
  arbitrary connections 108, 110, 241–242
worlds
  Popper's three worlds 15

Z

Zeno of Cytium 358
Zeno of Elea 48

Books by Bob Doyle

Free Will: The Scandal in Philosophy (2011)

Great Problems in Philosophy and Physics Solved? (2016)

Metaphysics: Problems, Puzzles and Paradoxes, Solved? (2016)

My God, He Plays Dice! How Albert Einstein Invented Most of Quantum Mechanics (2017)

Mind: The Scandal in Psychology (2017)

Chance: The Scandal in Physics

Life: The Scandal in Biology

Value: The Scandal in Economics, Sociology, Politics, and Ethics

PDFs of all of Bob's books will be available for free on the I-Phi website, both complete books and as individual chapter PDFs for easy assignment to students.

Colophon

This book was created on the *Apple Mac Pro* using the desktop publishing program *Adobe InDesign CC 2015*, with Myriad Pro and Minion Pro fonts. The original illustrations were created in *Adobe Illustrator* and *Adobe Photoshop*.

The author developed the first desktop publishing program, *MacPublisher*, for the Macintosh, in 1984, the year of the Mac, intending to write some books on philosophy and physics. After many years of delay and further research, the books are finally in production, completing work, in his eighties, on ideas that first emerged in his twenties.

About I-Phi Books

Information Philosopher books are *bridges* from the information architecture of the printed page, from well before Gutenberg and his movable-type revolution, to the information architecture of the world-wide web, to a future of knowledge instantly available on demand anywhere it is needed in the world.

Information wants to be free. Information *can make you free.*

I-Phi printed books are still material, with their traditional costs of production and distribution. But they are physical pointers and travel guides to help you navigate the virtual world of information online, which of course still requires energy for its communication, and material devices for its storage and retrieval to displays.

But the online information itself is, like the knowledge in our collective minds, neither material nor energy, but pure information, pure ideas, the stuff of thought. It is as close as physical science comes to the notion of spirit, the ghost in the machine, the soul in the body.

 It is this spirit that information philosophy wants to set free, with the help of Google and Wikipedia, Facebook and YouTube.

At a time when one in ten living persons have a presence on the web, when the work of past intellects has been captured by Google Scholar, we have entered the age of *Information Immortality*.

When you Google one of the concepts of information philosophy, the search results page will retrieve links to the latest versions of Information Philosopher pages online, and of course links to related pages in the Wikipedia, in the Stanford Encyclopedia of Philosophy, and links to YouTube lectures.

Thank you for purchasing this physical embodiment of our work. I-Phi Press hopes to put the means of intellectual production in the hands of the people.